Measuring
Student
Growth

Measuring Student Growth

Techniques and Procedures for Occupational Education

Richard C. Erickson
Northern Illinois University

Tim L. Wentling
University of Minnesota

Allyn and Bacon, Inc. • Boston, London, Sydney

Library of Congress Cataloging in Publication Data

Erickson, Richard C
   Measuring student growth.
   Includes bibliographies and index.
   1. Educational tests and measurements. 2. Grading and marking (Students) 3. Vocational education.
I. Wentling, Tim L., 1946- joint author. II. Title.
LB3051.E73   378.1'6'64   76-16018
ISBN 0-205-05506-0

Contents

Contents

Foreword

Measuring Student Growth: Techniques and Procedures for Occupational Education, by Richard C. Erickson and Tim L. Wentling, fills a long-recognized need for a comprehensive textbook on measurement applied to occupational education. The book will serve as a tool for classroom teachers in secondary and post-secondary schools and advanced undergraduate and graduate students in all areas of vocational education. Its readable style and organization, along with its comprehensiveness and the multiplicity and diversity of its examples, serve to ensure its usefulness as a textbook for the student and as a ready reference for the classroom teacher.

A balanced and updated treatment is given: general measurement considerations, teacher-made instruments, standardized instruments, and obtaining and using measurement information. One may find information on these subjects in a number of publications; what makes this book unique and of particular usefulness to those in vocational and technical education is the way in which the authors unfailingly make applications of each idea and each method to some aspect of occupational education. Their knowledge of and respect for their field of occupational education in its many dimensions are illustrated by this well-documented book.

In the first chapter, the authors note that, "Across the nation concerned students, parents, and governmental and civic leaders are calling for increased accountability in education." Skills in developing, selecting, and using the instruments of educational measurement and interpreting the results of their use may serve the purpose of accountability. Further, they contribute to the development and improvement of programs for the achievement of occupational competency. The development of these skills may be seen as the overall purpose of this textbook. It is apparent that, in purpose and related substance, through their book, Erickson and Wentling have made a significant contribution to the field of occupational education.

Elizabeth Jane Simpson, Dean
School of Family Resources
and Consumer Sciences,
University of Wisconsin-Madison

Preface

This book is directed toward the improvement of measurement and testing procedures within occupational programs. Current and future occupational instructors, counselors, and administrators are its intended audience. It is hoped that practicing occupational educators and advanced undergraduate and graduate students will find this book a basic resource and useful aid as they develop and sharpen their skills in measuring student growth.

Occupational education has been considered to include specific subject areas such as Home Economics Education, Industrial Education, Health Occupations Education, Business and Distributive Education, and Agricultural Education. Our objective was to prepare a comprehensive measurement text directed toward all subject areas in occupational education. Procedures and techniques for selecting or developing, using, and evaluating teacher-made and standardized instruments have been emphasized as well as specific ways in which measurement data and information are used in monitoring student progress and in developing, conducting, and evaluating occupational programs. Classic and contemporary concepts and developments in educational measurement are introduced as needed, and are presented with emphasis upon their application in one or more occupational program areas. Considerable attention has been given to providing example techniques, procedures, and forms that can be adapted to serve measurement needs in local occupational programs.

The focus of this book is on measurement of student growth and not on measurement of the many other facets of occupational programs. It is recognized that student evaluation and program evaluation are not mutually exclusive. The results of student evaluation can contribute to the evaluation of a program, but program evaluation must also include input from many other sources. The reader is referred to *Evaluating Occupational Education and Training Programs,* by Wentling and Lawson, for a comprehensive coverage of program evaluation.

This book is a happy combination of efforts by two persons whose professional preparation, experience, interests, strengths, and basic philosophy of measurement were mutually complementary. It represents an equally cooperative effort on the part of its authors and the ordering of their names reflects only an alphabetical happening, not an order of contribution. This joint authorship has resulted in a quality of work far beyond that which might have been attained through individual efforts. Though both authors share responsibility for the contents of the entire manuscript, the reader may find it useful to know who was primarily responsible for the initial drafts of particular portions. Chapters 1 thru 4, 10, 12, and 13 were the responsibility of RCE, and responsibility for the remaining chapters fell to TLW.

There were many individuals who have influenced the authors and who indirectly influenced what is included in this book and the manner in which it is presented. Among the most important of these are the advanced undergraduate and graduate students who have been enrolled in our measurement and evaluation classes. There are four individuals, however, who deserve special recognition for their direct contributions throughout the various stages of the book's development. Antoinette Wirth and Lea Zinke deserve many thanks for their assistance in editing and preparing the manuscript and in handling many administrative details in the preparation process. Appreciation is also due Barbara Brittingham and L. Allen Phelps, who critically reacted to several chapters of the manuscript.

Richard C. Erickson   Tim L. Wentling

Part I

General Measurement Considerations

Chapter 1

A Perspective on Measurement in Occupational Education

FUNCTIONS OF MEASUREMENT

Measurement is a systematic process that is concerned only with developing quantitative descriptions of student performance or behavior. Not to be confused with an evaluation, a measurement indicates no level of value or worth for the measured behavior. Measurement procedures and techniques by themselves cannot determine which students are competent to enter the world of work. In occupational programs they can be used only as tools for developing a quantitative description of each student's level of preparation. The occupational teacher or someone else must establish what level of preparation constitutes adequate preparation for entering the world of work; this latter activity is *evaluation,* which is distinctly different from measurement.

Measurement is a data- and information-gathering process. Evaluation is concerned with judging the adequacy or worth of a particular performance or sample of students' knowledge, understanding, skills, or feelings. Evaluative judgments in occupational programs should be based (at least in part) on data and information obtained through the use of sound measurement procedures and techniques. In many instances, several procedures and/or techniques will be used to obtain the data and information necessary for a sound evaluative judgment. Test scores, project ratings, grades on term papers and research reports, and teacher, peer, and employer ratings are but some of the types of measurements currently used as a basis for making judgments in occupational programs. Moreover, the current move toward accountability in education will demand intelligent and increased use of such measurements.

Across the nation concerned students, parents, and government and civic leaders are calling for increased accountability in education. Occupational education is no exception. Teachers, guidance personnel, and administrators associated with occupational education programs are and will continue to be held accountable for the amount and types of saleable skills developed in their programs. Those who have had professional training and have developed adequate skills in the application of measurement procedures and techniques will not only be able to apply these skills but will welcome this opportunity to evaluate and improve the instruction they extend to their students. They will recognize that properly applied measurement procedures and techniques can be used to monitor student progress and provide a measure of accountability or assurance that the "right" students are receiving the "right" instruction from the "right" teachers. An analysis of the functions of measurement in occupational education will show the relationship between measurement and such assurance to be real and important.

Monitoring Student Progress

Periodic monitoring of student progress on a regular basis is the most important function that measurement procedures and techniques serve in occupational programs. The primary foci of the monitoring process are to:

1. Facilitate program administration by providing occupational program staff with information and data needed for program planning, evaluation, and public relations activities
2. Facilitate instruction by providing records of student performance that will enable occupational teachers to identify when areas of instruction have been covered adequately and/or when areas of instruction are in need of further development

3. Facilitate learning by providing occupational students with up-to-date feedback on their performance in the program that, hopefully, will serve to motivate them to maintain or increase their current level of learning
4. Diagnose learning difficulties among occupational students who are having or would have an inordinate amount of difficulty with the instruction in the program and are in need of special attention

Aiding Career Guidance

One of the most valuable ways of insuring that the right students are enrolled in the right occupational programs is to include meaningful test data among the types of information that are available to those who make and those who assist in making career-guidance decisions: students, parents, teachers, and career-guidance personnel. This is not to say that appropriate test data alone will insure that good career-guidance decisions will be made every time. Currently, there are too many important but "unmeasurable" human variables for that to be the case. However, proper use of appropriate tests and test data does significantly reduce the number of mistakes that might be made in the career-planning process.

Classifying and Placing Students

One valuable way of insuring that occupational students are receiving the right instruction is to use their records of performance on achievement tests as a basis for classifying them according to their present levels of development and placing them in the program at levels that are compatible. Students should begin their occupational program at a level where the value added by the instruction is maximized. Data and information regarding students' vocational interests, aptitudes, and levels of readiness in mathematics and communications skills can make valuable contributions to this goal.

Aiding Program Evaluation

Occupational program evaluation, too, can provide assurance that students are receiving the right instruction. Data and information regarding the achievement of current students and graduates from the program are valuable input in determining program efficiency and effectiveness. A variety of measurement procedures and techniques can be used to provide meaningful information and data, which in turn can be used to determine the degree to which students are attaining the objectives established for the program. Records of student performance on objective-related instruments can provide valuable information and data when evaluating the efficiency and effectiveness of the occupational program.

Aiding Curriculum Improvement

If instruction in the occupational program is not right, then measurement procedures and techniques can play an important role in improving it and the curriculum as well. Subject matter that is neither related to nor necessary for competent and safe performance on the job is not the right subject matter for occupational instruction; it should not be included in the curriculum. Proper application of measurement procedures and techniques is a source of information and data that can be used to assess the adequacy of the curriculum materials used and help to insure that students are receiving the right instruction.

Improving Instruction and Hypothesis Testing

Proper application of measurement procedures and techniques can serve occupational programs in other ways to provide assurance that the right students are receiving the right instruction from the right teachers. One additional way would be concerned with improving instruction, or making it right. If measurement procedures and techniques are used in determining that occupational instruction is lacking with respect to either its level, method, or relevance, then measurement procedures and techniques can be used in determining when that instruction is right.

Hypothesis testing is an integral part of using measurement procedures and techniques to improve instruction in occupational education. Empirical tests of both formal hypotheses or informal hunches concerned with the efficiency and/or effectiveness of various instructional methods, media, sequences, and the like require appropriate and accurate measurement data. Such data can be obtained only through the proper application of appropriate measurement procedures and techniques. Moreover, such data are also used in testing formal research hypotheses in other areas of concern, such as the relationship between almost any human variable (i.e., age, sex, mechanical aptitude) and various aspects of the teaching–learning process (i.e., teaching method or instructional materials).

Assessing Teaching Effectiveness

Measurement procedures and techniques can provide one source of input for assessing teaching effectiveness. Proper use of such input in concert with data and information from other sources can help to insure that the right teachers are teaching in the occupational education program. Measurement of teaching effectiveness is admittedly "Peck's bad boy of educational measurement." However, if teacher self-evaluation is the emphasis, then assessment of teaching effectiveness loses some of its troublesome nature. Even under these conditions, if measurement of teaching effectiveness never develops beyond using achievement tests and ratings by students and peers, these techniques can contribute important information toward this end.

TYPES OF MEASURING INSTRUMENTS

Measurement procedures and techniques in occupational education use several types of instruments. However, all of them have one common characteristic: they possess well-defined and systematic procedures for comparing students' patterns of behavior or ability levels with those of others or with some predetermined standard of performance. Few, if any, of the relatively unstructured impressionistic techniques that clinical psychologists might use to "size up" individuals with respect to the nature of their personality and/or general mental abilities would be of value to professional personnel in occupational education. Consequently, little mention of them is made in this text.

There are many ways of classifying into types the measuring instruments or tests commonly used in connection with occupational education programs. Purpose, content, format, administration, and scoring are but a few bases that are currently in use. However, for the purposes of this text the best basis for classification is the "type of behavior" being measured, as presented in the following list of headings:

1. Achievement
2. General mental ability
3. Aptitude
4. Interest
5. Attitude

Achievement Tests

Achievement tests used in occupational education programs are designed to assess students' levels of accomplishment or achievement in a specified subject or occupation. Achievement tests can be classified into two main types: general achievement tests and diagnostic tests; it is important that occupational teachers and career-guidance personnel understand the distinction between the two. *General achievement tests* are composed of test items selected from a broad range of the subject or occupation being tested. They provide a single score indicating relative achievement with respect to all of the knowledge, skills, and understanding that are a part of that particular subject or occupation.

Diagnostic achievement tests are designed to identify specific strengths as well as areas of weakness in a given subject or occupation. Consequently, diagnostic tests are composed of items selected from a limited range of the subject or occupation in which the student is being tested. Although general achievement tests can be used for diagnostic purposes, a test that is limited in scope with more items devoted to fewer aspects of the subject or occupation will provide a stronger basis for diagnosis. For example, twenty test items devoted to measuring two specific skills would yield a better assessment of those two skills than would twenty test items devoted to measuring these two specific skills and three others. The former provides ten test items per skill while the latter provides only four. The consequences of either guessing an unknown item correctly or missing a known item affect the former by a factor of 10 percent and the latter by a factor of 25 percent.

Achievement tests also can be classified as verbal tests or performance tests. In a very broad sense, all tests designed to provide an assessment of human behavior are *performance tests.* That is, they require the individual being tested to perform—to provide an oral response to an oral or written question, to respond to a true–false item by marking a T or F, or to write a response to an essay question. However, in occupational education such tests are rarely regarded as performance tests. Performance tests in occupational education generally involve the application of psychomotor skills in conjunction with the manipulation of physical objects or apparatus. This would include testing situations involving the manipulation of paper and pencil as in a shorthand performance test or a performance achievement test in the areas of technical sketching or industrial illustration. However, the typical multiple-choice paper and pencil test that requires the student being tested to have and use highly developed verbal skills would not be considered a performance test. Other examples of performance achievement tests commonly used in occupational education programs would include typing, electronic and automotive troubleshooting, welding, sewing, and food preparation.

Performance achievement tests that require a student to perform a sample of work that one employed in a particular occupation would be required to perform are often referred to as *work-sample tests.* Development of skilled performance in the tasks associated with a particular occupation is the primary goal of occupational education. Work-sample tests are certainly some of the best instruments for measuring maximum ability to perform work-related tasks. Because their relationship to the job or occupational training for that job is so apparent, their degree of acceptance by students being tested is quite high. Work samples are rarely viewed as a threatening, superfluous, or ridiculous exercise, as is often the case with many other types of tests.

However, work-sample tests are not without their disadvantages. For example, they must be revised and revalidated each time even minor changes in tools, materials, equipment, or procedures occur in the job. In addition, most work-sample tests do not lend themselves to group testing. In instances where only one or two students in an occupational class can be tested at one time, this can cause problems for the instructor unless provision can be made for the remainder of the class. Finally, capable students occasionally become disturbed by the formality and pressure of the testing situation and are unable to perform at their best. These same students experience

9

the same difficulty with other types of tests and everyone seems to understand. But, somehow it seems ultra-traumatic when a student becomes "unglued" during a work-sample performance test and fails in his performance. Remembering that legendary professional golfers have been known to lose a big tournament by missing a short putt on the last hole should help keep in perspective this last disadvantage of work-sample tests.

There are a number of published achievement tests available to teachers of occupational courses. A partial listing is presented in chapter 10. The most complete listing can be found in *Vocational Tests and Reviews,* edited by O. K. Buros (1975). However, the majority of achievement tests used in occupational education classes will be developed by occupational teachers for use in their classes. Course content, objectives, and methods of instruction within specific subject areas of occupational education vary significantly from school to school. This variation has served to dampen efforts to develop and publish standardized achievement tests for occupational subjects.

General Mental Ability Tests

By contrast, measurement of general mental ability is the most highly developed area in all of mental measurement. Consequently, there is little occasion for occupational teachers (or any other teachers) to develop their own procedures or techniques for measuring general mental or scholastic ability. The question of whether professional personnel in occupational education should purchase a standardized instrument or develop their own is easy to answer when the purpose of the instrument is to provide an assessment of general mental ability. In the majority of situations the answer would be to use a published standardized instrument rather than to go through the rigors of developing such an instrument. Thus, the question is reduced to the problem of selecting an instrument from the many general mental ability tests that are available.

There is considerable variation among the types of general mental ability tests that are currently available from test publishers and there are several ways of classifying them. The distinction that is most important to professional personnel in occupational education is that between the individual and the group test. *Individual tests* are those designed to be administered to one individual at a time. *Group tests* are designed to be administered to groups of students or more than one person at a time.

The primary disadvantages of general mental ability tests designed to be administered on an individual basis are the large amounts of time required and the degree of skill needed for proper administration and interpretation. It can be readily seen that many more man-hours are involved in administering a one-hour test to 100 students on an individual basis than are involved in administering a one-hour group test to 100 students in one sitting. Not so apparent, however, is the variation in preparation or training required to be able to administer and interpret individual as opposed to group tests of general mental ability.

Preparation for administering individual tests of general mental ability usually requires successful completion of a university-level course in the administration and interpretation of the test to be administered, including successful completion of a long series of supervised administrations. This experience is preceded by graduate-level instruction equivalent to at least a master's degree in psychology. Most group tests of general mental ability, however, can be administered adequately by occupational teachers, administrators, or career-guidance personnel whose professional preparation has included one or more introductory courses in psychology or educational psychology and some advanced course work in measurement procedures and techniques.

The only real advantage that individual tests of general mental ability seem to have over those that are designed to be administered to groups is one of greater opportunity for clinical interpretation. That is, there is more opportunity to observe carefully the student taking the test and the manner in which he or she proceeds through this experience. Often, the test administrator in this one-to-one situation is in a position to make accurate judgments concerning motivation, physical constraints, emotional stability, and other behavioral aspects in addition to judging the student's general mental ability. Such information is valuable in interpreting a student's score on this type of test.

In addition, individual administration provides opportunity to reduce the ever-present error in measurement caused by things such as the student's failure to read instructions correctly, physical and mental fatigue, and lack of motivation or interest. These and other sources of error can be very rampant in group-testing situations. This is true particularly when testing students from educationally disadvantaged segments of the population who are disenchanted with "the system" and all the testing it seems to employ.

The advantages of measuring general mental ability on an individual basis make it a valuable adjunct to an occupational education testing program. However, since most of the measurement of mental abilities can be done quite satisfactorily with group tests it would be impractical for occupational education programs to use individual measures of general ability on anything but a supplementary basis.

Like achievement tests, tests of general mental ability may be classified as performance tests or verbal tests. *Performance tests* of general mental ability focus on the use and manipulation of objects such as form boards, picture puzzles, or blocks. Unlike the verbal tests of general mental ability, which require those being tested to have an understanding of the English language, the performance tests of general mental ability are useful in assessing ability among occupational students with language problems. These tests are appropriate for the non-English speaking and the educationally disadvantaged children and adults who have an urgent need to be enrolled in and receive instruction in an appropriate occupational education program.

Aptitude Tests

Aptitude tests used in occupational programs are concerned with measuring a particular mental ability that is important to achievement in some particular occupation or field of endeavor as opposed to measuring general mental ability that is important to most all occupations or fields of endeavor. Properly used, aptitude tests are valuable tools in estimating the probability that, with appropriate instruction or training, an individual will be able to succeed in a particular occupation or career field.

Examples of aptitude tests that are commonly used by career-guidance personnel in assisting occupational education students make appropriate career decisions would include tests of clerical aptitude, mechanical aptitude, verbal aptitude, mathematical aptitude, and the like. Such tests are not designed to measure future accomplishment. They are designed to measure a student's *current* capabilities in a particular area of endeavor. This assessment is then used as a basis for estimating the probability that this student will be successful in that area of endeavor. To the extent that the capacity to profit from further training can be expressed by the ratio between current level of achievement and the amount of training received to date, aptitude measures become useful tools for guiding students with respect to occupational choices.

The purpose of the measurement, rather than what is being measured, forms the basis for distinguishing aptitude tests from other types of tests. Any achievement test can serve as an aptitude test if concern for the measurement is with predicting future success. However, development of a good aptitude test involves considerably more than merely assembling a collection of performance tasks or paper and pencil test items that measure achievement in a given field of endeavor. Both newly developed aptitude tests and established achievement tests being used as aptitude tests are of little value in providing measures of aptitude until their predictive capabilities have been demonstrated to be of significant value. It is only after their value has been demonstrated that data from such tests can be used in making useful career-guidance decisions.

Interest Inventories

Interest inventories used in occupational programs are designed to assess a student's level of interest with respect to a variety of occupations or fields of study. Functionally, they are related to aptitude tests in that the primary use of interest inventories is in providing data for career-guidance decisions. However, it is important not to confuse these two types of instruments. Interest inventories do not provide direct measures of ability and, in fact, the relationships between measures of ability and interest are notoriously quite low. Students often do not report interests in areas in which they have considerable ability. Obviously, interest inventories and ability tests are concerned with two different aspects of fitness for a particular occupation or field of study. However, both are important to making career-guidance decisions. Interest in a particular occupation or field of study is certainly no substitute for the ability to function in that area. Likewise, the potential to develop the skills necessary to succeed in a particular occupation is no guarantee of success or satisfaction in that occupation.

Interest inventories are really nothing more than very lengthy questionnaires that employ a self-report technique, which assists students in listing or inventorying their likes and dislikes. This inventory or listing of likes and dislikes is then compared with inventories of preferences of groups of those who are successfully employed in various occupations. Significant similarities and differences in patterns of likes and dislikes are noted. To the degree that a student's patterns of preferences are found to be similar to those of individuals who are successfully employed in a particular occupational area, it is assumed that this student has an interest in that and other closely related occupations; lack of similarity in response patterns is indicative of a low level of such interest.

Of all the different types of measurement instruments used in occupational education programs, *interest inventories* are probably the least threatening. They may require a student to examine carefully his or her self-concept, but they are rarely responsible for threatening his or her self-image. Basically, this is because there are no correct or incorrect answers or passing or failing scores associated with interest inventories.

For most inventories, all that is required is that the student provide an honest indication of whether he or she likes, dislikes, or is ambivalent concerning each of a long listing of situations or activities. How an individual student responds to any single item has very little meaning in and of itself. However, responses to several hundred of these items produce a response pattern that can be useful in determining occupational areas and fields of endeavor in which that student's interests lie.

The primary reason for using interest inventories in occupational education programs has already been alluded to—to help in determining whether a particular student has a genuine interest in and would be happy employed in a particular occupation. Other reasons for using interest inventories in occupational education programs would include (1) determining the extent to which a student is interested in the same things as those already employed in a particular occupation and would make a congenial co-worker, and (2) calling attention to interest in a particular field to which the student has given little or no consideration. Interest inventories are used almost exclusively as aids in making career-guidance decisions. Scores on inventories are rarely used in prediction formulas to assist in making administrative decisions with respect to selection and placement of students in occupational programs. The primary focus of their use generally has been to assist students in making wise career choices rather than to assist occupational teachers and administrators in making institutional administrative decisions.

The rather unstable nature of vocational interests during adolescence is a major limitation on the use of vocational-interest inventories. In addition, interest inventories suffer from the various types of error that may accompany a student's report of his likes and dislikes. For example, students may not be truthful in their responses to inventory items concerned with tasks they consider to be too low in socioeconomic status. An adolescent boy from an upper-class family, whose parents hold working in the grease and grime of an auto shop with disdain, may tend to deny a real interest in working on cars. Students indicating a like for certain activities when they are misinformed about the activity is another potential source of error. Students who indicate a preference for engineering activities when they think of engineering as working outdoors and building things and give no thought to its scientific components inject this type of error. Students who tend to generalize from limited experience are prone to commit a third type of error: for example, an unsuccessful experience in attempting a major repair on a friend's bicycle as a child could be responsible for developing an aversion to all types of mechanical work. A young student with such an aversion could unjustifiably generalize for all types of mechanical work from this isolated experience and inject significant error into responses to items on an interest inventory.

In spite of such sources of error, interest inventories enjoy a satisfactory degree of validity and usefulness. Their correlation with measures of success and contentment in a variety of occupational areas, combined with their ease of administration and nonthreatening nature, make them one of the most popular and useful tools for those whose job it is to assist students in making adequate career-guidance decisions.

Attitude Measures

Very closely related to measuring interests or preferences is the assessment of attitudes. In fact, the relationship is so close that interest inventories are often considered a classification within the area of attitude measures. That is, students' attitudes toward different school subjects and occupations are often referred to as their interests or preferences. However, discussion of attitude assessment in this book focuses on attitudes as educational outcomes rather than interests or personal preferences. The primary concern is measurement of achievement associated with instructional objectives that have an affective nature. In occupational education programs such objectives are often expressed in terms of developing a degree of pride in craftsmanship, a sense of responsibility toward one's employer and co-workers, or a positive attitude toward the dignity in a job well done no matter how menial the task.

Like the measurement of interests in occupational programs, attitude assessment employs self-report techniques, which assist the student in describing his personal feelings about or attitude toward some particular attitude object. Quite often, the instrument is in a questionnaire format and consists of a series of brief statements.

Students respond either positively (yes, I agree) or negatively (no, I disagree) for each statement. For some statements a positive response is indicative of attitudes in a particular direction and for other statements a negative response would be indicative of an attitude in that same direction. Generally, no attempt is made to determine the degree of favorableness or unfavorableness to be associated with each statement. Each contributes a like amount. The degree of attitude toward the attitude object in question is obtained by summing algebraically the student's positive and negative responses. The larger the number of positive responses to positive statements about the phenomenon in question, the more positive the individual's attitude toward that phenomenon. Obviously, the inverse is true for negative responses.

Attitude-rating scales are also used in securing attitude data. *Attitude scales* employ the equal appearing intervals technique. Large numbers of statements expressing opinions toward the attitude object in question are collected. Each statement must express either a positive or negative attitude or feeling about the object in question. Neutral statements of fact are of no value in the development of attitude scales. The statements are sorted and ranged from the most favorable expression of attitude toward the object in question to the least favorable. Appropriate scale values are assigned to each statement. The number of statements are then reduced to form a final attitude scale composed of expressions that represent fairly equal steps along a continuum from most favorable to least favorable attitude toward the attitude object in question. Students respond to the scale by checking the statements presented that most closely express their opinion, feeling, or attitude toward that object. A student's score on the attitude scale is computed by averaging the scale values of the statements of opinion that were selected by that student as being representative of his or her feelings toward the attitude object.

Attitude measures are subject to the same types of error that are generally associated with self-report type instruments. Some students are prone to be something less than frank and honest about expressing their attitudes. This is particularly true in situations where socially defined "right" and "wrong" attitudes toward a particular attitude object are evident to the student. Moreover, correlations between scores on attitude measures and actual behavior of students in activities that might be considered related have tended to be quite low. The predictive validity of attitude measures is noticeably low.

However, some professionals counter such criticism of attitude assessment by indicating that expressed feelings for or against some attitude object are in themselves valuable. They provide added insight into the individual. For example, a student's expression of attitude toward the world of work is in itself an important expression because it represents that student's attitude. The most fundamental behavior toward any attitude object like the world of work would probably be some verbal expression. The fact that an expression of attitude often does not relate to other types of actual behavior is to be expected. Functionally, an attitude is rarely ever the single determiner of behavior. Environmental conditions, level of ability, and even other attitudes might be working at cross purposes with the measured attitude and producing a resultant behavior quite different from that anticipated on the basis of knowledge of the single attitude.

SUMMARY

Measurement procedures and techniques can be valuable tools for occupational teachers, administrators, and career-guidance personnel. As in the case of all other tools, the way in which measurement procedures and techniques are used in our occupational programs determines, to a large extent, their value to our programs. A hammer, for example, is a most valuable tool for building houses, furniture, and the like, but only if used properly. Improper use can result in a wide variety of conditions ranging from a sore thumb to a vandalized house full of broken windows. Rarely can we say that a tool itself is either good or bad. It is the way in which a tool is used that determines whether it makes a positive or negative contribution.

Properly used, measurement procedures and techniques are valuable tools in insuring that in our occupational programs the "right" students are receiving the "right" instruction from the "right" teachers. They can provide us with data and information that are useful in assisting our students to make sound career-guidance decisions. They can be used to good advantage in evaluating the level of instruction, the method of presentation, and the relevance of the content presented in occupational programs. They can be of some help in evaluating teaching effectiveness, in improving instruction, and in testing research hypotheses concerning occupational programs.

Finally, and probably of most importance, properly applied measurement procedures and techniques serve to facilitate learning. They induce students to prepare for "test day." They also provide a system for identifying and discussing with students any of the course content covered in the examination that they had not learned. Moreover, these procedures and techniques often assist in identifying those students who need and can benefit from remedial instruction and other special services to facilitate their attainment of all the knowledge, understanding, skills, and affective behaviors that will be required as they enter the world of work or continue their occupational preparation after leaving the occupational program.

There are many types of measurement instruments that have proven to be of value when properly used in occupational programs. Achievement tests, as their name implies, are valuable tools for determining what students have achieved or learned to date in some specific subject or occupational area. Those commonly used in occupational programs range in format from multiple-choice paper and pencil tests to work-sample performance tests.

General mental ability tests are valuable tools for determining students' levels of scholastic ability. They may be administered in a group setting or on an individual basis. The group tests will serve the needs of most occupational education students.

Aptitude tests are designed to measure a key or particular mental ability that is important to satisfactory performance in some particular occupation or field of endeavor. They are helpful in identifying and selecting from among a group of students those who have the most potential for succeeding in a particular occupational program and eventually as an employee in that occupation.

(Interest inventories can be useful tools to assist students in identifying occupational areas that would be of interest to them. They typically employ self-report techniques, have no "right" or "wrong" answers, and are probably the least threatening to the student's self-image of all the instruments currently used in occupational programs.)

Attitude measures that are used in occupational programs should be concerned with measuring work-related attitudes that can be modified or developed in the occupational programs. Such attitudes would include the importance and dignity of work and pride in craftsmanship.

In spite of the criticism and debate that continue to focus upon all the testing that we are subjected to throughout our lives, it is a certainty that proper application of the foregoing types of measurement instruments in occupational education has served the best interests of most students most of the time. Moreover, if instruments of these types were not available for occupational programs they would have to be developed. Just as whenever the other tools and equipment that we are using in our occupational programs cannot do the job required, we must either identify and purchase or develop new or better ones.

It is well to bear in mind, however, that it takes a knowledgeable and skillful worker to get the best results from any tool. If we are to look at measurement procedures and techniques as useful tools in occupational education, we must also look at ourselves as purchasers, developers, administrators, and consumers of tests and test data and information; all of which requires that as occupational teachers, administrators, and career-guidance personnel, we must develop the knowledge and skills necessary for proper use of these tools.

REFERENCES

Ahmann, J. S., and Glock, M.D. *Measuring and Evaluating Educational Achievement.* Boston: Allyn and Bacon, 1975.

Buros, O. K. *Vocational Tests and Reviews*. Highland Park, New Jersey: Gryphon Press, 1975.

Cronbach, L. J. *Essentials of Psychological Testing*. New York: Harper and Row, 1970.

Ebel, R. L. *Essentials of Educational Measurement*. Englewood Cliffs, New Jersey: Prentice-Hall, 1972.

Micheels, W. J., and Karnes, M. R. *Measuring Educational Achievement*. New York: McGraw-Hill, 1950.

Thorndike, R. L., and Hagen, E. *Measurement and Evaluation in Psychology and Education*. New York: Wiley and Sons, 1969.

Chapter 2

Essential Measurement Concepts

There are several basic measurement concepts that should be considered by occupational education teachers, administrators, and career-guidance personnel as they use measurement procedures and techniques in the conduct and administration of their occupational programs. A list of the most important of these basic concepts would include:

1. Validity
2. Reliability
3. Measurement error
4. Scales of measurement
5. Point of reference for measurement
6. Role of measurement

Knowledge and understanding of these concepts are fundamental and important to constructing, selecting, and administering measurement instruments and in interpreting the data and information obtained with these instruments. In fact, they are so fundamental and important that professional personnel associated with occupational programs should be able to demonstrate a thorough knowledge and understanding of these basic concepts prior to engaging in measurement activities associated with their programs.

VALIDITY

In a measurement context, *validity* refers to the degree to which a particular test or instrument is useful in measuring that which it was designed to measure. If a test or other measurement instrument produces an accurate assessment of the variable it was designed to measure, it is considered to be a valid instrument.

Validity is the first requisite of any test. No matter how satisfactory in all other respects, an instrument that does not provide to the decision maker accurate information of the type needed is worthless.

The measure of validity is related to the manner in which the problem of establishing the validity for a particular instrument is approached. Several approaches to the validation of measurement instruments are presented in the measurement literature. Each differs with respect to the record of outcome, procedure, or criterion used in the validation process and yields a particular type of validity. The most common of these types of validity are:

1. Predictive validity
2. Concurrent validity
3. Content validity
4. Construct validity
5. Internal validity

These five types of validity also vary with respect to the questions they are designed to answer and their principal uses in occupational programs. It is important to know the different types and understand their unique characteristics and contributions to measurement in occupation programs.

Predictive Validity

As its name implies, *predictive validity* is concerned with the degree to which an individual's score on a particular measurement instrument can be used to predict future success in some specified endeavor. For occupational education programs, this approach to validity is designed to answer the question, "Are the scores obtained with this instrument useful in predicting future performance on the job?"

Establishing predictive validity for many of the measurement procedures and techniques used in occupational education programs is important, particularly for those used in selecting and classifying students and the achievement tests used in determining course grades. One way to maximize the efficiency of an occupational program is to select only those students who appear to have the interest and ability to benefit from the program. Scores on selection and classification instruments should be related to program success criteria, that is, rank in graduating class, grade-point average, or teacher's ratings. Moreover, if grades in occupational courses are presented as being indicators of probable success on the job after graduation, then achievement-test scores upon which final grades are based should bear a positive relationship to job success criteria, that is, foreman's ratings, record of earnings, or record of job advancement.

Just how validly a particular instrument predicts can only be determined by a follow-up study—administering the instrument in question, giving those to whom the instrument was administered an opportunity to develop the behaviors that the instrument is supposedly useful in predicting, and then comparing predicted performance with a record of the outcome or actual performance. For example, a study to validate a mechanical aptitude test to be used in the selection of students for a vocational auto mechanics program would include:

1. Administering the mechanical aptitude test to a group of prospective vocational auto mechanics students

2. Developing for each student a prediction of expected success in the vocational auto mechanics program based on his or her score on the mechanical aptitude test

3. Enrolling these students in the vocational auto mechanics program

4. Upon completion of the program, collecting performance-criterion data reflecting each student's success or lack of success in the vocational auto mechanics program, that is, final grades, instructors' ratings, work-sample test scores, foreman's ratings, records of earnings, or records of job advancement

5. Using appropriate statistical techniques to correlate scores on the mechanical aptitude test with performance-criterion scores and arriving at a correlation coefficient expressing the degree of relationship between scores on the aptitude test and success on the program.[1]

1. Statistical techniques for computing validity coefficients are presented in chapter 9.

105323

It is expected that instruments used in making selection and classification decisions for a particular occupational program can provide useful data for predicting success in that program. It is also expected that student scores on achievement tests administered in occupational courses during the program can be of value in predicting success on the job after completing the program. To the extent that selection instruments and achievement measures fulfill these expectations, they have predictive validity. However, to the extent that predictions based upon data obtained from these instruments do not correspond to what happens in the end, the instruments are invalid. Instruments being used to make selection and classification decisions or to assess student achievement are worthless to the occupational program if they cannot demonstrate an acceptable level of predictive validity.

Concurrent Validity

Predictive validity and concurrent validity are closely related. Where predictive validity is concerned with an instrument's value in predicting *future* levels of performance in some specified endeavor, *concurrent validity* is concerned with the degree to which obtained scores on a particular instrument match *current* levels of ability for the behavior(s) the instrument was designed to measure. For occupational programs, this approach to validity is designed to answer the question, "Do the scores obtained with this instrument provide useful estimates of a student's present level of preparation in a particular occupational area?"

Establishing concurrent validity for instruments used in occupational education programs is important in two general situations: (1) when attempting to validate a test designed to measure level of skill development or competency in a particular occupational area, and (2) when attempting to substitute a new instrument for an established instrument that has demonstrated through the years an acceptable level of validity or accuracy. Examples of the first situation would include a cosmotology teacher attempting to determine the validity of his/her newly developed final examination that was designed to discriminate between those soon-to-be-graduating beauticians who would pass the state licensure examination and those who would not. The procedure for determining the concurrent validity of this teacher's final examination would be as follows:

1. Administering the teacher-made final examination to graduating cosmotology students shortly before they take the state licensure examination

2. Obtaining each of these student's scores on the state licensure examination after they have sat for this examination the first time

3. Using appropriate statistical techniques, correlate scores on the teacher-made final examination with the scores obtained on the first administration of the state licensure examination for beauticians and derive a correlation coefficient expressing the degree of relationship that exists between these two sets of scores

In this example, it would be expected that students who do well on the locally developed final examination for the cosmotology program, would do equally well on the state licensure examination the first time they take this test. To the extent that this expectation is fulfilled and that those who do well on the newly developed final examination also do well on their first attempt with the state examination, the test is a valid test. It can be used to discriminate between students who have completed the instruction and are ready to sit for the state licensure examination and those of lesser competence who are not ready. In short, the test is accurately measuring what it was designed to measure.

As previously indicated, concurrent validity is also a concern for personnel in occupational education whenever an attempt is made to substitute a new instrument or procedure for one that is currently being used in their program. This situation can arise when a new instrument is being introduced or considered as a replacement for an established one that is less convenient or perhaps too expensive.

Consider, for example, a foods service instructor, who for years has been using with much success a comprehensive two-hour essay test for the final examination in her advanced course. It places too much demand on her time and energies at the close of the semester. The examination that worked so well when enrollment in the course was small now causes her to spend long evening hours at the close of the semester just to get final grades submitted on time. Somewhat reluctantly, she agrees to develop a comprehensive multiple-choice examination that can be machine scored and to use it as a replacement for the comprehensive essay examination that, through the years, had demonstrated its ability to predict success on the job after graduation from the foods service program. The general procedure for determining the concurrent validity of the newly developed multiple-choice test would be as follows:

1. Administering the old established essay examination and the newly developed multiple-choice examination to all students who normally would be taking the final examination in this instructor's advanced foods service course
2. Scoring both the essay and multiple-choice examinations
3. Using appropriate statistical techniques to correlate students' scores on the essay examination with their scores on the multiple-choice examination and arriving at a correlation coefficient expressing the degree of relationship between these two sets of scores.

In this example, it is assumed that a high degree of predictive and content validity has been attained for the old, established essay examination. It would be expected that there would be a high positive relationship between the students' scores on the two examinations. In general, those who scored high on the essay examination would be expected to score high on the multiple-choice examination and those who scored low on the essay examination would be expected to score low on the multiple-choice examination as well. To the extent that these expectations are realized, the newly developed multiple-choice final examination would be said to have concurrent validity. Its use as a replacement for the old, established essay examination would be justified.

To the extent that individual students' scores on the newly developed multiple-choice examination are not positively related to their scores on the old, established essay examination, the old and the new examination are said to be measuring different abilities. The newly developed examination would be said to lack concurrent validity. It may have value for some other purpose, but it should not be considered a viable substitute for the time-consuming but valid essay examination. It should not be used as a replacement for the old, established essay examination even if it is more convenient.

It is important to note the procedural differences in establishing predictive and concurrent validity. In establishing concurrent validity, scores on the instrument whose validity is in question and the criterion data (rank of job classification with respect to competence in the auto mechanics area or score on the established essay examination) are obtained *concurrently* or at very nearly the same time.

Hence, the name concurrent validity. However, in the process of establishing predictive validity there is always a significant lapse of time between obtaining scores on the instrument whose validity is in question and obtaining the criterion data or record of the predicted outcome. The time lapse between obtaining a record of performance on the instrument whose validity is in question and obtaining the necessary criterion data is the single most distinguishing characteristic between predictive and concurrent validity.

Content Validity

Predictive and concurrent validity are empirical approaches to establishing validity. That is, they involve the collection and analysis of test and criterion data. Quite often, when developing achievement measures for occupational courses, it is neither convenient nor possible for an occupational teacher to submit newly developed instruments to an empirical validation. From a practical point of view many occupational teachers find the analytical approach of content validity the most appropriate approach to validating their teacher-made achievement tests.

Content validity, as its name implies, is concerned with analyzing the subject content of achievement tests. After such an analysis the test is either accepted or rejected on its face value. For occupational programs, this approach to establishing validity is concerned primarily with the question, "Does this test provide an accurate and comprehensive measure of the knowledges, skills, and understandings to be learned or developed in this course?"

Establishing content validity for instruments in occupational education programs has three major concerns: (1) is the subject matter included in the achievement test the same as that presented in the course? (2) is the subject matter presented in the test as comprehensive as that presented in the course? and (3) do the items in the test elicit the levels of learning indicated in the objectives for the course? Instead of empirically comparing scores on the test with quantifiable criterion measures or quantified judgments, as in predictive and concurrent validation, the test items are individually examined and compared with the course content and objectives presented in the course outline.

It would be expected that a test to measure achievement in

sewing would not contain test items concerned with measuring competence in areas such as baking, nutrition, or even knitting. Likewise, it would be expected that a final examination designed to measure achievement in a comprehensive vocational welding course would not focus either entirely or unduly on only one type of welding, for example, oxyacetylene or electric arc. Finally, it would be expected that a test to measure achievement in a vocational typing course would not focus either entirely or unduly on knowledge of the parts of the typewriter and either ignore or slight assessing typing accuracy and speed when the objectives for the course indicate that typing skills will be developed.

If examination of the test's content reveals (1) that it is the same as that presented in the course, (2) that it is as comprehensive as that presented in the course, and (3) that the competencies elicited by the test items are the same as those expressed in the objectives for the course, then the test is considered to have content validity. To the extent that one or more of the foregoing three conditions are not met, the test would be said to lack content validity.

It should be noted that content validity is not a requisite for either predictive or concurrent validity. There are many tests that, on the surface, do not appear to be useful in measuring what they purport to measure. Vocational interest inventories, for example, often appear to elicit behavior totally unrelated to vocational interests. However, many of these instruments have very acceptable levels of predictive and concurrent validity associated with them.

On the other hand, instruments that have content validity often do not have predictive or concurrent validity. The obvious approach to developing an alternate form of a test having high predictive or concurrent validity would be to construct the second test so that it has the same content coverage and types of items and measures the same knowledge, skills, and understandings as the original form. If this approach is followed, the newly developed alternate form will have content or face validity. However, this is no guarantee that it will have either the predictive or concurrent validity associated with the original form. It, too, must be submitted to an empirical validation before it can be determined whether it is truly an alternate form of the original. The presence of content validity in no way insures the presence of either predictive or concurrent validity.

Construct Validity

Few, if any, of the measurement procedures and techniques discussed thus far provide us with pure measures of the behaviors they were designed to assess. Most provide measures of qualities and/or abilities other than those implied in their names or specified in their descriptions. For occupational programs, construct validity is directed toward the question, "What does a student's score on this instrument *really mean* and how can it be explained in terms of known types of human behavior or psychological constructs?"

Construct validity uses both analytical and empirical methods of introspection. It is directed toward analyzing the meaning of performance records or obtained scores in terms of the behaviors actually measured by the instrument. In short, the psychological theory underlying the instrument is validated.

Establishing construct validity for instruments used in occupational education would be important in two instances: (1) when teachers or career-guidance personnel desire a better understanding of some particular instrument, and (2) when teachers or career-guidance personnel have a particular psychological construct they would like to measure. We have seen that predictive and concurrent validity can be established in one experiment. This is not the case with construct validity. The process involves a synthesis of observation, reasoning, and experimentation and, in practice, rarely reaches 100 percent completion. Construct validation for even the most well-developed of current psychological tests is far from complete. However, as the process proceeds, a listing of identifiable psychological constructs underlying performance on the selected instrument is gradually developed and attempts are made to determine the nature and strength of these constructs. In specific terms, the process involves:

1. Logical study of the instrument and intuitive identification of psychological constructs that might be involved in performance on that instrument
2. Logical study of the constructs identified and formulation of testable hunches concerning the extent to which they are important to performance on that instrument
3. Conduct of research studies to check out each hunch

The length and complexity of this validation process should not be used as rationale for completely avoiding it. For example, it is not uncommon for occupational teachers occasionally to find among their students individuals who exhibit superior performance in the laboratory, kitchen, shop, or drafting room and yet do very poorly on paper and pencil examinations designed to measure achievement in the occupational course. It is also not uncommon to find an occupational student who, in practice settings, can turn in a very adequate demonstration of a particular skill, but becomes "unglued" in a performance testing situation and is unable to demonstrate even a minimum level of that particular skill.

Situations such as these suggest that occupational teachers and career-guidance personnel should maintain some concern for the construct validity of the instruments they use in their programs. The depth to which they pursue this type of validation would be considerably less than that of developers of published standardized instruments, for example. However, when paradoxical situations similar to the two foregoing examples arise in their programs, they should begin to ask, "Just what is this test really measuring?" and then attempt to determine what psychological constructs are of *major* importance to performance on that test.

In the case of the obviously talented student who is unable to perform well on paper and pencil achievement tests, it might be hypothesized and construct validation might reveal the test to be measuring an undue amount of verbal skill, that is, reading comprehension and reasoning. In the case of the obviously talented student who becomes "unglued" in a testing situation, it might be hypothesized and construct validation might reveal the test to be measuring the student's anxiety threshold. Little formal research need be done to test these hypotheses.

In the first case, adapting the test to an oral format (reading the items to the student and having him provide an oral response) might serve to substantiate the hypothesis that a verbal construct accounts for too much of the variation in student performance on this test. In the second case, taking steps to remove any anxiety producing features from the test format, that is, time limits, implied drastic consequences of failure, strange tools or equipment, cold disposition of the test administrator, and the like, might serve to substantiate the hypothesis that an anxiety construct accounts for too much of the variation among students' scores on this test.

Granted, construct validation for the instruments in these two hypothetical situations would be far from complete. However, to proceed further in the process in an attempt to identify other constructs that are operant in these tests would require time and expertise not available to most occupational teachers. The major problems associated with these two instruments would have been remedied. The value gained from pursuing further the construct validation process would for these, and for many other instruments, not be worth the time and effort expended.

In short, construct validity is as important as predictive, concurrent, and content validity. The notion that only developers of published standardized instruments should be concerned with construct validity has no basis. The fact that the amount and value of the information gained in construct validation is so often inversely proportional to the degree to which the process is completed should serve to dispel this notion.

Internal Validity

Internal validation focuses upon statistical analysis of students' responses to individual items on a particular test and is sometimes used to validate or improve the validity of that test. For occupational programs, it attempts to answer the following question, "Does each item on this test measure what this test as a whole is measuring?"

This approach to validity does not employ any external criterion such as supervisors' ratings of performance on the job or record of advancement within the occupation. It is based on the following assumption: that the test as a whole provides a better measure of what it is designed to measure than does any single item in the test. This is generally a valid assumption, which serves as a basis for improving test reliability. However, when this assumption forms the basis for validating and improving the validity of measurement instruments some practical problems can arise.

Most variables that occupational teachers and career-guidance personnel want to measure are not pure. That is, they are made up of a number of subvariables or factors. For example, the variable "general scholastic aptitude" includes at least five factors: verbal ability, numerical ability, word fluency, comprehension, and reasoning ability. Careful analysis of a general scholastic aptitude test would reveal a small homogeneous group of items designed to measure the verbal factor, a group designed to measure the numerical factor, and groups designed to measure each of the remaining factors as well. Individually, these subgroups of homogeneous items would be of little value in measuring an individual's general scholastic aptitude or in predicting his or her success in a particular occupational program. This is because each is measuring a different and somewhat independent subvariable that is important to or a factor in general scholastic aptitude. Only when used in combination can these homogeneous groups provide an adequate estimate of an individual's general scholastic aptitude or be most useful in predicting success in a particular occupational program. When all the factors important to some measurement are present in the measurement instrument and performance on that instrument can be used to predict some concurrent or future performance, the instrument is said to have its maximum validity.

Attempts to increase predictive or concurrent validity that employ item-analysis data and internal-validation procedures actually run the risk of decreasing the instrument's ability to predict. Starting with the assumption that the test as a whole is a better measure of what it is intended to measure than any single item in the test, internal-validation procedures include:

1. Administering the instrument to a large sample of students for whom the test is intended
2. Scoring the test
3. Using appropriate statistical techniques to compute a correlation coefficient between performance on each test item and total test score
4. Eliminating from the test those items that correlate low or negatively with total test score
5. Developing more items for the test that are similar to those items that demonstrate a high positive correlation with total test score

If the instrument is measuring a single variable that has no subvariables or factors, then there is no problem with this procedure. However, if two or more factors are present in the instrument, then it is likely that many of the individual items that are "assigned" to measure one of these factors will not have high and positive correlation with total test score. Internal-validation procedures will call for revising these items or replacing them with items like those that have high and positive correlation with total test score.

As items are eliminated and replaced in this manner, one or more of the homogeneous groups of items will be reduced in size. Continuation of the internal-validation process generally results in eliminating, one-by-one, all but one of the groups of items designed to measure particular factors of a variable that contains more than one factor. The remaining subgroup of homogeneous items, even though larger in size, cannot provide an adequate measure of the original variable because all but one of the important factors or subvariables important to the original variable have been eliminated from the instrument. The end result of internal-validity procedures for instruments designed to measure variables having two or more factors is the development of purer and purer measures of less and less and a corresponding decrease in the ability to predict future or concurrent performance.

Occupational teachers who have readily available item-analysis data for the achievement tests used in their courses are often prone to eliminate from these examinations those test items that do not appear to measure what the test as a whole is measuring. In many instances, such action does in fact improve the validity of the examination. However, to follow blindly internal-validation procedures without regard for maintaining adequate coverage of course content, for example, will result in destroying the content validity of many achievement tests as well as much of the predictive, concurrent, and construct validity they might enjoy.

RELIABILITY

In a measurement context, *reliability* refers to the degree to which a particular test or instrument provides trustworthy or consistent measures of whatever it does measure. One simple way of thinking about reliability is with respect to the amount of confidence that can be placed in a ranking of occupational students based upon their performance on a particular achievement test. To the extent that these students would obtain nearly the same scores and retain their ranks in the group on a readministration of this test, the test would be considered reliable. On the other hand, to the extent that these same students failed to retain their ranks in the group on retaking the test, the test would be considered unreliable.

Consistency is a good synonym for reliability—consistency of results with repeated use of an instrument. A reliable instrument provides consistent assessments of the knowledge, skills, understanding, or other traits being measured. If a particular test is administered to the same group of students on two or more occasions, and their rankings within the group by test score changes little if any across these administrations, then that test is providing consistent and reliable assessments. Only instruments that can demonstrate a satisfactory amount of consistency or reliability in the scores they yield are of value to occupational teachers, administrators, or career-guidance personnel. This is because instruments that do not provide reliable or consistent measures are certain to provide invalid measures.

Purpose of Reliability Estimates

Estimates of reliability for a particular instrument may be directed toward one or both of two purposes: (1) providing an estimate of the *accuracy* of the instrument itself, and (2) providing an estimate of the *consistency* or *stability* of an individual's test score or record of performance on the instrument.

In the first instance, efforts would be directed toward determining if, for example, instructions for administering an instrument are unclear, some items included are ambiguous, and/or the printing is not intelligible. Individuals cannot be expected to perform reliably when the measurement procedures and techniques do not lend themselves to optimum performance. To the extent that one or more facets of an instrument are inadequate, it will tend to yield unreliable. estimates of performance.

Efforts directed toward the second purpose, providing an estimate of consistency, depend primarily upon the individuals involved in the testing. Even the best-prepared instrument cannot produce reliable estimates of performance if the individuals to whom the instrument is being administered are not capable of reliable behavior. For example, an occupational student suffering from severe anxiety or even a headache will probably give an uncharacteristic and therefore unreliable performance on the very best of instruments. Likewise, well-built achievement tests designed to measure high-level performance in electronics will yield unreliable results if they are administered to junior-high-age industrial arts students who are only capable of making random guesses in response to the items included in the test.

Types of Reliability Coefficients

The dual nature of reliability estimates is reflected in the types of reliability coefficients that have been developed and the methods that have been devised for computing them. Basic to each method is the use of statistical techniques for correlating performance on two "administrations" of the "same" instrument or intercorrelating performance on a single "administration." Three types of reliability coefficients commonly appear in measurement literature:[2]

1. Coefficients of stability
2. Coefficients of equivalence
3. Coefficients of internal consistency

Coefficients of Stability. A *coefficient of stability* is a quantitative expression of the correlation between scores obtained from a test and retest with some significant time period between the two administrations. For occupational education programs it is designed to answer the question, "Would the students obtain the same score on this test if they were to take it again at a later date?" It is often referred to as test–retest reliability and provides a good estimate of the stability of the students' performances on this test. Factors affecting stability of performance may be temporary conditions (illness, lack of motivation, etc.) or permanent changes that occur between the two administrations of the test (learning, maturation, etc.). There is no single estimate of stability for an instrument, only estimates for each of a variety of different time intervals. In general, the longer the interval the more opportunity for changes to occur and, consequently, the lower the correlation between the scores on the two administrations.

In occupational education programs, coefficients of stability must be viewed in light of the purpose of the instrument. If, for example, career-guidance personnel intend to make long-range projections based in part on students' performance on vocational-interest inventories and aptitude tests, then stability over a long period is important. The same would be true when measuring other traits that are supposed to remain relatively constant over long periods. For many other uses of tests, such as assessing student achievement in an occupational course, stability over long periods s of little importance.

---

2. Procedures for deriving these coefficients are presented in chapter 9.

For most classroom-testing situations in occupational programs, reliability coefficients that reflect accuracy and stability of performance over short periods are the most important. The interest is usually in whether students would have obtained the same test score if the test had been administered on some other day that week. It would be unfortunate to base course grades on test scores that might have been significantly different had the exam been given a day earlier or a day later.

The estimate of reliability should take into account temporary day-to-day changes in the student, but not be affected by learning occurring between administrations. This calls for a coefficient based upon two administrations separated by enough time for day-to-day changes that affect performance to be reflected in scores, but not so much time that permanent changes or learning have occurred. If the same form of the test is administered in both administrations, care should be taken to allow enough time between administrations to minimize the effect of memory. The practicalities of the situation, however, will dictate that for many occupational programs the equivalent forms and internal consistency techniques in the following sections will remain the most practical approaches to obtaining estimates of reliability for classroom tests.

Coefficients of Equivalence. Coefficients of equivalence are correlations between scores from two equivalent forms of an instrument that have been administered to the same individuals. For occupational education programs, this procedure is useful in answering questions such as, "Are forms A and B of this final exam such that students taking one form won't have an advantage over the students taking the other?" When the two forms are administered at essentially the same time, the concern is in answering only this question or obtaining an estimate of accuracy for both forms of the instrument. However, if a time interval (one day or so) is introduced between administrations of each form so the day-to-day variability of the individual is allowed to affect performance, this coefficient also can provide evidence concerning the short-term stability of the trait being measured as well as the accuracy or equivalence of the forms.

Coefficients of Internal Consistency. Coefficients of internal consistency are concerned with providing only quantitative estimates of the accuracy of the test itself. They are based on an internal analysis of scores obtained on a single administration of the instrument. For occupational education programs, this procedure is a quick and relatively easy way of answering the question, "Would the students obtain the same score on this test if they were to be retested right away?" Variation in scores that could be attributed to temporary environmental conditions or personal characteristics is held constant in the single administration. The most popular of these coefficients are the split-half and Kuder–Richardson techniques presented in chapter 9. They are particularly useful techniques for obtaining estimates of test accuracy in situations where time and other conditions permit only one form of a test to be administered, as in occupational classes.

Reliability and Validity

Reliability is the first requisite of validity. It places some very definite restrictions on validity. For example, statistically, its relationship to validity is such that the validity coefficient for a particular instrument cannot be any larger than the square root of its reliability coefficient. Instruments that provide accurate measures of what they are designed to measure must, by definition, provide consistent or reliable measures. However, the inverse is not necessarily true.

Instruments that provide consistent or reliable measures do not always provide accurate assessments of what they are said to measure. An instrument may be very reliable and still be invalid in many or all applications. It may provide the same score and rankings for the same individuals across two or more administrations and still not be providing accurate measures of what it was said to be capable of measuring. For example, procedures and techniques for measuring height and weight produce very reliable measures. They remain quite consistent for most individuals across repeated measurements. However, neither height nor weight could be considered valid measures of achievement in an occupational program no matter who said they were. In practice there are instances where this phenomenon is not quite so obvious. The numerous paper and pencil tests that provide consistent measures which consistently defy being related statistically to any meaningful variable are good examples.

Interpreting Reliability Estimates

Under ideal conditions, reliability coefficients would be derived from scores on two different but equivalent forms of an instrument that had been administered to an appropriate group on two occasions with an appropriate period intervening. Often it is not feasible for testing programs in occupational education to meet these conditions. For example, achievement tests for occupational courses are generally only available in one form. Often these tests are used as learning experiences and provide lasting variation in the form of increased learning. Consequently, reliability estimates based on some modification of the ideal procedure are very common for tests used in occupational programs. Fortunately, when such coefficients are properly interpreted they provide information that closely approximates that which would have been obtained had all the ideal conditions been met. However, proper interpretation requires an understanding of some of the factors that affect the interpretation of reliability coefficients. One of these factors, length of interval between the test–retest administrations of an instrument, has already been mentioned.

When two forms of an instrument are administered at a single sitting, the resulting coefficient is likely to overestimate the actual stability of the scores produced by that instrument. This is because temporary factors, which are not important to the instrument itself (i.e., environmental conditions, motivation, physical conditions, etc.), are likely to operate equally on both forms of the instrument. Each student's pair of scores would be more alike than they might be if a large time interval were injected between the two administrations. Overestimates of stability may be expected also when reliability is computed using a split-half or some other internal consistency technique based on a single administration of the instrument. These reliability coefficients describe the accuracy of the instrument itself but overestimate the stability of the scores by the extent to which fluctuation in the testing environment and temporary changes in the students tested might affect the stability of the scores. In short, coefficients based on administration in a single sitting do not provide accurate measures of stability of performance over long or even short periods.

Coefficients of stability provide estimates of how stable test data remain from day to day, week to week, month to month, or even year to year. However, they are likely to provide underestimates of an instrument's accuracy. Temporary factors like mental set and physical condition of students tend to decrease coefficients reflecting accuracy when the instruments are administered with an intervening time interval. For example, students who were ill or had an unrelated headache during one administration probably would not experience these same conditions during both. To the extent that such temporary factors tend to restrict performance during one of the two administrations, the resulting coefficient will underestimate the actual level of accuracy of which the instrument is capable.

Permanent changes in students' behaviors, which are directly related to performance on a particular instrument, can also affect an estimate of reliability. For example, during the time lapse between the two administrations of a vocational-interest inventory or aptitude test being checked for reliability, some students might become deeply involved in club activities in which they obtain some highly specialized knowledge and understanding that is reflected in their responses on the second administration of the interest inventory or aptitude test. The correlation coefficient for the instruments would be underestimated due to the effect of the differential learning.

At this point in the presentation of reliability as an important measurement concept it should be apparent that there is no such thing as a measurement instrument having a single estimate of reliability associated with it. Like validity coefficients, reliability coefficients relate only to the group of individuals whose responses to the instrument served as the data base for deriving the coefficient. Change significantly the nature or composition of the group, and a higher or lower coefficient will result.

MEASUREMENT ERROR

Nearly all occupational teachers, administrators, and career-guidance personnel know that the measurement techniques and procedures used in their occupational education programs are neither perfectly valid nor perfectly reliable. Scores on tests are, for the most part, determined by the talents, interests, or aptitudes of the students who take the tests. However, these scores are also influenced by other extraneous factors, such as distractions in the testing environment, student anxiety or illness, and even faulty construction within the tests themselves.

Components of a Test Score

Test scores obtained from instruments of the type presented in this text are said to have two components: an individual's true score plus an error component. A model equation for a score on any measurement procedure or technique used in an occupational program would be:

$$\text{Obtained Score} = \text{True Score} + \text{Measurement Error}$$

where the obtained score is the student's raw score or the score obtained on the test. The true score is a hypothetical concept—an unknown quantity. If we had a very large number of truly equivalent forms for our tests, we could administer all of them to a student at one sitting. As the student proceeded through all these forms of the test, we would see that his obtained scores for each form of the test were not equal. Some scores would be higher than others. Most would cluster around his average performance. Assuming that each form of the test is truly equivalent, we might conclude that the student's average score from this large number of administrations of the test would be characteristic of his performance on this test— his true score. In fact, this is one very good and practical definition of true score.

However, the difficulties of developing very large numbers of truly equivalent forms for any meaningful test, as well as our inability to eliminate the effects that things like practice and fatigue would have in such a testing situation, make this a very impractical approach to determining an individual's true score on some test. More practical techniques or approaches need to be developed. The most practical approach developed thus far focuses on, first, estimating the magnitude of the error component presented in the foregoing model, and, then, defining reasonable limits around the observed score in which we would be reasonably sure to find the true score

Standard Error of Measurement

Earlier in this chapter it was pointed out that the various types of measurement error that affect accuracy and consistency also were responsible for reducing in magnitude the estimate of reliability for a test. From this discussion you might surmise that an estimate of reliability for a given test would be useful in attempting to determine the magnitude of the error component. This is, indeed, the case.

The *standard error of measurement (SE)* is a quantitative expression of the magnitude of the error component that is based in part on the estimate of reliability for the test. Detailed procedures for computing the standard error of measurement are presented in chapter 13.

Occupational teachers and career-guidance personnel should have some knowledge of the size of the measurement error component of the scores students obtain on the tests used in the occupational program. Whether obtained from the manual for a purchased instrument or computed for teacher-made-tests, the *SE* is a very useful statistic for estimating the margin of error in obtained scores.

If, for example, the *SE* for a particular final exam in an occupational course were computed to be 2.5, then the teacher for that course would be able to make some useful probability statements about the accuracy of the distribution of students' scores on that exam. In this instance, the teacher could say that for about two-thirds of the students, their obtained scores are no more than 2.5 points (± 1.0 *SE*) away from their true scores on that final exam.

Of course, other types of statements are possible as well. For example, if the *SE* on a 100-point final exam were computed to be 10.5, then the teacher could say that two-thirds of the students who scored 70.0 on the exam have true scores ranging somewhere between 59.5 and 80.5—a confidence band so wide that this teacher should revise this exam in hopes of increasing its reliability and reducing the size of its *SE.*

Those who make evaluative judgments based upon test scores run a great risk of making poor decisions when the *SE* is large. Suppose, for example, the final written examination for an aviation mechanics program had an *SE* of 10.5 and the minimum acceptable score for graduation from the program were set at 70. A significant portion (approximately one-third) of those who graduated with a score in the lower 70s really should not have because their true scores are in the 60s on this exam and below the minimum accept-able score. On the other hand, with an *SE* this large some of those (approximately one-third) who scored in the upper 60s on this exam and failed to graduate should have graduated because their true scores are in the 70s and above the minimum acceptable score. Occupational teachers, administrators, and career-guidance person-nel are on very thin ice when they make pass–fail, go–no–go, and accept–reject decisions or even assign grades on the basis of scores obtained from instruments having large standard errors of measure-ment. In a like vein, they should not attach much significance to small variations between students' I.Q. scores, for example. The standard error of measurement associated with most popular meas-ures of general mental ability ranges from 5 to 8 points.

SCALES OF MEASUREMENT

Another consideration in maintaining an appropriate level of con-fidence in the precision of obtained scores involves understanding the scales used with various measurement procedures and tech-niques. All measurement data obtained in occupational education programs are based upon one of four different measurement scales. Each scale varies with respect to the level of accuracy and potential usefulness to measurement procedures and techniques in occupa-tional education. The four measurement scales are:

1. Nominal
2. Ordinal
3. Interval
4. Ratio

It is essential to have a thorough understanding of these four scales and to avoid the popular tendency to place too much faith in some obtained scores and credit them with having much more precision than they actually do.

Nominal Measurement Scales

A *nominal scale* is the most limited of the four types of scales and, hence, has the lowest level of precision. Nominal scales can only be used to number for purposes of identification and classification. For example, in our occupational programs we may have different groups of students with whom we might want to assign a number to act as a distinguishing label. All boys might be assigned to group 1 and girls to group 2, or vice versa. Or, we might classify those enrolled in the agricultural program as 1s, those enrolled in the business education program as 2s, those enrolled in the health occupations program as 3s, and so on until we have a numeric classification assigned to all students enrolled in our total occupational program.

The assignment of nominal numbers to different categories or groups is done for identification purposes only and is purely an arbitrary process. There is nothing meaningful that we can do with numbers on a nominal scale beyond merely using them as identifying labels for broad categories. This property of identification and classification also extends to the three higher level measurement scales. However, the identification and classification there is more refined and other properties of numbers are added at each level as well.

Ordinal Measurement Scales

Whereas a nominal scale is concerned with identification and classification based upon *descriptive* qualities, an *ordinal scale* is concerned with *quantitative* qualities that can be used to classify further by rank ordering individuals within broad categories. For example, we might observe three boys in a typing class and rank them on an ordinal scale 1, 2, and 3 in terms of their apparent typing speed.

All we really have at this point is an ordinal ranking of the boys in terms of their apparent typing speed. Though the *numbers* assigned are equally spaced on the scale of measurement, we have no assurance that the actual differences in the boys' typing speeds are spaced in a like manner.

Measurements on an ordinal scale can be used to rank students numerically on any continuous variable like speed of performance or class rank. However, when interpreting the assigned ranks we are not at liberty to make statements regarding the degree to which the first-ranking student's performance is superior to that of the second-ranking student, and so on. Nor are we at liberty even to add individual students' rankings on one or more variables in an attempt to obtain more precise information regarding their overall level of performance. The primary reason for these restrictions is that numbers from scales not having equal intervals cannot be compared or added in any meaningful way. However, ordinal data are not as useless as they may seem. Rank data, including data reporting frequency within two or more given classifications, are useful in computing correlations or estimates of relationship as in deriving estimates of validity and reliability.

Interval Measurement Scales

Interval scales have the identification and rank-order characteristics of the previous two scales. In addition, interval scales, as their name implies, have equal intervals between the numbers on the scale. For example, if we were to give our three male typing students the traditional speed and accuracy performance test, we might find that our first-ranked student was capable of 65 words per minute and our second- and third-ranked students, 35 and 20 words per minute, respectively. These three test scores would be on a scale of equal units of measurement, or an interval scale. The difference between 40 and 45 words per minute would be equal to that between 25 and 30 words per minute, and so on up and down this measurement scale.

When describing these boys in terms of their typing speed and accuracy, these scores provide significantly greater precision than our previous rankings. We can now make some rather exact statements about our students' performances. We can say that the first-ranked student is 30 words per minute faster than the second-ranked and that the difference between the first- and second-ranked student is twice as great as that between the second- and third-ranked. Moreover, we can add individual students' scores on several tests to obtain a more accurate picture of their overall performance, if the scores are all on at least an interval scale of measurement. Because an interval scale has equal units of measurement between the numbers on the scale, we can also legitimately perform nearly all the useful statistical operations with these test scores.

Ratio Measurement Scales

Many of the measurement procedures and techniques have or come very close to using an interval scale but very few except, perhaps, some physical measurements have a zero point—an essential requirement and distinguishing characteristic of a ratio scale of measurement. Most achievement tests in occupational education programs appear to be on something that approximates an interval scale. Very few approach a ratio scale. A score of zero on such tests does not usually mean that the student has achieved absolutely nothing from the instruction. It generally means that he/she failed to answer correctly any of the items included on that particular test. Had some of the many other items that might have been included on that test been included, the student's score might not have been zero.

The most precise of the four types of measurement scales is a *ratio scale*. It has the ability to identify—like nominal, ordinal, and interval scales. It has the ability to rank—like ordinal and interval scales. It has equal intervals—like interval scales. In addition, it has a zero point.

The few ratio scales used in conjunction with occupational programs are those concerned with assessing physical characteristics (i.e., height, weight, and age) or variables such as duration of employment or wages earned in dollar amounts. Scales of measurement used to assess these variables all have a meaningful zero point. Whenever we use a scale of this type we can legitimately make statements such as: "Students completing this particular occupational program on the average earn twice the annual salary that their peers who failed to complete the program earn." Moreover, where ratio measurements can be obtained, we can not only use a full range of statistical treatments, we can legitimately multiply and divide the obtained scores by constants and obtain meaningful results that can be readily replicated.

It would be nice if measurement data for all the variables that we are concerned with could be obtained on ratio or even interval scales. Unfortunately, for many abilities, aptitudes, and interests our measurement procedures and techniques are limited to the lower level scales. However, even these lower level scales can serve our needs to a moderate degree if we know them for what they are and can do for our programs, and then act accordingly.

Those who have a thorough understanding of these scales of measurement will not likely interpret ordinal data as though it were ratio or even interval data. Given any measurement procedure or technique, they should be able to classify it as to the scale of measurement used and interpret the obtained scores in a manner that does not exceed its limitations. Much of the legitimate criticism leveled against measurement procedures and techniques in occupational education and other areas of society is a result of a failure to understand these four types of measurement scales and their limitations.

POINTS OF REFERENCE FOR MEASUREMENT

Occupational teachers and administrators can consider measurement of student achievement in their programs from two different points of reference: norm-referenced measurement and criterion-referenced measurement. Like the scales of measurement, these, too, are essential measurement concepts that should be understood by those who want to use measurement procedures and techniques to their fullest advantage. Selecting a point of reference in assessing student competencies in occupational programs is like selecting an initial reference point for anything. Start with point of reference "A" and you end up somewhere, but start with point of reference "B" and you end up somewhere else. Norm- and criterion-referenced measurement as points of reference for measurement procedures and techniques in occupational programs are no exception to this rule.

Norm-referenced Measurement

Of the two, norm-referenced measurement is currently the most common. Most occupational teachers, administrators, and career-guidance personnel have received some preparation in using "the normal curve" of differences in students' achievement-test scores to assign student grades. Most, too, have had experience in comparing students with other students on the basis of test scores—either within a particular course, or by using an external norm group as a frame of reference. Hence, the term *norm-reference.*

The primary objective of this common type of comparison measurement is discrimination—separating students with regard to some variable, such as achievement in class, so that comparisons can be made among them. The objective is an old one dating back to the European system of education, which stressed selection of the gifted and permitted only those selected to continue on to higher education. If this is our sole point of reference, then the measurement procedures and techniques used in our occupational programs will be limited to tools designed to assist us in making comparisons among our students and making evaluative judgments based on these comparisons. Most of our current achievement tests, aptitude tests, teacher ratings, and course grades are based upon a norm-referenced approach to measurement. The primary concern seems to be rank ordering students with regard to some pertinent variable, making comparisons, and then making evaluative judgments based on the information obtained from these comparisons. The focus is not on what the individual student actually knows, understands, or can do.

Criterion-referenced Measurement

The focus of criterion-referenced measurement procedures and techniques is on obtaining assessments of student performance or test scores that are directly interpretable in terms of some criterion or specified standard of performance (Glaser and Nitko 1971). Hence, the term *criterion-referenced*. Examples of criterion-referenced tests that are of concern in occupational education would include the performance tests and written examinations used in licensing and certifying welders, cosmetologists, pilots, truck and heavy equipment operators, police and firemen, and nurses and other health-care professionals.

Interpretation of an individual's score on any one of these and similar tests neither invites nor requires one to make comparisons with the scores of others who are taking or who have taken the test. Specific standards for acceptable performance have been set in terms of what is and what is not an acceptable performance. Those whose test scores indicate that they have the ability to perform at or above the level of the standard set for that test, pass the test, and if applicable, are certified or licensed. Those who fail to perform at or above the minimum acceptable level, do not. Again, in criterion-referenced measurement how an individual's performance compares with that of others is of little or no concern.

Selecting a Point of Reference

As indicated earlier, the point of reference for measurement procedures and techniques in occupational education programs is very important. Occupational teachers and administrators should continually evaluate their choice of reference point to insure that their measurement procedures and techniques are leading them where they really want to go.

For occupational programs, the primary questions to be raised in selecting an appropriate point of reference are three: First, "What is the measurement task?" Then, "Is it to sort out, rank order, and make comparisons among our students in terms of some ability, aptitude, or interest?" Or, "Is it to identify among our students those who have actually attained some specified level of competency and those who have not?" In those instances where we want to know how students compare with others in their peer group, a norm-referenced approach to measurement should be selected. In those instances where we want to determine who among our students has obtained some specified level of knowledge, understanding, and/or skill, a criterion-referenced approach to measurement should be selected. Each should be selected as it is suited to the measurement task at hand. A detailed discussion of the advantages of norm- and criterion-referenced tests and guidelines for their development are presented in part II of this text.

ROLE OF MEASUREMENT

While closely related to the point of reference for measurement procedures and techniques, the role that measurement actually plays in an occupational program is determined largely by the time when the measurement process occurs. For most occupational programs, measurement procedures and techniques can be introduced prior to, during, and upon completion of instruction. It is important to understand the roles that measurement can play at these three points in the instructional process.

Formative Measurement

Measurement procedures and techniques assume a formative role (Bloom 1968; Bloom, Hastings, and Madaus 1971) when they are used to obtain diagnostic measures of student performance and these measures are used in formulating or forming the instructional objectives, content, and methods. Hence, the term *formative meas-urement*. Formative instruments can be used prior to or during a sequence of instruction. In the first instance, they are useful in identifying any deficiencies students might have that would work against their successful completion of the sequence of instruction. A formative test indicates such weaknesses to both teacher and student, and the need for alternative instructional objectives, content, and method becomes apparent to both.

Likewise, formative instruments administered prior to a sequence of instruction often indicate that some portion of the instruction really is not necessary. The students, through some prior learning, already have developed competencies enabling them to demonstrate achievement or mastery of one or more of the objectives upon which the instructional sequence is based. Instruction relating to these objectives would be unnecessary and the instructional sequence should be reformulated, eliminating these unnecessary elements.

Measurement also can play a formative role when introduced during an instructional sequence. For example, a short quiz administered during or at the close of a lesson in an instructional sequence that contains several lessons could serve to indicate to the teacher any deficiencies in the lesson. This feedback relative to the adequacy of the lesson could then be used to reformulate and/or improve that lesson. Moreover, for those students who receive positive reinforcement from such quizzes, attitude toward learning should become more positive. They should feel assured that their present mode of learning and approach to study is adequate and not in need of some modification or reformulation. This is a good feeling for the students to have.

Summative Measurement

A second and more common role for measurement procedures and techniques in occupational education comes after an instructional sequence has been completed. Its role is more conclusive in nature. Hence, the term *summative measurement* (Bloom 1968; Bloom, Hastings, and Madaus 1971). The actual role of end-of-instruction or summative measurement is to determine the extent to which the sequence of instruction has been successful—the extent to which all students have achieved all the objectives upon which the instruction was based.

For occupational programs, summative-measurement procedures and techniques are useful in determining not only the effectiveness of a particular instructional sequence, but whether particular students have attained the intended necessary job-related skills or are ready for more advanced training. Hopefully, the data and information obtained would be used as a basis for (1) modifying and improving instruction where needed, and (2) making evaluative decisions regarding individual students' readiness for entry into the world of work, pursuit of more advanced occupational preparation, or both.

Ultimate Measurement

The third role for measurement procedures and techniques in occupational education focuses on assessment that occurs after completion of both an occupational program and a significant period of employment. *Ultimate measurement* (Wentling 1970, 1973) corresponds to ultimate objectives (Lindquist 1951; Glaser and Nitko 1971)—the long-term objectives that can be assessed only some time after the completion of an educational program. This measurement concept is of particular importance.

For occupational education programs, ultimate measurement is concerned with evaluating the relationship between what students are taught in the instructional program and their actual performance on the job after completing their training. It may occur a week, a month, or a year or more after completing an occupational program and is directed toward assessing actual, on-the-job competencies.

Ultimate measurement, without doubt, is the most realistic and most valuable type of measurement if our goal is to evaluate (1) occupational students, and (2) occupational programs in terms of the overall success of our students after placement on the job—the ultimate criterion for determining success in these two instances. However, from a practical point of view, ultimate measurement in these two instances is also the most difficult role for measurement in our occupational programs. It is generally quite difficult to locate graduates, interview them, and obtain accurate direct assessments of their ability to perform on-the-job. For example, evaluating actual on-the-job effectiveness of graduates from a police science or fire safety program after a year or so of employment can become a time-consuming and quite difficult task if we use measurement procedures and techniques beyond mailing a short questionnaire to their captains or immediate supervisors.

Ultimate measurement often may prove to be rather involved and difficult to implement. However, occupational teachers and administrators should not, for that reason alone, refuse to consider it. Measuring the achievement of the ultimate objective for our occupational programs—preparation for a productive life—should be worth even the highest level of effort or involvement.

SUMMARY

A host of essential measurement concepts ranging from validity and reliability to the three roles of measurement in occupational programs have been presented here. All are important concepts for those who would make good use of measurement procedures and techniques in the development, conduct, and evaluation of occupational education programs. An understanding of these concepts forms much of the basis for selecting, developing, and using measurement procedures and techniques and for interpreting and using the data and information obtained with these procedures and techniques. Each of the concepts presented and discussed in this chapter will reappear in ensuing chapters of this text as the various measurement procedures and techniques useful to occupational education programs are presented and explained. The emphasis, however, will not be on repetition. It will be on a more detailed consideration of these concepts and their application to measurement procedures and techniques in occupational education.

REFERENCES

Bloom, B. S. "Learning for Mastery," *Evaluation Comment,* vol. 1, 1968.

Bloom, B. S., Hastings, J. T., and Madaus, G. F. *Handbook on Formative and Summative Evaluation of Student Learning.* New York: McGraw-Hill, 1971.

Cronbach, L. J. *Essentials of Psychological Testing.* New York: Harper and Row, 1970.

Glaser, R., and Nitko, A. J. "Measurement in Learning and Instruction." In Thorndike, R. L., ed., *Educational Measurement,* 2nd ed. Washington, D.C.: American Council on Education, 1971.

Lindquist, E. F., ed. *Educational Measurement.* Washington, D.C.: American Council on Education, 1951.

Wentling, T. L. "Quality Control for Education: A Closed Loop System," *Journal of Industrial Teacher Education,* vol. 7, no. 4, Spring, 1970.

Wentling, T. L. "Measurement Considerations of Competency Based Instruction," *Educational Technology,* vol. 13, no. 5, May, 1973.

Part II

Teacher-made Instruments

Basic Considerations for Teacher-made Tests

The first two chapters were concerned with reasons for using measurement procedures and techniques in occupational education programs, the types of instruments that might be used, and some concepts viewed by the authors as essential to a broad understanding of this area of study. Chapter 3 through 9 are concerned with applying some additional concepts that are of particular concern for preparing locally developed or teacher-made instruments for assessing student achievement in occupational programs.

TYPES AND LEVELS OF LEARNING

Occupational teachers should be concerned with the types and levels of learning included in their courses from two perspectives: (1) the development and teaching of their courses, and (2) the assessment of their students' achievement. When course objectives are expressed in terms indicating that the student will be able *to explain* some basic occupational concept, *to solve* some work-related problem, *to perform* some skilled operation, or *to produce* some saleable product, then the measurement procedures and techniques used to assess student attainment of these objectives should be directed toward measuring those specific behaviors. Normally, one would not expect to see such objectives being assessed with achievement-test items that call for students *to match* pictures of things with their proper names, *to list* the ingredients in particular mixtures, *to provide* missing words in incomplete statements, or *to label* true and false statements. The importance of occupational teachers being able to maintain the appropriate relationship between their instructional objectives and the measurement procedures and techniques they use to assess student attainment of course objectives cannot be overemphasized.

The most recent major achievement in conceptualizing levels of instructional objectives has been the development of the taxonomy of educational objectives. The taxonomy currently includes four rather broad categories or domains: cognitive, affective, psychomotor, and perceptual. Each is a result of much research and developmental effort on the part of several investigators.

Collectively, the four domains serve as one large classification scheme for all the variables or levels of achievement that might be evaluated in any instructional program, a taxonomy that is analogous to the taxonomy or scheme used for classifying plants and animals. The taxonomy of educational objectives is based on the premise that learning outcomes or objectives are most appropriately expressed in terms of student behaviors. Therefore, it is particularly useful to occupational education programs because the instructional objectives for these programs generally can be expressed in terms of what the students will know, understand, be able to do, or be upon completion of the instruction. Thus, the taxonomy becomes an extremely useful tool in helping occupational teachers and curriculum and test developers determine whether they have identified all the instructional objectives that should be included and measured in their occupational courses. A brief description of each of the four domains included in the taxonomy of educational objectives follows. For a more detailed presentation of each of these domains, the appropriate reference(s) listed at the end of this chapter should be reviewed.

Cognitive Domain

The *cognitive domain* (Bloom et al. 1956) includes all objectives that are concerned with the recall of knowledge and the development of higher levels of mental abilities and skills. It contains six major subdivisions of cognitive processes. Each in turn is subdivided into more specific levels of learning involving these major cognitive processes. In an abbreviated form, the six major classifications of the cognitive domain in increasing order of complexity are:

1. *Knowledge*—The recall of specifics, ways and means of dealing with specifics, and universals and abstractions in a field.
2. *Comprehension*—A type of understanding involving the abilities to translate, interpret, or extrapolate.
3. *Application*—The use of general ideas, rules of procedure, and generalized methods in particular and concrete situations.
4. *Analysis*—The breakdown of communications to clarify constituent elements, relationships, or organizational principles.
5. *Synthesis*—The production of a unique communication, plan or proposed set of operations, or a set of abstract relations.
6. *Evaluation*—Judgments about the value of material and methods for given purposes.

Bloom's taxonomy would be helpful in preparing occupational achievement test items to assess the cognitive processes developed in the instructional program. In its entirety, it offers a standard index and vocabulary for identifying, analyzing, classifying, and defining specific cognitive skills at various levels of learning. It also provides example behavioral objectives for each type and level of learning presented. The index of types and levels of learning is useful in identifying all the cognitive skills that might be included in a particular occupational achievement test. The example objectives are useful in developing the proper format for the objectives or occupational outcomes that should form the basis for the items included in such an achievement test.

Affective Domain

The *affective domain* (Krathwohl, Bloom, and Masia 1964) includes those objectives concerned with a student's personal–social development. In this taxonomy, the process of internalization serves as the basis for its five major subdivisions of types and levels of learning or development, and the subclassifications included at each level. Here, internalization is viewed as a developmental process having two or three identifiable stages: first, tentative adoption of the

specific personal–social behavior and, later, more complete acceptance. Therefore, this taxonomy includes a continuum of personal-
social behaviors at each of the five levels of development. In brief,
the five major classifications in ascending order of degree of internalization are as follows:

1. *Receiving*—The sensitization of the learner including awareness,
   willingness to receive input, and controlled or selected attention.
2. *Responding*—The interest to attend actively including acquiescence in responding, willingness to respond, and satisfaction in
   response.
3. *Valuing*—The recognition that a thing, phenomenon, or behavior
   has worth including acceptance of a value, preference for a
   value, and commitment or conviction.
4. *Organization*—The beginnings of the development of a value
   system when situations involving two or more values are encountered including conceptualization of a value and organization of a value system.
5. *Characterization by a Value or Value Complex*—The integration
   of beliefs, ideas, attitudes into an internally consistent total
   philosophy that serves to control the student's normal behavior
   including generalized set and characterization.

Krathwohl's taxonomy provides an excellent guide for identifying and classifying occupational program objectives concerned
with what each student should *be* upon completion of the program of instruction. It focuses on attitudinal factors such as feelings, emotions, and indications of acceptance or rejection that
are important to success in occupational programs and in the world
of work. For example, level-one objectives for occupational programs
would be concerned with students simply being able to attend to or
perceive occupational-content or career information. At level two,
the concern would be student interest in responding to such content
or information. The third level is concerned with students recognizing and accepting the value or worth of such content or information. At the fourth level, the concern is with intentionally responding
to the content or information in a value-oriented way and including
it in a personal value system. The fifth and final concern is with the
students characterizing their attitudinal structure in terms of consistent occupational- and career-development patterns.

The positive impact that occupational education programs have on developing appropriate attitudinal or affective behaviors is widely acknowledged but often overlooked when developing instructional objectives and assessing student attainment of those objectives. Without a receptive attitude toward occupational content, for example, students will experience difficulty acquiring the knowledge and understanding in the cognitive domain. They will not be ready to learn. Research has demonstrated that retention is dependent to a large degree upon the attitude that the learner brings to the class-room or laboratory. When the instruction and learner attitudes and values are not compatible, then the impact of the instruction is weakened considerably. Occupational teachers should make a serious effort to develop affective or "being" objectives for their courses as well as the instruments needed to assess attainment of these objectives. Measurement procedures and techniques for assessing affective objectives (rating scales, questionnaires, and Q-sort techniques) are presented and discussed in chapter 7.

Psychomotor Domain

The *psychomotor domain* (Simpson 1966) includes objectives that involve motor skills, the manipulation of materials and objects, and acts that involve neuromuscular coordination. Seven major sub-divisions are included. Each is based upon the degree of complexity in psychomotor behavior with consideration given for the sequence involved in the performance of the motor tasks. Briefly stated, the seven major types and levels of learning included in this domain are as follows:

1. *Perception*—The process of becoming aware of objects, qualities, or relations by way of the sense organs and involving sensory stimulation, cue selection, and translation.
2. *Set*—The preparatory adjustment or readiness for a particular action or experience including mental set, physical set, and emotional set.
3. *Guided Response*—The overt behavioral act under the guidance of an instructor or in response to self-evaluation where the student has a model or criterion for judging his/her performance, which includes imitation and trial and error.
4. *Mechanism*—The achievement of a degree of confidence and proficiency in performing an act.

5. *Complex Overt Response*—The attainment of complex skills or motor acts, which includes resolution of uncertainty and automatic performance.

6. *Adaptation*—The alteration of motor activities to meet the requirements of new problematic situations requiring a physical response.

7. *Origination*—The creation of new motor acts or ways of manipulating material objects based upon understanding, abilities, and skills developed in the psychomotor area.

Simpson's taxonomy is important for measuring competencies of the motor skill type developed in occupational programs. Many technical and occupational tasks require a high degree of motor skill development. These tasks can be identified and measured more readily by using this taxonomy.

However, as pointed out by Herschbach (1975), nearly all psychomotor skills include cognitive as well as affective elements. The occupational task of changing automobile tires, for example, involves a cognitive element (understanding the process), an affective element (being willing to work to specific standards), as well as the actual motor skills involved. The desired instructional outcome will determine which of the domains should be emphasized when constructing procedures and techniques for measuring attainment of instructional objectives involving two or more domains.

Perceptual Domain

The *perceptual domain* (Moore 1970) includes objectives that are concerned with sensory-dependent activity executed by the student in response to certain stimuli. The competencies indexed in the perceptual taxonomy are sequential behaviors ordered on the basis of increased information extracted by learners. Performance in this domain is affected more significantly by factors such as age, personality, and emotions than by the students' general levels of ability. The five major types and levels of learning included in this domain are as follows:

1. *Sensation*—The awareness of the informational aspects of the stimulus energy including detection and awareness of change.

2. *Figure Perception*—The awareness of entity including discrimination of unity, sensory figure-ground perceptual organization, and resolution of detail.

3. *Symbol Perception*—The awareness of figures that form denotive signs when associated meanings are not considered.
4. *Perception of Meaning*—The awareness of the significance commonly associated with forms and patterns and events and the ability to interpret and assign personal significance to them.
5. *Perceptive Performance*—The ability to make sensitive and accurate observations, complex decisions involving many factors, and change ongoing behavior in response to its effectiveness.

Collectively, the categories in this taxonomy constitute a series of perceptual activities of students in instructional settings, which is useful to many types of occupational programs. Wentling and Lawson (1975), for example, point out that beginning typing students initially become visually aware of the keyboard structure, then selectively discriminate key positions, perceive the symbolic relationship between keys and letters, indicate an awareness of correct sequencing for key (character) execution, and, finally, diagnose the resulting typed image.

The high degree of dependency between the perceptual domain and the cognitive and affective domains, and especially the psychomotor domain, should be mentioned. Many motor tasks depend upon accurate and complete perception for an adequate execution. For example, a welder must first perceive the appropriateness of the welding flame's color, shape, and sound before beginning to weld and must receive constant visual feedback regarding temperature, speed, and motion throughout the welding process. Successful welders also have, for example, a knowledge of the weldability of various metals (cognitive domain) and place much value in their being able to produce welds that meet and exceed accepted standards in the industry (affective domain).

Four behaviorally oriented domains of the taxonomy of educational objectives have been presented here. Although there is some dependency among them, the basic concern relative to each is the types and levels of learning that might be included and evaluated in an occupational education program. For practical reasons the four domains have been collapsed and introduced in chapter 4 as knowing, understanding, doing, and being. Effective employment of even these simplified levels and types of learning by occupational educators will do much to insure that the instruction in the occupational program and the locally developed or teacher-made instruments used to assess student attainment are congruent.

CRITERION-REFERENCED VS. NORM-REFERENCED TESTS

Another basic consideration for locally developed or teacher-made instruments is the choice of referencing to be reflected in the instrument. Will it be a norm-referenced or a criterion-referenced test? As indicated in our discussion of points of reference for measurement included in chapter 2, the point of reference should be selected on the basis of its suitability to the measurement task at hand.

Norm-referenced tests are appropriate when the primary purpose of the instrument is to make comparisons among individuals. Such comparisons are necessary when it is important to know how a particular individual compares with all others being considered before some decision about that individual can be made. For example, we might administer a large battery of automotive achievement tests to the students enrolled in our automotive classes for purposes of identifying the best team to enter into the National Plymouth Troubleshooting Contest competition. Such comparisons are necessary also when there is need to rank a group of individuals with regard to some variable, as in assigning letter grades A, B, C, D, or F to students with respect to their achievement in class.

Criterion-referenced tests, on the other hand, are appropriate when we are interested in determining who among a group of students has mastered a particular set of skills and who has not. We would want to use this type of test to identify who among those students enrolled in a particular class is ready to move on to the next level of instruction when success at the advanced level of instruction is dependent upon the development of the basic skills taught at the first level. Many occupational instructors, for example, do not begin "hands-on" instruction with some types of tools and equipment until the students have successfully passed the criterion-referenced safety test relating to that particular tool or piece of equipment. Certification or licensure for many occupations is based upon criterion-referenced tests or examinations. In criterion-referenced testing, the students are classified as having either passed or failed. In the case of evaluating a particular sequence of instruction, the instruction would be labeled as being either adequate or inadequate, depending upon the number of students who were able to pass the criterion test upon completing the instructional sequence.

If the measurement task calls for a locally developed instrument of the norm-referenced type, then the developer(s) must be concerned with producing a test that will provide a spread among students' scores and the more variability among these scores, the easier it will be to make comparisons among these students. Therefore, when preparing items for norm-referenced instruments, considerable thought must be given to including items that represent a wide range of item difficulty. The range should include a few very easy items (almost any student can answer them correctly) and a few very difficult items (only the extremely talented can answer them correctly) with the vast majority of the items representing the various shades of difficulty in between. Some thought also must be given to the number of items included in the instrument. Short instruments containing only a few items will not be able to provide much differentiation between students. Norm-referenced tests, then, should include enough items of such difficulty to insure discrimination between all levels of ability represented among those to be tested.

If the measurement task calls for a locally developed instrument of the criterion-referenced type, then the developer(s) will be concerned with producing a test that will differentiate between those students who have attained the minimum level of competence expressed in the criterion and those whose performance falls short of that level. Relative levels of performance within these two categories are of no concern, therefore, development of test items should focus on each item's relationship or importance to the task to be performed. For most applications in occupational programs the relationship between test items and the competency being measured will be a direct and obvious one. The numbers of items to be included in a criterion-referenced instrument will be determined by the number needed to adequately sample the behaviors that are important to performing at the minimum level of competence.

The choice of referencing is a fundamental consideration in the preparation of locally developed instruments for occupational programs. The purpose of the discussion here has been to draw some distinctions between these two points of reference and the basic considerations for local test development in occupational programs that are implied by each. No implications as to the superiority of either criterion- or norm-referenced testing have been implied. Each has its role to play in the occupational program.

GROUP VS. INDIVIDUAL
TESTS

Considerations relating to how the instrument will be administered (whether to groups of students or to individual students) are important and should be raised early in the process of preparing a locally developed or teacher-made test. Certainly, costs in terms of student time as well as teacher time will dictate that, for most occupational programs, group tests that can be administered to whole classes in one sitting be used when their use is practical.

There are some situations in occupational programs, however, when group tests do not adequately serve our needs. For instance, in individualized instructional programs where students are working and learning at their own pace, one or more students may be ready for his/her mastery exam at the completion of a unit of instruction when other students in the program are not. Achievement tests for this type of occupational program would probably be designed as individual rather than group tests.

Occupational programs often call for the use of individually administered achievement tests for some aspects of the program because there is no other way. Welding, truck driving, and heavy equipment operation programs, for example, must use individually administered achievement tests to measure at least the attainment of the instructional objectives concerned with the operational tasks of the occupation. Many performance tests in occupational programs like these use individually administered tests, particularly those that assess performance with some large and expensive piece of equipment like an airplane or caterpillar tractor.

On occasion, students with reading difficulties stemming from inadequate sight, language difficulties, or a low verbal ability will be enrolled in occupational programs. Such students will need individually administered achievement tests if their progress in the program is to be measured accurately.

Fortunately, from an economic view, most occupational programs can and do make good use of group tests of achievement for assessing attainment of the majority of their instructional objectives. Nevertheless, deciding whether to use a group or individually administered instrument remains a basic consideration in the preparation of locally developed or teacher-made tests.

POWER VS. SPEED TESTS

One additional basic consideration when preparing locally developed or teacher-made tests is whether to use a power test or a speed test. *Power tests* are tests designed to assess the full range of a student's skills or abilities, which place little or no emphasis on time limits. Students are allowed adequate time to consider carefully and respond to all items included in a power test. The items included in a power test range from very easy to very difficult. They are usually presented in the test in order of increasing difficulty. Variation in obtained scores is due almost solely to variation among students' actual abilities to respond to the items included in the test, without regard to a time factor.

Speed tests are tests in which a student's skills or abilities are measured by the number of test items that he/she can complete correctly within a given time limit. The difficulty level of all items included in a pure speed test are such that, given enough time, every student could provide a correct response to every item in the test. However, the time limit for pure speed tests is always set such that no student, no matter how capable, is able to complete correctly all the items included in the test. Variation in obtained scores, then, is due almost solely to variation among students' abilities to perform quickly these simple tasks.

Most locally developed instruments used in occupational programs are intended to be basically power tests but because there is often a time limit set for completing these tests, they sometimes take on a speed factor for some students, particularly those who have low reading abilities or are low in other verbal skills. To the degree that imposed time limits transform what are intended to be power tests into speed tests for some students, the validity of the tests must be questioned. For example, if, by imposing a time limit on a multiple-choice type achievement test in a vocational agriculture program, we restrict the number of students who complete the test because of their inability to read fast enough, then we must ask whether the test is for some students measuring reading skills as well as vocational agriculture skills. If so, the validity of the test has been reduced by imposing the time limit. The only way that we can be assured that this test is not measuring reading skills to any significant degree is to insure that each student has adequate time to read and comprehend all of the items included in the test.

Most achievement tests used in occupational programs are neither speed nor power tests, but some combination of the two. The most common combination is the mastery test. These tests have the liberal time limits of a power test and contain items having uniformly low levels of difficulty similar to a speed test. Their primary use in occupational programs is in determining if students have mastered all the knowledge and skills at the conclusion of a particular unit of instruction. Quizzes given at the end of an instructional unit or throughout programmed instruction are good examples of mastery tests.

From the foregoing discussion, it should be clear that locally developed instruments can be either power tests, speed tests, or some combination thereof. It is up to the test developer(s) to decide early in the preparation of the instrument the direction that will be taken. If a speed component is the variable to be measured (as in typing and shorthand achievement tests), then a speed test is appropriate. If the attainment of a broad range of knowledge, skills, and understanding (with little or no concern for speed) is the variable to be measured, then a power test is appropriate. If local conditions like length of class periods or the purpose of the measurement indicate that a combination speed and power test would be appropriate, then the test developer(s) should take precautions to insure that the resulting instrument does not become for some students a power test and for others (particularly the handicapped or disadvantaged) a speed test.

SUMMARY

Some basic points that should be considered early in the processes of preparing locally developed or teacher-made instruments have been presented. No specific decisions or hard and fast rules were offered regarding these basic points or decisions. Measurement tasks and local conditions vary too much for universal solutions to the considerations presented here to be possible.

After having reviewed the measurement task(s) for which the instrument is to be developed and having reached some decisions regarding the types and levels of learning to be assessed, the point of reference to be used, a group or individual administration, and the influence of speed and power factors, the local test developer(s) would be ready to prepare a table of specifications or some other type of blueprint for the instrument. Several specific approaches to preparing tables of specifications for locally developed or teacher-made tests are presented in chapter 4.

REFERENCES

Bloom, B. S., ed., Englehart, M. D., Furst, E. J., Hill, W. H., and Krathwohl, D. R. *A Taxonomy of Educational Objectives: Handbook* 1, *The Cognitive Domain.* New York: David McKay Co., 1956.

Herschbach, Dennis R. "Use of the Taxonomy of the Psychomotor Domain for the Writing of Performance Objectives," *Journal of Industrial Teacher Education,* vol. 12, no. 3, 1975.

Krathwohl, D. R., Bloom, B. S., and Masia, B. *A Taxonomy of Educational Objectives: Handbook* 2, *The Affective Domain.* New York: David McKay Co., 1964.

Moore, M. R. "The Perceptual-Motor Domain and a Proposed Taxonomy of Perception," *A V Communication Review,* vol. 18, no. 4, 1970.

Simpson, B. J. "The Classification of Educational Objectives, Psychomotor Domain," *Illinois Teacher of Home Economics,* vol. X, no. 4, 1966.

Wentling, T. L., and Lawson, T. E. *Evaluating Occupational Education and Training Programs.* Boston: Allyn and Bacon, Inc., 1975.

Chapter 4

Planning the Test

There is a long-standing maxim in occupational education that says you should plan your work and then work your plan. Occupational education teachers should follow this long-cherished principle when preparing locally developed or teacher-made instruments. This chapter focuses on procedures and techniques helpful to occupational teachers as they develop plans for their tests and begin to work their plans.

STUDENT-PERFORMANCE OBJECTIVES

Objectives should serve as the basis for all evaluation in occupational programs, whether focused on total programs or the achievement of the individual student learners enrolled in the programs. Well-stated objectives provide direction for developing and implementing the measurement procedures and techniques used to gather data and information for the evaluation.

Components of Objectives

The objectives that are of most value in serving as a basis for assessing student achievement in occupational programs are student-performance objectives, which contain at least the following three components (Mager 1962; Davis and Borgen 1974):

1. Task or outcome statement
2. Condition statement
3. Criterion statement

Task or Outcome Statements. The *task or outcome statement* identifies in behavioral terms precisely what it is that the students will be able to do upon completion of some specified segment of instruction. The segment of instruction may be a lesson, unit, course, or program. The following are all examples of task or outcome statements that would be appropriate for lesson objectives in occupational programs. Each presents in behavioral terms precisely what the student should be able to do upon completion of the lesson.

EXAMPLE TASK STATEMENTS

1. Prepare a tossed salad for fifty persons.
2. Determine a patient's blood pressure.
3. Set up and type a business letter.
4. Classify fires as to their being type A, B, C, or D.
5. Perform and interpret nitrate, phosphate, and potash plant tissue tests.

Condition Statements. The purpose of the *condition statement* is to further refine the task or outcome statement by defining the conditions under which the students would be expected to perform the indicated task or activity. The following are examples of condition statements that would be appropriate for the foregoing task statements. Each presents a specific condition under which students would be expected to perform its associated task.

EXAMPLE CONDITION STATEMENTS

1. Given an appropriate recipe and access to the necessary utensils and ingredients
2. In an appropriate clinical setting

---

3. Given the appropriate equipment, supplies, format, and copy
4. When shown color pictures of fires
5. In an appropriate field setting

Criterion Statements. The *criterion statement* is included in the objective statement to assist students and their teachers in determining when the objective has been achieved. It is a statement of the standard or criterion with which the student's performance will be compared. If student performance is judged as being equal to or exceeding the standard included in the objective statement, then that objective will have been met or achieved.

The following are criterion statements that might be combined with the foregoing task and condition statements:

EXAMPLE CRITERION STATEMENTS

1. As per the recipe and having a residual smaller than 3 percent after serving
2. With an accuracy of ±6mm. of that recorded for the same patient by the instructor
3. In mailable form as defined by the instructor and within 10 minutes
4. As per the *IFSTA Training Manual* and without error
5. Consistent with tissue testing practices outlined in *Agriculture Bulletin #723*

Example Objectives

When combined, the foregoing task, condition, and criterion statements form complete student performance or instructional objectives that are in a most useful format. Two examples assembled from our previous example statements follow:

EXAMPLE OBJECTIVES 1 & 2

1. Given an appropriate recipe and access to the necessary utensils and ingredients, the students will be able to prepare a tossed salad for

---

fifty persons as per the recipe and having a residual smaller than 3 percent after serving.

2. In an appropriate laboratory setting, the students will be able to determine a patient's blood pressure with an accuracy of ±6mm. of that recorded for the same patient by the instructor.

The utility of measurable student performance objectives that contain the three important components (task, condition, and criterion statements) is in some areas very apparent. For example, students, upon reviewing these instructional objectives, know precisely what types and levels of performance will be expected of them when they complete the instruction directed toward these objectives. Such knowledge can be a significant force in clarifying the intent of the instruction and in motivating the students enrolled in occupational programs. This type of instructional objective is also the very foundation of "individualized instruction" and "competency-based instruction," two related and currently important movements in occupational education.

Objectives as a Test Planning Device

Student performance objectives that contain task, condition, and criterion statements also can serve as the plan or blueprint for developing the measurement procedures and techniques necessary to assess *directly* student achievement in competency-based occupational programs. Drawing again from the components presented earlier, assume the following objective is from a competency-based secretarial course and we want to assess directly student attainment of this objective.

EXAMPLE OBJECTIVE 3

3. Given the appropriate equipment, supplies, format, and copy, the students will be able to type a business letter in mailable form as defined by the instructor and do so within ten minutes.

Direct assessment of student achievement of this objective would involve seating students at their typing lab work stations, presenting them with the copy to be included in the business letter to be typed, and informing them that they have 10 minutes in which to complete their letters in block format and present them to the instructor in mailable form (neat and clean appearance with no errors and no visible corrections). The actual procedures and techniques used to assess directly student attainment of this particular objective might vary somewhat from teacher to teacher, but the basic plan is embodied in the objective.

Occupational teachers who have developed and implemented student performance objectives of this type for the lessons in their programs and who want to assess directly attainment of *all* such objectives will have little need to develop extensive plans to insure that the measurement procedures and techniques they use are congruent with their instructional objectives. When the entire collection of the objectives to be covered by the assessment serves as the plan or blueprint for the measurement procedures and techniques used, the appropriate relationship between the objectives and the test is all but automatic.

This would be the ideal approach to assessing attainment of student performance objectives in occupational programs. It is the approach that should be used by occupational teachers whenever possible. However, the practicalities of the real world generally serve to make ideal approaches to most anything somewhat impractical at times. Assessing student attainment of instructional objectives in occupational education programs is no exception to this observation.

TABLES OF SPECIFICATIONS

Out of practical necessity occupational teachers often have need to (1) assess directly student attainment of *selected* student performance objectives, (2) assess *indirectly* student attainment of student performance objectives, or (3) use *course content* as the basis for developing achievement tests. In each of these instances, a special plan or blueprint for test preparation must be developed. These plans or blueprints are called *tables of specifications* and they are of three general types; each type relates to one of the foregoing three instances: direct assessment of selected objectives, indirect assessment of objectives, and content-based assessment. A detailed presentation of each and its use in planning locally developed or teacher-made tests follows.

Direct Assessment of Selected Objectives

In those instances where occupational teachers are either unable to or do not want to assess attainment of all student performance objectives developed for a particular segment of instruction, a plan or table of specifications is needed to insure that the test is designed to assess achievement of the most important of the objectives. For example, final examinations in occupational courses and achievement tests used to evaluate the effectiveness of occupational programs generally cover only the most important or critical competencies to be developed in the course or program. Much of the related or "nice to know" information is not covered in these exams. Usually, this is because there are limits to the available testing time. A plan or table of specifications is a useful tool to help insure that each student-performance objective is considered and used in preparing the final examination if it is found to be concerned with a competency that is critical to the occupation. The format for this type of table of specifications is presented in table 4.1.

Preparing and using this type of table are relatively simple processes. Occupational teachers should assemble all the student performance objectives that were to have been attained during the segment of instruction covered by the test. Each objective is then listed in the table of specifications by its related unit of instruction or content area.

TABLE 4.1 Table of Specifications for Direct Assessment of Selected Student-performance Objectives

Objectives by Unit or Content Area	Relative Emphasis of Unit or Content Area	Objectives to Be Included in the Assessment
I.		
1.		√
2.	25%	
3.		√
II.		
1.	15%	
2.		√
III.		
1.		
•		
•		
•		

The relative emphasis that each unit of instruction or content area is to be given in the development of the total test is listed in the column to the right of the objectives included in that unit or content area. For example, in table 4.1 the first and second units of instruction or content areas would contribute 25 percent and 15 percent respectively. The remaining units or content areas would contribute the additionally needed 60 percent.

The objectives selected to be assessed are then checked ($\sqrt{}$) in the last column of the form. In the example presented in table 4.1 objectives one and three in the first unit or content area will be assessed. Together, they constitute 25 percent of the total assessment to be achieved by the test constructed from the objectives checked in the table of specifications. The second objective in the first unit or content area has not been checked for inclusion in the assessment for which this test is being developed. In the selection process it was viewed, for one reason or another, as an objective that would not be assessed by the test being developed from this table of specifications.

Procedures for developing individual items for the test are the same as those followed when directly assessing attainment of all student performance objectives, except, in this instance, measurement procedures are developed only for those objectives that are checked in the far right column of the table of specifications. Student attainment of these objectives is directly assessed in the manner indicated in each objective. If, for example, the following objective was checked as one to be assessed:

EXAMPLE OBJECTIVE 4

4. When shown color pictures of fires, students will be able to classify the pictured fires as to their being class A, B, C, or D as per the *IFSTA Training Manual.*

---

then the testing procedure would involve showing students color pictures of class A, B, C, and D fires (in random order) and having them indicate the class of fire shown in each picture. It is important to note that this *direct* procedure for assessing student attainment of the above objective would *not* employ items of the following types or similar types of items:

Example Items 1 & 2: *True–False*

1. ____   ____   Gasoline fires are classified as class A fires.

2. ____   ____   Class C fires include fires in electrical wiring.

Example Item 3: *Multiple Choice*

3. Forest fires would be classified under which of the following IFSTA classes of fires?
   a. Class A
   b. Class B
   c. Class C
   d. Class D

The preceding items are certainly related to the foregoing objective. That is, the knowledge they elicit is important to being able to demonstrate the behavior expressed in the objective. They are in fact measuring "enroute behaviors" or knowledges that are developed enroute to attaining the expressed objective. Hence, they would be useful in obtaining an *indirect* measure of student attainment of the foregoing objective. However, they would not provide a direct measure of the behavior indicated in this objective.

Indirect Assessment of Objectives

Thus far we have discussed test planning based upon direct assessment of all or selected numbers of student performance objectives from a particular segment of instruction. Sometimes it is difficult, impractical, if not impossible, to obtain direct assessments of even well-stated student performance objectives. In such instances, it is necessary to use the *indirect* measurement procedures and techniques briefly alluded to above. They require a different approach to planning than do the direct procedures and techniques that have been emphasized. For example, the table of specifications for indirect assessment of student performance objectives takes on an expanded role in the planning process. Its purpose is not only to insure that the test is designed to assess achievement of all or the most appropriate objectives, but to insure that the test items used are adequate in content, scope, number, and level of learning. Drawing once more from the sample task, condition, and criterion statements presented earlier, assume the following objective is from a local vocational agriculture program and, while perhaps not impossible, direct measurement of student achievement is impractical.

EXAMPLE OBJECTIVE 5

5. In an appropriate field setting, the student will be able to perform and interpret nitrate, phosphate, and potash plant tissue tests consistent with tissue testing practices outlined in *Agriculture Bulletin #723.*

The table of specifications for assessing indirectly attainment of the above objective is presented in table 4.2.

All of the objectives to be assessed indirectly using the test to be constructed from the table of specifications are listed down the left column headed "Objectives." The next column, "Relative Emphasis," is used to record, as a percentage of the total test, the

TABLE 4.2 Table of Specifications for Indirect Assessment of Student-performance Objectives

| | | Types and Levels of Learning | | | | |
Objectives	Relative Emphasis	Knowing	Under-standing	Doing	Being	Item Totals
1. In an appropriate field setting, the students will be able to perform and interpret nitrate, phosphate, and potash plant tissue tests consistent with tissue testing practices outlined in *Agriculture Bulletin #723*	20%	4	2	1	0	7

relative emphasis that will be given the objective listed to the left. In this example, the test items relating to the first objective will constitute 20 percent of the total test, leaving 80 percent of the test items to be devoted to measuring indirectly student achievement of the remaining objectives covered by this test.

For practical reasons, the types and levels of learning indexed in the four domains of the taxonomy of educational objectives, presented and discussed in chapter 3, have been reduced to four broad categories: knowing, understanding, doing, and being. The first two, *knowing and understanding,* include all the abilities indexed in the cognitive domain of the taxonomy. The next category, *doing,* includes the tasks indexed in the psychomotor and perceptual domains. The *being* category is for those affective behaviors indexed in that domain.

The numbers entered under these categories indicate that the plan for this test will include four items devoted to measuring that which the student must know in order to perform the tasks specified in this objective, two items devoted to measuring that which the student must understand, one item of a perceptual or psychomotor nature, and no items that are directed toward attitudes, or values relating to this objective. Thus, the plan calls for the development of seven items, each directed toward indirectly measuring student attainment of our sample objective as expressed in the table of specifications. Example items that might be used to meet the requirements set for this objective by type and level of learning are as follows:

Example Item 4: Knowing

4. Which of the following time periods is recommended for making plant tissue tests?
   a. 8:00 A.M. to 5:00 P.M.
   b. 6:00 A.M. to 5:00 P.M.
   c. 8:00 A.M. to 6:00 P.M.
   d. All of the above time periods are recommended.

Knowing when to conduct tissue tests is an important part of being able to perform and interpret tissue tests. To answer this question, students would have to *know this one fact*—8:00 A.M. to 5:00 P.M. is the recommended time period.

Example Item 5: Understanding

5. If a nitrogen tissue test yields a light red reading during ideal growing conditions, what color reading would a tissue test from the same plant yield during a drought period?
   a. Pink
   b. Light red
   c. Cherry red
   d. Dark red

Understanding the relationship between nitrogen tissue test results and growing conditions is an important part of being able to interpret test results. To answer this question, students would have to *understand this relationship* and be able to apply it to this hypothetical situation. It should be noted that this item measures a higher level of cognitive learning than the previous knowing item.

Example Item 6: Doing

6. In the spaces below draw a picture of a normal ear of corn at maturity and a picture of a mature ear of corn from a plant that lacked sufficient phosphate during the growing season.

   Normal   *Phosphate Shortage*

   _____   _____

   _____   _____

Another important aspect of interpreting plant tissue tests involves using these test results along with information from other sources (e.g., soil tests and visual observations) to determine the adequacy of nutrient supplies. In corn, phosphate shortages cause ears to be small, sometimes twisted or bent, and to have underdeveloped kernals. To respond correctly to this item, students would have to *have a perception of these deficiencies* as compared to what is considered normal, and be able to *draw rather accurate pictures* of each. Again, this item requires a much different type and level of learning than that required by the understanding and knowing items.

It should be noted that the foregoing knowing, understanding, and doing items would contribute to an *indirect* assessment of the objective indicated in the table of specifications. In using an indirect approach to assessing achievement of this objective, the assumption is made that students who can provide correct responses to the seven test items indicated by the table of specifications could perform the tasks indicated in the objective. For any one student this may or may not be a valid assumption. However, a strong positive relationship would probably exist between performance on these seven test items and performance of the tasks indicated in the objective. Otherwise, use of the indirect approach to assessing student attainment of objectives would not be justified.

Assessing Student Attainment of Course Content

The development and use of student-performance objectives that are of the form presented and discussed here is far from being a universal practice in occupational programs. While objectives of this type have for years been advocated in the literature (Davis and Borgen 1974; Mager 1962; Popham and Baker 1970), they have also had their critics (Atkin 1968; Stake 1969). The primary criticisms focus on their placing restrictive limits on the learning process and the amount of time and effort required to develop such objectives not being in proportion to their consequential value in the instructional program. For whatever reason, many occupational teachers use instructional objectives that are less specific and often are not stated in terms of student behavior. These objectives are destined to play a less directive role in the test development process than that played by student-performance objectives of the type discussed thus far. When objectives are not expressed in such precise terms, the table of specifications for test development is based on course content. An example of a table of specifications based on course content from a fire fighter training program is presented in table 4.3.

All of the course content to be "covered" by the test is listed down the left column headed "Course Content." The remaining columns are the same as those incorporated in the objectives-based

TABLE 4.3 Table of Specifications for Assessing Student Attainment of Course Content

| | | Types and Levels of Learning | | | | |
Course Content	Relative Emphasis	Knowing	Under-standing	Doing	Being	Item Totals
I. Fire Behavior Science	25%					
1. Principles of combustion		1	1			2
2. Classes of fire		1				1
3. Flammable liquids						
a. Identification				1		1
b. Flashpoint		1				1
c. Ignition point		1				1
d. Transporting		1			1	2

table of specifications. In this example, about 25 percent of the items included in the total test are to be devoted to the content included in segment I of the course, Fire Behavior Science. The remaining 75 percent of the items to be included in this test will be devoted to covering the content included in the remaining segments of the course.

Again, for practical reasons the four domains of the taxonomy of educational objectives have been reduced to four broad categories: knowing, understanding, doing, and being. As in the objective-based table of specifications, the numbers entered under these categories indicate the number of test items to be developed to measure mastery of the content indicated at the level of learning indicated and included in the test for which this table of specifications has been prepared.

The numbers entered in the table thus far indicate that one item each will be devoted to what the student is expected to know and to understand relative to the principles of combustion. For example, the following two items might be used to fulfill the needs indicated in this portion of the table of specifications:

Example Item 7: Knowing

7. Which of the following elements of fire *is not* necessary to support combustion?

---

a. Heat
b. Fuel
c. Oxygen
d. Smoke

Example Item 8: Understanding

8. Which of the following elements of fire, if removed, would serve to extinguish a fire most rapidly?
   a. Heat
   b. Fuel
   c. Oxygen
   d. Smoke

The table of specifications presented in table 4.3 also indicates that the test will include one knowing item that is concerned with classes of fire. The following item might be used to satisfy this area of the plan for this test:

Example Item 9: Knowing

9. Match the following types of fires with their NFPA fire classifications by writing the appropriate classification on the line preceding each type of fire listed.

Types of Fires	NFPA Classes
____ Gasoline fire	A
____ Electrical transformer fire	B
____ Grass fire	C
____ Magnesium fire	D
____ Forest fire	

The remaining four items called for by the table of specifications presented in table 4.3 are concerned with the content area of flammable liquids. One doing item relating to identification and three knowing items (one each—relating to flashpoint, burning point, and transporting flammable liquids) are needed to fulfill this area of the plan. In addition, one being item is needed and it would be concerned with measuring, perhaps, some important attitude that students should have developed during the course of the instruction. The following four items might be used to satisfy the requirements of this area of the table of specifications:

Example Item 10: Doing

10. Vials of liquids numbered 1 through 5 at this testing station con- tain flammable and nonflammable liquids. Identify by their appear- ances and smell those that are flammable and record your answers by checking the appropriate boxes below.

Vial No.	Flammable	Nonflammable
1.	☐	☐
2.	☐	☐
3.	☐	☐
4.	☐	☐
5.	☐	☐

Example Item 11: Knowing

11. Which of the following changes occur to a flammable liquid when it is heated to its flashpoint?
    a. It ignites.
    b. It begins vaporizing.
    c. It begins condensing.
    d. It starts expanding.

Example Item 12: Knowing

12. What is the temperature relationship between the ignition point and the flashpoint of a flammable liquid?
    a. Ignition point is hotter.
    b. Flashpoint is hotter.
    c. Both are of equal temperature.
    d. Relationship changes depending upon the liquid.

Example Item 13: Knowing

13. For purposes of transportation, a flammable liquid has been defined by the NFPA as any ignitable liquid that vaporizes in air at a temperature of ___.
    a. 70°F or above
    b. 80°F or below
    c. 80°F or above
    d. 90°F or below

Example Item 14: Being

14. Teacher Rating of Student Attitude Toward Flammable Liquids

    | | | | | | | | | | | | | | | | | | |

    Student exhibits careless attitude and frequently violates safety precautions around flammable liquids.

    Student generally exhibits respect for flammable liquids and works carefully around them.

    Student continually exhibits healthy concern for flammable liquids and insists on his and others' compliance with all safety precautions.

SUMMARY

Three different approaches to planning for the preparation of locally developed or teacher-made tests to assess student growth and development in occupational programs have been presented. The first approach started with and used well-developed student performance objectives to serve as the plan for preparing such instruments.

It was pointed out that student performance objectives containing explicit task, condition, and criterion statements can constitute the plan for the test when direct measurement techniques are appropriate and can be used. These objectives leave no doubt in either the student's or the teacher's mind as to what the student is going to be able to do, under what types of conditions, and to what level or degree of performance. Direct assessment of student attainment of these objectives is equally straightforward. Students are given an opportunity to perform the stated task under the prescribed conditions and if they are able to perform at or beyond the expected level or degree of performance, then the objective is considered to have been achieved. If the expected level or degree of performance is not exhibited during the examination, then the objective is not considered as having been achieved.

When developing comprehensive final course examinations or tests to evaluate the effectiveness of a particular occupational program it is often necessary to concentrate on directly assessing student attainment of *selected* rather than *all* student performance objectives. In these instances, it is necessary to develop a table of specifications to assist in determining the overall emphasis of the test and the specific objectives that are to be assessed directly.

Because such a direct approach to testing is not always feasible for some occupational programs, an indirect approach to assessing student attainment of objectives was also presented. This approach to planning for test development uses a table of specifications, which lists student performance objectives to be assessed and the number of test items for each of the various types and levels of learning that will be needed to assess *indirectly* student attainment of each listed objective.

As a planning tool, this table of specifications serves to help insure that appropriate emphasis is given to each objective. Each should be covered in the test by an adequate number of items of an appropriate type and level of learning. If, for example, the objective called for students to be able to take a patient's temperature, then merely asking the student to identify from among pictures of a variety of thermometers the one that is appropriate for the task would not be, in itself, an adequate assessment of that objective. Certainly, additional items focusing, perhaps, on understanding the procedures involved would be needed to provide an adequate indirect assessment.

One final approach to planning for test development was offered for occupational programs that do not have student performance objectives that contain precise task, condition, and criterion statements. A table of specifications based upon course content was offered as a tool for planning locally developed or teacher-made achievement tests in these programs. Its purpose is to insure that the items included in the test are representative of the content presented in the instructional program and that the occupational teacher's expectations for student mastery of that content are indeed assessed by that instrument.

REFERENCES

Atkin, J. M. "Behavioral Objectives in Curriculum Design: A Cautionary Note," *The Science Teacher*, 1968, vol. 35, pp. 27–30.

Davis, D. E., and Borgen, J. A. *Planning, Implementing, and Evaluating Career Preparation Programs.* Bloomington, Illinois: McKnight, 1974.

Mager, R. F. *Preparing Instructional Objectives.* Palo Alto, California: Fearon Publishers, 1962.

Popham, J. W., and Baker, E. L. *Planning an Instructional Sequence.* Englewood Cliffs, New Jersey: Prentice-Hall, Inc., 1970.

Stake, R. E. "Language, Rationality, and Assessment." In Beaty, W. H., ed., *Improving Educational Assessment: An Inventory of Affective Behavior.* Washington, D.C.: Association for Supervision and Curriculum Development, 1969.

Chapter 5

Constructing
Measures of
Cognitive Achievement

Measurement techniques for assessing occupational students' achievement within the cognitive domain have been used much more extensively than those used to assess achievement in the affective, psychomotor, and perceptual domains. This is due primarily to the fact that student-performance objectives for cognitive skills and test items for assessing those skills are the easiest to prepare and administer when compared to affective, psychomotor, and perceptual behavior. Consequently, procedures and techniques for evaluating student performance within the cognitive domain of achievement are the most highly developed and most precise. Tests for assessing cognitive skills and abilities should be based, as mentioned in the preceding chapter, upon prespecified student performance objectives that specify the desired outcomes or changes in student behavior. Moreover, such tests should reflect the content and weighting as determined by the table of specifications prepared to aid in their development.

Items for eliciting and measuring cognitive achievement fall within one of two basic categories: recognition items or constructed-response items. *Recognition items* are those that present the student with a stimulus and a series of choices from which he/she can recognize a plausible response and choose that response. Examples of recognition items include multiple-choice, true–false, and matching. *Constructed-response items,* on the other hand, require the test taker or respondent to construct his/her response to the item. Examples of constructed-response items include definition, short answer, and essay.

RECOGNITION ITEMS

Recognition items, as mentioned previously, require the student to be presented with a stimulus, usually in the form of a question or declarative statement, and to make a judgment and provide a response based upon recognizing the correctness of the statement or a correct given alternative. Recognition items have many advantages over constructed-response items. The primary advantages exist in the means and simplicity of scoring. The uses of each of the item types, as well as presentation of advantages and disadvantages, are presented in the following sections. Also included are hints or suggestions in the development of each of the recognition-type items.

Multiple-choice Items

Multiple-choice items have been the most popular of all test items used within occupational education as well as within most other areas of education. Multiple-choice items consist of a stimulus statement, usually referred to as a *stem,* followed by a list of four or five possible responses or alternatives. The item stem may be in the form of an incomplete sentence or a direct question. In all cases, however, only one of the alternatives or responses should be correct. The remaining alternatives should be incorrect and, consequently, are often referred to as *distractors* or *foils.* The multiple-choice item, probably the most versatile of all items, can be employed to measure both knowledge and understanding as well as the higher order problem-solving skills of the cognitive domain. This type of item can also be used in the measurement of affective, psycho-motor, and perceptual behaviors. However, within this specific section, the multiple-choice item is only discussed with regard to the measurement of cognitive skill and achievement. Use of the multiple-choice item for assessing affective, psychomotor, and perceptual skills is described in chapters 6 and 7.

There is a considerable difference of opinion with regard to which is the most effective type of multiple-choice item—the incomplete sentence or the direct-question type of item. For instructional objectives that are basically concerned with knowledge (the lower end of the cognitive domain), there exists little difference between the two types of multiple-choice items. Example objective 1 is a knowledge-level cognitive objective.

EXAMPLE OBJECTIVE 1

1. Given a list of materials from which utensils are manufactured, the graduate of the food preparation program will be able to choose the correct utensil, as per manufacturer's suggestion, to be used with the three types of cooking containers.

This objective deals with the identification of proper types of utensils from a given list of materials from which they are manufactured. An example multiple-choice item that uses the direct question is shown in example item 1.

Example Item 1: Direct Question

1. What type of utensil should be used with cooking pans having a teflon coating?

   _X_ a. Nylon utensils

   ____ b. Steel utensils

   ____ c. Aluminum utensils

   ____ d. Glass utensils

Example item 2, on the other hand, presents the same question as example item 1, but this time in the form of an incomplete sentence.

Example Item 2: Incomplete Sentence

2. When using teflon-coated pans you should use utensils manufactured from:

   __X__ a. Nylon

   _____ b. Steel

   _____ c. Aluminum

   _____ d. Glass

Questions at the knowledge level that require knowledge of where, when, who, or what can be assessed quite easily by either type of multiple-choice item. However, the direct-question type of item is probably the easiest to construct since it simply involves the formulation of the question and the correct response, and then the preparation of three or four distractors.

When an occupational teacher is concerned with higher levels of knowledge involving behaviors such as applying knowledge or making analyses and inferring from previous known facts and principles, it is often useful to use the form of multiple-choice item that asks for the best answer. In other words, the alternatives will vary in degree of correctness; however, one will be the *best* alternative. An example of the best alternative multiple-choice item is present in example item 3.

Example Item 3: Best Alternative

3. Which of the following is the best reason for using nylon utensils with teflon-coated pans?

   _____ a. They are easier to clean than wood.

   _____ b. They are lighter in weight.

   __X__ c. They do not scratch the teflon.

   _____ d. They are dishwasher safe.

This item requires the student to identify the best reason for using nylon utensils with teflon-coated pans. This particular item goes further than the one presented as example objective 1, which simply requires the student to be able to identify the proper material. Example item 3 gets more specific and requires knowledge important to the reason for choosing a particular material. Even though the best-answer type of multiple-choice item can measure higher level skills and achievement within the cognitive domain, it is also a more difficult item to construct and often has more chance for misinterpretation on the part of the respondent. Example item 4 can easily be misinterpreted.

Example Item 4: Easily Misinterpreted

4. Which of the following woods is the best for constructing furniture?
   a. Oak
   b. Redwood
   c. Rosewood
   d. Pine

This item is open to misinterpretation because the term *best* in the item stem is undefined. The student would not know if the instructor was interested in determining the wood best for outdoor furniture, living room furniture, or for specific characteristics such as cost, weight, durability, and finishing qualities. Many of these varying definitions of *best* would require a different choice of given alternatives. Redwood is best for outdoor furniture; rosewood is the most glamorous; pine is the cheapest and lightest weight; etc. Through refinement, example item 5 is less vague.

Example Item 5: More Precise

5. Which of the following woods is most appropriate for constructing lawn furniture?
   a. Oak
   b. Redwood
   c. Rosewood
   d. Pine

The qualification of *best* with the term lawn furniture makes the correct response clearly redwood.

Advantages and Disadvantages of Multiple-choice Items. One of the major advantages of the multiple-choice item, which has already been mentioned, is its applicability to the assessment of many different levels of achievement within the cognitive domain. Another advantage is that a well-constructed multiple-choice item is usually less open to misinterpretation than constructed-response type items such as the short-answer and the definition type. Students know precisely what this task is and precisely how they should proceed to respond to the task. The multiple-choice item, obviously, is less ambiguous and more specific than most essay-type items. The third advantage focuses on overcoming the difficulties encountered by a typical true–false item. With true–false items, it is very difficult to have an item that is unequivocally true without some type of qualification. The best-answer type of multiple-choice item helps to overcome this type of difficulty. An additional advantage of the multiple-choice item over the true–false item is that the probability of guessing correctly is decreased with the multiple-choice item since more than two (and generally four or five) alternatives are usually included.

The multiple-choice item also has the advantage of providing input to the diagnosis of instruction and the diagnosis of student growth. The analysis of item responses, that is, which alternatives were chosen as being correct when, in fact, they were incorrect, can help to identify misconceptions or misunderstandings on the part of a student or a group of students. Hypothetical responses to example item 5 are shown in example item 6.

Example Item 6: Hypothetical Responses

6. Which of the following woods is most appropriate for constructing lawn furniture?
   a. Oak (10% chose this)
   b. Redwood (5% chose this)
   c. Rosewood (2% chose this)
   d. Pine (83% chose this)

By analyzing these responses the teacher could see that he or she had possibly failed in informing students of wood characteristics and their various applications. More specifically, the teacher may have provided information about pine that led to the wrong conclusion. Information of this type can ultimately lead to a clarification of points and the possible redesign of instruction in particular concepts. Another advantage of the multiple-choice item is that it is generally free from any response set that might be formed by students. *Response sets* are particular responding patterns within a test. For example, on a true–false test there may be a pattern of all true or all false items. Another advantage of the multiple-choice item is that this particular type of item requires considerably less response time than most constructed-response items, which include the formulation of a completion statement, a short answer, or even an essay. A final advantage lies in the ease and objectivity of scoring multiple-choice items. Like most recognition items, the multiple-choice items can be scored by clerical staff members or, when special answer sheets are used, by machine. Even if an instructor must score the items, the task of scoring a large number of items can be completed in a short period. And, no matter who scores or how they are scored, the same total score will be obtained.

Even though multiple-choice items have these many advantages, they still are open to some criticism. First, a multiple-choice item does not call for the student to organize and present ideas or learned material. Another criticism of the multiple-choice item is that it is totally verbally oriented. However, this type of criticism is usually true in most all paper and pencil type of items. Also associated with the multiple-choice item is the guessing factor. However, the chance of guessing correctly is not nearly as great in the multiple-choice as in other types of choice items. Another disadvantage, or at least criticism, of multiple-choice items is that they are often somewhat indirect in what they measure. That is, they measure a student's knowledge and understanding of how to do something, but do not really provide a direct measure of how well an individual can actually perform. However, this same criticism can be leveled at most paper and pencil test items. From a mechanical point of view, it is sometimes difficult to identify plausible alternatives or foils that form good distractors from the correct responses in multiple-choice items. This disadvantage, however, is overcome as the occupational teacher becomes more experienced with constructing this particular type of item. Also, the multiple-choice item, in most cases, requires more reading time on the part of the respondent than does a true–false item or most constructed-response items. However, this disadvantage also is usually overcome as the occupational teacher gains experience with constructing this type of item. Finally, the multiple-choice item usually requires more space on the test booklet than do many other types of items.

Development of Multiple-choice Items. There are many suggestions for the preparation of multiple-choice items, with many authors of measurement textbooks listing fifteen to twenty of these specific suggestions. In this section, many of these suggestions have been summarized and consolidated to focus on the most important aspects of item writing with simple and concise suggestions for preparing multiple-choice items for occupational programs.

Base Items on Relevant Information. As discussed in the previous chapter, all measures of achievement should be based upon a well-developed table of specifications, which outlines the objectives or course content to be covered by the test as well as the level of learning at which the material should be tested. The intersection of these two components then indicates the weight or emphasis that should be placed upon the specific content and levels of learning. In using the table of specifications for a broad category of items, it is often advantageous to review the instructional materials and identify specific content from which multiple-choice items can be developed. Texts, references, lecture notes, workbooks, and other such materials provide convenient sources for selecting key ideas and statements from which test items can be formulated. It is important to note, however, that multiple-choice items should not, in most cases, be formed using direct statements from written materials. When this happens the result may be the measurement of verbal memory when, in actuality, the intent is to measure understanding and problem-solving behaviors. However, there are cases where memorization is the intended measure as in remembering specific facts such as terminology and machine or utensil identification. In most cases, good items avoid this danger by rephrasing the idea or giving an illustration of the idea and asking for a response.

Formulate an Item Stem Using Simple and Concise Language. The stem of the item should set up a definite and explicit singular problem upon which the respondent or test taker can focus. It should set the task for the student. Caution should be taken when the incomplete-sentence type of multiple-choice item is used since oftentimes the statement may be too vague to pose a complete problem. However, on the other hand, caution must be taken to minimize the wordiness of item stems. Example items 7 and 8 present two forms of incomplete-sentence type multiple-choice items. Item 7 is somewhat too incomplete. The students really would not know how to respond until they had read the entire item. Item 8 is an improvement. Students could read the item stem and know that they would have to select from a list of possible functions the one that correctly relates to spark plugs.

Example Item 7: Faulty

7. The spark plug is:
   a. an element of the fuel system used to impede spark transfer.
   b. part of the ignition system with a function of igniting the gas-air mixture.
   c. a device used to stop sparks from escaping the exhaust pipe and entering the atmosphere.
   d. a rubber stopper in the firewall used to control incomplete combustion.

Example Item 8: Improved

8. Spark plugs perform which of the following functions in an engine?
   a. Impede spark transfer
   b. Ignite the gas–air mixture
   c. Stop sparks from entering the atmosphere
   d. Control incomplete combustion

It is also suggested that any words repeated in each alternative should be included in the stem of the item rather than relisting them within each alternative. Example items 9 and 10 show a faulty and an improved item with regard to repetition.

Example Item 9: Faulty

9. Spark plugs perform which of the following functions in an engine?

   a. They ignite the unburned gas of the exhaust.

---

b. They ignite the oil that leaves the fuel injector.

c. They ignite the gasoline vapor present in the valve covers.

d. They ignite the gas-air mixture in the combustion chamber.

Example Item 10: Improved

10. The function of the spark plugs in the engine is to ignite the:
    a. Unburned gas of the exhaust
    b. Oil that leaves the fuel injection
    c. Gasoline vapor
    d. Gas-air mixture in the combustion chamber

Another suggestion with regard to the construction of item stems is that the item stem should be worded positively. The use of negative words should be avoided. However, there may be instances where negative terms are important in the testing of a particular concept. In such cases, it is suggested that the negative portion of the item be underscored or set off some way from the remainder of the item stem. This helps the student in determining the correct task for that item. Example item 11 presents a negatively worded stem, and example item 12 provides a measure of the same behavior without the use of negative words.

Example Item 11: Less Desirable

11. Which of the following dictation machines does _not_ have reusable belts?
    a. IBM Executary
    b. Sony X61L
    c. IBM Portable
    d. Dictaphone _____

Example Item 12: More Desirable

12. Which of the following dictation machines uses disposable belts?
    a. IBM Executary
    b. Sony X61L
    c. IBM Portable
    d. Dictaphone ____

Construct Plausible and Unambiguous Alternatives. Alternatives to a particular stem of the multiple-choice item should appear equally attractive to the unknowledgeable student. Quite often construction of such foils or distractors is difficult since usually the test maker is knowledgeable and the correct answer is obvious and at the forefront of his/her thinking. An excellent way of obtaining plausible alternatives for multiple-choice items is to present an open-ended question or a constructed-response type of question to a small group of students, asking them to respond. The incorrect responses obtained from the students can then be incorporated as alternatives within the multiple-choice item. Example item 13 is a constructed-response item or a fill-in-the-blank item that is used to formulate alternatives in example item 14.

Example Item 13

13. When should the feeding of whole grain to pigs begin?

Example Item 14

14. At what age should whole grain be introduced in rations for pigs?
   a. At age 3 months
   b. Usually at 14 days
   c. As soon as they will eat it
   d. As soon as they can move about

There are several considerations that should be made when actually preparing the final draft of multiple-choice items and alternatives. First of all, each alternative should be grammatically consistent with the stem of the item. Specifically, if an incomplete-sentence type of stem is constructed, then each alternative should adequately complete that sentence with proper grammatical agreement. Example item 15 has improper grammatical agreement.

Example Item 15

15. The person responsible for reconciling complaints in a restaurant is the:

---

a. Waitress
b. Manager
c. Hostesses
d. Chefs

Obviously, only alternatives "a" and "b" have correct agreement. A student responding to this item could increase his chance of guessing correctly from a 25 percent to a 50–50 chance if he observed the agreement problem in alternatives.

If the direct-question type of item stem is used, then each alternative should adequately provide a feasible answer to that question. Additionally, care must be taken to insure that the given alternatives are parallel in either completing the sentence or in offering statements of fact. Alternatives should also be parallel with regard to detail and length. Oftentimes, the item writer will place too much detail in the correct alternative, trying to make it definitely the best and definitely the correct response. This will, at times, easily be identified by the "test-wise" student. Therefore, it is important to make sure that items are as close to equal length as possible and that they do possess the same type of structure and detail. Example item 16 presents poorly stated alternatives while example item 17 attempts to improve upon that item.

Example Item 16: Faulty

16. Which of the following financial considerations for childbirth requires the largest expenditure?
    a. Bath items and feeding equipment
    b. Obstetrician prenatal visits, delivery fee and hospital fees for the mother, and nursery charges for the baby
    c. Place for baby to sleep
    d. Storage space for baby's accessories

Example Item 17: Improved

17. Which of the following financial considerations for childbirth requires the largest expenditure?
    a. Bath items and feeding equipment
    b. Doctor and hospital fees
    c. Place for baby to sleep
    d. Storage space for baby's accessories

Another suggestion for multiple-choice alternatives has to do with the placement of the correct response. Some testing experts suggest that the correct response be randomly assigned to one of the four or five possible positions: a, b, c, d, and e. However, there are times when a logical arrangement of alternatives is advantageous. For example, time may be a logical factor. Example item 18 presents four dates in time.

Example Item 18: Logical Arrangement

18. The transistor was invented in what year?
   a. 1955
   b. 1959
   c. 1963
   d. 1967

The presentation of a chronological listing such as the one in example item 18 does not give the student any clue to the correct answer, and by randomizing this list the test maker may give an undue and incorrect clue to the correct choice. Time is just one factor by which alternatives can be arranged. Any type of mathematical measure can be presented in sequential order.

A final suggestion regarding alternatives focuses on the use of generalizing alternatives. The alternatives, "all of the above," "none of the above," and variations of these make up this type of generalizing alternative. It is suggested that these alternatives be used sparingly. As mentioned earlier, it is difficult to construct alternatives that are totally and always the correct choice. Likewise, constructing distractors to be totally incorrect, regardless of any application, is equally difficult. Therefore, by the presentation of a generalizing alternative, the student may be focusing on exceptions to the rules or unique examples rather than on the intent of the instructor and the test item. Even in cases where "all of the above" may be a correct response, an interpretation problem may evolve. Example item 19 presents such an item.

Example Item 19: Open to Interpretation

19. Gasoline mileage efficiency in automobiles is affected by:

---

a. Carburetor settings
b. Ignition time setting
c. Tire pressure
d. All of the above

If a student responded to example item 19 with "a," "b," or "c," he has displayed his knowledge of one factor that affects gas mileage. However, "all of the above" is the best answer. Interpreting incorrect responses and using the resulting information for diagnostic purposes is sometimes difficult. Also, if a student identifies two alternatives, which he knows are correct, then he knows the "all of the above" alternative is the correct one, thus, responding correctly without knowing all material in the item.

The generalizing alternative does have utility in measuring some cognitive behaviors and should not be overlooked. However, generalizing alternatives should not be added onto items just because plausible alternatives are difficult to formulate.

Vary Items to Incorporate Higher Order Cognitive Behaviors When Desired. As emphasized earlier, the table of specifications will guide the development of all items, including multiple-choice items. When problem-solving and application-type behaviors are the focus of measurement, multiple-choice items will, by necessity, look different from those that measure knowledge types of behaviors. Multiple-choice items will need to incorporate new material and new problems in which formerly learned principles and rules will be applied in the process of selecting the appropriate response, either in the form of completing a statement or of choosing an answer.

However, in the formulation of new applications of knowledge for multiple-choice items, care needs to be taken that too much novelty in the situation is not inserted or included. Situations presented in the item stem should, of course, be new to the student, but should not be so far removed from other examples used in class that the students cannot associate the two. Also, care needs to be taken to include enough information in the stem so that students have enough facts upon which to base a response. Often, new situations can be chosen that are real situations inherent in specific occupations being studied. By considering these real situations that the student may someday encounter, three functions can be served. First of all, the student can be informed of new situations that do exist and that he may encounter some day in the future. Second, occupational students are more receptive to and have more respect for test items that focus on real problems in their occupational fields. Finally, an item representing a real situation is much easier for the test maker to construct than some new or abstract situation. Example item 20 represents an application type of a multiple-choice item in which the student is asked to recall and apply a rule for calculating power consumption.

Example Item 20: Application

20. In a series electrical circuit where the current flow is 1.5 amp and the voltage is 110 volts, how much power is being consumed?
    a. 165.0 watts
    b. 110.0 watts
    c. 7.3 watts
    d. 1.5 watts

In this example the student is presented with a new situation, a series circuit, which has a certain amount of current flow and a certain amount of voltage applied. Answers or alternatives to the problem offer feasible results to the calculation. In this example, the student cannot just recall that one factor has a mathematical relationship with the other factor since alternatives include both multiplication and division, with the actual correct formula for the calculation being: power = current X voltage, thus making alternative "a" the correct response.

Make Allowances for Review and Revision of All Items. In the preparation of multiple-choice items, Ebel (1972) suggests writing only ten or twelve items per day, thus allowing the test maker to concentrate on few relevant items as opposed to the generation of a great number of items at one period. This also allows the test maker to go back and look at previously developed items on a different day. This can help in insuring that items are relevant and really represent what was intended. Another way of insuring the relevancy and correctness of the multiple-choice item is to have an independent person review the total test. This independent person can be another occupational teacher or advisory committee member knowledgeable of the content included in the test. If possible, the reviewer should share with the actual test developer his/her reactions to each item that is prepared. This is best accomplished in a one-to-one conference. There is a problem associated with this independent review technique. It involves the personal preference for style of the items. However, if both the test writer and the reviewer are aware of this fact, much of the problem can be avoided. By focusing on the accuracy, the material included in the items, and the correctness of the intended response and alternative responses, the reviewer can be more objective in reacting to the items. Several of the item characteristics that might be focused on in the independent review include: (1) approach used, (2) stem, (3) responses, (4) distractors, (5) wording, (6) clues, (7) difficulty, and (8) item arrangement and arrangement of alternatives. Other possible points of consideration include all of the suggestions and aspects of items that were discussed in the previous pages of this chapter.

True–False or Constant-alternative Items

The alternative-response item is generally composed of a declarative statement for which the test taker is asked to mark either true or false, right or wrong, correct or incorrect, yes or no, fact or opinion, agree or disagree, and so on. These items are considered *constant-alternative items* because two alternatives are presented for a number of items, that is, a list of true–false or correct–incorrect items is given. The true–false item is actually a subset or a major category of the constant alternative type of item. However, of the types used in occupational programs, the true–false item is the most popular and therefore is thoroughly discussed here. Probably the most common use of the true–false item is in identifying the correctness or accuracy of definitions, terms, statements of principles, and statements of facts. Because of their nature, they are usually confined to the measurement of these types of knowledge and abilities. Recall of facts can be assessed easily by the true–false item. Many times this requires a series of items to assess the attainment of a single objective. Example items 21 through 24 attempt to measure a student's knowledge of zinc and its composition as specified in example objective 2.

EXAMPLE OBJECTIVE 2

2. From presented statements, the student will accurately identify all the major alloys of zinc.

101

Example Items 21-24

21. T   F   Copper is a major alloy of zinc.
22. T   F   Lead is a major alloy of zinc.
23. T   F   Bronze is a major alloy of zinc.
24. T   F   Pewter is a major alloy of zinc.

Advantages and Disadvantages of the True-False Item.   A primary advantage of the true-false item is its efficiency. In terms of student time required to respond to true-false items, as compared to other types of items, it is the most efficient. Students can complete a great number of true-false items sampling a large body of knowledge in a very short time.

The second advantage is that the true-false item enables the test constructor to sample a broad body of knowledge in a very short time. In the knowledge categories of the cognitive domain, the recall of definitions, facts, and principles is a primary concern. The true-false item enables adequate sampling of this type of behavior. In addition, practice with true-false items assists students in learning to discriminate between alternatives, thus facilitating discrimination skills.

A third advantage of the true-false item lies in its ease of construction. Generally, it is easier to construct each true-false item and requires less time than constructing other types of items such as multiple-choice. This is not to say, however, that the true-false items are constructed without considerable thought and care. There still exists the need to minimize ambiguity and oversimplification in items of this type.

One of the more serious limitations of the true-false type of item is the types of learning and learning outcomes it can measure. Only the more elementary levels of the cognitive domain can be assessed by way of the true-false item. Determining an occupational student's knowledge of nomenclature, materials, tools, ingredients, definitions, and other knowledge-level behaviors can be assessed through use of the true-false item. Many critics suggest that other types of items, including the multiple-choice item, should be used in lieu of the true-false item since the true-false item adds little in terms of types of knowledge it can measure.

Another shortcoming of the true-false item (possibly the greatest shortcoming cited) is its susceptibility to guessing. With just two alternative choices, a student has at least a 50–50 chance of guessing the correct answer. This fact, coupled with the problem of constructing items that are clearly false or unequivocally true without providing any clue to the trueness or falseness of the items, can make the probability of guessing correctly even greater than 50–50. Gronlund (1965) cites three negative effects that result from successful guessing:

1. The reliability of each item is low, making it necessary to include a large number of items to obtain a reliable measure of achievement.
2. The diagnostic value of such a test is practically nil since analyzing a pupil's response to each item is meaningless.
3. The validity of the pupil's responses is questionable because of response sets.

There are scoring formulas that make corrections for guessing and can even affect or influence the responding behavior of the student. These formulas usually incorporate some type of heavier weight for incorrect responses, thus discouraging guessing on the part of the student. However, this type of formula has some negative effects. Many times it rewards the "chance-taking" type of student who has not studied, has little or no knowledge, and obviously nothing to lose in guessing. Another way of overcoming the guessing problem experienced with the true–false item is to modify the item slightly. One approach is to instruct the students to indicate why the particular item is false if they mark it false. This allows the student and the teacher using the results of the test to get a more accurate feeling of achievement. Valuable diagnostic information can be obtained from the true–false item when used in this way.

A final limitation or disadvantage of the true–false item is that many educators feel that it is harmful to expose a student to error. The presentation of false statements in writing may have a negative learning effect causing the student to believe and remember statements that were intended to be true. In other words, students may respond to a statement as being true, when actually it is false. Later the student may remember this statement rather than the actual correct fact as it was stated in a text or presented in a lecture. Thus, this type of item may confound learning or may promote learning of the wrong material or the wrong answer. An example of such an item from a crucial area of learning—safety—is presented in example item 25.

Example Item 25

25. T   F   It is not necessary to wear safety glasses in the machine shop unless you are operating power equipment.

This example is definitely false because eye protection is mandatory within any area where machines are being operated or other hazardous conditions exist. The unknowledgeable student may respond to this item incorrectly and never learn of his error, possibly until it is too late. This is an extreme example but other areas of learning could also be affected by learning from false statements.

Developing   True–False   Items.   As with multiple-choice items, construction of an effective true–false item should take into account rules of clarity, punctuation, and grammar. More specifically, there are several suggestions on the actual writing of true–false items. These suggestions include both things to do and things to avoid in the preparation of such items.

Avoid General Statements. General statements usually incorporate qualifiers that often give away the correct response to the item. These words or qualifiers are sometimes referred to as *specific determiners.* Examples include words such as generally, often, sometimes, usually, and their counterparts, always, never, all, none, and only. The test-wise student can usually identify these words and use them in guessing the right answer without knowing the intended subject matter.

Example Item 26

26. T   F   The president of the American Vocational Association is elected to that office.

Example Item 27

27. T   F   The president of the American Vocational Association is usually elected to that office.

In considering example items 26 and 27, item 26 might be marked false because it does not take into account the exceptions where a current president of the American Vocational Association (AVA) may become ill or may be in some way incapacitated to serve as president. In such cases, a vice-president, allowed for in the constitution of the AVA, would be appointed to assume those duties. Thus, example item 27, with the simple inclusion of the word "usually," makes the item true. However, the word "usually" might be a tip-off to the test-wise student. Example item 28 overcomes the problems posed in example items 26 and 27 by focusing more on the original intent of the item and eliminating some over-specificity and the specific determiner "usually."

Example Item 28

28. T   F   The presidency of the American Vocational Association is an elective office.

Avoid Oversimplification. When attempting to make statements unequivocally true or clearly false, it is often easy to identify statements that meet this criterion, but have little relevance to the assessment of achievement. Put another way, many times the occupational teacher will simply take sentences and statements of fact directly from a text or a workbook and present them in the form of true–false items.

Example item 29 presents a rather trivial fact regarding an IBM typewriter while example item 30 presents a more meaningful or more important advantage or concept related to the same typewriter.

Example Item 29: Trivial

29. T   F   IBM began producing the Selectric II in 1971.

Example Item 30: More Important

30. T   F   One primary advantage of the IBM Selectric II over other typewriters is its variable pitch.

Items such as the one presented in example item 29 tend to focus the student's efforts toward memorization of minute facts as opposed to more meaningful types of information such as that presented in the second example.

Present a Single Idea in the True–False Item. It is important to avoid including two or more ideas or statements within the same item. For example, consider example item 31, which makes two statements.

Example Item 31

31. T   F   Transistorized ignition systems will not function in subzero weather because of high resistance at low temperatures.

The first statement is that transistorized ignition systems will not function in subzero weather while the second statement within the item gives the reason why, that is, because of high resistance at low temperatures. When reacting to this item, the respondent must actually answer two questions before marking his response. First, he must judge the truth of the statement regarding malfunction, and, second, he must make a judgment regarding the reason. In this example, both statements are false; however, there are cases when one statement will be true and the other false, thus leading to confusion on the part of the student. The problem that an item of this sort can pose is obvious. Therefore, when at all possible, limit true-false items to a singular problem.

Avoid the Use of Negative Terminology and Especially Double Negatives. Many times, use of negative terms, such as no or not, tends to be overlooked on the part of the test taker and consequently results in an erroneous choice of answer. Example item 32 presents a faulty type of a true–false item in which a double negative is used. Example item 33 improves upon this item by making the item totally positive.

Example Item 32: Faulty

32. T   F   It is not unwise to never wear safety glasses in the wood technology laboratory.

106

Example Item 33: Improved

33. T   F   It is wise to wear safety glasses in the wood technology laboratory.

In special cases, negative terminology is necessary to emphasize certain concepts. In these cases, it is suggested that the negative term, whether it is a not, none, or no, should be underlined or set in italics so that the student will not pass over the word so easily when reading the item.

Avoid the Use of Unfamiliar Language and Terminology. With most true–false items, the intention is to assess students' knowledge of the content area and not vocabulary outside the content area. Therefore, it is imperative that language familiar to the student be used within the items. Example item 34 presents an item that uses terminology possibly unfamiliar to the student.

Example Item 34: Unfamiliar Language

34. T   F   Success in business is contingent upon an aggregate of functions and personnel with a compendium of competencies.

Terms such as contingent, aggregate, compendium, and competencies may be terms that are not in the repertoire of the responding student. Example item 34 is restated below without the use of the unfamiliar terms.

Example Item 34: Improved

34. T   F   Success in business relies on a total system that involves a group of individuals with necessary skills.

This revision does more to measure the student's knowledge of components of a successful business, where the original item 34 relies heavily upon the vocabulary of the individual in first understanding what the item is saying.

Attempt to Make the Length of True Items Equal to the Length of False Items. There is oftentimes a tendency to make true items more lengthy than false items because of an attempt to make them clearly true. However, this can lead students to identify this characteristic in responding to the length of items and thus improving their chances of guessing correctly on true–false items.

Include Approximately the Same Number of True Items as False Items. Another technical aspect of test development with regard to true–false items involves the number of each type of item included. It is usually suggested that an approximately equal number of true and false items be included. This will help to prevent response sets from being established by the students. However, when preparing true–false items, it is not necessary and even not suggested that an exactly equal number of each be included. If an equal number is included consistently from one test to the next, this may be a tip-off to the students and may also influence their responding behavior.

Matching Items

A third major type of recognition item that is used extensively in assessing cognitive achievement within occupational education is the matching item. Actually, the *matching item* is a variation of the multiple-choice item. While the multiple-choice item is comprised of an item stem and a list of plausible alternatives, the matching item provides multiple stems as well as multiple alternatives. The traditional matching item is usually presented in two columns, one for stems or premises and one for alternatives. However, there may be cases where more than one column of alternatives will be offered. Example item 35 presents a traditional type of matching item. Note also that with most matching items instructions or directions to the student precede the item.

Example Item 35

35. *Directions:* Column A contains a list of electronic components found in most AM radios. Column B contains a list of materials that electrical parts are constructed from. Select the material from column B that the component listed in column A is made of. Place your choice in the

space provided in column A. Column B items can be
used only once. When responding, think of commonly
applied components (AM radio) and not special purpose
components.

A	B
____ Resistor	1. Germanium
____ Capacitor-fixed	2. Mica
____ Capacitor-tuning	3. Carbon
____ Circuit board-structure	4. Copper
____ Circuit board-conductor	5. Bakelite
____ Diode	6. Aluminum
____ Controlled rectifier	7. Zinc
	8. Silicon

Example item 35 can be modified slightly to ask the student to
identify visually the electronic component in addition to choosing
the material from which it is made. Example item 36 contains this
modification.

Example Item 36

36. Addition to directions in item 35: Column C contains a series of
pictures of electronic components. After you have matched construction materials with components choose a picture from column
C and list its letter in the space provided next to the appropriate
component in column A.

A	B	C
____ Resistor	1. Germanium	a.
____ Capacitor-fixed	2. Mica	b.
____ Capacitor-tuning	3. Carbon	c.
____ Circuit board-	4. Copper	d.
structure	5. Bakelite	e.
____ Circuit board-	6. Aluminum	f.
conductor	7. Zinc	g.
____ Diode	8. Silicon	h.
____ Controlled rectifier		

The matching item can be used to measure a student's knowledge of associations. The attainment of objectives that emphasize the identification of relationships can usually be assessed through the matching item, if sufficient material (both premises and alternatives) is available and is homogeneous. Examples of relationships that can be assessed include:

1. Inventors—Inventions
2. Tools—Applications
3. Ingredients—Recipes
4. Machines—Uses
5. Plant diseases—Treatments
6. Symbols—Concepts
7. Terms—Definitions
8. Plants—Classifications
9. Problems—Solutions

To this point the presentation of the matching item has been limited to discussion of measuring basic knowledge. With care in construction, adequate tryout, and revision, matching items can be developed to assess higher level cognitive behaviors. Cause-and-effect relationships comprise one area of cognitive functioning that might be sampled. Or, the identification of plausible solutions to presented problems in a matching item can also require high level functioning. Example item 37 presents the beginning of a problem-solving matching item.

Example Item 37

37. *Directions:* Column A presents a problem or malfunction of an automobile. Column B contains possible causes for malfunctions. Column C contains plausible solutions for solving or remedying malfunctions in column A. First choose a possible cause from column B and place its number next to the malfunction in column A. Then choose a suggested solution from column C and place its letter next to the malfunction in column A.

A	B	C
Starting Problem	*Possible Cause*	*Possible Solution*
___Starter disengages before car starts	1. Weak battery	A. Replace spring

---

| ____ Engine back-
fires through
carburetor | 2. Weak bendix | b. Adjust voltage regu-
lator |
| ____ Engine cranks
hard before
starting | 3. Advanced
timing | c. Adjust distributor |

This type of item requires the student to apply knowledge he has acquired and to analyze and solve a problem. There are, of course, many adaptations to this type of item.

Advantages and Disadvantages of the Matching Item.   A primary advantage of the matching exercise lies in its efficiency in sampling a large amount of related material in a short period. A cited advantage of the matching item is the ease with which matching items may be constructed. In reality, it can be somewhat difficult to develop truly good matching items. As with multiple-choice items, it is difficult to formulate alternatives that are plausible and attractive choices to a given item stem. With the matching item, this concern is amplified since alternatives must be plausible and attractive to an entire series of item stems.

A main limitation of the matching item, at least the most often cited, is its limitation on what types of behavior it can measure. Most test critics limit the matching exercise to the assessment of factual information—usually the memorization of relationships. However, as indicated in example items 36 and 37, this limitation can be overcome with care in construction.

A second major limitation was mentioned above; it dealt with the difficulty of obtaining sufficiently homogeneous material from which to construct premises and alternatives. Often, irrelevant material is included in an item simply to complete it without regard to an original test plan or table of specifications.

Developing Matching Items.   *Use Only Homogeneous Material.* Content material used in the formulation of both premises and alternatives should be homogeneous and should match an original test plan. Usually, homogeneity is a matter of degree. Something that appears to be homogeneous to one individual may not be to another.

111

Example Item 38

(Tools)	*(Applications)*
Column A	**Column B**
Pliers	Tighten screws
Screwdriver	Splice wires
Side cutter	Cut sheet metal
Aviation shear	Cut wire
Lug wrench	Raise car
Auto jack	Loosen wheel bolts

For example, the item elements presented in example item 38 appear to be rather homogeneous—tools and application of those tools. However, to the student in advanced electronics, the last two items are definitely out of place with regard to his needs and consequently are irrelevant giveaways in terms of the cues they provide.

Formulate Clear and Concise Directions. The matching item is probably familiar to most occupational students, and the basis of matching is usually obvious after reading the list of item stems and list of alternatives. But, directions should leave no doubt in the students' minds about the basis of matching and should not require the student to figure it out. Additionally, as the more complex or modified matching items are used, such as those with more than three columns, directions become even more important.

Keep the Number of Item Elements Small. Ten elements in a matching exercise are usually the maximum. It is generally very difficult to construct an item of much greater length unless there exists a larger body of information that is very similar or a large number of terms are to be matched. When placing elements in columns, usually the longer elements (in terms of number of words) should be considered premises and should be placed in the left column of the item.

Include an Unequal Number of Premises and Alternatives. To decrease the student's chance of guessing items correctly on the basis of elimination, columns should be of unequal length. Directions or instructions to the student should state whether alternatives may be used once or more than once, and should alert the student if some may not be applicable at all. This will help decrease successful guessing.

The Entire Item Should Be Included on a Single Page. It is much easier for the student to make his choices if he does not have to flip pages constantly to view the total list of alternatives. Also, by placing all choices on the same page, there is less chance of the student overlooking the choices on the second page.

Place Lists in a Logical Order. As with the multiple-choice item, some logical arrangement of lists should be used. Alphabetizing, numerical sequencing, chronological sequencing, and so on are possible means around which organization can focus.

CONSTRUCTED-RESPONSE ITEMS

The constructed-response item comprises the second major type of item that can be used in assessing cognitive behavior within occupational education. Basically, as its name implies, the *constructed-response item* includes a stimulus of some kind to which the student must construct a response or answer. There are two fundamental classes of constructed-response items: short answer and essay. As with the item types presented in the previous section, the following pages discuss the uses, advantages and disadvantages, and suggestions for constructing short answer and essay items.

Short-Answer Items

Short-answer items can take one of three forms: completion, definition, and identification. The most basic of the three is the completion item. The *completion item* is simply an incomplete sentence, which the student must complete with a word or phrase to make it correct. Example item 39 is a completion type of short-answer item.

Example Item 39

39. The alloying of tin and lead forms a material called _____.

The second kind of short-answer item asks the student to

construct from his memory a definition for a given term, to state a principle or convention, or to list the steps of a process or method. The definition item is very useful in occupational education for assessing an individual's knowledge of definitions and processes. Example items 40, 41, and 42 present varying forms of this type of short-answer item.

Example Item 40

40. Define the automotive term "ignition tune-up."

Example Item 41

41. Briefly describe the principle of air flow in the venturi of an automotive carburetor.

Example Item 42

42. State, in proper order, the five necessary steps in adjusting the ignition timing on an eight cylinder, 350 C. I. Chevrolet engine.

    1. _____

    2. _____

    3. _____

    4. _____

    5. _____

The third type of short-answer item is focused on assessing a student's knowledge of certain objects. The student is usually presented with a stimulus in the form of a sensory object and is asked to use his visual, olfactory, auditory, or kinesthetic senses to identify the object. The student is then asked to write or construct the name of the object. Example item 43 presents a visual-stimulus identification exercise and example item 44 asks the student to

Example Item 43

43. Identify the following tools:

A. _____   B. _____   C._____

Example Item 44

44. Wood Identification Exercise

Directions: In the box given to you there are eight blocks of wood with a number from 1 to 8 on each block. Write the name of the wood that corresponds to each number.

1. _____
2. _____
3. _____
4. _____
5. _____
6. _____
7. _____
8. _____

use both visual and kinesthetic senses to identify wood samples. Other types of special stimulus items might include the presentation of odors of several different medical solutions to the health occupations students, requesting that the students identify each odor. Similarly, malfunctions of an automobile may be tape recorded or malfunctions of a television set may be filmed. The student may be asked to listen or view these presentations and to identify the malfunctions or even their possible causes. Possibilities for the identification item are almost limitless.

Advantages and Disadvantages of the Short-answer Item. The greatest advantage of the short-answer item is its accuracy in assessing knowledge of facts, principles, and processes. With this type of item the student is required to recall the correct response rather than simply recognize the correct response as is the case with multiple-choice, true–false, and matching items. Thus, the short-answer item minimizes the chances of students guessing successfully.

An additional advantage lies in the form of the short-answer item: most students can associate well with the simple question–answer routine of most short-answer items. This form of item is possibly the most natural in terms of its approach.

Also, the short-answer item can allow for the assessment of a student's knowledge of complex processes or procedures without extensive elaboration such as in an essay item. This type of item can also expand testing to include more than just paper and pencil testing as illustrated in the preceding sections. These advantages make the short-answer item a very useful and efficient means of assessing cognitive achievement.

However, like all item types, the short-answer item is not without limitation. The obvious limitation that relates to this item type is related to objectivity of scoring. The acceptability of different wordings can often pose a problem. With procedure listings, if a student misses one step or if two steps are reversed, does he receive no credit or partial credit for the item? In stating a definition, if the student is not totally accurate in his use of the English language, is he incorrect or does scoring take into consideration verbal skill? These are questions that need answering prior to the scoring of any short-answer item. A predetermined plan for scoring is a necessity, and usually a knowledgeable person should do the scoring as opposed to a clerical person. This will insure that alternative responses are wrong if they are not included in the key, and if they are correct, the key could be revised to include them.

Developing Short-answer Items. Require Short and Concise Answers. The question should be focused closely enough so that a student's response is limited and consequently is simple to score. Example item 45 is too general while example item 46 attempts to improve upon it.

Example Item 45: Faulty

45. A compass is _____

 _____

Example Item 46: Improved

46. A tool used by draftsmen to draw circles and arcs is a/an

 _____

Completion Items Should Have Singular Completing Words or Phrases. Items that have several blanks to be filled in should be avoided. Too often multisplit statements lead to confusion or misinterpretation on the part of the student. Example item 47 emphasizes the problem that can result from a mutilated item. Example item 48 is an improvement.

Example Item 47: Faulty

47. The _____is a device used in tearing _____of clothing.

Example Item 48: Improved

48. The device used in tearing seams of clothing is called a _____.

With too much incompleteness in an item, the student has trouble knowing what knowledge the item is focusing on and likewise, in observing incorrect responses, the instructor may have trouble using the resulting information diagnostically.

Avoid Using Direct Statements from Textbooks. As with the true–false item, the use of verbatim sentences as items is discouraged. It is usually better to obtain a concept and paraphrase it to focus on the desired knowledge. This will discourage students from trying to memorize direct statements from texts or related documents.

Place Blank or Incomplete Section at End of Sentence. Beginning an item with a blank can cause undue confusion to the student. A complete phrase should begin each item with the missing portion coming at the end of the item. Example items 49 and 50 portray this point.

Example Item 49: Faulty

49. The _____ is used to cut curved lines on small gage sheet metal.

Example Item 50

50. The tool used to cut curved lines on small gage sheet metal is the _____ .

Allow for Synonyms or Similar Answers in the Scoring Key. In developing a key for scoring, the correct response, along with nuances that are acceptable, should be included. In definition types of items, the major parts of the definition should be delineated. Also, decisions regarding partial credit for partially correct answers should be made. Flexibility in the key should be maintained to allow for responses obtained that are correct but that are unthought of by the instructor at the time the key is constructed. Example item 51 presents such a case.

Example Item 51

51. The mixing of air and gasoline in various ratios for an internal combustion engine is a function of the _____ .

The correct answer to item 51 is carburetor; however, it is feasible that a student might respond with the answer "fuel injector." This answer is correct in that a fuel injector is a special form of carburetor. The scoring key would need to make allowances for answers such as this one.

Essay Items

An item familiar to all of us, the *essay item,* has its greatest utility in assessing the attainment of objectives that require the student to recall, organize, and present ideas. In addition, the essay item can assess students' ability to express themselves and to supply rather than select interpretation and application types of information. The essay item should be used to measure more than factual knowledge. It is capable of assessing higher level objectives from the cognitive taxonomy of objectives. Understanding and problem solving skills become a primary focus of the essay item.

Essay items can vary considerably in terms of their specificity. An item might require a limited response such as a paragraph, or two or three sentences. Or an item might be broader and require several pages in response. Based upon this difference, essay items have been classified as either restricted-response items or extended-response items.

The *restricted-response type* of essay item limits a student's response by including specific delimiters within the question statement. Items can be restricted in two ways: in content and in form. The content of an item is limited or restricted by the scope of the topic to be discussed or written about. The consumer or business education question posed in example item 52 restricts the student's response by asking that only four factors be discussed. Also, the item limits the student's response to the economic state of our community as opposed to the state, nation, or world. The form of the item can be restricted further by adding either a preceding or following sentence that tells the student how detailed or restrictive he should be in his response.

Example Item 52

52. Discuss four factors that have contributed to the current economic state of our community.

Example item 53 restates item 52 with a form delimiter added.

Example Item 53

53. Discuss four factors that have contributed to the current economic state of our community. Write a paragraph for each factor and include an example of how each factor has affected an aspect of our economy.

This additional statement informs the student of expected detail and quantity. The restricted-response item is adequate for measuring cognitive performance within a specific area of content and it does allow for measuring understanding and limited application. This type of essay item is also easier to score since the substance of the item is more closely defined.

The *extended-response item* provides for a sampling of cognitive behavior within even higher levels of functioning. The extended-response item poses a very broad question or problem. The student is expected to select any factual information he feels is pertinent to organizing and synthesizing this information and to present it along with personal judgments and evaluations. With this type of item, the student has almost unlimited freedom to relate his learning. Even though this item type does allow for assessment of high levels of functioning, it is limited in focusing on specific content and its related objectives. It also can create a more difficult task in scoring. Example item 54 is an extended-response essay item.

Example Item 54

54. Describe the effect of increases in the prime interest rate on the housing industry.

This item allows the student to react as he wishes to the extent and detail he wishes.

Advantages and Disadvantages of the Essay Item. An important advantage of the essay item has already been mentioned and discussed in previous pages of this chapter. It is the ability of the essay item to elicit and measure complex cognitive behavior. The essay item can measure problem-solving skills and expression skills that no other type of item can. Because of this, the use of the essay item should be incorporated in a test where the test plan or table of specifications necessitates the measurement of higher order behaviors.

A second advantage of the essay item is that it can help improve the expression and writing skills of the student. In most occupational areas, the requirement for writing and other forms of verbal communication is increasing. Report writing, budget justifications, quality control reports, and others are but examples of work-related writing requirements. The essay item can provide the occupational student with practical experience in writing and the opportunity to gain feedback from the instructor. This function of the essay item is, of course, secondary to the assessment of cognitive achievement, but writing skill should not be overlooked.

A third advantage of the essay item lies in its ease of construction. It is relatively easy and requires little time to write a series of essay items. This fact has led to the fairly widespread use of the essay item. However, many times instructors will write essay items in a hurry without regard to the complex behaviors they intend to assess. A good essay item that relates closely to a test plan, and that elicits adequate information for evaluating the attainment of intended objectives, requires the same care and time that other types of items do.

The major disadvantage of the essay item is related to the lack of reliability in scoring. Research studies have shown that different teachers scoring the same essay items have scored them very differently. Additionally, it has been shown that the same teacher scoring the same item at two different points in time has resulted in dissimilar scores. This disadvantage makes it very important for the instructor to develop a special scoring key for each item and to develop a weighting system for various item components. More attention to the scoring of essay items as well as other item types is paid in chapter 12.

A second disadvantage is that an exam or instrument that is comprised of all essay items cannot sample a broad body of knowledge and understanding that other item types can. Even though the essay item can focus more closely on specific behaviors, to do so usually requires a lot of testing time and a broad sample is sacrificed.

The combining of several item types into a single instrument can help to gain both breadth and depth in assessment.

The usually great amount of time required in scoring essay items is a third disadvantage of this type of item. To score conscientiously only a few essay items requires a considerable amount of time. This is especially true if comments and reactions are written on the test papers by the instructor. The scoring task becomes even greater when class size is large. Therefore, the number of essay items included on a test may be influenced by the size of the class and time available to the instructor, as well as by the original table of specifications.

Developing Essay Items.   Insure That the Item Is Eliciting the Proper Behavior. It is often easy to formulate an essay item that is related to instruction, but it is more difficult to formulate an item that will always reflect the overall emphasis of a unit or course. The preparation of an essay item must be based upon one or more objectives and the item must solicit information that will relate to that or those objectives. It is much easier to insure the direct relationship between essay items and objectives when the restricted-response type of item is used. With the extended-response item, direction and detail of the response will be much more in the control of the student.

Use Essay Items to Measure Behaviors That Cannot Be Measured by Other Item Types. Somewhat related to the above suggestion, the essay item should be used to assess behaviors that the multiple-choice, true–false, matching, and short-answer items cannot. For efficiency's sake, the essay item should not be used to assess knowledge of facts. For knowledge assessment, other item types are more appropriate—requiring less student response time and less scoring time in addition to being more reliable.

Include Specific Instructions to the Student. The student should know enough about the teacher's expectations to be able to approach the problem or answer the question properly. A vaguely stated question may lead a class of students to each respond differently to the same question. Example item 55 is a vaguely stated restricted-response essay item.

Example Item 55

55. Briefly discuss two types of grass utilized for golf course greens.

Example item 56 improves upon item 55 by offering more direction to the student.

Example Item 56

56. Briefly discuss two types of grass used for golf course greens. In your response focus on differences in (1) watering requirements, (2) cutting requirements, (3) golfer preferences, and (4) repairability.

Indicate an Approximate Time Limit for Each Essay Item. An indication of time to be spent in answering each item should be given either on the test or orally prior to the testing. The estimate should be based on the time the teacher feels it should take to construct an adequate response. The time estimates should also communicate to the student the priority to be given to each item. If one item is allowed 30 minutes, while another is allowed only 10 minutes, one is obviously more important to the total assessment. Also, if part of a test is devoted to recognition items, an indication of how much time should be allowed for that section should be given.

Limit the Use of Optional Essay Items. The practice of including six items, requiring each student to answer only four or five of them, is not encouraged. This practice affects the comparability of test papers when they are being scored. This is especially important when scores are to be norm referenced. Also, by giving students an option, it tends to reward or favor the student who is not prepared and may not reward the student who is better prepared and capable of answering all items correctly. Additionally, a test should be designed to measure a student's achievement. If he is weak in one area, the test should reflect this fact. By providing options, the teacher may not obtain a good indication of what a student does not know. This has relevance for the diagnostic use of test results.

An Ideal Answer Should Be Written Before an Item Is Included in a Test. The formulation of an ideal answer or response at the time an item is drafted can serve several purposes: first, it can provide a check on the reasonableness of a question. This can lead the test maker to restrict, expand, or otherwise improve the item. Also, an estimate of time can be obtained through this writing exercise. This can aid in determining total test length and in giving students an estimate of how much time to spend on each item. A final outcome of this task can be a model to which student responses can be compared. In this sense, this ideal item can provide a form of scoring key.

REFERENCES

Ahmann, J. S., and Glock, M. D. *Evaluating Pupil Growth,* 5th ed. Boston: Allyn and Bacon, 1975.

Bloom, B. S., Hastings, J. T., and Madaus, G. F. *Handbook on Formative and Summative Evaluation of Student Learning.* New York: McGraw-Hill, 1971.

Ebel, R. L. *Measuring Educational Achievement.* Englewood Cliffs, New Jersey: Prentice-Hall, Inc., 1972.

Gerberich, J. R. *Specimen Objective Test Items: A Guide to Achievement Test Construction.* New York: Longmans, Green, 1956.

Green, J. A. *Teacher-Made Tests.* New York: Harper and Row, 1963.

Gronlund, N. E. *Measurement and Evaluation in Teaching.* New York: Macmillan, 1965.

Payne, D. A. *The Specification and Measurement of Learning Outcomes.* Waltham, Massachusetts: Blaisdell, 1968.

Thorndike, R. L., and Hagen, E. *Measurement and Evaluation in Psychology and Education.* New York: Wiley and Sons, 1969.

Wood, D. A. *Test Construction.* Columbus, Ohio: Merrill, 1960.

Chapter 6

Constructing Measures of Performance

Performance measurement or testing in occupational education is concerned with assessment of occupational skills, usually physical or motor skills. At one time, measurement specialists and researchers separated an individual's behavioral processes into two distinct areas: cognitive and motor. With the current emphasis on competency-based individualized instruction and the use of student-performance objectives, theorists as well as practitioners have identified distinct categories of objectives and developed the taxonomy of educational objectives discussed in chapter 3. The taxonomy includes cognitive, affective, psychomotor, and perceptual domains. However, even though student behavior can be so categorized for discussion purposes, measurement and testing techniques cannot be separated so neatly. In this regard, there is considerable overlap and interrelatedness among the domains.

For example, a skilled sewing machine operator must possess knowledge and other cognitive skills to be able to perform various operations. Also, he/she must be able to manipulate physically materials and equipment (psychomotor) and must rely on visual, auditory, and kinesthetic perceptual inputs to guide movement to sew accurate and adequate seams. Likewise, a farmer must have knowledge and understanding of a variety of agricultural machines and their functions in order to operate these machines physically and cultivate, plant, harvest, and transport farm products successfully.

In chapter 5 cognitive assessment was presented as a discrete entity (except for making physical responses to items by writing or checking). In some on-the-job situations, purely cognitive performances must be made by managers and other supervisory personnel. However, there are few occupationally oriented psychomotor and perceptual activities that do not require associated cognitive behavior. Recent characterization of human behavior indicates behavior existing on a cognitive-motor continuum with different actions varying in the degree of motor and cognitive skill required. (See figure 6.1)

/ _____ /

Cognitive   *Perceptual-Motor*

FIGURE 6.1. Behavior Continuum.

A common misconception is that an individual's level of achievement with respect to some complex skill can be assessed by only focusing on part of his behavior, usually the cognitive. The assumption that high cognitive achievement indicates proficiency in performance involving cognitive, psychomotor, and/or perceptual skills is usually a false one. For example, having knowledge of traffic laws, automobile controls, driving etiquette, and automobile care does not insure that an individual can drive adequately and safely. Likewise, a person having a broad knowledge and understanding of the anatomy of the eye, surgical techniques, and maladies of the eye may not have the surgeon's skills necessary to remove a cataract successfully. This is not to say that assessing knowledge and understanding is an inadequate approach because it does provide some very useful information. However, most learning, especially in occupational education, involves the application of cognitive, motor, and perceptual abilities in unique combinations that result in skilled job performance.

The ultimate in performance measurement for occupational education is the assessment of a student's ability to perform important job-related tasks in an actual job setting. This type of measurement has not been used extensively by occupational educators for obvious cost and logistical reasons. The design and use of simulated work samples and other performance tests has received some attention by occupational educators. However, expanded and improved efforts would contribute significantly to this program. Even though performance measurement requires more preparation and time to administer than most paper and pencil types of measurement, its benefits in helping to understand what an occupational student can do or cannot do are useful to occupational educators and students as well. Specific points in this regard are developed throughout this chapter.

Traditionally, performance tests have focused upon both aptitude and achievement. Probably the best known to occupational educators in general has been the aptitude performance test. The manipulative aspects of the General Aptitude Test Battery (GATB), Ravens Progressive Matrices, and the Purdue Pegboard are examples of aptitude performance tests. These tests, like other aptitude tests, have aided in identifying students' potential with regard to certain occupational tasks. For example, McDonald's hamburger chain used the Purdue Pegboard to assess trainees' motor aptitudes for working in their food service operations.

The primary use of performance tests in occupational programs, however, is in assessing student achievement; this is the emphasis of this chapter. Examples of achievement-oriented performance tests date to 800 B.C. in the form of Greek athletic competition. The tournaments and games of athletics employ principles of performance testing in assessing the skill of individuals and teams of individuals. In addition, the skill of artists and musicians has been assessed through ratings and judgments even though the evaluation structure may have been somewhat informal. In education, the handwriting test was probably the first formally structured or standardized performance test. Since then, the use of performance tests has expanded to almost every area of occupational education as well as areas such as physical education and military and industrial training. However, for the reasons presented in chapter 3, the actual number of standardized performance tests used in occupational programs is not very large. The driving portion of driver license exams used by all states is an example of a performance test that is based on local needs and standardized for each state. The Plymouth Trouble-Shooting Contest is a good example of a standardized performance test used on a national basis. All performance tests employ

one or both of two basic approaches to assessing performance:
(1) observing and rating the procedures used in performing, and (2)
observing and rating the end product of the performance.

PROCESS AND PRODUCT MEASUREMENT

In assessing student performance in occupational education programs,
either or both the process or the product of the task should be
measured. Both product and process assessments have their advantages—a decision must be made regarding which should be used.
However, in many situations it will be advantageous to look at both
process and product. For example, in assessing an individual's typewriting skill, the product of performance can easily be judged. This
can be done by observing and assessing a typed letter or manuscript segment on the basis of specified criteria such as spacing,
indentation, neatness of corrections, and accuracy. In addition to
focusing on the product of the typewriting exercise, it may also be
important, especially at the early stages of learning, to focus on the
process used in completing the typing exercise. It may be important
for the occupational teacher to see whether the student is sitting up
straight, has the correct fingers on the correct keys, has his/her feet
flat on the floor, has his/her wrists up, and keeps his/her eyes on the
copy. It is possible in certain typing exercises that an individual
student may be able to use the hunt and peck method to produce
an adequate product. However, in terms of later speed and performance in a secretarial position, this method of typing would be inadequate. By focusing simply on the product in this situation, the teacher may overlook some performance inadequacies. It is important
to focus on both process and product measures of performance in
cases such as this.

Characteristics of Process Measurement

Process variables are generally more difficult to measure than product variables. In many instances, observation techniques are used.
This involves one person (an occupational teacher) making a rating of
another's performance (an occupational student). Such a measurement

can be quite objective when there is one and only one way of performing a certain task. However, many occupational tasks can be performed successfully in more than one way. Making up a hospital bed is a good example. An occupational student may use a certain method of making a bed and be rated negatively by an observer who is an experienced nurse's aide. This negative rating may simply be based upon differences in technique used by the student when compared to the technique usually employed by the rater. This subjectivity in rating is probably the greatest disadvantage of measuring processes.

Even though many process measures tend to be subjective, one can attempt to objectify most process measures through a thorough analysis of the task being performed. Basically, two groups of measures can be used in observing and assessing processes used in performance: (1) those relating to an estimation of quality, and (2) those having to do with efficiency of the operation in terms of rate, speed, or movement. In the performance of some tasks, measurement of one of these characteristics is definitely more important than the others. In other cases, measures of both quality and efficiency are important. Consider the example of an automechanic student who is faced with the task of replacing a thermostat in an automobile. It is important that the thermostat be installed properly. There should be no leaks and the thermostat should operate properly following installation. However it is also important that the task be completed within a reasonable amount of time. This is the case when students are being prepared for entry into the world of work and particularly for entry into occupations where time means money. An employer will not want only quality of performance if he has to pay in terms of added time for adequate completion of a task. Therefore, it is important in most occupational tasks to consider the quality of performance as well as the speed or rate at which the task is completed.

In process measures, time may be used in assessing the number of units of work that can be completed or produced within a certain period, thus, indicating a production rate. Or time can be considered in estimating the duration that it takes to complete or produce a certain product. These are two ways of looking at time with regard to performance: even though time and quality are the most important aspects to assessing process as it relates to performance, there are several others that may be important; they include learning time, accident rate, and attitude toward the job. These are sometimes considered side effects or incidental consequences to the actual job task.

Characteristics of Product Measurement

It is easier to apply specified standards of measurement when assessing the product of performance, projects, samples of manipulated fixtures, or devices. For example, it is easier to measure a machine part that is the product of a machine lathe operation than it is to rate the sequence and adequacy of the processes used in machining that particular product. This is true because devices such as micrometers, rulers, and gauges can be used to objectify the measurement. In product assessment, the characteristics to be considered can be specified as standards concerned with appearance, usability, and conformance to prespecified instructions. The product of a baking performance test—an angel food cake—can be assessed by observing its external appearance, texture, and density. Thus, the product evaluation or assessment is basically the evaluation of conformance to prescribed dimensions, standards of general appearance, freedom from error, strength, and/or suitability for use.

The complexity of product evaluation is determined by the complexity of the tasks or procedures used in preparing the product. The assessment of a wooden kitchen cabinet that has been built will be more complex than that of a wooden cutting board. This is due to the fact that more operations, pieces, or parts, and more complex procedures had to be used to develop one product over the other.

Advantages and Disadvantages of Performance Tests

The greatest advantage of any performance test, regardless of whether it focuses on process or product, lies in the fact that it can assess a number of behaviors as well as complex behaviors in a realistic situation. This type of assessment has impressive face validity and credibility in occupational programs because it generally relates very closely to a job situation. There are many disadvantages of performance measures. The greatest of these disadvantages is the time required for administration and the extra time usually needed for development and preparation. This extra time can include both student and staff time. Also, most performance tests require some type of special equipment, apparatus, or specialized situational materials. These materials or devices generally cost more than the paper and pencil necessary for most cognitive achievement tests. Another disadvantage of performance tests is the rater subjectivity. The rating of either process or product of performance involves making ratings based upon human observation and judgments. This human element in the observation process can lead to unreliable information. However, this disadvantage is minimized when proper rating scales are used by occupational teachers who have been trained in observation techniques. A final disadvantage, and minor one at that, is the fact that rating of processes or products requires a one-to-one relationship for many performance tests. Thus, testing large groups of students will take a great amount of time. Moreover, this poses the possibility that earlier tested students may pass on information about proper and improper responses and procedures to students to be tested at a later time. However, in most performance tests that focus on other than cognitive achievement this disadvantage will be minimal.

It is difficult to cite advantages and disadvantages of product measures versus process measures since the behavior and task being used in the performance measure will more or less dictate the necessary focus. However, overall product measures tend to be more reliable since more specific, standardized scales and, hence, more objective measuring instruments can be used to evaluate the product. Also, product measures take less teacher time to organize, administer, and score. That is, a number of different students can produce the same product at one time with the products being evaluated later at the teacher's convenience. Process measures, on the other hand, have to rely on scheduled observations and observation scales as indicated earlier. Another major disadvantage of a product-type assessment is that certain errors may be introduced into the product in the early stages of the production process which may be irreparable and may affect the final product. Yet, procedures may have been adequate from the point of the mistake to the completion of the project or product. Many product measures may not be sensitive to the actual degree of error in the product in this case.

The greatest advantage of process measures lies in the fact that diagnostic information that will aid in upgrading a student's performance can be achieved through observation of deficiencies. Also, in many operations it is imperative that safety precautions be observed and that the process conform to specified guidelines. In evaluating a student semi-truck driver by simply looking at product, that is, did he/she arrive at a specified point or location within a specified amount of time, can be easily assessed. However, if the driver had endangered, for example, the lives of other individuals on the road in the transporting task, this may be an important consideration in evaluating the driving function. Where at all possible, it is usually advantageous to obtain measures of both product and process. However, time, cost, and other constraining factors will need to be considered by the occupational teacher in determining the focus of performance measures.

Types of Rating Systems

Instructor or Supervisory Ratings. Perhaps the oldest and most used type of rating system in the evaluation of either process or product as a performance measure is that conducted by an instructor or a supervisor. Within occupational education, the teacher conducts many different types of informal performance assessments through informal observations. That is, when a group of home economics students is working at sewing machines on specific projects, the instructor is usually walking around and observing how the students operate the equipment. Likewise, in the automechanics laboratory, individuals working on different components of the automobile are observed by their instructor. These informal observations are generally all part of the individualization of instruction within occupational education programs. However, with regard to more formalized performance tests or measures, the rating of student performance must be objectified through the use of guides or rating forms, which also serve to record the ratings once they are made. In most situations, occupational teachers must organize and set up specific performance tests in which students can be observed or in which the products of students' performance can be rated.

Employer or supervisor ratings conducted within the realm of a cooperative education program or in postinstructional or job settings provide the most realistic appraisal of the student's performance. Most employers and supervisors within employment settings use some type of assessment system to aid them in determining an employee's retention in the job or for purposes of salary or wage increase or adjustment. However, occupational educators should devise specific rating forms to be filled out by employers of graduates of their programs to aid in the assessment of student performance and the ultimate revision and improvement of their instructional programs. This process has been used fairly extensively within cooperative education programs; however, these techniques should not be limited to that end. Specific suggestions for constructing supervisor–employer rating forms and their use are included in the last section of this chapter.

Peer Ratings. With any type of rating system, just as with any other type of student assessment, information is collected to aid the teacher in assessing instructional techniques as well as in determining the proficiency level of students. In both of these cases, the measurement or assessment provides feedback regarding the teaching–learning process. It has recently been suggested that the involvement of students in the assessment process has many benefits. Bloom (1974) indicates that involving students in the evaluation of performance can meet three goals: (1) to introduce the student to the complexity of performance evaluation; (2) to encourage the student to evaluate his actions and efforts; and (3) to encourage the student to become more actively involved in the teaching–learning process. In addition, it is believed that students evaluating other students' performance can provide for a recapitulation of the task and therefore reinforce the retention of the particular task. The practical aspects of applying a peer or student evaluation system can be organized in several ways. First of all, each member of the class can evaluate each of the other members of the class in terms of their process or in terms of their product. However, in most cases, this approach ends up being too time consuming and the gained advantage of using such a system is generally outweighed by the additional time requirement. A second approach is to involve a special committee of students or a segment of the class as an evaluation committee that will be responsible for rating projects or the processes of all students in the class. Third, students can be divided and assigned the responsibility for assessing three or four other members of the class, thus involving multiple ratings of each student in the class by different student or peer raters. It is important within the student or peer evaluation or rating process to incorporate appropriate rating scales and instruments for the recording of ratings. It is important also to have a means of combining ratings or averaging ratings, especially when multiple ratings are taken of each student's product or processes. The involvement of students in the identification of important components of product and processes and the establishment or formulation of rating forms can also aid in the instructional or learning process in addition to facilitating the measurement or assessment processes involved.

Self-assessment of Process and Product Performance.   The process of having occupational students evaluate their own work, both processes and products, is something that occurs in most all occupational programs although again on an informal basis. It is often advantageous to formalize the process by providing students with a rating form, possibly the same rating form that is used by the occupational teacher. By making students aware of the rating process and giving them the opportunity to evaluate their own work, the rating process probably provides the best available diagnostic information to the student about his/her performance. Such information can aid occupational students in improving their competencies prior to an evaluation by their teachers.

The rating forms and instruments used within each one of these three types of ratings involving teacher or supervisory, peer, and self-assessment can be very similar and, in many cases, identical. In the development of rating forms and scales, their purpose should be determined prior to development so that specific allowances can be made within the instruments to accommodate their use.

Types of Rating Scales or Instruments

Rankings.   The ranking of processes or products of performance is the most basic measure that can be used in performance assessment. *Ranking* involves comparing processes or products within a group of students and then ordering each from the best in the group to the poorest. Obviously, ranking is strictly done in a norm-referenced way and a student's performance is reported with regard to how he/she compared to the others in the norm group. This type of measurement or rating system has many shortcomings in that the system does not really indicate adequacy of performance or product.

134

It simply shows how an individual compares to others included in the ranking. The ranking of products or processes can be a reliable process in occupational programs if the teacher is an expert judge. Moreover, the fewer tasks involved in a specific procedure, or the fewer complexities in a specific product, the more reliable the rating process. That is, if the task is to assess dental hygiene students with regard to their ability to expose X-ray film, then it becomes somewhat easy to rank several students with regard to their performance. However, it becomes more difficult with the addition of more processes or an increase in complexity of the product to be completed. In the case of our example, if dental hygiene students are being ranked on their performance regarding exposure and development of X-ray film, it becomes more difficult to rank them on the multiple processes, thus leading to possibly lower reliability in overall rankings. Example item 1 provides a sample ranking form to be used by peer or student ratings of classroom projects.

Example Item 1

1. On the following ranking form, indicate the best project first and most deficient last. In your ranking, consider the following criteria:
   a. Accuracy of construction (per blueprint)
   b. Design changes
   c. Workmanship

Project 31	_____	Rank
Project 20	_____	Rank
Project 19	_____	Rank
Project 12	_____	Rank
Project 3	_____	Rank

Product Scales. Product scales incorporate a means of taking measures similar to rankings and allowing for a criterion reference rather than relying solely upon intergroup comparisons of products. Basically, a *product scale* is a collection of samples of products that vary in degree of accuracy or quality. The samples are usually arranged on a board or display panel from the outstanding or very good samples to the less acceptable or poor samples, depending on the focus or product. Numbers are then generally assigned to each one of the samples along the line of quality. Evaluating a student's product with a product scale simply involves the comparison of the student's product to the scale and then identifying or awarding the number that corresponds to the sample on the scale which most closely represents the student's product. Example item 2 presents a picture of a product scale used in judging the excellence of arc welds made by welding students. Other example scales might include a series of bread or cake samples, a series of woven fabric samples, a series of exposed X-rays, or a set of ink and pencil lines used in drafting. These are but a few examples. The possibilities for the development of product scales for occupational programs are extremely varied.

Example Item 2

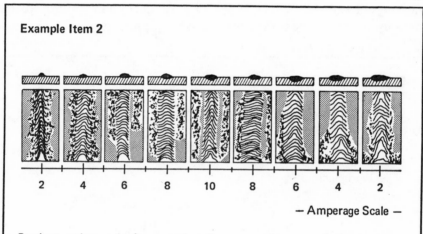

— Amperage Scale —

Product rating scale for assessing the appropriateness of the amperage setting for welds made by students. Ten points are awarded to welds made at the appropriate amperage (heat) setting and proportionately fewer points are awarded to welds that are judged as being either too "hot" or too "cold."

Product scales are easy for occupational teachers to develop. If they take the products that are produced by a particular class or a number of classes, choose those products that can be ranked one better than another, they can place them along a scale. The scale may be updated as additional products are developed that do not compare with any of the products already included on the scale. Hence, additions are always made between two existing points on the scale. It can be seen that by using a product scale rather than the ranking method, occupational students are compared to a developed standard and any number of the students within a class can have outstanding products. In other words, an entire class may perform in an outstanding manner when compared to other classes. Yet, if class rankings are used, someone in the class has to receive the lowest rank. An extreme but potential happening is that the lowest rank in one class could exceed the highest rank in another class when actual products are considered. Therefore, the product scale can help minimize this problem and allow for a criterion reference of performance.

Checklists. Checklists are simply lists of behaviors or activities that are checked by an occupational teacher as being observed during a particular observation session. Checklists are valuable instruments for determining what a student does or does not do and can be extended to record the number of times a particular activity or technique has been used. Example item 3 is a checklist for observing an individual using an overhead projector. In addition to recording the existence and frequency of actions the checklist can also be modified to record the proper sequence or occurrence in time of particular acts or maneuvers, as shown in the medical technology program example, example item 4.

Example Item 3

Instructor's Actions	Occurrence
Position projector.	√
Plug projector into recepticle.	√
Place sample transparency on projector table.	√
Turn on projector.	√
Adjust position of machine.	√
Focus projector.	√
Turn off projector.	√
Insert first transparency.	√
Turn on projector.	√

Turn off projector while changing transparencies.	√

Example Item 4

Student's Actions	Sequence of Actions
a. Takes slide	1
b. Wipes slide with lens paper	2
c. Wipes slide with cloth	
d. Wipes slide with finger	
e. Moves bottle of culture along the table	
f. Places drop or two of culture on slide	3
g. Adds more culture	
h. Adds few drops of water	
i. Hunts for cover glasses	4
j. Wipes cover glass with lens paper	5
k. Wipes cover with cloth	
l. Wipes cover with finger	
m. Adjusts cover with finger	
n. Wipes off surplus fluid	
o. Places slide on stage	6
p. Looks through eyepiece with right eye	
q. Looks through eyepiece with left eye	7

This type of checklist is exceptionally useful when there is more than one way or sequence for completing a task. In addition to focusing on correct maneuvers or actions, the checklist can also include incorrect actions to indicate an individual's lack of proper response in certain instances. Many times this type of information is useful to the occupational teacher for diagnostic purposes and in aiding both teacher and student in correcting deficient behavior.

Numerical Scales.   *Numerical-rating scales* measure characteristics by assigning numbers to specific rating categories. For example, a typing student may be rated on his/her adequacy in positioning the paper in the typewriter on a scale ranging from one to ten—one being poor and ten being excellent. Example item 5 provides a numerical rating scale for evaluating machine tool operations in the formation of convex and concave radii. This type of scale simply asks that a check mark be placed in the appropriate box.

Example Item 5

5. Forming of radii on the engine lathe

		Accuracy			
		1	2	3	
a. Convex		□	□	□	3 = best
		1	2	3	
b. Concave		□	□	□	3 = best

Source: Reproduced from *Handbook of Performance Testing, A Practical Guide for Test Makers,* by Boyd, J. L., and Shimberg, B., 1971, with permission of Educational Testing Service, Princeton, New Jersey.

Other rating scales ask that check marks be placed along a continuum ranging from zero or one to a higher number ranging anywhere from three to ten. Example item 6 is an expansion of example item 5. In addition to measuring the accuracy of convex and concave radii, the workmanship of that formation is also being judged at the same time through the use of an additional three-point scale.

Example Item 6

6. Forming of radii on the engine lathe

		Accuracy			*Workmanship*		
		1	2	3	1	2	3
a. Convex		□	□	□	□	□	□
		1	2	3	1	2	3
b. Concave		□	□	□	□	□	□

Another alternative for numerical scales involves using bipolar adjectives for assessing performance or products. Example item 7 incorporates such a rating scale for assessing food service operations.

Example Item 7

7. Setup of the food preparation area
   a. Disorganized   1   2   3   4   5   6   7   Systematic

| b. Slow | | 1 | 2 | 3 | | 4 | 5 | | 6 | 7 | Fast |
| c. Loud | | 1 | 2 | 3 | | 4 | 5 | | 6 | 7 | Quiet |

As can be noted from this example item, a series of ratings can be achieved for the same area of behavior, each focusing on a different aspect of that behavior. The numerical-rating scale has the advantage that it is simple and easy to summarize the observed ratings by adding and averaging ratings and combining these to formulate an overall or total score for the occupational task.

Graphic-Rating Scales. The *graphic-rating scale* is simply an item stem followed by a straight line with rating categories positioned along the line. The scale can assume many different forms with or without descriptive categories or numbers for the scale units. Usually, however, the graphic scale does not have numbers. Example item 8 presents an item with five categories described in two or three words. These descriptions, of course, can be extended to a more specific delineation of each category—up to a paragraph for each. Example item 9 presents an expansion of example item 8 with detailed descriptions of categories.

Example Item 8

8. Rate this individual on gross motor coordination as you have perceived him in this work situation.

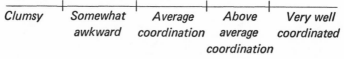

| *Clumsy* | *Somewhat awkward* | *Average coordination* | *Above average coordination* | *Very well coordinated* |

Example Item 9

9. Rate this individual on gross motor coordination as you have perceived him in this work situation.
   a. *Clumsy.* Very clumsy in the handling of objects such as tools, equipment.
   b. *Somewhat awkward.* Has trouble manipulating objects such as tools, equipment, but with practice can improve on a specific task.

> c. *Average coordination.* Performs at an average level as compared to others in the group.
> d. *Above average coordination.* Possesses a high level of coordination on most tasks but may have trouble with some.
> e. *Very well coordinated.* Demonstrates a high level of coordination across all manipulating activities.
> f. *Insufficient information.*

This particular item, which focuses on teacher, supervisor, or employer rating of gross motor coordination, can provide more consistent and reliable information than a simple numerical-rating scale. One of the problems with a numerical-rating scale without graphic descriptions is that the scale of one to five or one to ten is basically the scale possessed by the individual rater. In other words, a score of "5" to one occupational teacher may be a score of "3" to another. The graphic scale serves to standardize ratings. That is, it provides a number of different raters a more consistent description of the behavior that represents each category along the scale.

Graphic items can also be grouped with a number of stems using the same categories for rating. This can be a great advantage in terms of saving space and preventing the occupational teacher from changing his/her response mode for each item. On many rating scales, the line or continuum of a characteristic is divided into unit distances, usually of equal length. Sometimes numbers are even assigned to points along the continuum. This facilitates scoring, summing, and averaging the item responses. Remmers (1963) has presented the following nine suggestions for constructing graphic-rating scales.

1. The line, whether horizontal or vertical, should be unbroken.
2. The line should be five or six inches long, enough to allow indication of all discrimination of which the rater is capable.
3. The direction of the lines should be the same, that is, the socially desirable end should be the same for all traits.
4. Guilford (1954) suggests that for unsophisticated raters the good end of the line should come first.
5. If several objects are to be rated, the best arrangement of the page is that which rates all of them on one characteristic before proceeding to another characteristic.

6. Descriptive categories should be as near as possible to the points of the scale they describe.
7. The categories need not be equally spaced.
8. In other than machine scoring, a stencil divided into numbered sections makes a convenient scoring device.
9. Guilford (1954) suggests that segmented lines should not call for any finer discriminations than will be used in scoring.

These basic rating scales comprise the majority of those that are appropriate to performance appraisal. There are others, and many times those presented here are given different names; for example, the graphic scale is often called a descriptive scale or Likert scale, and the numerical scale is often referred to as a qualitative scale. In addition, there are many other types of rating scales that are used for purposes such as rating teachers and other types of rating, but they are not as appropriate to performance testing as the scales presented here. For a more detailed description of rating scales and their use, see Remmers (1963).

These types of rating scales used in the measurement of process and product of performance provide a good basis for systematically judging and recording judgments. However, a performance test or measure requires more than simply a rating scale. It requires a systematic way of organizing the proper stimuli for eliciting performance and for standardizing the elicitation of evaluative information. The following sections focus on the construction of specific performance tests that incorporate the rating scales discussed in this section. Basically, there are three performance measures that are discussed: (1) identification tests; (2) work-sample and simulation tests; and (3) employer–supervisor ratings.

IDENTIFICATION TESTS

Identification tests for occupational programs are designed to assess students' ability to identify objects or parts of objects, to distinguish between correct and incorrect procedures, to identify basic elements of a process, and to identify the adequacy of products.

Traditionally with occupational programs, identification tests have tended to focus upon measuring students' skills at identifying tools and equipment and the controls or component parts of equipment. Figure 6.2 is an example identification test for an electric typewriter. Other popular identification tests include the wood identification test in which a box of numbered wood samples is presented to the student with instructions to identify each type of wood by its proper name. Similar measures are used in identifying types of fasteners, fixtures, and other associated devices in all areas of occupational programs including agricultural education, home economics and public service education, business and marketing education, health occupations education, and industrial education. Example item 10 presents an example of a tool identification item.

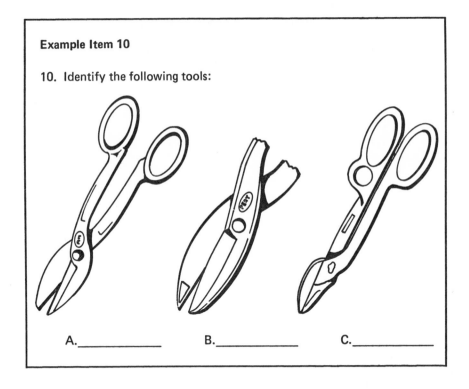

Example Item 10

10. Identify the following tools:

A._____   B._____   C._____

From the above description of traditionally used identification tests, the distinction between the performance-identification test and the special form of cognitive-achievement test item discussed in chapter 5 is not clear. Some may argue that an identification test only involves knowing and does not really measure an individual's skill at doing. Knowing the parts and controls of an electric typewriter does not insure that an individual can type adequately. Likewise,

1. *Paper Guide:* A movable plate back of cylinder; set at "0" and rest paper against it.

2. *Line Space Regulator:* Adjusts carriage for single, double, or triple spacing.

3. *Carriage Release Levers:* Depress to move carriage right or left.

4. *Carriage Return Lever:* Returns carriage and spaces paper to a new line of typing.

5. *Tab Set Key:* Sets stops at intervals along carriage for typing tabulations, indenting.

6. *Back Space Key:* Moves carriage one or more spaces to the right.

7. *Paper Release Lever:* When pulled foward releases paper from cylinder.

8. *Cylinder Scale:* Guide in setting margins; indicates number of strokes across paper.

9. *Variable Line Spacer:* A button, usually in left cylinder knob, when depressed permits the cylinder to roll freely.

10. *Cylinder:* The roller (platen) around which paper turns; cylinder knobs at each end.

11. *Paper Bail and Rollers:* Long bar resting on cylinder; holds paper in position. Adjust rollers an equal distance from each edge of paper.

12. *Tabulator Bar or Key:* Moves carriage to position where a tab stop has been set.

13. *Tab Clear Key:* To remove a tab stop, go to that position and depress tab clear key.

14. *Ribbon Change Lever:* Determines if key will strike upper or lower part of ribbon (red or black); if set on white (stencil) no part of ribbon is used.

15. *Margin Release Key:* Permits temporary typing beyond the margins without actually changing the margin settings.

FIGURE 6.2. Electric Typewriter Identification Test.

an individual may be able to memorize and recall pictures or objects using the same knowing-level cognitive memory as would be used in memorizing words. However, the main difference between performance-identification tests and cognitive-identification tests is that performance-identification tests are using a perceptual input other than words. As discussed in chapter 4 and mentioned earlier in this chapter, perceptual skill is important in the completion of most psychomotor tasks. Visual, auditory, kinesthetic, and olfactory perceptions can be assessed through the most basic of performance tests—the identification test.

Identification tests can be designed so that any occupational teacher can measure students' perceptual skills. A test can be designed rather easily to measure students' abilities to identify specific devices from a broad array of devices using any or a combination of any of the senses. For example, in a foods program, a series of breads can be numbered and arranged on a table. Then each student can be given an answer sheet and instructed to identify each type of bread. An alteration of this type of test could include, for each type of bread, a variety of excellence in product. Then, in addition to identifying the type of bread, the students must also identify, say, which of three is the best baked bread.

Another adaptation of the identification test can ask the examinee to identify parts of products and then further indicate the function of the part. Obviously, this type of test can be used on numerous types of materials from microscopic slides to plumbing valves. Comer (1970) has developed an automotive test of this type, which could be adapted to all occupational areas. This particular test is composed of fifty small automobile parts or sections of large parts. The automotives student is required to: (1) identify each part, (2) tell what is wrong with it, and (3) explain what caused the damage. An example is a cross section of a radial tire that is worn on the inside edge. The student would have to identify it as a radial tire, indicate that it is worn unevenly, and indicate that the toe in or caster and camber were out of adjustment.

The most popular of the identification tests have usually relied upon visual cues. All occupational areas have many possibilities for expanding and overcoming this limitation. Recently, tests have been designed for measuring the auditory skill of auto mechanics trainees in identifying engine malfunctions. These tests (Swanson 1968) consist of tape recordings of actual engine malfunctions with an answer sheet to record the examinee's responses. Example item 11 is a practice question used in acquainting an examinee with such a test.

Example Item 11

11. You will hear a V8 engine starting in this recording. Your job is to identify the manufacturer of the car.

(sound)

_____ A   General Motors Corporation

_____ B   Ford Motor Company

_____ C   Chrysler Motor Corporation

_____ D   American Motor Corporation

A test of this type has been shown to discriminate between experienced and inexperienced mechanics. Likewise, a test of machinist skill (Becker 1969) at identifying improper machine setups and faulty equipment has also been developed. Example item 12 presents one item from such a test.

Example Item 12

12. This question concerns grinding wheels. Four disc-type grinding wheels, suspended from string, are tapped lightly with a small plastic mallet. Indicate which one of the four wheels is cracked.

(sound)

_____ 1.

_____ 2.

_____ 3.

_____ 4.

Similar tests have been developed for assessing kinesthetic skill in determining finish quality of material and texture of woven material. Tests for cooks, medical technicians, agribusiness workers, and others can all be constructed to measure various types of perceptual skills.

Identification tests can also focus on procedures and adequacy in the sequencing of procedures. A list of steps can be presented to an occupational student directing him/her to number the steps in correct sequence. Example item 13 presents such an item.

Example Item 13

13. Number the following processes in the order in which they would occur in the growing of corn in a field that had been used for corn the previous year.

_____ Plant

_____ Disc

_____ Apply liquid nitrogen

_____ Apply starter fertilizer

_____ Apply herbicide

_____ Apply corn borer killer

_____ Harvest

_____ Cultivate 2nd and 3rd time

_____ Harrow

_____ Plow

_____ Roto hoe

_____ Cultivate 1st time

Advantages and Disadvantages of Identification Tests

One advantage of identification tests over cognitive tests is that they can assess an individual's skill at identification and discrimination among real objects. The identification provides for measuring students' perception—visual, kinesthetic, auditory, olfactory, and gustatory. In addition, the identification test can assess an individual's ability to identify steps in a process without actually being involved in it.

Another advantage is that most identification tests do not require expensive or complex equipment. Also, most identification tests can be administered to groups rather than individuals. There are certain considerations in administering a group-identification test that may be more elaborate than those required for administering group cognitive-achievement tests. However, in most instances, they do not require a one-to-one relationship of examiner to examinee as do some other forms of performance tests.

The greatest disadvantage of the identification test is that it does not provide a direct measure of an individual's skill at performing occupational tasks other than identification tasks. Like many cognitive and perceptual measures, the identification test provides an indirect measure of understanding, doing, and being types of performance. The identification test has another disadvantage in that it often requires a large number of parts or products. This, in many cases, will necessitate some additional expenditures. The trade-off of time, equipment, and other costs must be weighed to determine the utility of these indirect measures over direct ones.

Developing Identification Tests

The construction or development of identification tests will vary with the format of the objects or other stimuli as well as with the mode of responding. However, there are some general and specific suggestions for construction. Since many identification tests involve some type of printed recording form and an instruction form, many of the suggestions made in chapter 5 regarding multiple-choice and short-answer items are appropriately applicable to identification tests. Marshal and Hales (1971) make the following suggestions for preparing identification tests:

1. Insure that the problem statement clearly establishes one and only one frame of reference for responding to the item.
2. Insure that the item is concise, unambiguous, and grammatically correct.
3. Insure that superfluous and unnecessarily technical words and phrases are not used.

4. Insure that directions for the test state explicitly the general procedures for responding to the tasks presented and for recording responses.

In addition to these general considerations for developing identification tests, there is a more specific procedure or series of steps that can be either applied in total or adapted to meet the specific need for and nature of an identification test.

STEP 1. Identify Desired Behavior. Before any test or measuring instrument is developed, it is obviously necessary to define very specifically what is to be measured. As suggested in chapter 4, the test should be prepared from a plan or table of specifications, which is based upon either prespecified student-performance objectives or course content. Of course, in either case, an analysis of the job or occupation would precede the preparation of objectives or the development of a course outline. This insures relevancy of both course content and testing procedures. Whichever the case, the content of the identification test should be indicated in the table of specifications.

STEP 2. Select Items or Products to Be Included in the Identification Test. Based upon the information specified in step 1, objects to be included in the identification test should be located and obtained. In cases where procedures are the focus of the identification test, either actual equipment or devices in which the procedures will be displayed should be arranged. Or, if paper and pencil identification tests are to be used, then appropriate stimuli should be drawn, tape recorded, or recorded in some other manner.

STEP 3. Develop an Operating Plan for the Test. After the testing problem has been defined and the necessary products or devices gathered, it is important to organize the testing procedure. The development of an operating plan can provide the vehicle for this organizational effort. This plan initially should be considered tentative and open to change based upon tryout of the test. Also, the operating plan can be filed for reuse in future testing situations within subsequent course or problem offerings. Ryans and Frederiksen (1951) suggest that the operating plan contain the following four elements:

1 Directions for preparing the equipment or other materials for administration

2. Directions for training the test administrator and other assistants or judges who may be involved
3. Directions for checking the condition of the equipment
4. Directions for the actual conduct of the test

In addition, a plan for physically organizing the room or laboratory for testing should be included. This is especially pertinent if physical objects and not paper and pencil representations are the forms of the test. Figure 6.3 presents an example plan for a valve identification test.

STEP 4. Develop and Reproduce a Recording Form and Other Related Documents. The preparation of a form or answer sheet for recording examinee responses is a simple task. However, its importance in objectively assessing a student's performance should not be overlooked. Additionally, the format of the answer sheet can simplify scoring and summarizing the test results. Figure 6.4 presents an answer sheet designed to be used in the valve identification test described in figure 6.3. In addition to an answer sheet, many times there will be a need for other documents to support the identification test. For tests that use a multiple-choice type of format or a format other than constructed response, either a printed booklet or a printed card such as the one used in the valve identification test must be developed. (See figure 6.5.)

STEP 5. Develop Instructions for the Test. A necessary component of any test is a set of directions on how to take and respond to the test. The complexity of the test will determine the extensiveness of the directions. Furthermore, if the size of the examinee group is large and a person other than the test developer will be involved in administering the test, it is suggested that a set of directions for the test administrator and/or proctor be developed. Table 6.1 provides examinee instructions and administrator instructions for the valve identification test mentioned previously.

STEP 6. Try Out and Revise the Test. Tryout of the test can be viewed as occurring in two phases or stages: the first phase involves a simulation of the actual test administration. This simulated testing should include a small sample of examinees who are similar to the ultimate population. The testing situation should be set up as outlined in the operating plan, using the recording form, printed and verbal directions, and other components of the test. The test should then be administered to the small group of students, paying very

VALVE IDENTIFICATION TEST

PLANNING SHEET

I. **Purpose of the test.** This test is designed primarily to measure the trainee's acquaintance with the various kinds of valves that he disassembles and assembles by testing the trainee's knowledge of (a) the names of the various parts, and (b) how these parts function. This test uses actual valve parts instead of verbal descriptions or pictures.

II. **Items (Valve parts to be identified).** This test consists of 29 valve parts selected from the following types of valves: gate, globe, check, bottom blowdown, pressure relief, pressure regulating, boiler feed stop and check, safety, steam trap, boiler feedwater regulator, and main steam stop valve. (An odd rather than an even number of items is chosen for the test in order to permit a smooth flow of students from station to station.)

III. **Time required per student.** A trial run on the identification of the 29 selected parts of valves shows that each identification and determination of function requires no longer than 50 seconds. Allowing time for giving directions and collection of papers, a period of a half-hour is needed to administer this test to 29 students. (If the number of students exceeds slightly the number of items included in the test, dummy stations with blank item cards are included in the circuit to accommodate the few extra men. The total testing time will be slightly increased.)

IV. **Assistance needed.**
  a. Twenty-nine selected valve parts.
  b. Twenty-nine cards (one for each valve part) on which has been typed the test item consisting of a list of five names of parts and a list of five functions of parts. Each part and test item card are known as a station. Each card is numbered to indicate the item and station.
  c. Tables arranged in a hollow rectangle. The arrangement is illustrated in Figure 4.

	14	28	13	27	12	26	11	25	10	24	9	23	
29		PROCTOR			TEST SUPERVISOR				PROCTOR				8
15													22
1	16	2	17	3	18	4	19	5	20	6	21	7	

Figure 4

This diagram indicates how the cards (test items) are arranged. The numbers of the two halves of the series are laid out alternately. By moving *two* stations to the right each man answers all items in correct numerical order. By this arrangement, trainees on either side of a man are not working on adjacent parts of the test. This layout reduces the likelihood of mutual assistance, and it also makes it easier for proctors to detect copying. A man must make two complete circuits of the table to complete the test.

  d. Separate answer sheets. Answer sheets are needed for each man. Each item has two blanks for recording answers; one blank for the name of the part, the second blank for the function. The answer sheets are laid out at the stations before beginning the test. At each individual station the item number corresponding to the station is circled in red pencil on the answer sheet to indicate at what part of the test the man is to begin.
  e. A watch with a second hand or a stop watch.
  f. A whistle. The blowing of the whistle at 50-second intervals is the "change stations" signal.
  g. Timekeeper's card with an arrangement of numbers as shown below.

TIMEKEEPER'S CARD				
60	60	60	60	60
50	50	50	50	50
40	40	40	40	40
30	30	30	30	30
20	20	20	20	20
10	10	10	10	10

This card will help the supervisor keep account of the 50-second intervals.

V. **Assistance needed.** Two proctors. Test supervisor will act as timekeeper.

Source: Reproduced from *Handbook of Performance Testing, A Practical Guide for Test Makers,* by Boyd, J. L., and Shimberg, B., 1971, with permission of Educational Testing Service, Princeton, New Jersey.

FIGURE 6.3.   Valve Identification Test Planning Sheet.

Station	Name	Function	Station	Name	Function
1	——	——	2	——	——
3	——	——	4	——	——
5	——	——	6	——	——
7	——	——	8	——	——
9	——	——	10	——	——
11	——	——	12	——	——
13	——	——	14	——	——
15	——	——	16	——	——
17	——	——	18	——	——
19	——	——	20	——	——
21	——	——	22	——	——
23	——	——	24	——	——
25	——	——	26	——	——
27	——	——	28	——	——
29	——	——			

Name _____

Section _____ Date _____

Source: Reproduced from *Handbook of Performance Testing, A Practical Guide for Test Makers,* by Boyd, J. L., and Shimberg, B., 1971, with permission of Educational Testing Service, Princeton, New Jersey.

FIGURE 6.4.   Answer Sheet for the Valve Identification Test.

close attention to their responses and reactions. Many times it is advantageous to ask one or two students to think out loud to the test developer as he or she is going through the test. By observing the small group of examinees, major obstacles and problems in the testing procedures, hardware, or software can be identified and revised prior to administration of the test to the larger group.

PART PLACED HERE

The valve part for this item is the piston of the pressure regulating valve (Leslie CP type).

17

Part-Name	Function
1. Main valve	1. Aligns and supports lower cross-head.
2. Spring seat	2. Opens auxiliary valve when pushed by discharge pressure.
3. Diaphragm	3. Opens main valve when forced down by steam pressure admitted through controlling valve.
4. Piston	4. Provides a means of opening and closing steam ports.
5. Slide	5. Acts as a buffer and guide for adjusting spring.

Source: Reproduced from *Handbook of Performance Testing, A Practical Guide for Test Makers,* by Boyd, J. L., and Shimberg, B., 1971, with permission of educational testing Service, Princeton, New Jersey.

FIGURE 6.5. *Sample Card for Specifying Valve Part Used in an Identification Test.*

TABLE 6.1. Directions for Administration of the Valve Identification Test and Directions to the Examinee.

I. Directions for administration of the test.

1. Before the test begins make sure that all preliminary arrangements have been attended to by checking to see that each item card matches the valve part, that stations are properly numbered, that the answer sheet at each station is properly marked with a red circle around the item number that corresponds to the station, and that a scoring key has been prepared.

2. Place the trainees around the tables so that *one and only one* man is at a station and that there are no vacant stations between the men. In case the number of men being tested is less than the number of items in the test, remove the extra answer sheets.

3. See that each man has a pencil. Have a few extra in reserve in case trainees break their pencil points.

4. Read "DIRECTIONS TO STUDENTS" aloud. Answer questions. Then say "READY, BEGIN."

5. At the end of each 50-second interval blow the whistle as the "change station" signal. Use the timekeeper's card to indicate the elapse of 50 seconds by crossing out the appropriate figure in the vertical columns each time the whistle is blown. Give the directions for starting when the second hand of your watch is on 60. Cross out the "60" at the top of the first column. The figure 50 which appears below tells you to blow the whistle when the second hand of the watch reaches 50. Continue in this manner until the test is completed.

6. During the progress of the test, make sure that the proctors continue to check the work of the students, seeing that the answers are recorded in the proper places on the answer sheet.

7. When the test is completed, collect the answer sheets and send the students to their next assignment.

II. Directions to students *(To be read aloud by the test supervisor).*

1. "This is a test designed to measure your ability to *identify parts of various types of valves and the function or use of each part.*

2. "Write your name, section number, and the date in the spaces on the answer sheet.

3. "Notice the large number at the top of the card in front of you. This tells you the number of the station at which you are now standing. Find this same number on your answer sheet. It has been circled with a red pencil. This circled number shows you where to start marking your answers.

4. "Above the card you will find a part from a valve. You may pick up the part and examine it if you wish. On the left side of the card are five names of parts; one of these is the name of the part before you. Select the correct name of the part and notice the number 1, 2, 3, 4, or 5, in front of it. This is the number you are to write in the first blank space beside the red circle on your answer sheet. If you are not sure of the correct name, make the best guess you can. On the right hand side of the card are five statements of part functions. One of these statements describes a function or a purpose of the valve part. Select the correct function and notice the number in front of it. This is the number you are to write in the second blank space to the right of the item number. If you are not sure of the answer, make the best guess you can. If you wish to change an answer, erase and write in your new answer.

5. "As you change stations leave the card and part where you found them. When the whistle blows, take your answer sheet with you and move TWO stations to your right, to the station with the next higher number. After you reach the highest number (29 for this test), your next station will be 1.

6. "After you finish at each station, put your answer sheet face down on the table and stand by that station until the whistle blows.

7. "Are there any questions?" (Allow time to answer any legitimate questions.)

8. "READY, BEGIN." (Give this signal when the second hand of your watch is on "60".)

Source: Reproduced from *Handbook of Performance Testing, A Practical Guide for Test Makers,* by Boyd, J. L., and Shimberg, B., 1971, with permission of Educational Testing Service, Princeton, New Jersey.

The second phase or tryout occurs when the test is administered to the larger group. At this time, of course, problems of the larger group may be encountered that can lead to a revision in procedures and associated materials. Of equal importance, results can be collected and analyzed from the test administration to aid in refinement. This statistical analysis of the identification test is similar to the analysis performed on the paper and pencil test in relation to reliability, validity, discrimination ability, etc. For more detailed suggestions on analysis of the identification test, refer to chapter 9.

WORK-SAMPLE AND SIMULATION TESTS

The *work-sample test* of performance is basically a controlled test that is administered using the actual conditions of the work or job situation. The examinee is required to use exact procedures that would be employed in the actual job situation. *Simulation tests,* on the other hand, are tests designed to duplicate or simulate the real-life work situation by using specialized equipment or making modifications in existing equipment. From an examinee's performance on a simulation test, his/her actual performance in a real-life work situation can be inferred. Even though the task is artificial in a sense, it is generally easier to administer than its work-sample counterpart and usually provides a fairly accurate assessment.

Types of Work-samples and Simulation Tests

Work-samples and simulation tests can be broken down into three basic categories: (1) paper and pencil performance tests; (2) performance tests using simulators; and (3) actual work samples using realistic equipment and conditions.

Paper and Pencil Tests. The common conception that paper and pencil tests of performance can only measure cognitive functioning is not entirely true. Many paper and pencil tests can provide direct assessment of job performances. For example, the National Architectural Registration Board examination requires that a candidate develop a site plan for a specific structure when given a topographical map. In this sense, the architect is actually displaying his ability through drawings by using paper and pencil. Also, the preparation or drawing of schematics, both for plumbing trades and for electrical trades, is often required on licensure examinations. Figure 6.6 is an example of the paper and pencil performance test in which the examinee is required to indicate appropriate locations for electrical outlets on a residential home layout. Another form of a paper and pencil performance test (this form approaching a simulation test) is the use of photographs or a printed layout of a measuring instrument, which the examinee is asked to read. For example, a student may be asked to make the readings from a vernier scale and a micrometer as shown in figure 6.7.

The diagram below shows the floor plan of a master suite in a private residence. Directly on the diagram, locate the electric outlets and switches that are necessary and desirable for the entrance hall, bathroom, and bedroom.

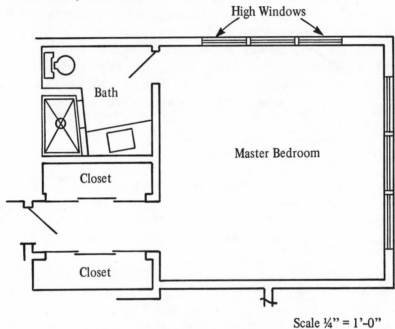

Scale ¼" = 1'-0"

Source: Reproduced from *Handbook of Performance Testing, A Practical Guide for Test Makers,* by Boyd, J. L., and Shimberg, B., 1971, with permission of Educational Testing Service, Princeton, New Jersey.

FIGURE 6.6.   Paper and Pencil Performance Test.

As was mentioned, a paper and pencil performance test of this nature is more of a simulation test because the student is not required actually to use the measuring instrument, applying it to a standard or a specific piece of material and then making the necessary reading. In this respect, the student is measured on his/her ability to read the scale of the instrument rather than on his/her ability to actually use the measuring instrument.

Another form of paper and pencil performance test, which can very easily be extended to fulfill the requirements of an actual work

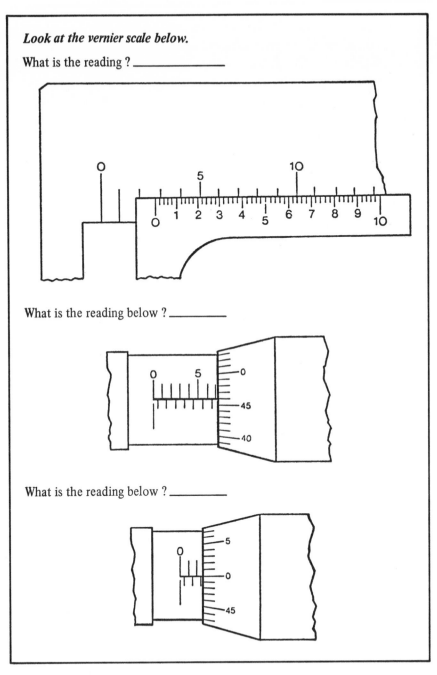

Source: Reproduced from *Handbook of Performance Testing, A Practical Guide for Test Makers,* by Boyd, J. L., and Shimberg, B., 1971, with permission of Educational Testing Service, Princeton, New Jersey.

FIGURE 6.7. Performance-test Items on Measuring Instruments.

sample, is the development or the writing of a computer program. Students can be presented with a problem that requires the design of a computer program. They can be asked to write out their programs on coding sheets and flow chart them according to the operation and iterations within the program. An instructor or examiner can then grade or score the computer program according to the theoretical ability of completion. This test can be extended to keypunching the program cards and running the cards through the computer with associated data cards to determine if the program actually works.

An additional paper and pencil performance test that approximates very closely the work sample is a bookkeeping test. Since bookkeeping is actually done with paper and pencil, this test can provide a realistic measure of a student's bookkeeping skills or competencies. Figure 6.8 presents an example of a bookkeeping test in which the student is required to prepare a profit and loss statement from a presented worksheet.

One other type of paper and pencil performance test is the *variable-sequence test.* Variable-sequence tests lend themselves well to assessing troubleshooting skills. *Troubleshooting skills* are the skills related to looking for malfunctions or deficiencies in a particular piece of equipment or operation. Troubleshooting can range from the analysis of a malfunctioning automobile engine by an auto mechanic to the diagnosis of an ailing individual by a medical professional.

The most sophisticated form of the variable-sequence test is sometimes referred to as a *tab test.* Tab tests have a series of tabs presented on a heavy paper or cardboard pad. The student is presented with a problem to be solved and responds by pulling one or more of the tabs at a time. For example, the student may be presented with a problem such as "an automobile engine will not start." Tabs located on the answer sheet in this case would correspond to different observations or tests that a mechanic could choose in his diagnosis of the starting problem. For example, there may be tabs for: (1) measure battery charge; (2) check starter terminals; (3) check ignition coil; (4) check carburetor function; and so on. An experienced or trained mechanic would know which of these items or functions to check and then which functions to go to next once a negative or positive reading has been found on any of the responses. The measure of a student's performance on the tab

Directions: *Prepare a Profit and Loss Statement from the work sheet shown below. Possible score--20 points.*

NASH PAINTING SERVICE

Work Sheet for Quarter Ended March 31, 19--

Account Title	Acct. No.	Trial Balance Dr.	Trial Balance Cr.	Profit & Loss Expense	Profit & Loss Income	Bal. Sheet Assets	Bal. Sheet L&P
Cash	1	2,215				2,215	
Painting Equipment	2	545				545	
(Acct. Rec.) Davis Mills	3	260				260	
(Acct. Pay.) Pittsburgh Paint Co.	22		225				225
Walter Nash, Capital	31		1,950				1,950
Service Sales	41		1,200		1,200		
Rent Expense	54	300		300			
Advertising Expense	57	55		55			
		3,375	3,375	355	1,200	3,020	2,175
Net Profit				845			845
				1,200	1,200	3,020	3,020

Solution:

Nash Painting Service
Profit and Loss Statement
For Quarter Ended March 31, 19--

Income		
Service Sales		1,200
Expenses		
Rent Expenses	300	
Advertising Expense	55	
Total Expenses		355
Net Profit		845

Source: Reproduced from *Testing and Evaluation in Business Education*, 1966, with permission of South-Western Publishing Company, Cincinnati, Ohio.

FIGURE 6.8. Example Bookkeeping Test.

test is indicated by the number of appropriate and inappropriate tabs that have been pulled.

Another form of technical presentation of the tab test uses an opaque ink placed over typewritten or mimeographed lettering, which can easily be removed with a pencil eraser. Rather than pulling tabs, an individual simply erases a selected response, thus indicating a particular reading or a correct or incorrect response. An excellent example of this type of item presentation is the diagnostic test prepared by the National Board of Medical Examiners. One page of this test, including two sample problems, is included in figure 6.9.

Obviously, the use of a professionally prepared tab test or one using the opaquing overlay would require additional expense. However, Boyd and Shimberg (1971) have suggested several alternatives to the tab test that overcome this expense or technicality problem. They suggest using 3" X 5" cards with a choice on one side of the card and the consequence of the choice on the other side. Also, choices can be placed on sealed envelopes with the consequences indicated on a card contained in the envelope. This second form, of course, makes evaluating the performance test easier because it is more obvious that a response has been made by opening of the envelope as opposed to simply looking at the opposite side of a card.

Tests Using a Simulator.   The second major classification of work-sample and simulation tests includes tests that rely on a simulator or a piece of apparatus that simulates an actual work setting for testing. Simulation tests do not always require complex and expensive simulators or equipment. The traditional connotation of simulators causes one to think of the complex aircraft simulators that are used in the training of single and multiengine aircraft pilots. They are used to examine the student pilot's performance before he is actually given control of the said aircraft. However, in the electronics lab, when an individual is given a schematic and asked to "bread board" the specific schematic using components with quick fasten terminals, this is also a simulation both in terms of an experience and a test.

Simulators have been used extensively in the military services for both the training and testing of individuals. During World War II a simulator was used to train and evaluate the skill of navigators and aircraft gunners with scores being based, in the case of the gunners, on the number of objects hit in the simulator experience. Also,

160

SAMPLE PATIENT

You are called to the emergency room of the hospital to see a comatose patient. You find a man about 40 years old, unaccompanied by family or friends. There is no obvious evidence of trauma. There is Kussmaul breathing and the breath has an acetone odor. The skin is dry. The eyeballs are soft to palpation. Examination of the heart and lungs shows nothing abnormal except for labored respiration and a rapid, regular heart rate of 120 per minute. The abdomen is soft. There is no evidence of enlarged liver or spleen or abnormal masses. Deep tendon reflexes are somewhat hypoactive bilaterally. The rectal temperature is 98.0°F (36.7°C). Blood pressure is 100/70 mm Hg.

SAMPLE PROBLEM S-1

You would immediately

1. Order serum calcium determination
2. Order carbon dioxide content determination
3. Measure venous pressure
4. Catheterize
5. Perform lumbar puncture
6. Order blood sugar determination
7. Order electroencephalogram
8. Order electrocardiogram
9. Request neurological consultation

For Problem S-1 the correct answers are:

SAMPLE PROBLEM S-2

You would now

10. Order digitalis
11. Order morphine sulfate
12. Order insulin
13. Order coramine
14. Start intravenous infusion with normal saline
15. Withdraw 500 ml of blood by phlebotomy
16. Admit patient immediately to cardiac ward
17. Admit patient immediately to neurosurgical service
18. Admit patient immediately to medical service
19. Keep patient in emergency room for further observation

For Problem S-2 the correct answers are:

Source: Reproduced from *Proceedings of the 1963 Invitational Conference on Testing Problems.* Copyright © 1964 by Educational Testing Service. All Rights reserved. Reprinted by permission.

FIGURE 6.9. Variable-sequence Response Sheet with Erasable Overprint.

a simulator to train and evaluate United States Navy machinists has been used. Figure 6.10 presents a representation of such a device.

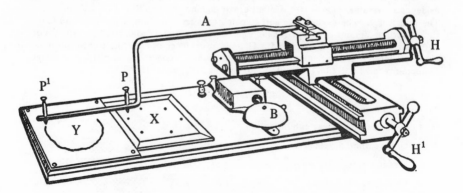

Source: Reproduced from *Industrial Psychology,* by M. S. Vitteles, 1932, with the permission of W. W. Norton & Co., Inc., New York, N.Y.

FIGURE 6.10.   Test Apparatus for Engine–Lathe Operation.

In the past decade, commercially produced simulators have been introduced in occupational education programs at a fairly rapid rate. These simulators have focused on assessing students' trouble-shooting ability. For example, electronic circuit boards have been prepared, which an instructor can disturb by entering malfunctions to the circuit. Then the student has the responsibility of making various tests in the circuit and identifying the malfunctions. Figure 6.11 presents an example of an electronic transistor radio simulator. Also, simulators have been marketed for assessing the ability of clothes washer and dryer repairmen. The more sophisticated simulators of this type have a built-in examiner control panel in which the examiner can enter the malfunction simply by slipping switches or turning dials. Figure 6.12 presents a picture of an automatic clothes washer simulator and table 6.2 presents an associated malfunction list for the automatic clothes washer.

Simulators can be developed by individual occupational teachers or they can be purchased through commercial manufacturers. The complexity of simulators should not be a constraining factor in the preparation of instructor-made simulators. Many occupational competencies can be assessed through simple simulators requiring no special or expensive types of equipment.

Work-Samples.   The third category of work-sample and simulator tests includes the true work-sample. As mentioned earlier, *work-*

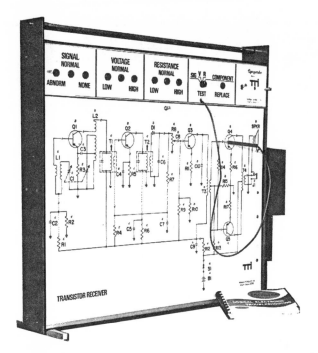

Source: Reproduced with the permission of Training Technology, Inc., Atlanta, Georgia.

FIGURE 6.11. Electronic Transistor Radio Simulator.

samples are selections taken from an actual work setting and systematized for objective assessment or testing procedures. The differences between the use of simulators and actual work-samples are sometimes very small and not really important. But, the basic differentiation is that the material and equipment in the work-sample are identical to those in the actual work setting. For example, basic components and basic schematic configurations were presented in the simulators mentioned in the foregoing section for assessing a student's ability to troubleshoot and repair a washing machine or to troubleshoot and repair a transistor radio. However, in a true work-sample, the student would be presented with an actual washing machine or transistor radio that had a malfunction in it and asked to diagnose and repair the equipment. Obviously, it can be seen that the materials, equipment, and preparation required would be much greater with regard to the work-sample than with the simulator. An example of a work-sample that does not require complex equipment is the Blum sewing machine test. This test involves presenting to the sewing student a pattern with instructions to sew

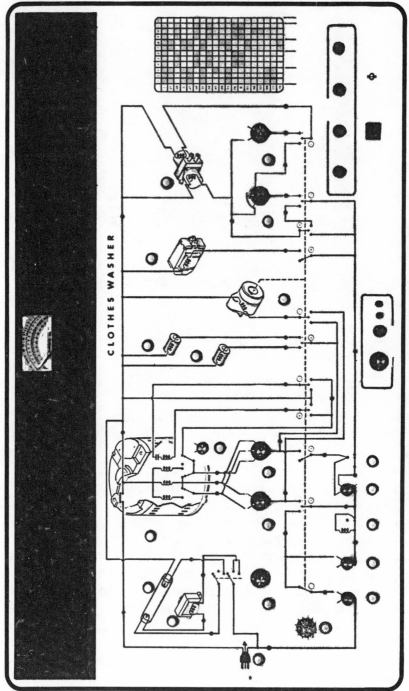

FIGURE 6.12. Automatic Clothes Washer Simulator.

TABLE 6.2. *Malfunction List for Clothes Washer Simulator.*

Malfunction List

Malf. No.	Symptom	Defect	Replace No.	Item
1	Fluorescent lamp does not light	Open light switch	4	Lamp switch
2	Fluorescent lamp does not light	Open ballast (choke)	2	Choke
3	Fluorescent lamp does not light	Open lamp filament	3	Fluorescent tube
4	Fluorescent lamp does not light and machine does nothing	Open motor protector	11	Motor
5	Fluorescent lamp lights and machine does nothing	Open ON/OFF switch	6	ON/OFF switch
6	Operation good until spin, then sequence stops	Open vibration limit switch	8	Vibration limit switch
7	No water enters tub	Open water level switch	9	Control pressure switch
8	No water enters tub	Open cam 10, bottom contacts	5	Timer
9	No water enters tub on hot wash	Open hot water solenoid	21	Water valve (solenoid)
10	No low speed agitation	Open agitate switch, low cont.	13	Agitate speed switch
11	No medium speed agitation or spin	Open motor, medium winding	11	Motor
12	No agitation at any speed	Open cam 3	5	Timer
13	No agitation	Open cam 4, bottom contacts	5	Timer
14	No agitation or spin	Open motor, direction winding	11	Motor
15	Operation sequence stops at end of agitate cycle	Open cam 7, top contacts	5	Timer
16	Operation sequence does not advance from any cycle	Open timer coil	17	Timer motor
17	Bleach not added to wash	Open cam 6, top contacts	5	Timer
18	Tub empties, but basket does not spin	Open cam 8 contacts	5	Timer
19	Bleach not added to wash	Open bleach dispenser solenoid	15	Bleach dispenser solenoid
20	Wash water temperature ok, but rinse water always cold	Open rinse temperature switch	20	Rinse temperature switch
21	No agitation at any speed	Open water level switch	9	Control pressure switch
22	No water enters tub on cold wash or cold rinse	Open cold water solenoid	21	Water valve (solenoid)
23	No water enters tub on hot wash	Open cam 11, top contacts	5	Timer
24	Operation good until spin, then sequence stops	Open door switch contacts	7	Door switch

165

along the line in one case and between two lines in another case. Figure 6.13 presents an example of the Blum sewing machine test.

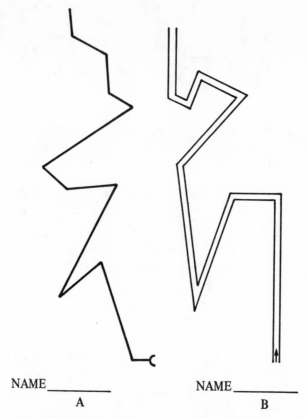

NAME_____   NAME_____

       A   B

Source: Reproduced from "Selection of Sewing Machine Operators," *Journal of Applied Psychology,* Vol. 27, p. 36, 1943, with the permission of American Institutes for Research, Silver Spring, Maryland.

FIGURE 6.13. Blum Sewing Machine Test.

The list of potential and existing work-sample tests is almost endless. They can include things such as presenting to a machinist student a blueprint and requiring him or her to produce the particular part specified in the blueprint. Also, a test of a dental hygiene student's ability to adequately clean an individual's teeth is another form of a work-sample. Table 6.3 presents an example of a work-sample test for evaluating an office occupations student's ability to operate a keypunch machine. This table includes directions for preparing and administering the test, directions to students, as well as a checklist

TABLE 6.3. *Example Test for Evaluating Office Occupations Students.*

Performance Test: Operation of IBM 083 Sorter*

NOTE: *There are six possible versions or combinations of the job-required task of operating an 083 sorter. These six possible versions are alpha sorting, numeric sorting, card counting, block sorting, selection by sorting, and selection by rejection. The test illustrated in the following paragraphs examines performance of numeric sorting, card counting, and block sorting.*

1. Directions for preparing for, and administering, the test.

a. Preparation for the test.
(1) Place a deck of 250 cards with punched information on each 083 sorter.
(2) Insure that the machine is on and warmed up.
(3) Depress all suppression keys.
(4) Set edit and edit stop and sort test switches in the ON position.
(5) Set the card count switch in the OFF position.
(6) Reset the card count indicator.
(7) Set sort selection switch in an erroneous position.

b. Administration of the test.
(1) Issue the student the "Directions to Students" (para 2 below).
(2) Direct the student to read the entire problem before beginning.
(3) Observe the student's performance. Record the student's performance on the scoring sheet (para 3 below). Score the student's performance as he proceeds through the steps. If after a reasonable time the student is unable to proceed, score that step "NO", help the student only on that step, and allow the student to proceed.
(4) Insure that the student gives his card count orally at the end of the problem. If incorrect, score item 12 "NO". After completion of the test, determine the reason for the incorrect card count and correct the error.

2. Directions to students: 083 Sorter Test.

a. General instructions. This is a graded examination. All work in this examination must be your own. You are not authorized to communicate in any way with other students, give or receive assistance, refer to notes, make a record of your answers, or pass on information about the examination to other students. Any conduct contrary to the above will be the basis for appropriate disciplinary action.

b. Special instructions.
(1) The deck of cards placed on the machine is the deck you will work with on this problem.
(2) Insure that your machine is operating properly.
(3) If you think it is appropriate, you may accomplish more than one step in the same operation.
(4) Using the block sort method, sort the cards as follows:
  (a) Sort columns 26 through 28 numerically:
    Column 28 minor.
    Column 27 intermediate.
    Column 26 major.
  (b) Card count all cards.
(5) Upon completion of the operation outlined above, assemble your cards in proper order and return the entire deck to the instructor, informing him of your card count.
(6) Leave the machine on.

c. Material required. A deck of cards to be sorted will be supplied by the instructor.

d. Time limit. There is no time limitation. However, if you are not able to proceed after a reasonable time at any step of the operation, the instructor will assist you and you will be evaluated accordingly.

3. Directions for scoring: 083 Sorter Test.

Student Name _____	Student Number _____	Date _____	
1. Cards joggled before being placed in hopper.		YES	NO
2. Cards placed properly in hopper.		YES	NO
3. Suppression keys checked.		YES	NO
4. Sort test switch in SORT position.		YES	NO
5. Edit and edit stop switches in OFF position.		YES	NO
6. Sort selection switch set properly for each sort.		YES	NO
7. Sort brush set on proper column for blocking.		YES	NO
8. Sort brush set on proper column for minor sort.		YES	NO
9. Sort brush set on proper column for intermediate sort.		YES	NO
10. Cards removed properly from machine.		YES	NO
11. Sight check performed.		YES	NO
12. Card count made at beginning and end of operation.		YES	NO
13. All cards in correct sequence when returned to instructor.		YES	NO

Instructor _____

Source: Reproduced from *Handbook of Performance Testing, A Practical Guide for Test Makers,* by Boyd, J.L., and Shimberg, B., 1971, with permission of Educational Testing Service, Princeton, New Jersey.

for evaluating a student's performance on this particular work-sample. It would be impossible to list all of the potential work-sample tests in a chapter such as this. Refer to Boyd and Shimberg (1971) for a more detailed listing and presentation of various work-sample tests.

Advantages and Disadvantages of Work-sample and Simulation Tests

The greatest advantage of work-sample or simulation tests is that their face validity is high. That is, they appear to occupational students and to everyone else to be measuring what they are supposed to measure. Also, these tests provide direct or nearly direct measures of a student's skill in performing some important occupational task, whether on paper, on a simulator, or in a real work-like situation. An additional advantage is that these types of tests provide excellent measures of troubleshooting skills, which are so important in many of the service occupations. Work-sample and simulator tests also can provide good learning experiences for occupational students. They provide realistic experiences in doing job-related tasks with the opportunity to gain feedback from an instructor, usually on a one-to-one basis, regarding the appropriateness of actions and of product. And finally, the paper and pencil form of work-sample and simulator tests is a very efficient means of assessing the performance of a group of examinees, even though it cannot be used to assess all occupational tasks.

With regard to disadvantages, work-sample and simulator tests, with the exception of the paper and pencil versions, require a great amount of time to administer since one-to-one observation is usually necessary. This, of course, requires a greater investment in the examination process. Also, most tests of this type require simulators or on-the-job type of equipment. This equipment can be costly and can sometimes prohibit adequate performance testing. Another significant shortcoming of some work-sample and simulator tests that incorporate rating forms for either procedural or product assessment is the possibility of rater error and low rater reliability. Of course, the preparation of good rating scales and the training of raters can help in overcoming this potential deficiency. A final disadvantage is that the work-sample and simulation tests can assess student performance in only a limited sample of the job or occupation without obtaining an overall rating of job performance.

Developing Work-sample and Simulator Tests

The specific occupational area as well as the complexity of the task to be measured will influence the exact procedures that are used in constructing the actual test. However, there are some general steps that will aid occupational teachers in the developmental process. Also, many of the points made in the previous section of this chapter concerned with developing identification tests have application in developing work-sample and simulator tests.

STEP 1. Select a Sample of the Job or Occupation. Experts indicate that the sample of the job to be included in the work-sample or simulator test should be chosen following a job or task analysis of the occupation. This suggestion is emphasized here, but in many occupational programs, such analyses have already been conducted and course objectives and instruction have been based upon these analyses. In these instances, the selection of a job sample is an easier task. From the job analysis or course objectives, the occupational teacher should choose behaviors that are important, frequently used, difficult to measure with other tests, or a combination of these three. Ryans and Frederiksen (1951) suggest that the test developer perform the task or job himself to learn the job subtleties that may not appear in the job analysis or in the objectives. Of course, if the test is to be developed by the occupational teacher, it is assumed that he/she already possesses this skill. Ryans and Frederiksen (1951) also suggest going beyond objectives once a job segment has been selected. They believe that observing someone in the job situation can not only aid in developing the performance test but may also have the side effect of increasing the relevancy of the instructional program.

STEP 2. Develop a Rating or Recording Form. Once a job segment and corresponding tasks or qualities to be included in the performance test have been selected, the next step is to determine the important features of the performance or the product of performance and to develop a rating form that focuses on them.

If the performance components being assessed have distinctly recognizable go or no-go qualities, then the checklist is probably the best type of rating form to be used. However, if the measure of quality of performance must be expressed as a judgment of a rater, the numerical scale or the graphic scale is suggested. Each of these scales was discussed in detail in a previous section of this chapter.

When the product of performance is to be measured, important characteristics of the product should be delineated and ranking forms or product scales should be developed that focus on these characteristics. It may also be necessary to develop separate or several rating forms if more than one approach to rating is used. That is, if both self-appraisal and teacher appraisal are to be used, then possibly two separate forms will be needed.

STEP 3. Survey Practical Limitations of the Testing Environment. Practical limitations of the testing environment must be known to the occupational teacher to aid either in overcoming them or in working within them. The first limitation that should be surveyed is the amount of time available for testing. Usually, testing time must be reviewed in light of total available instructional time because, in most occupational programs, testing will usually take away instructional time. Another consideration should be personnel requirements, particularly personnel time needed to develop and administer such tests. Available teacher time will often place constraints on the number and extensiveness of performance tests to be developed and used. And finally, the amount and availability of equipment for testing should be determined. By considering these factors, the test constructor can better design an operating plan for the performance test.

STEP 4. Develop an Operating Plan. The operating plan for work-sample or simulation tests is similar to the operating plan used with identification tests. The operating plan should include an outline or set of directions for the setup and conduct of the performance test. Reiterated, the suggestions by Ryans and Frederiksen (1951) include:

1. Directions for preparing the equipment or other materials for administration of the test
2. Directions for training the test administrator and other assistants or judges who may be involved
3. Directions for checking the condition of the equipment
4. Directions for the actual conduct of the test

Table 6.4 is a plan for a comprehensive thirteen-hour dental hygiene exam. The plan will help in standardizing procedures from one administration to another as well as simplifying use of the test at a later time or by another occupational teacher.

TABLE 6.4. Comprehensive Dental Hygiene Examination.

Comprehensive Practical Examination (13 hours)

Courses Presented To: Dental Specialist (Basic)

Place: Hygiene Clinic – Radiology Clinic

References:

All previous references

Study Assignment: Review classroom notes

Tools, Equipment, and Materials: Three SF 603's, three Dental Treatment sheets, and three Buck Slips per student, autoclaves, resuscitators, straight and angle handpieces, hand instruments and materials, and dental operatories (as required).

Personnel: Nine primary instructors

Type of Instruction: Examination.

I. **Introduction (5 min)**

A. Opening Statement: The following 12 hours of practical examination conducted in 4-hour blocks in the fourth, fifth, and sixth weeks of the course will be the method used to determine the extent of the student's comprehension of the course of instruction. An additional one hour practical examination will be administered during the fourth week to determine the student's comprehension of the SF 603.

B. Objectives
   1. Ability to prepare dental amalgam, silicate cement, root canal, and prophylaxis setups.
   2. Ability to operate and perform maintenance on dental equipment.
   3. Ability to expose and process dental X-rays.
   4. Ability to maintain dental health records.
   5. Ability to perform resuscitative procedures.

II. **Examination (575 min)**

A. Administrative Instructions
   1. NCOIC – schedules instructors for examination
   2. Duties section leader
      a. Students
         (1) Divide students into groups
         (2) First hour – one group of students to X-ray section; the other half to Hygiene clinic
         (3) Second hour – switch student groups
      b. Chairside examination
         (1) Assign instructors
         (2) Supervise activities
      c. Sterilization and resuscitation examination
         (1) Assign instructors
         (2) Supervise activities
      d. Maintenance examination
         (1) Assign instructors
         (2) Supervise activities
   3. Radiography instructor
      a. Give students instruction
      b. Assign students to booths
      c. Designate radiographs desired
      d. Supervise student activities

B. Directions to Students
   1. Remain seated in waiting area until called

Source: Reproduced from *Handbook of Performance Testing, A Practical Guide for Test Makers*, by Boyd, J. L., and Shimberg, B., 1971, with permission of Educational Testing Service, Princeton, New Jersey.

STEP 5. Try Out and Revise the Test. Also, like the identification test, the work-sample or simulator test should be placed into operation for a trial run to help in identifying problems in process, equipment, rating forms, and procedures. This should also be done following the first large administration of the test. In both cases, the purpose should be to revise the test and make it more reliable, more efficient, and easier to administer.

EMPLOYER–SUPERVISOR MEASURES

Ratings made by supervisors or employers of the graduates of occupational programs can provide an ultimate measure of an individual's performance, that is, measurement of actual on-the-job performance. Employer surveys are not new to occupational education programs. Most programs, which incorporate some type of cooperative instructional setting, use employer ratings. These cooperative arrangements, usually under the aegis of diversified occupations, distributive education, office occupations, cooperative vocational education programs, cooperative work training programs, and so on, involve a student working in a supervised job setting for part of the school day. The programs incorporate employer–supervisor ratings for grading purposes as well as for assessing students' job-related skills or competencies. Employer or supervisor assessments of students' job skills can focus on two basic types of behavior: first of all, they can focus on the general traits that students possess with regard to work, such as ability to get along with others, attitude toward work, appearance and grooming, and so on. Example items 14, 15, and 16 focus on these kinds of traits or behaviors.

Example Item 14

14. *Dependability:* promptness, reliability in attendance	*Low*	*Average*	*High*
	1 2 3	4 5 6	7 8 9

Example Item 15

15. *Responsibility:* willingness with which work is accepted and performed	*Low*	*Average*	*High*
	1 2 3	4 5 6	7 8 9

Example Item 16

16. *Initiative:* ability to plan and direct own work	<ins>Low</ins> 1 2 3	<ins>Average</ins> 4 5 6	<ins>High</ins> 7 8 9

Second, the employer or supervisor evaluation can focus on specific competencies to be developed by the student employee. These types of behaviors or competencies relate to the specific occupation in which the student is employed and being prepared. Example items 17, 18, 19, and 20 present examples of competency assessment relating to automotive and machine trades.

Example Item 17

	Very Adequate	*Adequate*	*In-adequate*	*Cannot Determine*
17. Use of micrometers	☐	☐	☐	☐

Example Item 18

	Very Adequate	*Adequate*	*In-adequate*	*Cannot Determine*
18. Use of compression gauge	☐	☐	☐	☐

Example Item 19

	Very Adequate	*Adequate*	*In-adequate*	*Cannot Determine*
19. Use of vacuum gauge	☐	☐	☐	☐

Example Item 20

	Very Adequate	*Adequate*	*In-adequate*	*Cannot Determine*
20. Use of ammeter	☐	☐	☐	☐

Figure 6.14 presents an example employer survey instrument that focuses on general job traits. And figure 6.15 presents an example employer evaluation which focuses on the specific competencies in addition to general job traits within the food service occupations.

EVALUATION OF EMPLOYEE'S
HIGH SCHOOL PREPARATION
FOR EMPLOYMENT

To the Employer or Supervisor of:

Employee's Name

1. In what capacity are you related to the employee named above? (Check the box.)

   1 ☐ Employer   2 ☐ Supervisor   3 ☐ Other_____
                                                  (Write in)

2. What is the title of the job for which this employee is hired?_____
                                                        (Job title)

3. In the following aspects of employment, how well prepared was the employee previously named for the job for which hired? (Circle the number below the answer.)

-25

	Not at all	Poorly	Some-what	Well	Does not apply
1. Job know-how, application of technical knowledge and skill	1	2	3	4	5
2. Use of tools and equipment	1	2	3	4	5
3. Selection and care of space, materials, and supplies	1	2	3	4	5
4. Quality of work, ability to meet quality demands	1	2	3	4	5
5. Quantity of work, output of satisfactory amount	1	2	3	4	5
6. Cooperativeness, ability to work with others	1	2	3	4	5
7. Accepting advice and supervision	1	2	3	4	5
8. Dependability, thorough completion of a job without supervision	1	2	3	4	5
9. Initiative, doing jobs that need doing	1	2	3	4	5
10. Attendance, reporting for work regularly	1	2	3	4	5
11. Appearance, presenting a business image	1	2	3	4	5
12. Adaptable to new situations	1	2	3	4	5
13. Being able to talk to the boss about job related problems	1	2	3	4	5
14. Serving the public, patient, etc.	1	2	3	4	5
15. Safety habits, minimizing chance for accidents	1	2	3	4	5

4. How would you rate the suitability of the employee previously named for the kind of job held? (Check the box that applies.)

   1 ☐ Exceptionally able   26
   2 ☐ Well
   3 ☐ Acceptable
   4 ☐ Poorly
   5 ☐ Not at all

5. Below is a list of personal qualities and job skills. Check the box before <u>the three you consider most important</u> for a person entering the job held by the previously named employee.

                                                     27-29
   1 ☐ Ability to get along with others--other workers, customers, patients
   2 ☐ Initiative
   3 ☐ Positive attitude toward work
   4 ☐ Appearance and grooming
   5 ☐ Judgment--ability to make decisions, ability to plan and organize
   6 ☐ Competency in using job tools, machines, and materials
   7 ☐ Dependability
   8 ☐ Accuracy, quality, and thoroughness
   9 ☐ Attendance and punctuality
   10 ☐ Work quantity
   11 ☐ Other_____
                        (Write in)

Use the back of this sheet for other suggestions concerning high school occupational training.

FIGURE 6.14.   Example Employer Survey Instrument.

Both of the evaluation or rating forms presented in figures 6.14 and 6.15 are designed to be mailed to employers with a request for completion and return to the educational or training institution. This, however, represents only one method of gathering information

EXAMPLE EMPLOYER EVALUATION OF PROGRAM GRADUATE*

(FOOD SERVICE OCCUPATIONS)

CONFIDENTIAL: The information reported in this survey will be used for career program planning purposes only, and the source of the information will not be divulged to any other agency or party.

1. Employee
2. Program from which employee graduated
3. Name of employing organization
4. Mailing address of organization _____ ZIP
5. Name of respondent _____ Telephone number of respondent (AC)
6. Total number of employees in your organization _____ your department
7. Primary product(s)

Please rate the general traits of the employee according to those listed below. Circle the rating on the following scale.

	need to know*	performance of skill**
	U D E	VA A I CD
	low average high	
	1 2 3 4 5 6 7 8 9	
A. Integrity; trustworthiness, honesty, loyalty	1 2 3 4 5 6 7 8 9	VA A I CD
B. Dependability: promptness, reliability in attendance	1 2 3 4 5 6 7 8 9	VA A I CD
C. Responsibility: willingness with which work accepted is performed	1 2 3 4 5 6 7 8 9	VA A I CD
D. Initiative: ability to plan and direct own work	1 2 3 4 5 6 7 8 9	VA A I CD
E. Judgment: ability to make sound decisions	1 2 3 4 5 6 7 8 9	
F. Cooperation: ability to work with others in harmony	1 2 3 4 5 6 7 8 9	
G. Leadership: ability to understand people and direct others	1 2 3 4 5 6 7 8 9	
H. Attitudes toward work: enthusiasm with which work is performed	1 2 3 4 5 6 7 8 9	
I. Emotional stability: poise and self-control	1 2 3 4 5 6 7 8 9	

*Adapted from survey used by: Springfield Area Vocational Center, Springfield, Illinois.

TASK LIST FOR COMMERCIAL COOKING AND FOOD SERVICE

Please rate the importance of knowing each skill listed below and then rate the employee according to his performance of the tasks which apply to his or her work.

	need to know*	performance of skill**
	U D E	VA A I CD
ORIENTATION to FOOD SERVICE OCCUPATIONS		
Take orders from superiors	U D E	VA A I CD
DIETETICS and NUTRITION		
Identify basic food groups	U D E	VA A I CD
Make calorie counts	U D E	VA A I CD
Plan basic menus for one week	U D E	VA A I CD
Identify primary nutrients in various foods	U D E	VA A I CD

*U = Unnecessary D = Desirable E = Essential
**VA = Very Adequate A = Adequate I = Inadequate CD = Cannot Determine

	need to know*	performance of skill**
	U D E	VA A I CD
SERVING FUNDAMENTALS		
Handle food, beverages, equipment, utensils, table settings, etc., in a way to avoid contamination	U D E	VA A I CD
Replenish serving stations	U D E	VA A I CD
Acquire napkins, utensils, plates, etc., from proper locations	U D E	VA A I CD
Set tables for dinners, parties, etc., as required	U D E	VA A I CD
Carry filled trays	U D E	VA A I CD
Carry filled containers without spilling	U D E	VA A I CD
Observe safety precautions in food handling	U D E	VA A I CD
Wipe spills of food or liquid	U D E	VA A I CD
Keep serving areas clean and uncluttered	U D E	VA A I CD
Wash food preparation equipment	U D E	VA A I CD
Inspect equipment and utensils for cleanliness and sanitation	U D E	VA A I CD
Know sanitation laws	U D E	VA A I CD
SANITATION and SAFETY		
Identify areas where safety equipment is located, e.g. fire blankets, and extinguishers	U D E	VA A I CD
Inspect equipment, glassware, utensils, etc... for cleanliness and spotlessness	U D E	VA A I CD
Use precautions to avoid accidents	U D E	VA A I CD
Shut off main electrical switch when cleaning equipment	U D E	VA A I CD
Keep equipment, utensils, etc., in neat, orderly arrangement	U D E	VA A I CD
Identify faulty steam valves and equipment	U D E	VA A I CD
Identify faulty electrical equipment	U D E	VA A I CD
Identify gas jets which need cleaning or replacement	U D E	VA A I CD
MAINTENANCE and HOUSEKEEPING		
Sort, count, and store utensils in designated areas	U D E	VA A I CD
Lubricate power equipment as necessary	U D E	VA A I CD
Police area to see that hazards do not exist	U D E	VA A I CD
Keep utensils sharp and equipment in good working order	U D E	VA A I CD
Replace worn or dull blades on slicers, cutters, peelers, etc.	U D E	VA A I CD
Check periodically steam tables, heating elements, gas jets, etc.	U D E	VA A I CD
INTRODUCTION to COMMERCIAL KITCHEN EQUIPMENT		
Select proper equipment for job desired	U D E	VA A I CD
Identify each piece of equipment by appropriate name	U D E	VA A I CD
Identify good and poor features of each tool or utensil	U D E	VA A I CD
Operate electrical controls in kitchen for food preparation	U D E	VA A I CD
Operate control valves on gas and steam lines for heat control	U D E	VA A I CD
BASIC TECHNIQUES of FOOD PREPARATION		
Read recipes	U D E	VA A I CD
Follow recipe procedures	U D E	VA A I CD
Measure food quantities and weights accurately	U D E	VA A I CD
Know food preparation terminology	U D E	VA A I CD
Wash food stuffs	U D E	VA A I CD
Peel, seed, and chop vegetables and fruits	U D E	VA A I CD
Prepare raw foods for cooking and serving	U D E	VA A I CD
Prepare meats for cooking	U D E	VA A I CD

*U = Unnecessary D = Desirable E = Essential
**VA = Very Adequate A = Adequate I = Inadequate CD = Cannot Determine

FIGURE 6.15. Example Employer Survey Form for a Specific Program.

Source: Reproduced from Planning, Implementing, and Evaluating Career Preparation Programs, by J. Borgen and D. Davis, 1974, with the permission of McKnight & McKnight Publishing Co., Bloomington, Illinois.

from employers or supervisors. The personal interview and the telephone interview have proven to be worthwhile techniques for gathering information from employers in the private or service sector. However, when interviews are used, it is necessary for the occupational teacher to develop an interview form or schedule to guide and objectify the interviewing process. Figure 6.16 represents one segment of an employer interview form that was used in the assessment of deaf students who had graduated from an occupational education program.

1. Have you found that employment of a deaf person hinders progress or production of your operation in any way?

    Yes.1
    No..2

2a. Are there any special considerations necessary for the employment of a deaf person?

    Yes.1
    No..2 (*skip to* 3)

 b. (*If yes*)   Please describe them. _____

    _____

3. Does the presence of a deaf person make other employees in your business uncomfortable?

    Yes.1
    No..2

4a. Was_____prepared to enter his/her job?

    Yes.1 (*skip to* 5)
    No..2

 b. (*If no*)   In what skils was he <u>not</u> prepared?_____

    _____

5. How does_____get along with other workers?

    Is isolate from group...........1
    Associates with a few...........2
    Associates with many...........3
    Associates with almost everyone.4

6a. Do you feel that _____'s enthusiasm for his work is better, the same, or poorer than that of other workers?

    Better.1
    Same...2 (*skip to* 7)
    Poorer.3

 b. Why do you think this is so? _____

    _____

FIGURE 6.16.   *Employer Interview Form Used in the Assessment of Deaf Students.*

Even though the employer–supervisor rating or evaluation can provide the most accurate measure of a student's performance with regard to occupational skills, it is still one of the most difficult procedures of assessment. It is difficult in the respect that students must be located after leaving the occupational program. Many times this can be a major task compounded by the mobility of many students. There is the additional problem of impressing upon the employer–supervisors the importance of their taking the time to complete carefully such a rating and return it to the school or educational institution. This has great consequences on the number of employers who will participate in this activity, especially when the mail questionnaire or survey is used.

Advantages and Disadvantages of the Employer-Supervisor Rating

The greatest advantage of the employer-supervisor evaluation has already been mentioned: that it provides an ultimate measurement of an occupational student's performance. Another advantage is that the employer–supervisor forms focus only on behaviors that are relevant to the specific job. If behavior listed on the form is not relevant, then the employer can indicate so. Therefore, the student is rated solely on what is important. Also, the employer–supervisor evaluation can provide some secondary information that can be useful to program managers and instructors. The form can include space for soliciting from employers suggestions for improving the occupational program. This can provide both an informational input with regard to program inprovement and it can also provide a public relations vehicle for the occupational program. That is, by involving employers from the community in making suggestions for program change and improvement, the school and community can be drawn closer together in a unified effort toward preparing students for a more rewarding productive life in the community.

One of the greatest disadvantages of the employer-supervisor evaluation is that students are evaluated by different raters, that is, two occupational students graduating from the same program are, in most cases, going to be rated by different employers. This introduces a variability in interpretation of rating forms and rating scales, thus possibly resulting in inconsistent measures from one student to another. However, the other advantages of this measurement technique will probably outweigh this disadvantage. This disadvantage also places responsibility on the occupational teacher who develops the rating scale to really specify standards and give very definite instructions with regard to completing the forms. Two final disadvantages of the employer–supervisor form when used in a mail format have already been mentioned: these are the problems of locating graduates and employers and receiving an adequate return from employers. But, in this case also, adequate precautions and preventative measures can be taken to insure an adequate return.

Planning the Employer–Supervisor Survey

As in the case of any other measurement activity, it is important to plan in detail the employer–supervisor survey. Planning must be based upon a well-conceived objective or desired outcome and must involve both those individuals who will conduct the survey and those who will use the results. Also, decisions must be made regarding the method to be used in the survey and in the selection of employers or supervisors who will be surveyed.

STEP 1. Determine the Desired Outcome. Although the general purpose of determining the postprogram performance of former students might be the desired purpose, it is yet necessary to define the scope in terms of what class or what program is to be assessed for what time frame. For example, a specific purpose might be the assessment of postprogram performance of the former students of the electronics technician program for last year. Of course, the scope could be much broader than this; it could be assessment of the graduates of all industrial-oriented programs, of all business education programs, or of all sales training programs. The desire of the institution and its staff along with the consideration of financial and personnel resources for conducting the survey will be factors that will contribute to the decision regarding the scope of the survey. To delineate the purposes and scope of the survey, and to aid later development of the instrument, it is suggested that one or more broad key questions be stated. One possible key question is, "How do the graduates of our electronics technician program perform in a work setting?" Another key question might be, "How do the graduates of our electronics technician program compare to those employees who have been trained on the job?" For some surveys, just one of these questions may be sufficient; however, if a broader survey is being conducted with emphasis on more than postprogram performance of graduates, then a number of these key questions should be formulated. These key questions provide an overall focus of the survey.

STEP 2. Determine the Method to Be Used in the Survey. Basically, there are three methods that can be used in the conduct of the employer–supervisor survey: the personal interview, the telephone interview, and the mail survey.

The personal interview is probably the most costly technique for collecting employer–supervisor follow-up information. However, this method allows the interviewer the opportunity to establish rapport with each employer–supervisor, and to convince him/her of the importance of the study. Also, the personal interview allows the interviewer to probe into the underlying reasons for specific responses to questions. If improvement of public relations is one function of the employer survey, then the personal-interview technique is probably the most efficient means of achieving this goal. These attributes make the personal interview one of the most potentially accurate methods of gathering information. The primary disadvantage of the personal interview is its cost in terms of required personnel time and travel to employment sites. This in itself could limit the gathering of information from employers who are not in the immediate community.

The telephone interview can overcome some of the disadvantages of the personal interview, while maintaining some of its advantages. The telephone interview allows the interviewer to explain the purpose and importance of the study and to ask a set of prepared questions. Although the cost of interview personnel is still a sizeable one, travel costs are avoided with the telephone interview.

The mail questionnaire is probably the most efficient way of gathering employer–supervisor information. Costs for this method are very low and the mail questionnaire can reach any employer-supervisor regardless of his/her location. Probably the greatest disadvantage of the mail questionnaire is its rate of return. Precautionary measures should be employed to insure that the employer is motivated to complete and return the survey instrument. Weighing these advantages and disadvantages against personnel and financial resources available to the local agency, the staff should select one of these methods to be used in the survey. Selection of one of these techniques will further require special considerations for the development of the particular type of instrument that is used.

STEP 3. Develop the Employer–Supervisor Survey Instrument. Once the survey method has been chosen, attention should be given to the development of an instrument to be used for structuring the interviews, and for recording results from the survey. An instrument, whether used with a personal, telephone, or mail questionnaire survey, usually contains a series of questions to be asked of the employer–supervisor with categories for his/her response. The entire instrument, including each of its items, must relate to the key questions and the overall purposes of the employer–supervisor survey, which were discussed previously.

Key questions such as, "How do the graduates of our electronics technician program perform in a work setting?" delineate the focus of the survey. Given just this one example key question, it can be seen that there are many facets to the performance of graduates in a work setting. Therefore, it is necessary to define even more precisely the focus of the employer–supervisor survey. Taking this key question relating to the electronics technician program, the evaluator would want to specify another series of questions, which we will call *criterion questions.* Criterion questions make more specific our general concern about the electronics technician program. Some example criterion questions are: How are general job traits of our graduates perceived by employers? How are specific job competencies of our graduates perceived by employers? Many similar questions can be derived from our general key question. Once criterion questions have been developed, then specific instrument items can be formulated. A number of instrument items can be written to correspond to the single criterion question, "How are general job traits of our graduates perceived by employers?" Items may make direct reference to any of several job traits, including dependability, responsibility, initiative, and so on. The instrument item simply asks the respondent to rate an employee on a specific job trait. Example items 14, 15, and 16 presented earlier in this chapter are examples of this type of item. Graphic and numerical rating scales can be used in employer–supervisor surveys. Also, multiple-choice and ranking items are often adequate.

To summarize, the survey instrument begins in the form of a key question, becoming more specific with the delineation of criterion questions from which instrument items are developed. Figure 6.17 presents schematically how this progression flows.

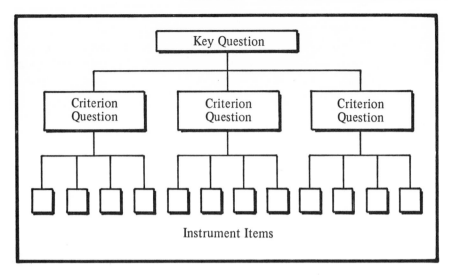

FIGURE 6.17.   Schematic of Instrument-item Development.

Once items have been prepared, there are two other concerns that should be considered. First, the items must be organized into an instrument in a consistent and meaningful format. Items should be grouped both according to similar format, that is, items with similar rating categories should be combined, and according to criterion questions. Grouping facilitates response to the questionnaire and allows the employer to see the logic and significance of each individual item, which adds to the entire face validity of the instrument.

The final consideration for instrument development is the formulation of directions to go along with the instrument. Directions should be instructive to the employer–supervisor, both in terms of the overall instrument and in terms of specific directions for each type of item included in the instrument. Overall directions should stress the importance of the survey being conducted, as well as include an indication of who is conducting the survey.

STEP 4. Try Out and Revise the Instrument. Once the instrument items have been assembled and directions developed, the instrument should be perfected via a trial run—and reviewed by several groups. A first step to the testing of the survey instrument is to have the staff of the program review each item contained in the instrument. This can be done either on an individual basis or in a group. If done individually, each staff member should be asked to read the instrument and to make comments on the form. The instrument should then be returned to the person in charge of instrument development for his synthesis of the comments and resultant revisions. In the case of a group review, the staff should discuss each item with the person in charge of the instrument development, who may make notations for subsequent changes. The second important task in the testing of the instrument is to have the advisory committee review it. Advisory committee members, many of them employers, are in a very good position to judge the content and format of the employer survey instrument. Also, this is an excellent way to involve the advisory committee in the total effort of the employer survey. In addition, it may be worthwhile to mail out the instrument to several employers, asking them to react to the content of the instrument. But usually, this information can be gained from advisory committee members.

STEP 5. Select Employers–Supervisors. The first step in the actual administration of the employer–supervisor survey should be the identification of employers or supervisors to be surveyed. This will also require that addresses or telephone numbers be obtained for each of the selected employers. If a student or learner follow-up study has been conducted within the last several years, then this study may be used as a source of employer–supervisor names. Or, if a student or learner follow-up is being conducted in conjunction with or simultaneously with the employer survey, then an item may be included in the student follow-up survey asking the name and address of the student's employer or immediate supervisor. For an employer-supervisor survey, it is important to specify each individual's name rather than simply sending the survey to the employing agency. Because this personalizes the survey, it helps to insure an adequate return or response to the instrument.

If a student follow-up is not being conducted, then it may be necessary to telephone each former student and ask him the name of his immediate supervisor or employer, or it may prove to be just as easy to conduct a student follow-up. In many cases, this type of activity can be conducted by clerical or secretarial staff members. Also, it is often possible to telephone the student's parent, whose name can be obtained from student records, requesting that he indicate the student's place of employment and immediate supervisor.

STEP 6. Develop a Cover Letter or Interview Introduction. If a mail survey is being conducted, a cover letter must be prepared to accompany the instrument. This letter should attempt to establish rapport between the educational or training agency and the employer-supervisor, indicating the purposes of the survey and giving some indication of how the results will be used. Since the mail-survey instrument pretty much stands alone, it is important that the employer–supervisor be convinced that his contribution will be of some use and will warrant the time spent on completing the instrument. Many times it is advantageous to involve the advisory committee in the development of this letter. Figure 6.18 presents an example cover letter, designed to accompany a survey instrument. In addition to involving the committee in the development of the letter, it may prove fruitful to duplicate this letter on the letterhead of the advisory committee chairperson, adding his/her signature. This indicates that the advisory committee has sanctioned the survey and employers and supervisors within the community may be more likely to respond to such a survey instrument than to an instrument mailed solely by the educational or training institution. If a telephone interview is used in the employer–supervisor survey, then an introduction to be delivered by the interviewer must be developed. This introduction must establish rapport, indicate the purpose of the survey, and, in some way, convince the employer–supervisor that the survey is of importance and worthy of the time that it will require. This introduction should not necessarily be read to the employer–supervisor, but the interviewer should be given adequate guidelines for conducting this portion of the interview.

STEP 7. Follow Up Nonrespondents. A good response requires that the response rate be representative of all employers of the students of a particular program. The size of the survey, of course, will determine the exact response rate required. However, in most instances 70 or 80 percent return of a mail questionnaire is thought to be adequately representative. It is possible to resurvey a sample of those individuals who did not respond and to compare their responses with those of the initial responding groups. If no differences occur, then it can be assumed that the obtained sample is representative of the total group being surveyed. However, if differences do occur, then it will be necessary to take further remedial action in obtaining a better response to the survey.

In order to follow up on those individuals who have not responded, of course, it is necessary to have a record of the individuals whose responses you have received. Individuals who have not responded become the focus of the follow-up of nonrespondents. For the mail survey, normal procedure involves the mailing of a second follow-up letter or card to those individuals who have not responded, along with an additional copy of the survey instrument.

Hamilton Vocational Institute
1523 Main Street
Hartford, Connecticut 02360

Dear Employer or Supervisor:

    We are currently evaluating the effectiveness of the occupational training we provide high school youth. One of our occupational training objectives is to equip students with job skills required to enter the world of work. As the employer or supervisor of one of our former students, you can help us determine if we are doing what we have set out to do.

    Will you take a few minutes to assess the preparation for employment of the employee named on the enclosed evaluation form? This is designed to give us vital information for determining the effectiveness and identifying strengths and weaknesses of present occupational training programs. No employee, employer, supervisor, or business will be identified in the results of this study. All responses to questions will be kept in strict confidence.

    Would you complete the evaluation form as soon as possible and mail it in the enclosed stamped envelope? Thank you for your valuable contribution to the improvement of job training for future students.

                                  Sincerely,

                                  Mrs. G. Alibrandi
                                  Principal

FIGURE 6.18. Example Employer-Supervisor Survey Cover Letter.

Figure 6.19 represents a second follow-up letter that should be mailed if the particular respondent has not responded within a specific period.

```
                    Hamilton Vocational Institute
                          1523 Main Street
                    Hartford, Connecticut  02360




Dear Employer or Supervisor:

     In case you did not receive our earlier letter, this second copy
of the evaluation form is being sent so you will have the opportunity
to let us know how you feel about the high school occupational training
provided youth.

     The early responses to our request for information from the
employer/supervisors of our former students have been rewarding.  An
analysis of returns seems to indicate that employer/supervisors welcome
the opportunity to assist school personnel in providing realistic em-
ployment education for students.

     Won't you help us improve the occupational training of future
students by mailing your completed evaluation form today?  We have
enclosed, for your convenience, a stamped envelope addressed to the
data processing agency at our institution.  Again let me assure you
that your answers will be kept in strict confidence.

     Thank you for your assistance.

                                        Sincerely,



                                        Mrs. G. Alibrandi
                                        Principal
```

FIGURE 6.19. Example Follow-up Letter for Mailing to Non-responding Employers.

Another means of following up nonrespondents to the mail survey is to contact those individuals by telephone, asking them to react or respond to the survey by mail—or collecting their verbal response on the phone. In the case where the telephone interview is used for the entire survey, then continual contact should be attempted with those individuals of the survey until an 85 or 90 percent return has been achieved. Of course, in most instances it will happen that not all employers will wish to spend the time in answering questions over the telephone. In these cases, the fact will simply need to be accepted. However, if a great number of employers express a negative attitude toward the survey, then possibly the administrators of the survey should reassess their approach.

REFERENCES

Becker, D. W. "Auditory Diagnostic Performance as a Criterion Measure for Machinists." Doctoral dissertation, University of Illinois, 1969.

Bloom, T. K. "Peer Evaluation—A Strategy for Student Involvement." *Man/ Society/Technology* vol. 33, no. 5, February 1974, pp. 137-138.

Boyd, J. L., and Shimberg, B. *Handbook of Performance Testing.* Princeton, New Jersey: Educational Testing Service, 1971.

Comer, John C. "A Diagnostic Work Sample Instrument for Assessing Automotive Trade Competence." Doctoral dissertation, Wayne State University, 1970.

Guilford, J. P. *Psychometric Methods,* 2nd ed. New York: McGraw-Hill, 1954.

Marshal, J. C., and Hales, L. W. *Classroom Test Construction.* Reading, Massachusetts: Addison-Wesley Publishing Co., 1971.

Remmers, H. H. "Rating Methods in Research on Teaching." In Gage, N. L., ed., *Handbook of Research in Teaching.* Chicago: Rand McNally, 1963.

Ryans, D. G., and Frederiksen, N. "Performance Tests of Educational Achievement." In Lindquist, F. E., ed., *Educational Measurement,* pp. 455-493. Washington, D. C.: American Council on Education, 1951.

Swanson, R. S. "Auditory Automotive Mechanics Diagnostic Achievement Test." Doctoral dissertation, University of Illinois, 1968.

Chapter 7

Constructing Measures of Affect

The importance of affective learning has long been emphasized in all education. The fact that the major reason given for lack of success in jobs is "failure to get along with others" speaks strongly for the need to prepare potential workers with proper and congruent affective skills. It is not enough to possess only technical skills. Appropriate attitudes, interests, values, and appreciations are important to success on the job. Many job failures are highly competent in the cognitive skill and psychomotor area. Traditionally, occupational educators have perhaps been more attuned to the need for education that focuses upon work-related attitudes, interests, values, and appreciations.

It should be emphasized, however, that, like the psychomotor, perceptual, and cognitive behaviors, "affective" behavior cannot be isolated except for discussion purposes. That is, affective behavior has cognitive as well as performance components. Even in sleep, dreams that involve affective feelings also involve some cognitive thinking and psychomotor activity. So, when we speak of assessing affective behavior we often must consider it as one facet of some rather complex observed behavior.

For example, in assessing an occupational student's interest in certain occupations, his or her knowledge of those occupations is an important requisite. First, it must be determined whether the student possesses knowledge of an occupation before we can determine his or her level of interest in it. Without this knowledge a negative response with regard to interest may be misconstrued.

There are several schemes for classifying affective behaviors. Among the best known is *The Taxonomy of Educational Objectives, Handbook 2, Affective Domain* (Krathwohl, Bloom, and Masia 1964). This scheme was described in chapter 3. Other categorization schemes are presented by Girod (1973) and Wight et al. (undated). Each is useful in preparing and classifying objectives, but strict adherence to these schemes often leads one beyond the practical limits of use as viewed by the typical occupational instructor. Basically, occupational instructors should know that an affective continuum exists and that it is a reaction continuum that ranges from initial reactions of receiving something to internalizing something and making it a part of day-to-day behavior.

Tyler (1973) in his broad range of experience with behavioral objectives has identified four basic categories of affective objectives. They include: (1) interests, (2) attitudes, (3) values, and (4) appreciations.

Interests are commonly defined either as "liking something" or as "voluntary attending to it or engaging in it" (Tyler 1973). Interests are very important to occupational education since motivation and desire to learn the skills of an occupation often rely on students' interests.

An *attitude* is defined as the degree of positive or negative feelings associated with some object. Attitudes are generally exhibited when a student is presented with some kind of stimuli. For example, students drawing back from the sight of blood would be indicative of at least an uneasy feeling about blood. Occupational educators are concerned about the attitudes that students have toward jobs, job tasks, themselves, co-workers, equipment, tools, and so on. For example, if a student could not stand the sight of blood—a behavioral disposition—then he or she probably would not be successful in many health-related careers.

Values are formalized attitudes that have become permanent. Values tend to be group determined and held, as opposed to attitudes that are more individual. A value such as loyalty to an employer is generally a group-held value. A negative attitude toward a co-worker is generally held by an individual, whereas, in many cases, a whole group of employees rarely has such an attitude toward one individual.

Appreciations are a fourth type of affective behavior. Briefly, an appreciation is defined as "knowing or recognizing the worth of certain things." These things could be works of art or a manufactured or constructed product or service. Appreciation in educational programs generally tends to be associated with literature, art, and music. However, occupational education has responsibilities for developing appreciations and their measurement. For example, developing an appreciation for good workmanship is a worthy objective for occupational programs. Also, developing students' interest in providing an adequate service such as medical care can be essential.

Wick (1973) combines attitudes, interests, values, and appreciations into one category called *acquired behavioral dispositions.* Each indicates a tendency to act or react in a certain way when faced with a situation or object.

If an airline pilot is faced with a ceiling too low for landing at a small airport, whether he tries to land will depend on several affective components: What is his attitude toward his job and toward maintaining it? Is he interested in the safety of others? How do the FAA regulations and the law relate to his value system? All of these components interact and result in certain actions or behavior. Similarly, an individual's interest in his job, his attitudes toward his employer and his co-workers, as well as the value he places on his union, may affect his job performance. All of this is aside from his cognitive and psychomotor skills necessary for successful performance on the job.

Attitudes, interests, values, and appreciations are similar, and can be assessed using similar measurement techniques. This is because each is directed toward or in reaction to some object. Wight et al. (undated) have identified four objects of affect. These objects are:

1. *Self* (i.e., self-awareness, self-concept, self-understanding, self-control, etc.)
2. *Others* (i.e., friends, acquaintances, strangers, family, teachers, specific groups, other cultures, religions, races, nationalities, etc.)
3. *Man-made world* (i.e., institutions, society, learning, work, school, political and economic systems, human achievements in the arts, sciences, and humanities, etc.)
4. *Nature* (i.e., ecology, environment, natural resources, wild life, pollution, etc.)

In preparing students for the work force, it is important that

189

occupational educators work toward the development of positive attitudes toward self, work, and others and that an interest in learning and in careers be nurtured as well.

USES OF AFFECTIVE MEASURES

There are many uses for affective measures. Probably the primary use that can be made of attitude and interest measures is in assessing a student's entrance level of behavior. That is, what attitudes and interests does a student have when he enters or enrolls in an occupational program? Additionally, assessments should be made to determine changes that have occurred in affective behavior during or following instruction. So, both current affective status as well as achievement can be assessed.

A related use of affective measurement lies in curriculum development of the design phase of instruction. Obviously, the statement of objectives should precede any instructional design, instruction, or measurement. As more occupational educators become skilled in measuring affective behavior, emphasis on affective objectives and related instruction will increase. This should result in a more relevant and comprehensive occupational program.

The results of affective measurements have many group and individual uses. The most popular use of interest measures is in career guidance. Many counselors administer an interest inventory to aid in identifying areas of occupational interest to integrate with other measures.

Results of affective measures can also be used to facilitate learning. Occupational teachers can use student interest and attitude information to guide the choice of instructional material and the design of instruction. If a teacher knows that a particular group of students is highly motivated and interested in a particular occupation or cluster of occupations, he may build upon this interest to teach principles and other related competencies. By having indications of students' attitudes, the teacher also can individualize instruction to change undesirable or build desirable behavior.

A final use that can be made of affective assessments is in program planning. With information about the attitudes and interests of student groups, new courses and programs can be designed and existing courses can be revised. For example, if a group of electronics students is interested in computer design and job supply and demand information supports the need for computer design personnel, then a course or program in computer design may be designed and instituted.

PROBLEMS OF AFFECTIVE MEASUREMENT

There are many reasons why affective measurement has received a disproportionate emphasis when compared with measurement in other areas such as the cognitive, psychomotor, and perceptual domains. This disproportionate emphasis has existed within occupational education programs and other education programs as well as within textbooks, journals, and curriculum guides. There are a number of reasons for the lack of coverage.

Duration of Learning Experiences

It is often assumed that the achievement of affective behavior or changes in affective behavior cannot be accomplished in a period as short as a semester or a year. This is contrary, however, to the long-held belief that cognitive achievement can be attained in a fairly short period. The usual response made by teachers when asked about affective behavior implies that their affective goals for a course or program are of long range and intangible. Teachers often indicate that attitudes, values, and appreciations may not manifest themselves until long after a student completes the educational program. It is true that many affective behaviors will not appear until after schooling; however, the same is true with many cognitive- and performance-type behaviors. Therefore, many of the assumptions held with regard to short-term and long-term attainment of affective objectives appear to be in error.

Vagueness of Terminology

When we compare affective behavior to cognitive behavior, in terms of the amount of research and writing done in each, affective behavior tends to be emphasized less. Researchers within the last several decades have only begun to better understand affective components of human behavior. A consequence of this lack of emphasis has been vagueness in the terminology used to describe behavior in the affective domain and a resultant lack of instruction and measurement within this area. Terms like interest and appreciation are somewhat difficult to translate into specific understandable behavioral terms. However, the recent writings of Bloom, Hastings, and Madaus (1971), Girod (1973), Lee and Merrill (1972), and Tyler (1973), in addition to Handbook 2 of the *Taxonomy of Educational Objectives* (Krathwohl, Bloom, and Masia 1964), have helped to standardize the terminology used for affective behavior. This standardization of terminology should facilitate an increased emphasis on affective behavior.

Indoctrination vs. Education Dilemma

A concern with affective education and measurement is that teachers have no right to "brainwash" or "indoctrinate" students. Many fear that value and attitude education may develop into indoctrination or behavior modification rather than preparation of students with appropriate and adequate affective behaviors. M. Scriven (1966) makes a distinction between values acquired in conjunction with cognitive learning such as the valuing of objectivity in scientific methods and moral values such as empathy and sympathy, which cannot be taught with cognitive techniques. Scriven (1966) feels that educators are failing if they do not address themselves to cognitive-related affective behaviors. By preparing individuals with the proper attitudes both toward objectivity and toward indoctrination, individuals will in the long run be less likely to become indoctrinated. Essentially, emphasizing these affective behaviors, as Bloom, Hastings, and Madaus (1971) indicate, will help avoid indoctrination and the type of society that Orwell described in *1984*.

Privacy of Affective Behavior

A second philosophical concern with measuring affective behavior is individual privacy. Legislation in recent years has tended to emphasize this concern. Many believe that affective education and affective measurement are private rather than public concerns. A person's feelings, attitudes, opinions, and values are viewed by many as subject to the privacy guaranteed by our constitution. Others have felt that the development of feelings and other affective behaviors is the task of the home and the church, not of the school. These concerns are important to all educators, and particularly occupational educators, when considering affective education. However, there are many affective behaviors, as mentioned earlier, that are important to success in an occupation or career. Development of these specific behaviors is, of course, of concern to occupational educators and, generally, of little concern to parents or others in the community. Tyler (1973) emphasizes that occupational educators and test developers need to remind themselves continually that although there are many kinds of affective behavior, educators should emphasize only those behaviors that students are expected to develop and are appropriate to assess as educational achievement. That is, occupational educators should not focus on behaviors that are not within the scope of their instruction, which is to prepare students for success on the job.

False Assumptions About Learning Affective Behavior

Instructional techniques that are typically used in teaching concepts, principles, and other knowledges are rather well developed. These methods include lectures, demonstrations, and discussions incorporating the use of instructional materials. However, methods used in teaching affective behaviors are not as well developed. A basic assumption held by many educators is that appropriate feelings and attitudes will develop automatically with the acquisition of knowledge and experience, and therefore, do not require any special instructional attention. It is true that many attitudes and other types of affective behavior are affected by cognitive learning. Smith (1966) points out, "to teach any concept, principle, or theory is to teach not only for its comprehension, but also for an attitude toward it— the acceptance or rejection of it as useful, dependable, and so forth." It should be noted that the attitude developed in conjunction with cognitive achievement will not necessarily be positive. For example, too much emphasis on a cognitive skill component by an instructor may precipitate a negative attitude toward the content area. Many times it is necessary to incorporate special instructional methodology to insure that proper attitudes are being built at the same time that cognitive learning is occurring. Instruction toward affective goals and objectives, then, is an important and relevant component of any occupational education program.

Lack of Well-developed Procedures

As mentioned in the section on vagueness of terminology, research and experience have not been as extensive within the affective domain as they have been within other domains. It becomes very obvious when one reviews measurement and testing textbooks and other procedural guides that the assessment of cognitive achievement receives far more attention in these works than does measurement in the affective domain. This lack of attention to the affective domain is not a result of lack of interest or concern; many times it is the lack of technological development in affective measurement. Oftentimes measurement of attitudes, interests, values, and appreciations tends to be associated with standardized instruments. Typically when occupational interests are mentioned, the Kuder, the Strong, or the Ohio Vocational Interest Survey come to mind. For some reason occupational educators have assumed that affective instruments require developmental techniques that are beyond the competency of individual teachers. It is unfortunate, however, that this assumption has been made, since attitude and interest measures for some purposes are no more difficult to construct than the average cognitive-achievement test. Many teacher-made or locally developed instruments can be prepared with simpler and less formal techniques than are typically used by developers of standardized instruments.

Inconsistency Between Affect and Its Manifestation

Most measurement techniques such as the interview, the questionnaire, the self-report, and even observation may provide an inaccurate measure of affect. This limitation is often given as an excuse for not measuring affective behavior, even when it would be more appropriate to try to overcome the limitation. There are several reasons for the inconsistency between real affect and its manifestation or exhibition. First of all, we cannot always be sure that a given behavior is the result of a given affective quality. Many times students or individuals react in different ways even though they possess the same affect. Also, a particular action or reaction may result from several different affects.

A second reason for the inconsistency is that students may respond in a desirable way or even an undesirable way simply because they know they are being observed or assessed. In this case, students are simply acting in a way that their instructor or test administrator feels appropriate or inappropriate, and not really in a way that is internalized by the individual being examined. These problems can be overcome in several ways. Items on questionnaires and on self-report instruments can be written in such a way that the student has difficulty determining the desired response. Another way of helping to insure honesty in response is to remove the grading component from affective-achievement measurement.

DEVELOPING AFFECTIVE MEASURES

Like cognitive-achievement testing, affective behaviors can be assessed through a number of different approaches. As with all types of measurement, it is usually advantageous to gain more than one measure—more than one perspective—of an individual's affective behavior. Five possible approaches to the assessment of affective behavior have been identified: these include direct observation, interviews, questionnaires and inventories, projective techniques, and unobtrusive measures. These five approaches are briefly described below.

1. *Direct observation:* Viewing and recording a student's behavior with regard to a stimulus object and making inferences about the underlying affective causes for the behavior.
2. *Interview:* Asking a student open- and closed-ended questions in a face-to-face situation regarding a certain stimulus object.
3. *Questionnaires and inventories:* Presenting a student with a printed set of questions similar to interview questions or seeking a student's self-report of affect through a checklist or rating scale.
4. *Projective techniques:* Presenting a task or object to a student for reasons unknown to the student. An example would be

requiring a student to write an essay on a value-laden topic.

5. *Unobtrusive measures:* Observing, either directly or indirectly, the behavior of students without their being aware that their behavior is being measured.

The questionnaire and inventory are probably the most popular in terms of traditional use. However, the other four approaches have considerable potential for expanding and improving our affective-measurement efforts.

Direct Observation

The direct observation of behavior to assess affect requires viewing an individual or group of individuals in a real-life or simulated situation. Generally, the student's reaction to a selected object is watched. Direct observation was presented in chapter 6, which discusses the assessment of performance. In the assessment of performance, direct observation cannot be surpassed in its adequacy by any other means of measurement. However, when assessing affective behavior, this is not always the case.

When observing students' affect toward many objects (work, co-workers, etc.) in a real-life situation, it is very difficult to observe a large number of students. Observation generally requires a one-to-one relationship, which demands a great deal of staff time. The time required to observe a student and complete a rating form is far more than that required to interview a student.

An additional limitation of direct-observation methods is in the stimulus situation. Observing a group of students' attitude toward supervision is not something that can be rated in a short period. Usually, either very long observation periods or simulated situations are necessary to facilitate accurate observations. By simulating situations or presenting students with an affective object, accurate measurements can often be made immediately; whereas waiting for an individual to have an encounter with a supervisor in a natural setting may take days or weeks.

However, if students know that their affective behavior is being measured or observed, they may respond differently than they ordinarily would in a natural setting. For example, a dental hygiene student may display a very pleasant attitude toward patients when in the company of the dentist or dental instructor. However, in the absence of the dentist or instructor, the student may display attitudes that may be less than desirable. In some situations most everyone has concealed attitudes that might be considered undesirable. If an individual invited to a dinner where fish is served is not fond of fish, most likely the individual would not overtly express this attitude unless it was very strong. It should be remembered that group pressure, whether it be social or otherwise, and observer or rater pressure may influence a student's true expression of affect.

Another limitation of direct observation lies in the inability to isolate all of the variables that may be influencing behavior. For example, a student who is observed sewing a dress or suit until late hours of the night is not necessarily displaying a positive attitude toward sewing. The student may be sewing because of social pressure to wear attractive clothes. Likewise, showing up 30 minutes early for school each day may not reflect attitudes toward the occupational program but instead may reflect local bus scheduling or the working hours of a parent or the class schedule of a fellow student. Due to the complexity of behavioral causes, it becomes difficult to make strong inferences about attitudes from observed behavior. This emphasizes the need to make multiple measures of affect using one or more of the four approaches (interviews, questionnaires and inventories, projective techniques, or unobtrusive measures).

The final limitation in obtaining measures of affect is the difficulty in determining the magnitude of interest, attitude, value, or appreciation. Included in the definition of attitude is the term *degree,* which also is relevant to the other affective components. Usually it is difficult to assess degree by quantifying an individual's actions. For example, it is difficult to determine *how* positive is an attitude of a student food service worker toward his or her work by observing facial expressions. It is not always correct to assume that an individual who smiles five times in an hour has a more positive attitude than someone who smiles only three times.

Girod (1973) has suggested a classification scheme to aid in determining the degree of affect toward a certain object. This scheme incorporates five stages of behavior ranging from little affect to a great deal of affect. The stages are briefly described below, and an occupational example is presented for each stage. These example behaviors are those that can be assessed through direct observation. Examples of behaviors within the stages that can be assessed through other means are presented in the subsequent sections of this chapter.

1. Experiment stage
   a. *Type of behavior*—indication that something has been tried.
   b. *Example behavior*—student is observed reading an occupational course catalog or brochure.

2. Choice stage
   a. *Type of behavior*—indication that a choice has been made between two (or more) alternatives.
   b. *Example behavior*—student chooses to enroll in an occupational program rather than a liberal arts program.

3. Concurrence stage
   a. *Type of behavior*—indication that an individual has actively shared or participated in an activity with other enthusiasts.
   b. *Example behavior*—student attends occupational classes regularly.

4. Proselyte stage
   a. *Type of behavior*—indication that an individual has involved others in an activity.
   b. *Example behavior*—occupational student convinces two friends to enroll in an occupational program.

5. Sacrifice stage
   a. *Type of behavior*—indication that an irreversible choice has been made to participate in an activity.
   b. *Example behavior*—occupational student sells his antique car to pay tuition and fees for the upcoming semester.

These stages can aid the observer in assessing affective behavior. However, it is often difficult to know what kinds of choices and what kind of behavior an individual is manifesting when not being observed. For example, instructors would not be aware of a student selling his car unless they had been verbally informed. This point emphasizes the need to augment observation methods with self-report and other verbal measures of affect.

All educators, especially occupational educators, assess students' affective behavior through direct observation. Instructors have used their observation of students in classrooms and laboratories to appraise individuals. However, most of these observations have been informal—informal in the sense that specific behaviors have not been rated and/or recorded. Also, observation has often not been based upon well-formulated affective objectives. Assistance in preparing affective objectives is not offered in this text; however, several suggestions for developing observation instruments are provided. Basically, three types of instruments or instrument scales can be used in the direct observation of affective behavior: these include checklists, numerical scales, and graphic scales. These scales were discussed in chapter 6 as they relate to performance testing. They are discussed here as they relate to affective measurement.

Observer Checklists. Checklists are forms that contain lists of behaviors that reflect positive or negative affect toward something. For example, a checklist could be developed for use by a laboratory instructor or a clinical or co-op education supervisor to indicate those behaviors that a student has displayed. Obviously, the same checklist or a similar one could be used to record the occurrence of undesirable as well as desirable behavior.

Example item 1 is a checklist used by truck driver instructors to assess the driving courtesy of trainees.

Example Item 1

1. Place a check mark ($\sqrt{}$) in the space next to each observed behavior.

_____ 1. Stop for a motorist attempting to park.

_____ 2. Pull into right lane on upgrades.

_____ 3. Slow down when pedestrians are present.

_____ 4. Pass small cars slowly.

_____ 5. Flash lights to aid passing motorist.

_____ 6. Maintain adequate spacing.

_____ 7. Stop to aid motorist in distress.

_____ 8. Warn motorists of danger ahead.

Obviously, the results of this checklist could be misconstrued if procedures for completion and results utilization were not standardized. For example, if item 7 of the checklist is not checked, it is possible that the trainee did not encounter a motorist in distress during observation, and so the item was not applicable. The checklist could be improved by adding a column to indicate the potential for the behavior to be manifested. Example item 2 expands upon example item 1.

Example Item 2

2. Place a check mark (√) in the space next to each observed behavior.

Opportunity occurred	*Behavior occurred*	
_____	_____	1. Stop for a motorist attempting to park.
_____	_____	2. Pull into right lane on upgrades.
_____	_____	3. Slow down when pedestrians are present.
_____	_____	4. Pass small cars slowly.
_____	_____	5. Flash light to aid passing motorist.
_____	_____	6. Maintain adequate spacing.
_____	_____	7. Stop to aid motorist in distress.
_____	_____	8. Warn motorists of danger ahead.

A checklist also can be used to assess safety consciousness. Example item 3 presents a safety checklist for operating a table saw.

Example Item 3

____ 1. Check tightness of blade.
____ 2. Wear proper eye protection.
____ 3. Stand aside from blade while turning on machine.
____ 4. Use fence guard.
____ 5. Use push stick.
____ 6. Keep fingers 6″ or more away from blade.

Similar checklists can be used for all types of equipment, tools, and general laboratories.

Numerical Scales for Observation.   *Numerical scales* are used to rate a particular object of affect with numbers that correspond to various points along a line. Usually, the ends of the numerical scale are described in some way with words such as good–bad, poor–excellent, high–low. Example item 4 is a numerical scale for assessing a student's motivation.

Example Item 4

4. This student's motivation to work is:

1	2	3	4	5	6	7	8
Low							High

One advantage of the numerical scale is that affect toward a number of different objects can be assessed through use of the same scale. This increases efficiency in terms of rater time and use of instrument space. Figure 7.1 presents a numerical-rating instrument for use in assessing food service personnel in their affective reactions to common job occurrences.

Graphic Scales for Observation.   *Graphic scales,* often referred to as descriptive scales, use a statement or item stem followed by a line with words or descriptions rather than numbers. The primary advantage of a graphic scale over a numerical scale lies in its ability to increase consistency among raters. By describing behavior with words, it is easier to classify an observed behavior. Example item 5 is an item directed at rating an individual's flexibility when faced with a new situation.

Example Item 5

1	2	3	4	5
Displays adequate flexibility	Exhibits flexibility under most conditions	Exhibits tendency to resist change	Displays consistent resistance to change	Displays excessive rigidity

---

WAITER OR WAITRESS
AFFECTIVE-ASSESSMENT FORM

Name _____

Rate the above named student or employee on the following nine points by placing an X along the rating line to the right of each statement. If you have insufficient information to make a rating, leave the item blank.

	Poor							*Excellent*	
1. Pleasantness of greeting	1	2	3	4	5	6	7	8	9
2. Reaction to order change	1	2	3	4	5	6	7	8	9
3. Reaction to request for individual checks	1	2	3	4	5	6	7	8	9
4. Reaction to request for special arrangements (high chair, two tables)	1	2	3	4	5	6	7	8	9
5. Reaction to dissatisfaction with food	1	2	3	4	5	6	7	8	9
6. Awareness of customer needs	1	2	3	4	5	6	7	8	9
7. Cooperation with co-workers	1	2	3	4	5	6	7	8	9
8. Reaction to children	1	2	3	4	5	6	7	8	9
9. Reaction to amount of gratuity	1	2	3	4	5	6	7	8	9

FIGURE 7.1. Waiter or Waitress Affective-Assessment Form.

The extensiveness of the description for each category of the item can vary. Many times the experience of the rater and his or her familiarity with the behavior being rated will influence the amount of description necessary. Example item 6 is an expansion of example item 5.

Example Item 6

6. (FLEXIBILITY) When faced with change this student:
   a. *Displays adequate flexibility.* Student is able to accommodate a variety of changes.
   b. *Exhibits flexibility under most conditions.* Student is able to accommodate ordinary changes.
   c. *Exhibits tendency to resist change.* The student is able to accommodate most change but under certain circumstances reacts with considerable resistance.
   d. *Displays consistent resistance to change.* Student is able to accommodate change only with assistance.
   e. *Displays excessive rigidity.* The student is incapable of accommodating necessary change.

Figure 7.2 is a portion of an instrument used to assess several aspects of affective behavior of hearing-impaired cooperative education students. It is often helpful to use an expanded description on a separate page to be used as a reference by a rater. An expanded description also is useful in training raters or observers.

Nine suggestions for constructing graphic scales were presented in chapter 6. They are reiterated here:

1. The line, whether horizontal or vertical, should be unbroken.
2. The line should be five or six inches long, enough to allow indication of all discrimination of which the rater is capable.
3. The direction of the lines should be the same, that is, the socially desirable end should be the same for all traits.
4. If several objects are to be rated, the best arrangement of the page is that which rates all of them on one characteristic before proceeding to another characteristic.
5. Guilford (1954) suggests that for unsophisticated raters the good end of the line should come first.
6. Descriptive categories should be as near as possible to the points of the scale they describe.
7. The categories need not be equally spaced.
8. If machine scoring is not used, a stencil divided into numbered sections makes a convenient scoring device.
9. Guilford (1954) suggests that segmented lines not call for any finer discriminations than will be used in scoring.

ILLINOIS SCHOOL FOR THE DEAF - DIVISION OF VOCATIONAL REHABILITATION
Evaluation and Career Planning
Summer Program 1975

SUPERVISED WORK STUDENT RATING FORM

STUDENT NAME
RATER NAME
DATE OF RATING _____ WEEK 1 2 3 4 5 6

DIRECTIONS: Rate the student on each of the following items by circling the appropriate numbers. If the item does not apply circle "a". If you do not have sufficient information to respond to a particular item, circle "b". Add comments to the last page which may help in understanding and counseling the student. This form is to be completed weekly and returned to the appropriate person each week.

	1	2	3	4	5	a	b
1. I WOULD RATE THIS STUDENT:	very independent	independent except when faced with change	dependent only on non-routine tasks	dependent	very dependent	does not apply	insufficient information
2. WHEN FACED WITH CHANGE, THIS STUDENT:	displays adequate flexibility	exhibits flexibility under most conditions	exhibits tendency to resist change	displays consistent resistance to change	displays excessive rigidity	does not apply	insufficient information
3. WITH REGARD TO MATURITY, I WOULD RATE THIS STUDENT'S BEHAVIOR AS:	always stable	generally stable	occasionally unstable	frequently unstable	generally unstable	does not apply	insufficient information
4. IN WORK SITUATIONS INVOLVING A GROUP, THIS STUDENT:	seeks to be involved	participates willingly	participates when encouraged	avoids participation	refuses to participate	does not apply	insufficient information
5. IN RESPONSE TO SUPERVISION, THIS STUDENT:	accepts direction	passively accepts authority	accepts but resents authority	resents and rejects some direction	rejects authority	does not apply	insufficient information
6. I WOULD RATE THIS STUDENT'S RECEPTION OF COMMUNICATION AS:	excellent	very good	average	fair	poor	does not apply	insufficient information

FIGURE 7.2. Segment of a Work Supervisor's Affective-assessment Instrument.

Affective Interviews

The interview involves a one-to-one relationship between a question asker and a respondent or occupational student. The interview can provide measures of an individual's affect toward different things. It has the advantage over other affective-measurement techniques in that it provides an opportunity to probe into the reasons or causes for certain observed behavior. Occupational instructors can use the interview technique to identify students' interests as well as attitudes toward certain objects. The classification scheme presented in the previous sections for determining degree of affect can also be used with the interview. In an interview, the five stages—experiment, choice, concurrence, proselyte, and sacrifice—can be used to classify a student's statements about his actions rather than actual observed behaviors. Girod (1973) summarizes these stages as follows:

1. *Experiment stage:* Expression of willingness to try something.
2. *Choice stage:* Expression of a choice between an attitude object and something else of value.
3. *Concurrence stage:* Expression of willingness to share an activity with other enthusiasts.
4. *Proselyte stage:* Expression of willingness to involve others in an activity.
5. *Sacrifice stage:* Expression of willingness to sacrifice something of great value for another object or activity.

Structured interviews, as do any objective data-gathering techniques, require the use of a standard format for asking questions and recording responses. Generally, a form or instrument referred to as an *interview schedule* is used. These instruments include: (1) the exact questions that are to be asked, (2) categories for responses or space to write out responses, and (3) special instructions to the interviewer. Example item 7 presents these three components. The instructions to the interviewer are in italics.

Example Item 7

7. Generally, how many times during the last month have you gone to the open laboratory rather than to other places during your free hour? *(circle one response.)*

1. Never
2. Once
3. Twice
4. Three times
5. Four times
6. Five or more

This particular item (example item 7) is a choice stage item that is designed to measure a student's affect toward the open laboratory situation. Another form of an interview question, the open-ended item, can be used to follow up on responses to closed-ended items. Example item 8 attempts to identify a student's reasons for not using the open laboratory.

Example Item 8

8. *(If response was 1 or 2 to item 7)* Why did you choose not to visit the open laboratory?

_____

_____

_____

_____

Interview items can also include a form of rating scale, as long as it is not too complex. Example item 9 is such an item for identifying the value students place on jobs or careers.

Example Item 9

9. How important would each of the following characteristics be to you in picking a job or career? *(Circle one number for each statement.)*

	Of No Importance	Of Little Importance	Of Some Importance	Of Great Importance
a. Making a lot of money	1	2	3	4
b. Opportunity to be original and creative	1	2	3	4
c. Opportunity to be helpful to others	1	2	3	4
d. Avoiding high pressure	1	2	3	4
e. A chance to be a leader	1	2	3	4
f. A stable, secure future	1	2	3	4
g. A chance to be my own boss	1	2	3	4
h. Living in a place where both my spouse and I will be able to find meaningful work	1	2	3	4

The interview schedule also can be used to assess an individual's affect toward instruction and toward a course or program. Table 7.1 presents a segment of a course-attitudes interview schedule.

It is cautioned that occupational instructors not be interviewers when obtaining judgments about a course or subject of great personal importance to them. This will help minimize pressure on the students to respond in favor of the teacher. One plausible alternative is to have a neutral party such as a counselor or an advanced student conduct the interview. A member of the advisory committee for the occupational program could also serve as an interviewer in these situations.

Interviews that use an interview schedule are an excellent means of determining affect of students who are poor readers or who have handicaps that inhibit their verbal communication. The interviewer can interpret and clarify questions in ways that would be impossible if a printed questionnaire were used.

TABLE 7.1. Segment of Course-attitudes Interview Schedule.

1. How much do you like your Home Economics course?
   a) A lot
   b) Indifferent
   c) Not much
   d) Don't know

2. Why?
   a) Teacher
   b) Subject matter
   c) Fact that it's a special class
   d) Friends are not in it
   e) Get credit without work
   f) Hardness or easiness
   g) _____

3. What is the most important thing you've learned in your Home Economics course so far?
   a) All teachers are not bad
   b) A good teacher can make a subject interesting
   c) Content response
   d) I can do something well
   e) A new respect for school
   f) A new understanding of other school topics
   g) A better understanding of current events
   h) The relation between what goes on in school and out of school
   i) _____

4. What do most other students in the course think about it?
   a) Like
   b) Dislike
   c) Indifferent
   d) Don't talk about it
   e) Afraid to say

5. What do students not in the class think of it?
   a) A good idea
   b) Wish they had a course like it
   c) Don't ever say
   d) Dislike it
   e) _____

A second approach to interviewing is the unstructured interview. The unstructured interview does not rely on a set of presented questions or an interview schedule. Instead, a limited number of key or leading questions are used to guide the interview. This technique requires a more skilled interviewer than the structured interview. The interviewer has the responsibility of listening and probing when necessary in addition to leading the interview. The unstructured interview allows for a more natural and personal expression of values, interests, and attitudes and allows for an indication of the reasons for particular expressed feelings.

Caution must be taken in the unstructured interview not to lead the respondent to an expected response. Bloom, Hastings, and Madaus (1971) list four uses of the unstructured interview:

1. It can provide information that cannot be obtained through other techniques.
2. It can suggest ideas for writing structured items.
3. It can allow for a validity check of structured data.
4. It can add flesh and blood to the skeletal forms of the structured approach or other techniques.

There are five suggestions for conducting interviews. These include:

1. *Be friendly and informal but, at the same time, professional.* Remember that everything said or done should help to gain the student's confidence in the interviewer as well as in himself.

2. *Be a sympathetic, interested, and attentive listener.* Encouraging nods, "uh-huh's," "I know how you feel," and similar gestures will convey to the respondent that he is understood and that his opinions are valued and appreciated. But don't overdo it! There is nothing quite so distracting to the average person as the listener who keeps up a running stream of "uh-huh," "is that so," when it is not needed. A nod of the head is usually a much more articulate way of showing interest than a constant clucking in the background, which many respondents will feel is a camouflage for a lack of genuine interest in them and their problems.

3. *Be neutral with respect to the subject matter.* Do not express personal opinions either on the subjects being discussed by the respondent or on the respondent's ideas about those subjects. Never present feelings of shock, surprise, indignation, or disapproval

at what the respondent is saying either by word or involuntary gesture. Understand and accept what he is saying, do not approve or disapprove of it, nor agree or disagree with it.

4. *Be observant.* Be alert to the way in which the respondent expresses himself and to the gestures he uses. These signs may serve as cues that the respondent is becoming uncomfortable and ill-at-ease or that he is not expressing what he really feels.

5. *Last but not least, be at ease in the interview situation.* If the interviewer feels hesitant, embarrassed, hurried, or awkward, the respondent will soon sense this feeling and begin to behave in a like manner.

Questionnaires and Inventories

Questionnaires can assume many different forms, but basically they involve the presentation of printed questions with the request to the respondent to either check an appropriate response or construct a response. Fundamentally, the questionnaire is a printed-interview schedule that has been adapted for individual administration and independent response. An inventory is not distinctly separate from a questionnaire since many times inventory items are included in a questionnaire. Basically the *inventory* includes either lists of items that a student checks or on which the student makes some form of rating.

The questionnaire has several advantages over the interview. First, the questionnaire or inventory can minimize bias by insuring anonymity of responses. Also, the questionnaire or inventory can be administered to a group rather than on a one-to-one relationship, minimizing personnel time. Time for recording responses is also decreased. The primary shortcoming of the questionnaire or inventory relative to the interview is that ambiguous responses may go unclarified since the opportunity to probe is eliminated. Many of the same types of rating scales and items that were described in chapters 5 and 6 and in the direct observation section of this chapter are also applicable to affective questionnaire use. However, there are some specific differences that deserve recognition and discussion in this section. Questionnaire and inventory items can be broken down into five major categories: these categories include checklists, multiple-choice items, open-ended items, rating items, and Q-sort items. Each item type is discussed and, for some, example items as well as larger segments of existing instruments are presented.

Self-report Checklists

Checklists were discussed in the direct observation section of this chapter. Checklists also have utility in self-report forms of measurement. Checklists have been used most extensively in interest measures. The most basic form of the *affective checklist* incorporates a series of items or statements and asks the student to check those that he feels are important or that reflect his feelings. Figure 7.3 is an occupational-values checklist that focuses upon an ideal job. Note that the checklist is adapted in the second part, so that the respondent is also asked to rank the checked items on the list. This ranking yields a relative comparison, which can be useful to understanding job-related values. A similar checklist could be developed for numerous other objects such as individual courses, school, or co-workers.

Occupational Values

Consider to what extent a job or career should satisfy each of these requirements before you would consider it IDEAL. Check the responses that best describe your feelings.

The ideal job for me would have to:

___ 1. Provide an opportunity to use my special abilities or aptitudes

___ 2. Provide me with a chance to earn a good deal of money

___ 3. Permit me to be creative and original

___ 4. Give me social status and prestige

___ 5. Give me an opportunity to work with people rather than things

___ 6. Enable me to look forward to a stable, secure future

___ 7. Leave me relatively free of supervision by others

___ 8. Give me a chance to exercise leadership

___ 9. Provide me with adventure

___ 10. Give me an opportunity to be helpful to others

Now go back and look at the requirements you checked. Rank them in order of importance to you by entering a "1" for the most important, a "2" for the next in importance and so on for all checked items.

FIGURE 7.3.   An Example Occupational-values Checklist.

Another adaptation of the checklist has proven successful in the form of the *Gordon Occupational Checklist*. The Gordon checklist is made up of 240 short, simple descriptive phrases of job requirements taken from the *Dictionary of Occupational Titles*. The respondent is asked to circle the job descriptions he likes and underline the ones he dislikes. This particular instrument focuses upon five general components: business, outdoor, arts, technology, and service. Items can be taken from the Gordon checklist and incorporated into a teacher-constructed instrument to aid in assessing specific interests. Or, a group of Gordon-type items can be constructed from the review of more specific job analysis information. The *Dictionary of Occupational Titles,* the *Occupational Outlook Handbook,* and the *Encyclopedia of Careers* can all be used as starting points for the development of interest checklists.

It is obvious that similar checklists can be used to inventory not just the things or tasks that an individual likes and dislikes but also to distinguish the kinds of activities an individual participates in, reads about, and so on. Used the latter way, the checklist can provide measures of attitudes and appreciation as well as interests.

Another form of the checklist allows for a dichotomous response rather than a simple check or choice. The dichotomy can vary from yes–no, necessary–unnecessary, good–bad to almost any bipolar pair of adjectives. An example form that gives an indication of how an individual views his job is presented in figure 7.4.

On this form the respondent is asked to place a "Y" next to items that describe his or her job and an "N" next to those that do not. Some may contend that when adjectives such as high–low and good–bad are used, the instrument becomes a rating scale rather than a checklist. However, since no real scale exists (other than two extreme points) it should be considered a checklist.

The final type of checklist to be presented includes small groups of items from which the respondent is asked to make a choice. One of the best-known instruments that uses this form of checklist is the *Kuder Preference Record.* This instrument incorporates triads of objects or job-related activities. The respondent is asked to choose from three items the item he likes most and the one he dislikes most. The *Minnesota Vocational Interest Inventory* has a similar format— also called the *forced-choice format.* This type of checklist can be useful for determining affect toward certain objects. It requires that a relative choice be made and, as Girod's (1973) second stage of

---

JOB-DESCRIPTION INDEX

Directions: Place a "Y" beside an item if the item describes the particular aspect of your job (e.g., work, pay, etc.) and an "N" if the item does not describe that aspect.

Work	Supervision	People
___ Fascinating	___ Asks my advice	___ Stimulating
___ Routine	___ Hard to please	___ Boring
___ Satisfying	___ Impolite	___ Slow
___ Boring	___ Praises good work	___ Ambitious
___ Good	___ Tactful	___ Stupid
___ Creative	___ Influential	___ Responsible
___ Respected	___ Up to date	___ Fast
___ Hot	___ Doesn't supervise enough	___ Intelligent
___ Pleasant	___ Quick tempered	___ Easy to make enemies
___ Useful	___ Tells me where I stand	___ Talk too much
___ Tiresome	___ Annoying	___ Smart
___ Healthful	___ Stubborn	___ Lazy
___ Challenging	___ Knows job well	___ Unpleasant
___ On your feet	___ Bad	___ No privacy
___ Frustrating	___ Intelligent	___ Active
___ Simple	___ Leaves me on my own	___ Narrow interests
___ Endless	___ Around when needed	___ Loyal
___ Gives sense of accomplishment	___ Lazy	___ Hard to meet

Pay	Promotions
___ Income adequate for normal expenses	___ Good opportunity for advancement
___ Satisfactory profit sharing	___ Opportunity somewhat limited
___ Barely live on income	___ Promotion on ability
___ Bad	___ Dead-end job
___ Income provides luxuries	___ Good chance for promotion
___ Insecure	___ Unfair promotion policy
___ Less than I deserve	___ Infrequent promotions
___ Highly paid	___ Regular promotions
___ Underpaid	___ Fairly good chance for promotion

FIGURE 7.4. Job-description Index.

attitude indicates, the choice can be an adequate measure of attitudes. Example item 10 is a medical-related item.

Example Item 10

10. Choose the activity you enjoy most:

_____ 1. Reading medical journals

_____ 2. Talking with patients

_____ 3. Setting up facilities and instruments

The use of this type of checklist requires time and effort to construct, but it can provide valuable information. Technically, consideration must be given to keeping the comparisons that are made heterogeneous to insure ease of interpretation of results. It is possible to use the same items in many different triads or groups (there is nothing sacred about the number 3). Example items 11 and 12, which employ four alternatives, might be used in a student's attitude checklist. For those items, the respondent is asked to choose the item that is the most descriptive of him and the one that is the least descriptive.

Example Item 11

_____ I am emotionally disturbed at home.

_____ I get school assignments in on time, all the time.

_____ I have good ability in relating to teachers.

_____ I have constant complaints about school.

Example Item 12

_____ I enjoy life in general.

_____ I must be led through new school routines.

_____ I have sincere interest in the welfare of my fellow students.

_____ I will lie to my teachers.

A special-stimulus checklist, which incorporates the forced-choice technique, can also be used, although it is somewhat difficult to construct. These special-stimulus item types use pictures or sketches rather than verbal statements. This type of measure has many advantages for handicapped and/or disadvantaged individuals who possess less than adequate verbal skills. Example item 13 is a picture item that incorporates a choice of three alternatives.

Example Item 13

13. Put an "X" under the picture of the workers who have jobs that you would be interested in doing.

A _____   B _____   C _____

The Geist Picture Interest Inventory is a performance instrument for assessing interests without relying on verbal skill. In its present form, the Geist instrument consists of 8½″ × 11″ line drawings that are presented to the respondent. There are many ways to adapt this kind of picture interest for group use. For example, overhead transparencies or slides can be used to project the choices to a group of students.

The following suggestions are offered for preparing and using checklists to assess affective behavior:

1. Base items on predetermined objectives or needs.
2. Keep statements brief.
3. Test the interpretation of items with one or more sample students.
4. When using a forced-choice format, limit the choices to five or six.
5. Provide adequate directions for the instrument.

Multiple-choice Items

Multiple-choice items are certainly not new to anyone involved in occupational education. Their use has been extensive in the assessment of cognitive behavior. However, the intent of the item is somewhat different within the affective domain. Within the cognitive domain, the multiple choice is used to test knowledge and other higher level cognitive skills. Within the affective domain, the intent is not only to test achievement, but to acquire information about a student's feelings. Therefore, the basic difference is that cognitive items are strictly for testing achievement, while affective items can play a dual role.

The multiple-choice item is very similar to the typical interview schedule item, which presents a question or item stem that is followed by a series of feasible choices or alternatives. With a cognitive-achievement item there exists only one correct response, and the remaining are foils or distractors. Affective items do not have a single correct alternative. The alternatives are various ways of feeling or responding to the stem and as such should not be viewed as being correct or incorrect.

The stem of the multiple-choice item can be either a question or an incomplete statement. Example item 14 is a question directed at determining a student's attitudes toward labor unions.

Example Item 14

14. Does the union interfere seriously with how the company is managed?

    a. It is no problem.
    b. It interferes a little but not seriously.
    c. It interferes quite often.
    d. It seriously interferes with management.

Example item 15 presents the incomplete-sentence type of multiple-choice item.

Example Item 15

15. I prefer a job in which I can:

---

a. Use my skill and knowledge.
b. Be in contact with many different people.

Example items 16 through 18 are items that focus on determining a student's attitude toward his supervisor.

Example Item 16

16. Does your immediate supervisor avoid you when he knows you want to see him about a problem?

    a. Usually
    b. Occasionally
    c. Never

Example Item 17

17. Does your immediate supervisor explain to you the "why" of an error in order to help you prevent recurrence of the error?

    a. Usually
    b. Occasionally
    c. Never

Example Item 18

18. If something happens that puts your immediate supervisor "on the spot," what is he most likely to do?

    a. Almost always takes the responsibility himself
    b. Usually takes the responsibility himself
    c. Usually puts the responsibility on an employee
    d. Almost always puts the responsibility on an employee

Many of the suggestions for writing multiple-choice items that were offered in chapter 5 are applicable to affective multiple-choice items. Those that also relate to affective measurement are reiterated here.

1. Base items on relevant affective objectives or desired behavior.

2. Formulate an item stem using simple and concise language.
3. Construct plausible and unambiguous alternatives.
4. Vary items to incorporate higher level affective behaviors when desired.
5. Make allowances for review and revision of all items.

Open-ended Items. The open-ended item presents either a question or an incomplete sentence that the respondent must answer or finish. Several examples of affective items are presented in example items 19 through 22.

Example Item 19

19. When I have free time during study hall or open class, I like to_____

_____.

Example Item 20

20. Some of the students in this program want only to _____

_____.

Example Item 21

21. If given the opportunity in this class, I would like to _____

_____.

Example Item 22

22. When I complete my schooling I would like to_____

_____.

The open-ended item can do much of what the unstructured interview can. It allows free expression of feelings without appearing like some type of test. The open-ended item can provide valuable information for understanding an individual or revising a curriculum. Also, like the unstructured interview, the open-ended item can provide alternatives that may be included in future developed closed-ended questionnaires.

Even though the open-ended item has these advantages, it also has some shortcomings. The greatest disadvantage of the open-ended item lies in the time it takes to read and analyze. Also, many times the written responses may be hard to read. Finally, it assumes adequate writing skill on the part of the student. Many students may have trouble expressing their true feelings in writing.

Oftentimes, it is advantageous to administer the open-ended item as a writing assignment rather than as an affective scale. In secondary schools and community colleges, cooperation between occupational education teachers and other teachers such as English and speech and communications instructors can help each meet his or her instructional responsibility while making assignments and projects more meaningful to students.

Rating Items. The rating item has traditionally been the most popular item type used in affective measurement. There are three basic forms of commonly used rating items for assessing affective behavior: these include the Likert item, the Thurstone item, and the semantic differential. Each of these items can aid in determining the intensity or magnitude of an individual's affect toward an object.

Likert Item. The Likert item is a numerical scale that consists of stimulus statements about some affective object followed by a scaled set of responses. Stimulus statements generally indicate a strong direction, either positive or negative. A common set of scaled descriptions includes agreement-type statements. Example item 23 incorporates such a scale.

Example Item 23

23. Business careers have a great deal of appeal to me.   SA A U D SD

Notice that example item 23 possesses a very positive statement about business careers exemplified by the phrase "great deal of appeal." Responses to the agreement scale give an indication of an individual's adherence to this statement. A statement such as the one offered in example item 24 is not as directional and may lead to misinterpretations when analyzing responses.

Example Item 24

24. Business careers are okay.   **SA A U D SD**

Also, it can be noted that the third or middle rating category of items 23 and 24 is "U" or undecided. Many authors and measurement specialists believe that a neutral response such as undecided does not provide information about affect. Therefore, many suggest omission of the middle category for agreement-type rating scales.

Table 7.2 presents a segment from a scale designed to assess an individual's attitude toward automation. This scale incorporates a 5-point Likert agreement scale.

There are many attitude and interest scales, both published and unpublished, that use the agreement-type Likert scale. One of the greatest advantages of this type of scale lies in the ease of adapting existing items or developing new ones.

The agreement scale can be adapted to facilitate the responses of verbally disadvantaged individuals or elementary career education students. Example items 25 and 26 present such item scales.

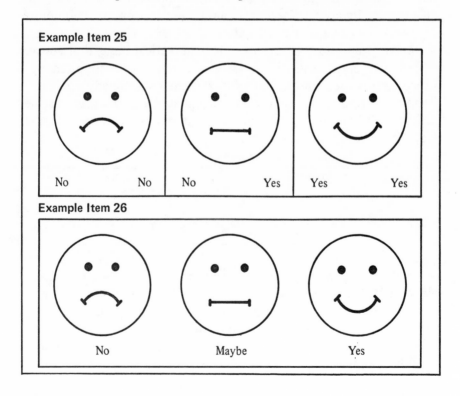

TABLE 7.2. Segment of the Attitudes Toward Automation Scale.

All items utilized a five point answer category system. The order and response weights were as follows: (1) Disagree a great deal, (2) Disagree slightly, (3) Neither disagree nor agree, (4) Agree slightly, (5) Agree a great deal. Items marked with an asterisk (*) should be scored in reverse, i.e., 5 = Disagree a great deal, 4 = Disagree, etc.

*1. Automated plants will be noisier than the more traditional assembly line.

2. Automated factories will be cleaner than non-automated plants.

3. Increased shift work during the night hours will be acceptable by the majority of workers.

4. Bad odors in the air within the factory will be greatly reduced because of automation.

5. Automation will lead to improved lighting in the factory.

6. Automation will lead to an expanded economy with new jobs.

*7. Those displaced by automation will have considerable difficulty in finding new jobs.

*8. Unemployed workers displaced by automation will be forced to find new opportunities in other areas of the country.

9. Automation will raise our standard of living.

*10. Automation displacement will eventually throw the country into another depression.

11. Wages under automation, will increase at an even faster rate than before automation.

12. Workers in automated plants will earn a greater salary than those doing the same type of work in non-automated plants.

*13. Under automation, wages will buy less because of increasing inflation.

*14. In an era of automation, wages will become increasingly more important to worker happiness than before automation.

*15. Part of future wages may be used for retraining programs and therefore proportionately reduce take home pay.

*16. Training may be the answer to the automation problem, but no one really knows what to train for.

17. On-the-job training will increase because of the needs created by automation.

*18. Less than half the industries that are considering automated installations will invest their money for retraining.

19. Automation will produce more semi-skilled and fewer non-skilled workers.

20. The idea of retraining will be gladly accepted by workers, especially if the company pays for it.

21. Automation will increase group morale of workers on the job.

22. Automation will improve individual job satisfaction on the job.

23. Operating an automated piece of equipment should, in general, be more interesting than operating older machines that once performed the same function.

Source: Reproduced from *Perception of Automation Issues, Worker Background, and Interpersonal Behavior,* by J. M. Rosenberg, 1962, with the permission of J. M. Rosenberg.

The stimulus statement or question for such response scales should be read aloud to students or interpreted manually to hearing-impaired students. In many cases it is advantageous to provide both printed and oral stimuli.

The Likert scales can have descriptors other than agreement types. Importance and frequency, as well as general numerical ratings, can be incorporated. Example item 27 presents a Likert scale with importance values.

Example Item 27

27. How important is your work to you?

very important   *no importance*

             1   2   3   4   5   6   7

The scale used in example item 27 ranges from very important to no importance with seven possible categories. More than one scale can be used with the same item stimulus statement or stem. Table 7.3 is an instrument that has been designed to measure career-oriented occupational values (Marvick 1954).

This instrument uses two separate Likert scales for each item: the first scale asks for an importance rating of job characteristics, while the second asks the respondent to indicate the degree to which his current job provides each characteristic.

O'Hara (1958) describes an interesting and valid way of assessing vocational self-concept in the areas of interests, general values, work values, and aptitudes. Basically, the procedure involves taking a construct and having an individual rate himself in terms of the construct. Example item 28 has been taken from the artistic interest category of the *Kuder Preference Record* and adapted to a 9-point descriptive or graphic scale.

TABLE 7.3. *Career-oriented Occupational-values Instrument.*

FACTORS IMPORTANT IN A JOB

	How important is this to you in most jobs?			Does your job in ONR actually provide this?		
	Very important	Fairly important	Not important	Quite a bit	In some ways	Not at all
1. Opportunity to learn (Acquiring new skills and knowledge)	☐	☐	☐	☐	☐	☐
2. Influence (Being able to make important decisions—exercising authority—having help of important people)	☐	☐	☐	☐	☐	☐
3. Getting ahead in the organization (Having a chance to get a better job in the organization)	☐	☐	☐	☐	☐	☐
4. Getting ahead professionally (Furthering professional career—being with people who can help one get ahead)	☐	☐	☐	☐	☐	☐
5. Full use of abilities (Having enough freedom, responsibility, and authority to do a job the way it should be done)	☐	☐	☐	☐	☐	☐
6. Salary (Earning enough money for a good living)	☐	☐	☐	☐	☐	☐
7. Prestige in organization (Having an important job in the organization—one with status and prestige)	☐	☐	☐	☐	☐	☐
8. Originality (Working with new ideas—being original—using initiative)	☐	☐	☐	☐	☐	☐
9. Availability of support (Working with people who will stand behind a man—who can help out in a tough spot when needed)	☐	☐	☐	☐	☐	☐
10. Importance of task (Having a job that means something—that is necessary and valuable and essential)	☐	☐	☐	☐	☐	☐
11. Competence (Knowing the job—being fully competent to do the work)	☐	☐	☐	☐	☐	☐
12. Prestige in community (Having a job seen by people outside the organization as being an important and meaningful job)	☐	☐	☐	☐	☐	☐
13. Respect for co-workers (Working with people who are competent and respected by others for their abilities)	☐	☐	☐	☐	☐	☐
14. Work enjoyment (Enjoying the work itself)	☐	☐	☐	☐	☐	☐
15. Security (Being reasonably sure that the job is fairly permanent)	☐	☐	☐	☐	☐	☐
16. Good personal relations (Being with people who are congenial—easy to work with)	☐	☐	☐	☐	☐	☐

Source: Reproduced from *Career Perspectives in a Bureaucratic Setting*, by D. Marvick, 1954, with the permission of University of Michigan Press, Ann Arbor, Michigan.

Example Item 28

28. *Artistic Interest:* Artistic interest means liking to do creative work with your hands—usually work that has "eye appeal" involving attractive design, colors, and materials.

  1. My interest ranks with the lowest group in this field
  2. I have a great deal less interest than most people
  3. I have much less interest than most people
  4. I have less interest than most people
  5. I have the same amount of interest as most people
  6. I have a little more interest than most people
  7. I have much more interest than most people
  8. I have a great deal more interest than most people
  9. My interest ranks with the highest group in the field

In developing an affective instrument using the Likert-type item, there are several suggested procedures:

STEP 1. Identify affective objects and subobjects. The delineation of broad objects and subobjects focuses the entire instrument. For example, an instrument that focuses on occupational students' attitudes toward a course may have several major subobjects or foci. It may focus on course materials, course organization, teacher planning, teacher presentations, allowance for individual differences, and so on. Likewise, an instrument focused on job attitudes might include major areas such as opportunity to advance, working conditions, noneconomic stability and security, personal relations, compensation, and communication. This step should define exactly what the instrument will focus on.

STEP 2. Write items. Write a number of items that relate to one or more of the categories identified in step 1. In many instances adapting or using items from existing instruments can save time and provide models for new items. A. L. Edwards (1957) has suggested fourteen points to consider in the development of affective rating items:

1. Avoid statements that refer to the past rather than to the present.
2. Avoid statements that are factual or can be interpreted as factual.

3. Avoid statements that may be interpreted in more than one way.
4. Avoid statements that are irrelevant to the psychological object under consideration.
5. Avoid statements that are likely to be endorsed by almost everyone or almost no one.
6. Select statements that are believed to cover the entire range of the affective scale of interest.
7. Keep the language of the statements simple, clear, and direct.
8. Statements should be short, rarely exceeding twenty words.
9. Each statement should contain only one complete thought.
10. Statements containing universals such as all, always, none, and never often introduce ambiguity and should be avoided.
11. Words such as only, just, merely, and others of a similar nature should be used with care and moderation.
12. Whenever possible, statements should be in the form of simple sentences.
13. Avoid the use of words that may not be understood by those who are to review the results of the scale.
14. Avoid the use of double negatives.

STEP 3.   Try out instrument. After items have been written or adapted they should be organized into an instrument. The instrument should then undergo a review and tryout phase. This phase is important to the development of almost every type of instrument. However, with the affective instrument, the need for review and tryout is paramount. Colleagues should check the instrument for ambiguous or poorly worded items. The instrument should then be administered to two or three students. Either go through the instrument orally with them or ask them to respond and indicate any ambiguous items. Following review and tryout, the instrument should be revised and duplicated. Of course, a more extensive statistical evaluation of the instrument can be done after it has been administered to a large group. Procedures for the latter type of evaluation are presented in chapter 9.

Thurstone Items. The Thurstone item is a type of item that provides a weighted score for each individual item included in the instrument. In other words, one item may have a higher value than another item. The Thurstone instrument is much more difficult to construct, refine, and score than other types of rating scales. For this reason, measurement specialists are usually more interested in using the

Thurstone item than are occupational educators. However, since many standardized affective instruments incorporate the Thurstone item, a brief description of its developmental procedures is offered here.

- *STEP 1.* A series of items that pertain to a certain object is written or collected.
- *STEP 2.* A panel of expert judges is assembled.
- *STEP 3.* The judges sort the items into eleven categories ranging from the least desirable to the most desirable.
- *STEP 4.* A sample of items from each category is selected for the instrument with each receiving the average scale value awarded by the panel of judges.
- *STEP 5.* Items are then randomly placed on the instrument and the numerical values are recorded for later use in scoring of the instrument.

Example items 29, 30, 31, and 32 are Thurstone items with their scale values presented in parentheses.

Example Item 29

29. My instructor presents his subject matter better than any other instructor. (8.2)

Example Item 30

30. If this course were an elective, I'd still enroll. (6.3)

Example Item 31

31. This company treats its employees better than any other company. (10.3)

Example Item 32

32. Doing it all over again, I'd still work for this company. (7.2)

Semantic-differential Items. The semantic differential is a type of rating scale that has many uses, including the measurement of generalized attitudes. Basically, the semantic differential consists of the statement or description of an affective object followed by a series of bipolar adjectives with a 5-point scale between the adjectives.

Example item 33 presents a partial item that focuses on a student's perception of the ideal job.

Example Item 33

The Ideal Job

Irregular	____:____:____:____:____	Systematic
Changing	____:____:____:____:____	Static
Private	____:____:____:____:____	Public
Office work	____:____:____:____:____	Factory work
Easy	____:____:____:____:____	Difficult

Source: Reproduced from *Measurement of the Meaning of Work,* paper presented at the American Psychological Association, September 4, 1965, with the permission of R. Guion, Bowling Green, Ohio.

The semantic-differential item can be very efficient in terms of the time that is required for completion and the amount of information that can be obtained. C. Osgood, G. Suci, and P. Tannenbaum (1967) offer many good suggestions for constructing and using the semantic differential for *attitude* measurement. They suggest that evaluative adjectives such as good–bad, beautiful–ugly, clean–dirty, valuable–worthless, beneficial–harmful, and pleasant–unpleasant be used.

Q-sort Techniques. W. Stephenson (1953) developed a method to assess attitudes: the Q-sort technique. The Q-sort has several advantages, including the elimination of response or answer sets such as denial, hedging, or lack of consentience. Since its introduction, the technique has been used in the analysis of many types of occupational and career problems related to attitude. The objective of the Q-sort method is to *map* a respondent's opinion of a concept or object by asking that he sort a given number of attitudinal statements about the concept or object into piles representing a range of attitudes. Q-sorts may be employed to assess any changes in attitude that may result over time, perhaps as a function of instruction given between measures. For example, an evaluator may use the Q-sort to determine a respondent's attitudes toward managerial or supervisory training prior to and upon completion of the training seminar. Or an occupational instructor might use Q-sorts with his students several times during the semester to determine their dynamic feelings and attitudes toward numerous occupational or career-learning experiences.

The stages for developing and administering a Q-sort are as follows:

Stage 1. Decide on the standard upon which the scoring will be based (e.g., the agreement or disagreement with a statement).

Stage 2. Assemble attitudinal statements (words, phrases, sentences) relevant to the attitude or task being assessed. Usually thirty to fifty statements are used.

Stage 3. Determine the number of intervals or response categories into which statements will be sorted.

Stage 4. Decide on the number of statements to be placed in each category to insure that the final responses tend to cluster between the two statements. For example, if twenty statements are to be sorted into seven intervals, the number of statements assignable to each category would be as follows:

	Strongly Disagree					Strongly Agree	
Category	1	2	3	4	5	6	7
Number of times	1	2	4	6	4	2	1

Stage 5. Present cards containing one statement each to the student, with directions for sorting. The directions should include: (1) the criterion, (2) the number of piles, and (3) the number of cards to be sorted into each pile.

The individual statements are scored using the numbers assigned to the successive categories that relate to a degree of favorableness. For example, if seven categories are used, the statements included in the first pile would be assigned a score of 1. This same procedure would be repeated for the remaining six piles of statements with the most agreeable statements receiving a score of 7. Q-sort administrations both before and after instruction may be used to study any changes in a respondent's level of agreement with regard to each statement.

Projective Techniques

Projective techniques are used to help reveal an individual's deeper feelings without using direct questions or person-to-person techniques. Typically, projective techniques have been used by clinical psychologists to understand better an individual's behavior. The Rorschach or ink blot test is a well-known projective measure.

The projective technique has some utility in measuring affective behavior but does not receive major attention here. The sentence-completion type of item, which was mentioned in the open-ended item section of this chapter, can be thought of as a projective item. Another kind of projective item is picture interpretation. Example item 34 precedes the presentation of four pictures to which an individual must respond.

Example Item 34

34. The first section of the booklet contains four pictures. You are to look at a picture and think up a story about it. Try to think up as imaginative stories as possible. After each picture there is a blank page on which you can write your story. Write only one story on each sheet. You may use both sides of the page. In order to build a complete story, there is a set of questions which you could use as guidelines in writing your story. These are the questions:

What do you think is going on?
Who are the people?
What happened in the past?
What are the people thinking?
Do any of them want anything?
What do they want?
What will happen afterward?
What will be done?

These questions are only a guide to help you write a story...a complete story with a beginning, a middle, and an end. Let your imagination supply the details. When requested to do so, you may turn the page and look at the first picture. You will have about twenty seconds to look at each picture. Then you will be asked to turn to the blank page following the picture and write your story. You will have only three minutes to write the story so you will have to work quickly. You will be warned when the time is almost up for each story. When the time is up, you will turn to the next picture.

There aren't any right or wrong kinds of stories. Any story is all right. You don't have to figure out exactly what is going on in the pictures. Just write the story that comes into your mind when you look at the pictures. You don't have to worry much about spelling or grammar. Stories won't be graded. What we are interested in is how imaginative a story you can write.

Another projective technique is to have individuals write stories or essays on certain value-laden topics. Stone et al. (1966) describe a computer technique that can be used to identify recurring words and phrases to aid in objectively evaluating and interpreting the responses to all types of projective items. Raths, Harmin, and Simon (1966) have compiled listings of key words and phrases that are useful in appraising interests, attitudes, and aspirations from projective responses.

Unobtrusive Measures

Unobtrusive measures are made without the knowledge of the individual or individuals being measured. As mentioned in an earlier section of this chapter, many times an individual who knows he is being observed or tested will respond in a desirable way, which may not necessarily reflect his true affect.

Direct observation can be considered an unobtrusive or non-reactive measure if subjects do not realize they are being observed. However, most unobtrusive measures are indirect or secondary. For example, after taking a class on a field trip to a local plastics manufacturer, an instructor may want to determine whether attitudes toward the plastics industry have changed. Unobtrusive measures might include monitoring of the reference book shelf in the laboratory to see if plastics books have been used more frequently than before. Requests for additional information about plastics could provide yet another measure. Choice of projects that involve plastics would also be a nonreactive measure. Asking students for suggestions about areas or topics they would like to expand upon is not as obtrusive as most direct measures but can still provide an attitude measure.

An unobtrusive measure such as the observation of writing or carving on desks and benches, writing on restroom walls, and other forms of vandalism often reveals student affect. Also, theft of tools and materials can be used as unobtrusive measures. Even the number of laboratory accidents can provide an unobtrusive measure of students' safety consciousness. There are some affective behaviors like honesty, safety consciousness, and respect for authority figures that are reflected in loss of small tools and materials, accident rates, and the graffiti on washroom walls respectively. Occupational teachers should not hesitate to use such information and data in assessing student attainment of objectives. Of course, every attempt should be made to gather and record such information in a systematic manner and to interpret it in light of other evidence when possible.

Even though unobtrusive measures may provide a more honest measure of a student's affect, in some instances they may not be the best measure. There are some obvious shortcomings in using indirect measures that make it difficult to infer affect. Also, and possibly more important, students need to gain confidence in performance under pressure or under observation. A golfer who can play fantastic rounds of golf by himself but goes to pieces while playing with others or while being observed will certainly fail as a professional.

REFERENCES

Bloom, B. S., Hastings, J. T., and Madaus, G. F. *Handbook on Formative and Summative Evaluation of Student Learning.* New York: McGraw-Hill, 1971.

Edwards, A. L. *Techniques of Attitude Scale Construction.* New York: Appleton-Century-Crofts, 1957.

Girod, G. R. *Writing and Assessing Attitudinal Objectives.* Columbus: Charles E. Merrill Publishing, 1973.

Guilford, J. P. *Psychometric Methods,* 2nd ed. New York: McGraw-Hill, 1954.

Hopke, W. E., ed. *Encyclopedia of Careers.* Chicago: J. G. Ferguson Publishing, 1972.

Krathwohl, D. R., Bloom, B. S., and Masia, B. *A Taxonomy of Educational Objectives: Handbook 2, The Affective Domain.* New York: David McKay Co., 1964.

Lee, B. N., and Merrill, M. D. *Writing Complete Affective Objectives: A Short Course.* Belmont, California: Wadsworth Publishing, 1972.

Marvick, D. *Career Perspectives in a Bureaucratic Setting.* Ann Arbor, Michigan: University of Michigan Press, 1954.

O'Hara, R. P. "A Cross-Sectional Study of Growth in the Relationship of Self-Ratings and Test Scores." Doctoral dissertation, Harvard University, 1958.

Osgood, C., Suci, G., and Tannenbaum, P. *The Measurement of Meaning.* Urbana, Illinois: University of Illinois Press, 1967.

Raths, L., Harmin, M., and Simon, S. *Values and Teaching: Working with Values in the Classroom.* Columbus: Merrill, 1966.

Scriven, M. "Student Values as Educational Objectives." In *Proceedings of the 1965 Invitational Conference on Testing Problems,* pp. 33–49. Princeton, New Jersey: Educational Testing Service, 1966.

Smith, B. O. "Teaching and Testing Values." In *Proceedings of the 1965 Invitational Conference on Testing Problems,* pp. 50–59. Princeton, New Jersey: Educational Testing Service, 1966.

Stephenson, W. *Study of Behavior: Q Technique and Its Methodology.* Chicago: University of Chicago Press, 1953.

Stone, P. J. et al. *The General Inquirer.* Cambridge, Massachusetts: M.I.T. Press, 1966.

Taylor, E. K. *Manual for Sales Attitude Check List.* Chicago: Science Research Associates, 1960.

Tyler, R. W. "Assessing Educational Achievement in the Affective Domain." From a series of special reports by the National Council on Measurement Education, vol. 4, no. 3, Spring 1973.

U.S. Department of Labor. *Dictionary of Occupational Titles,* 3rd ed. Washington, D.C.: U.S. Government Printing Office, 1965.

_____. *Occupational Outlook Handbook.* Washington, D.C.: U.S. Government Printing Office, 1974.

Wick, J. W. *Educational Measurement.* Columbus: Merrill, 1973.

Chapter 8

Assembling the Teacher-made Instrument

The preparation of a test or other measuring device is almost complete once items have been written or adapted, reviewed by colleagues or others, and revised to incorporate reviewers' suggestions. However, the task of assembling the items and several other technical points remain.

Specific suggestions were given in chapter 6 for assembling and administering performance tests. This chapter focuses on finalizing paper and pencil measures for administration. Six tasks or technical points are presented: using a card file, arranging items, writing directions, reproducing the test, preparing an answer sheet, and preparing a scoring key.

USING A CARD FILE

The use of test-item cards and a card file to store test items offers several ways to use and improve test items continuously. Basically, the item card can be used as items are written, or as existing items are taken from presently used tests and transferred to item cards. The cards may be 3" × 5" or any other convenient size. Blank or used IBM cards make good test item cards. It is recommended that cards be preprinted with spaces for certain information to be provided later; however, this step is not a necessity. Figure 8.1 provides a sample item card with preprinted spaces for information such as course, topic, objective number, and taxonomy. Used in the format

Which of the following is the best reason for using nylon utensils with teflon-coated pans?

    a. They are easier to clean than wood.

    b. They are lighter in weight.

    c. They do not scratch the teflon.

    d. They are dishwasher safe.

Diff. _____

Course _____   Disc. _____

Topic _____

Obj. # _____

Taxonomy _____   Correct Response _____

FIGURE 8.1.   Example Item File Card.

suggested, the item card is not only a copy of the item but also a source of descriptive information about the item. Additionally, evaluation information about the item can be stored and updated each time the item is used.

Item cards can be filed in several different ways. First, a file can be organized according to objectives. That is, all items that pertain to the assessment of objective 1 of an electronics course would be grouped. Or, item cards can be organized by course. Figure 8.2 presents a course and objective combination system. This type of item-organization scheme is particularly helpful when the teacher wants to prepare a test for a particular unit of instruction or a particular group of objectives.

Another way of filing the items takes slightly more time but offers several advantages. This second organizational scheme uses a card that has been notched in the appropriate places to aid in selection. Figure 8.3 presents such a card. Note the coding system at

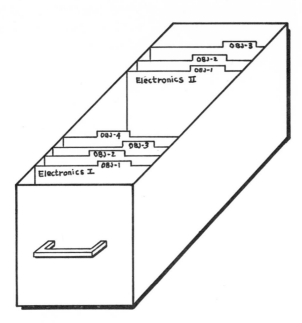

FIGURE 8.2.   Objectives by Course-item Card File.

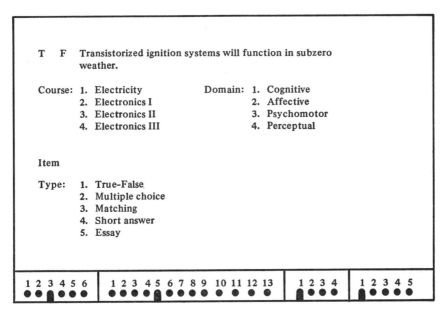

FIGURE 8.3.   Example Sort Card for Test Items.

the bottom of the card, which corresponds to categories printed on the midsection of the card. Also, note the notches that have been punched within each of the four broad coding categories. These notches describe the item typed at the top of the card by indicating, as in figure 8.3, that the item is from course 3, unit 5, the knowing domain, and that it is a true–false item. This type of system can be used by placing the notched card upside down in a card file tray. Then if items pertaining to course 3 (Electronics II in our example) are desired, a long rod or knitting needle is slid through the holes in row 3 as shown in figure 8.4. When the rod is lifted, all cards that have been notched will fall out, providing a group of items for

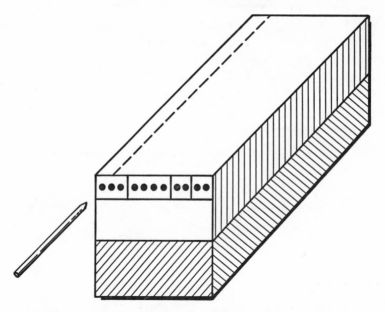

FIGURE 8.4.   Sample Item Deck with the Use of Sorting Needle or Rod.

course 3. Next a further sort to identify items by unit and type of learning can be made in a similar fashion.

This system allows for the selection of items without physically organizing them within the file. After items have been used or as new items are written, they can be inserted any place in the file. This system works especially well if an instructor is teaching multiple courses and/or multiple occupational areas.

Specially printed and punched item cards can be obtained from a commercial firm, or they can be locally developed. McBee Corporation

(Peoria, Ill.) provides an extensive line of sortable cards. In addition to the cards, special paper punches can be purchased. However, punch cards also can be developed using ditto, mimeograph, or offset printing and a paper punch.

ARRANGING ITEMS

Items that have been written or selected from an item file must next be placed into a sequence and technically reproduced. In arranging the items, several factors should be considered. These factors include (1) item difficulty, (2) item type, (3) content, and (4) use of results. Standardized instruments usually incorporate all four of these features simultaneously; the occupational instructor may wish to use one or more.

Item Difficulty

Many testing specialists suggest ordering items within a test from the easiest to the most difficult. This practice has several advantages. First, it tends to encourage the student as he begins taking the test. This encouragement can help decrease anxiety toward the test and may allow for more accurate measures of students' performance. Second, by leaving the most difficult items to the end of the test, the chance of a student being stumped on an item early in the test and taking too much time on it is reduced. Item difficulty measures for norm-referenced tests are based upon a group administration of items. If items have been used previously, and appropriate item analysis data are available, the difficulty indices are known and can be used to order the items within the test. But for new items, and for criterion-referenced items, determining a difficulty level for each individual item will be a judgmental decision on the part of the occupational instructor. Since most difficulty indices are based on group performance, applicability to a similar group will be fairly accurate. As with many other things, what is true for a group is not always true for an individual. However, with the lack of a better index, the group measure is generally better than a teacher's judgment.

Item Type

For instruments that contain more than one type of item (e.g., multiple choice, true–false, and short answer), items should be grouped within the instrument according to their type. All multiple-choice items should be in one section, all true–false items in another section, and so on. There are several reasons for such grouping. First, the student is not constantly required to change his response mode as he proceeds through the test. Students generally like to respond to a series of items of one type before switching to another type of item. Moreover, it is less likely that students will become confused by a shift in response mode and mark their answer incorrectly on the answer sheet. Finally, it is usually easier to score a test when items of a similar format are grouped.

Combining item-type grouping with difficulty grouping is a simple process. It is suggested that within a particular type of item group, the items be ordered according to difficulty. For large or long tests, this process is easily accomplished. For short tests or quizzes of 25 items or less, Noll and Scannell (1972) suggest that grouping by any basis other than item type is not often practical or useful.

Item Content

Items may also be grouped according to the content areas that form the scope of the test. For example, a final examination for an electricity course might focus on terminology, mathematical formulas, and building-code regulations. The test could be divided into three sections, each including items for one of the three foci. This type of grouping has advantages to students in establishing relationships among items that pertain to the same topic or subtopic. Also, it is often easier for the instructor to interpret scores and to use the results of subsections or subscores of the test to aid in evaluating his instruction for certain topics. For example, it is useful for an instructor to know that as a group, students did not perform well in one area of his course. This knowledge can aid in developing remedial instruction or in revising the course content for future instruction. Also, subscores from various sections or content areas can be useful to students in helping them better understand their strengths and weaknesses.

Use of Results

If an instrument is being developed to meet one or more of the functions identified in chapter 1 and discussed in chapter 8, such as aiding in career guidance, classifying and placing students, or diagnosing learning difficulties, items may be grouped according to the use to be made of the scores. For example, if an instrument is to be used in aiding career guidance, it may be useful to group items that will provide measures of cognitive and affective functioning within several areas such as mathematical reasoning and occupational awareness.

Items can be arranged according to any or all of the four factors discussed here: difficulty level, item type, item content, and use of results. The use of item cards can facilitate organizing the test since items can be easily placed or moved within the desired sequence. If item cards of the type described and shown in figures 8.1 and 8.3 are used, a rough draft or review copy of the instrument can easily be prepared. Such a copy can be made by placing item cards facedown on a Xerox or other type of photo copying machine with cards overlapping an appropriate amount. Figure 8.5 shows a series of cards organized in this manner.

This quickly prepared initial copy can be used for review purposes. Subsequent changes in items or in the sequence of items prior to final typing and reproduction of the instrument can be made by merely shifting the item cards and making another photo copy.

PREPARING DIRECTIONS

Once items have been sequenced and reviewed, the next step is to develop the directions or instructions for the instrument. Directions should be designed to provide the student with everything he or she needs to know about taking the test or completing each of the items included in the instrument. General directions should be prepared for the total instrument. In addition, directions should be prepared for individual subsections of the instrument as needed.

Traxler (1951) has suggested several guidelines for preparing general and specific directions:

239

Gasoline mileage efficiency in automobiles is affected by:
  a. Carburetor settings
  b. Ignition timing setting
  c. Tire pressure
  d. All of the above

Which of the following woods is the best for constructing furniture?
  a. Oak
  b. Redwood
  c. Rosewood
  d. Pine

Which wood is best for constructing lawn furniture?
  a. Oak
  b. Redwood
  c. Rosewood
  d. Pine

Which of the following is the best reason for using nylon utensils with teflon-coated pans?
  a. They are easier to clean than wood.
  b. They are lighter in weight.
  c. They do not scratch the teflon.
  d. They are dishwasher safe.

FIGURE 8.5.   Suggested Use of Cards for Preparing a Review Copy of Test.

1. Assume that the examinees know nothing about tests.
2. Use clear, succinct style.
3. Make the more important directions stand out through the use of different sizes or styles of type.

240

4. Give the examiner and/or proctor instructions on what to do prior, during, and after the test administration.
5. Check on all possible misunderstandings and inconsistencies by having several people try out the directions.
6. Keep various directions for subsections parallel with each other.
7. When necessary, include sample items with the directions.

In addition to Traxler's seven guildelines there are several other suggestions regarding the type of information that should be included in directions. First, an indication of the time available or time limit for the test as well as an indication of the total number of items in the test should be included in the directions. These facts should also be emphasized in oral instructions given by the administrator.

Second, when feasible, the worth or weight of each item or each type of item should be specified in the directions. This will enable the respondent to focus attention and time on the more important items in the instrument. The specification of item weight is especially desirable for essay tests that have a small number of items of varying importance.

Third, directions should state whether guessing may be to the student's advantage. If a special scoring procedure designed to minimize guessing is used, then it should be explained in the directions.

Fourth, instructions for recording responses on the instrument or an answer sheet should also be given. These instructions should indicate, for example, whether to write in, check, or circle the desired response, either directly on the test booklet or the answer sheet.

Two other considerations are also necessary: directions should spell out what the students should do when the instrument has been completed and how they should change answers if they feel they have made a mistake. If machine scoring is used, the process for changing answers is especially critical since a machine will sense and tally marks and pay no attention to notes or other changes. The sample directions offered in figure 8.6 incorporate many of the aforementioned suggestions. The directions should make the test as close to self-administering as possible, even if someone will emphasize orally the key points. Clear directions are one way to help insure accurate measures of student achievement.

DIRECTIONS

This section of the test contains 45 true-false statements. Read each one carefully. If you think a statement is true, place a T in the blank provided. If you think a statement is false, place an F in the blank. You will receive one point for each correct answer. If you are not sure of the correct answer, but can make an intelligent guess, mark the statement; if not, omit it. Do not guess wildly. Your score on this part of the test will be the number of right answers minus the number of wrong answers. You will have 30 minutes in which to complete the true-false section of the test. When you have completed it, do not stop, continue to the next section.

FIGURE 8.6.   Example Directions for a True–False Segment of an Instrument.

DEVELOPING AN ANSWER SHEET

The use of separate answer sheets rather than recording responses on the instrument itself has become a rather widespread practice. There are reasons for such widespread use. Basically, answer sheets are inexpensive, and they make it possible for the same instrument or test booklet to be used more than once. Also, answer sheets can provide for up to 150 responses on a single sheet of paper. From the standpoint of speed and accuracy, the use of a separate answer sheet is much preferred to responding on the instrument itself.

The separate answer sheet is not without shortcomings. Usually, more desk space is required when a separate answer sheet is used. Certain demands on the students' motor skills and spatial perception are made when a separate answer sheet is used. However, such problems are usually significant only with young or handicapped students. Some teachers are critical of separate answer sheets because they believe it is more difficult to use the instrument for diagnostic and remedial purposes if they have to refer to an answer sheet as well as to the test or instrument.

Even though there are some shortcomings in using separate answer sheets, efficiency and accuracy in scoring will, in most cases, outweigh the shortcomings. Research has indicated that separate answer sheets do not affect instrument reliability or accuracy in assessment. Therefore, the decision to use or not use a separate answer sheet is usually one of personal preference.

Both Science Research Associates and the University of Minnesota have produced test booklets with articulated answer sheets. These booklets are designed to overcome some of the shortcomings associated with the use of a separate answer sheet. The booklets include an answer sheet with multiple columns, which becomes the last page in the test booklet. Each of the other pages in the booklet is of a succeedingly smaller width so that they align with their respective column on the answer sheet. A similar type of test booklet–answer sheet format could be prepared for locally developed instruments.

Kinds of Answer Sheets

There are several types of answer sheets. Each has advantages for certain applications or uses in the occupational program.

Hand-score–Single-sheet. The *hand-score single-sheet answer form* is probably the easiest to construct and most used. This type of answer sheet simply provides a space for responding to each item on the instrument. The space provided can be either a blank for the insertion of a letter or it can be a series of blanks, and the respondent must check ($\sqrt{}$) the correct one. Figure 8.7 is an example single-sheet hand-score answer form.

Answer Sheets Using Carbon Paper. By using carbon or carbonized paper, answer sheets can be designed to provide for ease in scoring as well as for immediate feedback to students. This can be accomplished in several ways.

One method involves using two regular answer sheets with a sheet of carbon paper placed between them. The answer sheets should be mimeographed or printed in a format similar to the answer sheet shown in figure 8.7. The two identical sheets are then stapled together with the carbon paper placed between them. A student then completes the instrument and places his responses on the answer sheet. After completion, the answer sheet and its duplicate can be separated. The original is submitted to the instructor and the instructor gives the student the answer key so he/she can self-score the carbon-copy answers. Thus, the students gain immediate feedback regarding their performance on the test without placing unworkable scoring requirements on the instructor.

Name _____ Student number _____

Test name _____

	A	B	C	D			A	B	C	D
1.	☐	☐	☐	☐	21.		☐	☐	☐	☐
2.	☐	☐	☐	☐	22.		☐	☐	☐	☐
3.	☐	☐	☐	☐	23.		☐	☐	☐	☐
4.	☐	☐	☐	☐	24.		☐	☐	☐	☐
5.	☐	☐	☐	☐	25.		☐	☐	☐	☐
6.	☐	☐	☐	☐	26.		☐	☐	☐	☐
7.	☐	☐	☐	☐	27.		☐	☐	☐	☐
8.	☐	☐	☐	☐	28.		☐	☐	☐	☐
9.	☐	☐	☐	☐	29.		☐	☐	☐	☐
10.	☐	☐	☐	☐	30.		☐	☐	☐	☐
11.	☐	☐	☐	☐	31.		☐	☐	☐	☐
12.	☐	☐	☐	☐	32.		☐	☐	☐	☐
13.	☐	☐	☐	☐	33.		☐	☐	☐	☐
14.	☐	☐	☐	☐	34.		☐	☐	☐	☐
15.	☐	☐	☐	☐	35.		☐	☐	☐	☐
16.	☐	☐	☐	☐	36.		☐	☐	☐	☐
17.	☐	☐	☐	☐	37.		☐	☐	☐	☐
18.	☐	☐	☐	☐	38.		☐	☐	☐	☐
19.	☐	☐	☐	☐	39.		☐	☐	☐	☐
20.	☐	☐	☐	☐	40.		☐	☐	☐	☐

FIGURE 8.7.   Example Hand-score Answer Sheet.

Another carbon-paper type answer sheet facilitates scoring by the teacher or test administrator. This answer sheet is very similar to the one previously discussed; however, in this instance correct responses are provided on the second sheet. Figure 8.8 shows an example of the sheets. Note that the second sheet has only the

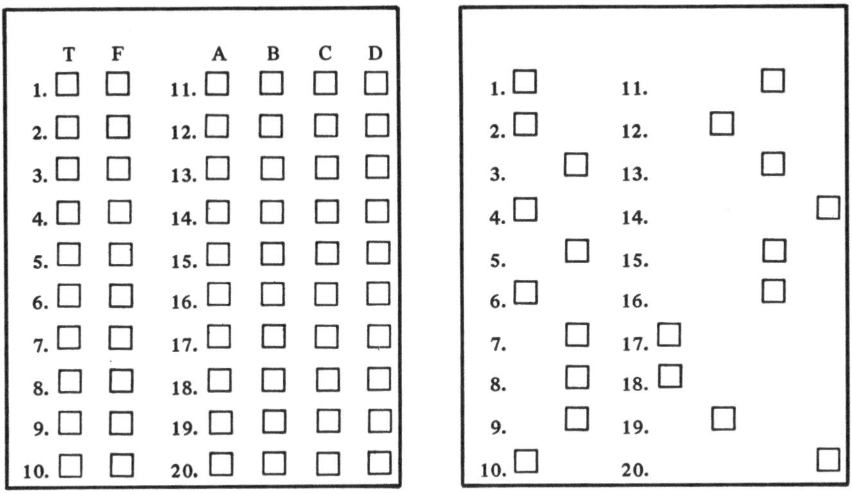

Answer Sheet   **Score Sheet**

FIGURE 8.8. Example Carbon Duplicate Answer Sheet Designed for Ease in Scoring.

correct response spaces printed on it. The two sheets are sealed together with carbon paper between them. It is important that the sheets be sealed with tape or staples so that students cannot see the second sheet. In scoring this answer sheet, the instructor needs only to count the number of check marks that fall *within* the printed spaces to determine the number of correct responses. It should be noted also that if carbonized paper is used in printing either of the foregoing types of answer sheets, then carbon paper need not be placed between the two answer sheets.

An alternative to this type of answer sheet, which may save time in preparation of the second or carbon answer sheet, involves using a duplicating master. After the initial run of answer sheets is made on the mimeograph or spirit duplicating machine, the correct spaces are circled on the master and a second set of sheets is made. The original and circled answer sheets are then attached and sealed. This process can save preparatory time.

Stylus-punch Answer Sheets. *Stylus-punch answer sheets* are very similar to the second type of carbon answer sheets described above. Rather than using carbon paper to record the response on the second page or answer key sheet, a stylus such as the one shown in figure 8.9 is used by the students to punch a hole through both answer sheets as they respond to each item on the test. The stylus-punch approach

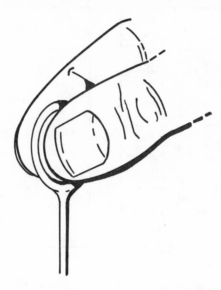

FIGURE 8.9.   Stylus Used to Respond on Stylus-punch Answer Sheets.

has the same advantages as the carbon sheet. It provides immediate feedback and facilitates scoring. The stylus-punch form is neater than the carbon smudging but requires a soft surface below the answer sheet to allow the stylus to pass through the sheets.

An additional advantage of the stylus-punch and the carbon answer sheet is that multiple copies of the form are available for filing in different places or offices for use by different individuals. This advantage has special utility with interest or attitude inventories, which may be used by teachers as well as counselors.

Opaqued Answer Sheets. *Opaqued answer sheets* provide spaces for responses that have been coated with an opaque solution. In responding, a student erases the opaque material to indicate his choice and is informed as to the correctness of this response by a symbol that appears beneath the opaquing. This standard type of answer sheet as shown in figure 8.10 is an adaptation of the performance

NAME _____ RIGHT _____ WRONG _____

CLASS/COURSE _____ MODULE/TEST NO. _____ SCORE _____

DATE _____ TIME _____ ITEMS OF DIFFICULTY _____

Self-Scoring PATENTED · VVN&N · TRADEMARKED **TRAINER-TESTER** * **Response Card**

Directions—Variable Alphabetical Response Mode:
Erase the block where you think correct answer is. Preferably use clean, firm, non-plastic pencil eraser, with reasonably sharp edge. Your instructor will **designate** the correct answer response for a **particular** exercise, for example **Correct Answer Designated:** Then other responses are:
"T" = Right "H", "E" or "L" = Wrong etc.
"H" = Right etc. "T", "E" or "L" = Wrong etc.
If your instructor wishes you to learn the correct answer, continue answering (erasing) until the response designated as correct is revealed; make as few erasures as possible. For self-scoring, grading and item-of-difficulty identification see Direction Sheet. Indicate sequence of responding—your step numbers—if requested.

Item of Difficulty

Item of Difficulty Mark

ITEM NUMBER	ANSWER RESPONSE/ CORRECTIVE FEEDBACK				SCORING POINTS	ITEM NUMBER	ANSWER RESPONSE/ CORRECTIVE FEEDBACK				SCORING POINTS
UNIT	(a)	(b)	(c)	(d)		UNIT	(a)	(b)	(c)	(d)	
1					___	21					___
2						22					
3						23					
4						24					
5					___	25					
6						26					
7						27					
8						28					
9						29					___
10					___	30					___
11					___	31					___
12					___	32					___
13					___	33					___
14					___	34					___
15					___	35					___
16					___	36					___
17					___	37					___
18					___	38					___
19					___	39					___
20					___	40					___

SEPT 1975 Total ___ Total ___

T-T No. Z11B Second Series

Source: Reproduced from Self-Scoring ® TRAINER-TESTER Response Card, T-T No. Z11B, with the permission of Van Valkenburgh, Nooger & Neville, Inc., New York, New York 10038.

FIGURE 8.10. Example Opaque Answer Sheet.

test that uses opaquing, as described in chapter 6. These standard sheets can be purchased with response patterns in several different forms so that students cannot, through trial and error on different exams, determine keyed-response locations. Along with each form comes a key that indicates the placement of certain symbols below the opaque. For example, for items 1 and 2 on the same sheet, the following symbols might appear:

1. Z   Y   J   4
2. Y   4   Z   J

For a particular test, the instructor can either organize alternatives so that the same symbol is the correct response throughout the test or can indicate on the test, the correct symbol for each item. This type of answer sheet has the advantage of providing immediate feedback as to the correctness of the student's response. Additionally, if students respond incorrectly, they can erase a second or third response until the correct one has been located. Used in this way, students can learn from the test. Scoring is not confounded by multiple responding because a multiple response is automatically scored as an incorrect response by the teacher. Teachers can also use the number of incorrect responses made for each item in a special scoring formula that provides partial credit for partial knowledge and/or understanding. For example, with four alternatives, the following schedule might be used in computing each student's score:

- 3 pts.—1 correct response
- 2 pts.—1 correct response and 1 incorrect response
- 1 pt.—1 correct response and 2 incorrect responses
- 0 pt.—1 correct response and 3 incorrect responses

Machine-scorable Answer Sheets. Machine-scorable answer sheets are used with special optical scanning equipment to produce either a punched card for computer summarization or a printed output or score. This special equipment is often available for use in large educational institutions and universities but few small school systems can afford to purchase the necessary equipment. Test service bureaus do offer scoring services through contractual agreements. However, such arrangements are of very limited practical value for small-scale testing in individual occupational programs. If a large-scale testing program is planned to serve an entire school, it may be beneficial to use machine scoring. But for most small-scale teacher-made instruments, it is not cost effective to use machine scoring.

Machine-scorable answer sheets can be purchased from IBM or from the Optical Scanning Corporation. These sheets have a standard format such as the one shown in figure 8.11 or they can be specifically printed to suit local needs. Usually, the latter is used only for large-scale administration where added expenditures would be warranted. For most machine-scorable answer sheets a soft lead pencil is required for responses and special care must be taken to respond accurately and to make clean erasures when responses are changed.

Mechanical Answering Devices. Mechanical devices can be used in answering multiple-choice and dichotomous-response items. These devices usually provide each student a responding console with four or five buttons that can be used to respond to item alternatives. Each of the student consoles is connected with a monitor unit, which the teacher or test proctor controls. The monitor provides a visual display of how each student responded to a visually presented item. Some monitors will tally and keep a cumulative score for each student. This type of device has utility in working with students who have verbal deficiencies and might require a verbal explanation of items in addition to the written form. Also, such a device can be used during instruction to gain feedback from students regarding their comprehension of previously discussed material before moving on to new topics. This method does, however, have the disadvantage of generally requiring each student to proceed through the exercise or instrument at the same rate of speed. Gifted students tend to get bored, impatient, and/or lose interest while slower students tend to feel pushed, lost, and/or inadequate. Of course, none of the foregoing feelings are conducive to effective learning.

SCORING KEYS

Within the discussion of each of the item types in chapters 5, 6, and 7, scoring was mentioned in terms of ease and objectivity. The short-answer, essay, open-ended, and projective items are the most difficult

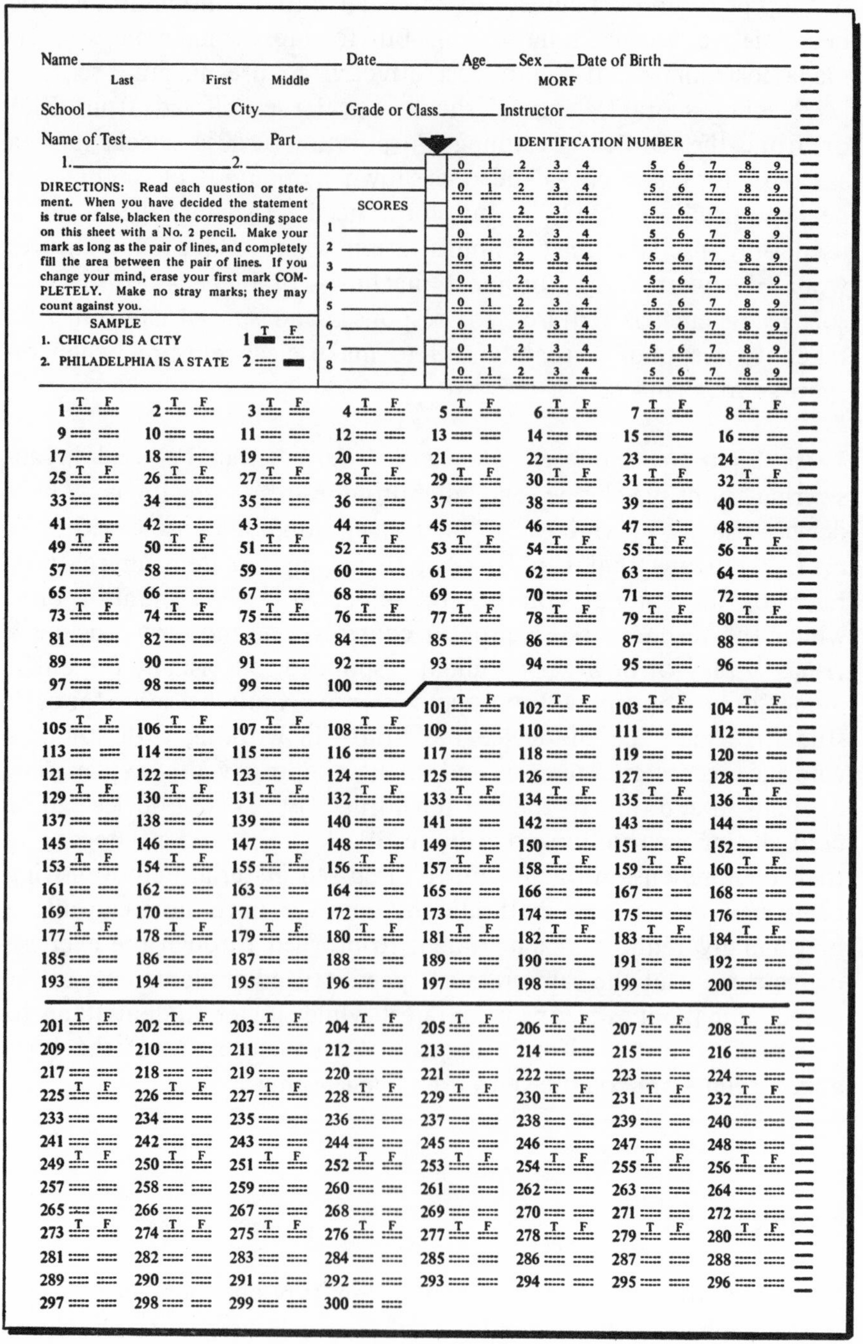

Name_____ Date_____ Age_____ Sex_____ Date of Birth_____
 Last   First   Middle   MORF

School_____City_____ Grade or Class_____ Instructor_____

Name of Test_____ Part_____   IDENTIFICATION NUMBER
1._____2._____

DIRECTIONS: Read each question or statement. When you have decided the statement is true or false, blacken the corresponding space on this sheet with a No. 2 pencil. Make your mark as long as the pair of lines, and completely fill the area between the pair of lines. If you change your mind, erase your first mark COMPLETELY. Make no stray marks; they may count against you.

SCORES
1 _____
2 _____
3 _____
4 _____
5 _____
6 _____
7 _____
8 _____

SAMPLE
1. CHICAGO IS A CITY   1 ▬ ▭
2. PHILADELPHIA IS A STATE   2 ▭ ▬

FIGURE 8.11. Machine-scorable Answer Sheet.

250

to score, and in most cases require professional judgment in rating the adequacy of response. However, multiple-choice and rating types of responses are much easier and less time-consuming to score. Additionally, many times a clerical staff member or student assistant can relieve the teacher of the scoring task. Regardless of who does the scoring, it is advantageous and necessary to use some type of scoring key.

Strip Key

A *strip key* is designed for use with test booklets that have answer spaces aligned vertically, or with answer sheets that use blanks for responses. Basically, the strip key is a strip of paper or cardboard upon which answers or correct responses are typed with the appropriate spacing. The strip key is simply aligned with the proper page of the student's test booklet or the proper column of his or her answer sheet. A special form of the strip key incorporates a number of columns on a paper or cardboard sheet that is folded like a fan or accordion. Each column on the key corresponds with a page of the test booklet or a column of the answer sheet. Figure 8.12 is an example accordion-type strip key.

Punched or Cut-out Key

Punched keys can be used for scoring test booklets or answer sheets where students mark or check boxes in responding. Holes are punched through a sheet of cardboard or heavy paper in the appropriate locations. By placing the punched key over an answer sheet, scoring simply involves counting the number of checked boxes that appear through the punched holes. Of course, the entire field of answers must be scanned by the scorer to insure that only one response is marked for each item. Placing a contrasting colored mark through the punched holes that are not marked correctly can be useful to students in reviewing their test. This provides feedback of not only the correctness of their response but also tells them which response is correct. Figure 8.13 is an example punched key for an answer sheet.

A *cut-out key* is a special form of a punched key. The cut-out

Column 1	Column 2	Column 3	Column 4
A	T	3	A
C	F	1	C
C	F	6	B
B	F	4	D
D	T	5	D
D	T		A
C	T		A
C	F	1	C
A	T	4	C
A	F	5	D
D	F	3	A
A	T	2	A
A	F		B
C	T		C

FIGURE 8.12. Example Strip Key.

key is designed to be used in scoring short-answer or fill-in-the-blank types of items, or for items where the student writes down a letter or number indicating a response. Figure 8.14 is an example cut-out scoring key.

An adaptation of the punched or cut-out key is the transparent key. The *transparent key* is made of transparent acetate plastic such as that used for making overhead projector transparencies. This type of scoring key is punched in the appropriate places and provides the advantage of ease in alignment. Also, it allows the scorer to check

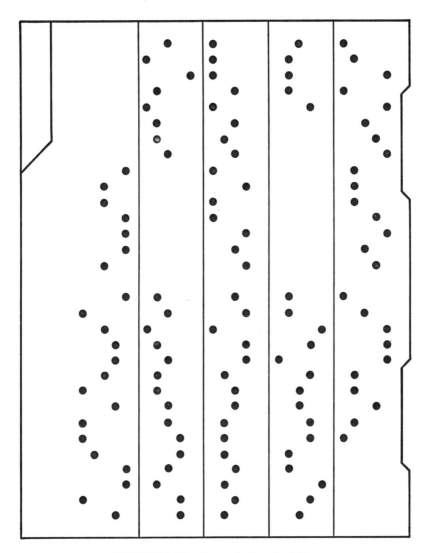

FIGURE 8.13.   Example Punched Key.

for multiple checks or responses for individual items. Some measurement specialists cite as its major shortcoming the visual interference caused by being able to view incorrect responses.

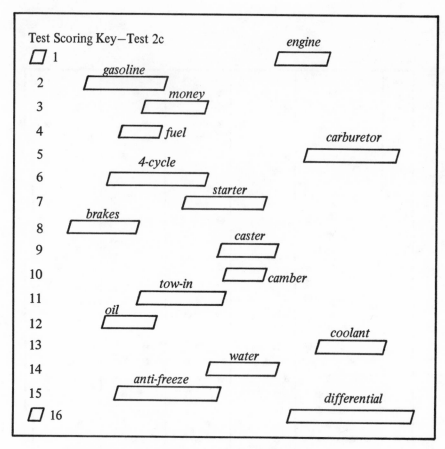

FIGURE 8.14.   Cut-out Scoring Key for Short-answer Items.

Overprinting

Overprinting of answer sheets is a technique used in lieu of a strip or punched key. This technique involves running completed answer sheets through a mimeograph, spirit duplicator, or multilith machine to print the scoring key in a contrasting color onto each answer sheet after it has been completed by the student. Scoring involves counting the number of student marks that appear in the appropriate position on the overprinted key. This technique has advantages in providing feedback to students and in overcoming alignment problems of punched or strip keys. Figure 8.15 is an example overprinted answer sheet.

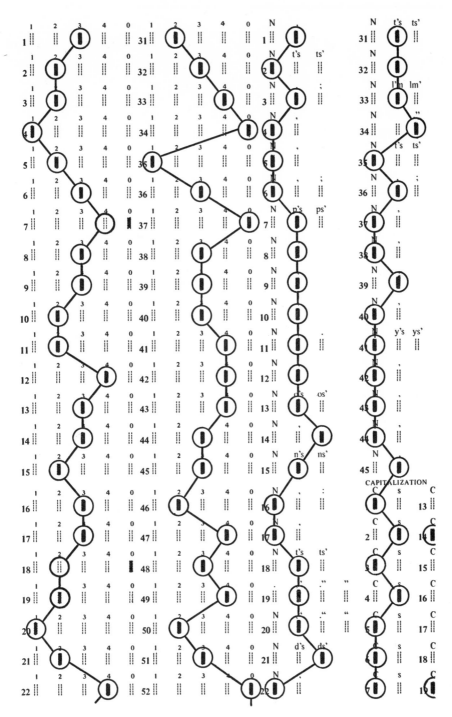

FIGURE 8.15. Example Overprinted Answer Sheet.

One alternate to this method is called the *Dog Patch IBM*. It involves placing the answer key and a number of completed answer sheets in an aligned stack, fastening the stack to a board backing, and either drilling holes or driving a nail or awl through the sheets where the correct answers were to be marked. Scoring then involves counting the marked responses that correspond with holes.

REPRODUCING THE TEST

The final step in preparing an instrument for administration is reproduction or duplication. There are four basic means of reproduction that often are available to most occupational instructors. Decisions about which method to use are usually dependent upon the availability of equipment and the number of copies needed. The four methods include photocopying, spirit duplicating, mimeographing, and offset printing.

Instrument Layout

Instrument layout is a rather simple process that is often taken for granted and often left up to the discretion of a typist. There are several points, however, that should be made known to whoever is responsible for laying out and typing the instrument.

Use Two Columns for Multiple-choice Items. When multiple-choice items are used, it is usually more efficient in terms of space use to list the items in two vertical columns numbered from top to bottom in the first column and then to the top of the second column. This format not only is efficient in terms of space but it is easier for the student to follow.

Do Not Split Items. When the bottom of a page is reached and there is insufficient space for an entire additional item, put the entire item on the next page. When an item is split, it is very difficult to flip pages to refer to alternatives or to review an item stem.

All Item Information Should Be Printed Left to Right. When descriptive information is used on graphic rating scales and other items, it should be typed parallel to the bottom of the page. In no instance should students be required to rotate the test booklet in order to read any part of an item.

Directions Should Stand Out from the Rest of the Instrument.   Directions should be easily distinguished from other parts of the instrument. This can be accomplished by using a different colored carbon master when spirit duplicating is used, or by using a different type style when any other method of reproduction is used. When typing interview schedules, it is common practice to use italics for instructions given to the interviewer and bold type for items presented to the interviewee.

Item Cards Can Be Used in Special Cases. When typing time is a problem or typing services are not available, it is possible to reproduce a test from item cards such as those described in the first section of this chapter. Directions can be prepared and added to the instrument review form produced by photocopying (figure 8.5). Either spirit masters or mimeograph stencils can be made by using a heat-type thermofax machine and special materials designed for these purposes. These special masters can then be used in the same manner as a typed master. The quality of this method is usually not comparable to that obtained with typed masters but in most instances is adequate.

Reproduction Methods

Photocopying. *Photocopying* is probably the most economical method for reproducing a small number of copies. It requires no special masters or techniques, just a clear typed original copy of the instrument. However, if more than fifteen but less than 100 copies are needed, spirit duplications may be a better method for reproduction than photocopying.

Spirit Duplicating. *Spirit duplication* requires that a special master be prepared by using a typewriter or ball-point pen. The copy produced by this method is usually in purple, although other colors are available and multiple colors can be incorporated on the same master. The spirit duplication machine is simple to operate and most educational agencies have one available. Given a demonstration, most occupational instructors can operate the machine without further assistance.

Mimeographing. If more than 100 but less than 300 copies of an instrument are needed, *mimeograph* is probably the best method. This method requires the use of a special master that is cut on a regular typewriter or by using a special hand-held stylus. The copy produced is usually in black ink and is generally clearer and more professional looking than the spirit-duplicated copy. Only one color of ink is possible per run with the typical mimeograph process. A second run with a contrasting colored ink would require a complete cleaning of the machine's ink drum. This is a very messy and time-consuming task.

Offset Printing. For quantities of instruments exceeding the recommended run for the mimeograph, *offset printing* is recommended. The process requires a special machine to make paper or metal printing plates and an offset printing press. Many schools do not possess this expensive equipment, so it may be necessary to job out the printing of instruments when large quantities of a test are required. In addition to its usefulness in producing large quantities, the offset printing method produces the best copy in terms of clarity and professional appearance. Most published standardized tests are prepared via the offset method.

REFERENCES

Noll, V. H., and Scannell, D. P. *Introduction to Educational Measurement.* Boston: Houghton Mifflin, 1972.

Traxler, A. E. "Administering and Scoring the Objective Test." In Lindquist, E. F., ed., *Educational Measurement,* pp. 329–416. Washington, D.C.: American Council on Education, 1951.

Chapter 9

Evaluating Teacher-made Instruments

Our society relies very heavily on measurement instruments. When one considers any day of his life, numerous measuring devices are encountered. Auto speedometers, grocery store scales, gas pump meters, rulers, highway mile markers, and clocks are all examples of measuring devices. The federal government has established definite standards for measures and employs agencies to insure adherence to set standards. With measuring instruments in education and specifically occupational education, the same types of standards and quality control agencies do not exist. Instead, teachers and other test developers and users must continually monitor their instruments and make improvements in them when needed.

Preceding chapters have focused on writing items and developing composite measures by assembling items and preparing ancillary materials such as directions and scoring keys. This chapter focuses on evaluating instruments after they have been developed, reviewed, reproduced, and administered. Logically, the step or task referred to in each of chapters 5, 6, and 7, which suggests a review of instrument components and total instruments by students and colleagues, can be considered part of "evaluating the instrument." The procedures described in this chapter occur after an instrument has undergone this initial review and revision, and after the instrument has been administered to a group of students.

As indicated in chapter 1, *evaluation* implies determining worth or identifying weaknesses of something. The greatest use of evaluative results is in the improvement process. If an occupational program is being evaluated, the paramount purpose for the evaluation should be the improvement of the program. Likewise, evaluation of measurement instruments should focus on improvement of the instruments.

The evaluation of an instrument can be focused in two ways. First, the evaluation can focus on the individual parts of an instrument, for example, the specific items of a paper and pencil test or specific stages of a performance measure. Second, the instrument evaluation can focus on the instrument as a whole and consider such things as reliability and validity. Evaluation that focuses on individual items is often referred to as *item analysis* and ultimately contributes to the reliability and validity of an instrument. However, there are specific holistic concerns about the instrument such as reliability, validity, directions, and item organization that, too, must receive specific attention in the evaluative process. There are several purposes for partial and holistic approaches to evaluating instruments used in occupational programs.

PURPOSES FOR EVALUATING INSTRUMENTS

Improve the Instrument

The most important purpose for evaluating any instrument, as already mentioned, is to improve the instrument. Item-analysis procedures can aid the test developer in selecting adequate items from an item pool and in discarding items that are identified as inadequate. Additionally, item analyses can focus attention on items that need to be revised to help them more adequately measure what they were designed to measure. As the individual parts of an instrument are improved, indirectly, the instrument as a whole is improved. However, a holistic analysis of instruments can provide information that can directly aid the improvement of the instruments. Faulty or difficult procedures for administering or scoring a performance measure may be identified and deficient holistic aspects of a paper and pencil test such as directions and item organization may also be identified. As these types of deficiencies are identified, direct action can be taken to revise and improve the instruments. Other more sophisticated holistic-analysis measures can be used to judge the overall consistency or reliability and validity of an instrument. Refer to chapter 2 for a review or more detailed discussion of reliability and validity.

Facilitate and Reinforce Learning

Item-analysis information is useful in structuring student discussions regarding specific instruments. Items that were easy (having a high easiness index) may receive little or no discussion while items that had a variation in responses can be considered. For students who responded incorrectly to difficult items, discussion can clarify thinking, and they can learn from their mistakes. For those who scored correctly, the discussion can reinforce learning. Class discussion has a secondary, although important effect, in that it can often illuminate, for the teacher, item ambiguities and justification for responses other than the correct response. In these cases, learning can be clarified, scoring inequities remedied, and individual items improved.

Form Basis for Remedial Work

In addition to facilitating learning through class discussion of items, item-analysis information can also provide indications of students' strengths and weaknesses. For example, in reviewing students' response patterns on a Business Law exam, it is determined that one individual knows the appropriate terminology but is having trouble relating legal principles. This information can aid an instructor and student in planning remedial instruction or study to overcome the identified deficiency. Likewise, analysis of student-response patterns for performance tests could identify certain procedures or skills that should be practiced and worked on in greater depth.

Improve Instruction

Just as item-analysis information can be used to plan remedial instruction or to prescribe practice activity for individuals, the same information can be combined for a group to aid in making needed groupwide or course changes. For example, if an entire class of Business Law students experienced difficulty in relating legal principles, then this might indicate a deficiency in instruction. Possibly inadequate time was spent on the topic. Maybe the instructor did not use enough examples. Maybe students did not have the opportunity to apply principles during instruction. These are all feasible thoughts that an instructor might have after reviewing item-analysis data. Based upon judgments made by the instructor about the instruction, along with additional student input and suggestions, the instructor might consider and plan a remedial unit of instruction to reemphasize the relating of legal principles. Additionally, this information will undoubtedly affect the design of a subsequent offering of the same course. In this way item-analysis information can be used both to remediate current students and to aid in improving the future instructional program.

Provide Credibility Indices for Instruments

As discussed in chapter 10, reliability and validity indices should be considered in selecting and purchasing a standardized instrument. These holistic analysis measures or indices are important when selection decisions are made. However, they are important also for locally developed instruments. Everyone's goal is to maximize instrument reliability and validity. By calculating and reviewing reliability and validity indices, the test developer can determine if and when an instrument needs to be improved. It may be determined that the test should be lengthened or that it needs minor or total revision. In either case, improvement is the concern. However, as higher indices are achieved for locally developed instruments, they should be publicized to counselors and administrators to gain some recognition for a conscientious effort at test improvement.

Increase Skill in Test Construction

One additional positive side effect of evaluating tests and other instruments is an increase in skill, on the part of the instructor or test developer, in instrument development. This should ultimately lead to the future development of more valid and reliable instruments.

Also, the instrument development task will become more efficient. This increase in test development skills, when coupled with the use of an item file for keeping records of item-analysis data, will result in an overall improvement in the measurement procedures and techniques for the occupational program.

ITEM ANALYSIS

Item analysis, as mentioned earlier, has as its purpose (1) selecting items that are proven adequate, (2) identifying structural defects of items, (3) aiding in designing remedial instruction for individuals, and (4) aiding in instructional improvement. Traditionally, item analysis has focused on analyzing items in light of two basic statistics or indices: a difficulty or easiness index and a discrimination index. The *difficulty index* is the percentage of students tested who respond correctly to an item. A difficulty index of 85 for an item indicates that 85 percent of the examinees responded correctly to that particular item. Nunally (1972) suggests calling this index an easiness percentage because as a difficulty index, it is numerically backwards; the higher the number value such as 95, the lower the difficulty. The easiness percentage index has a direct numerical relationship rather than an inverted relationship and is easier for teachers and measurement specialists to remember and use.

The *discrimination index* provides a measure of how well an item discriminates between high scorers and low scorers on a test. It is based on the assumption that the total test provides a better measure of what it measures than does any single item included in the test. In essence, the discrimination index provides an index of how an item correlates with the total test.

Norm-referenced measures, as discussed in chapter 2, are used when it is important to know how a student performs when compared to other students. Norm-referenced measures are good when they can discriminate or separate individuals on the skill being assessed. They are even better when they can widen these differentiations. Difficulty is also related to discriminative power. Items must be difficult enough to cause segments of the group tested to respond incorrectly—thus widening the discrimination gap. The difficulty index, easiness percentage, and discrimination index all are appropriate for use with norm-referenced tests. However, only the latter has some value for mastery or criterion-referenced tests.

Criterion-referenced measures relate an individual's performance to an achievement continuum ranging from zero to maximum performance. A mastery test is a criterion-referenced measure for which a certain point on the achievement continuum has been determined as a mastery level. For instructional purposes, the goal is to bring each student to the point of mastery without regard for relative group comparisons. For this type of measure, a difficulty or easiness index is inappropriate since many items will be achieved by all but still contribute to the overall assessment of performance in regard to the continuum. Traditional discrimination indices have some value for criterion-referenced measures. A negatively discriminating item on either a norm-referenced or criterion-referenced instrument is equally suspicious. A negatively discriminating item is one for which more low scorers on the test respond correctly to the item than do high scorers. Cox and Vargas (1966) suggest a discrimination index that shows how an item discriminates between individuals who have received instruction and those who have not. This type of index has promise for assessing criterion-referenced items.

Conducting an Item Analysis—Norm-referenced

An item analysis can assume many different forms. A number of specific procedures are described by Downie (1958) and a number of those procedures have been adapted for computer use. If a test-scoring service is available in the educational agency, chances are that an item-analysis program is among the services available. If it is not, a program can be easily written or purchased. The *MERMAC Manual* (Costa, 1971) describes one set of available item-analysis software for IBM computer systems. Such programs can simplify the task of the item analysis and in most instances, provide for a more accurate analysis than could be computed by hand or with the aid of a calculator, and in less time.

There are, however, procedures that can be followed by occupational teachers to provide item-analysis data efficiently for small numbers (twenty to forty) students. If larger numbers are involved, the use of data processing equipment is suggested.

The basic procedure for computing the easiness percentage and the discrimination index for norm-referenced items is shown below.

STEP 1. Arrange scored answer sheets in rank order from highest score to the lowest. An alternate approach involves a class of students. In the alternate approach, students are lined up in the order of their test scores.

STEP 2. Identify a high- and a low-scoring group. These groups are taken one each from both ends of the ranked papers or students. The size of the total group is a factor in determining how many should be included in each of the high and low groups. For computer analyses, R. L. Brennan (1972) suggests that each group contain 27 percent of the total. For local analysis, between 25 and 35 percent should be included in each group. However, if a very small total group exists such as ten to fifteen students, 50 percent should be included in each group. Since group size is not really critical, each group should contain an even number to facilitate later calculations. For example, for a class of thirty-three students, the top ten and the bottom ten should be selected.

STEP 3. Separately record the responses for each group to each item alternative. This task can be completed by recording responses on two blank test answer sheets as shown in figure 9.1, or a special form or item card can be used such as the one shown in figure 9.2.

STEP 4. Sum for each item the total that responded correctly from both the high and the low group. Simply total the number of correct responses to each item and record this number on the answer sheet or form used for recording alternative responses.

STEP 5. Divide the number of correct responses for each item by the total number in the high and the low groups and multiply by 100. Each product is the easiness percentage or the difficulty index for its respective item. It approximates the percentage responding correctly to the item.

The formula for calculating the easiness percentage is:

$$EP \text{ (easiness percentage)} = \left(\frac{\text{high correct} + \text{low correct}}{\text{high } N + \text{low } N} \right) \times 100$$

where N = number of students in the group.

Item 1 of figure 9.1 would have an easiness percentage of 40 percent as shown below.

$$EP = \left(\frac{6 + 2}{20} \right) \times 100 = 40\%$$

High Group

Item	A	B	C	D
1.	~~1111~~1 *		111	1
2.		~~1111~~111 *	1	1
3.		111	111 *	111
4.		~~1111~~1 *	1111	
5.	11	1	1111 *	111
6.	~~1111~~1 *	11	1	1
7.	1	1	1111 *	
8.	~~1111~~	11		1111 *
9.	11	1	1111 *	111
10.	1111 *	1111	11	
11.	11		~~1111~~11 *	1
12.	11	111		1111 *
13.		~~1111~~11 *	11	1
14.	~~1111~~ *	1	11	11
15.	11	11	~~1111~~ *	1
16.		1111	1	~~1111~~ *
17.	11	1	~~1111~~ *	11
18.	111	11	1111 *	1
19.	1111 *	11	111	1
20.		~~1111~~ *	11	1111

Low Group

Item	A	B	C	D
11.	11	~~1111~~	1 *	11
12.		111	111	1111 *
13.	11	1 *	111	1111
14.	~~1111~~1 *		1111	
15.	111	1111	1 *	11
16.	11	111	111	1 *
17.	11	~~1111~~1	1 *	1
18.	~~1111~~	1	111 *	1
19.	11 *	111	111	11
20.	1	11 *	11	~~1111~~

*Correct Response

FIGURE 9.1. ***Blank Answer Sheets Used for Recording High and Low Group Responses.***

		T	F		
		A	B	C	D
Item 1	Upper	6 *	0	3	1
	Lower	2	0	6	2
Item 2	Upper	0	8 *	0	2
	Lower	8	2	0	0
Item 3	Upper	0	1	0	9 *
	Lower	3	1	2	4
Item 4	Upper	8 *	1	0	1
	Lower	3	2	5	0

*Correct Response

FIGURE 9.2. Special Form Used for Recording High and Low Group Responses.

The higher the easiness percentage, the easier the item.

STEP 6. For each item, subtract the number of correct responses in the low group from the number of correct responses in the high group. Using the same example item as used in step 5, the result would be 6 – 2 = 4: the difference between the high and low group correct responses for that item.

STEP 7. For each item, divide the difference between high and low groups by the number of students in one of the subgroups. The resulting decimal is the discrimination index. The formula for the discrimination index is:

$$DI \text{ (discrimination index)} = \frac{\text{high correct} - \text{low correct}}{\text{high } N}$$

where N = the number of students in the group.

Referring back to our example:

$$DI = \frac{6-2}{10} = 0.40$$

The procedures presented here for calculating easiness percentages and discrimination indices are adaptable for multiple-choice, true-false, and matching as well as other types of recall items. Additionally, some types of constructed-response items can be analyzed with similar techniques.

Swanson (1965) has suggested the use of a nomograph for determining the discrimination index of items that eliminates lengthy mathematical manipulations. This process is summarized in six steps.

STEP 1. Separate the test papers into three groups on the basis of total test scores.

- Group I—the best 25% of the papers
- Group II—the poorest 25% of the papers
- Group III—the middle 50% of the papers

STEP 2. Determine the percentage of group I getting the item correct.

STEP 3. Locate this point on the left scale of figure 9.3.

STEP 4. Determine the percentage of group II getting the item correct.

STEP 5. Locate this point on the right scale of figure 9.3.

STEP 6. Connect the two points (steps 3 and 5) with a straight edge. At the point of intersection on the center scale read the discrimination index.

Conducting an Item Analysis—Criterion-referenced

The item analyses used for norm-referenced measures are not appropriate for criterion-referenced measures except for the use of discrimination indices to indicate gross deficiency such as in identifying items that discriminate negatively. The development of item and test "adequacy indices" for criterion-referenced instruments is in

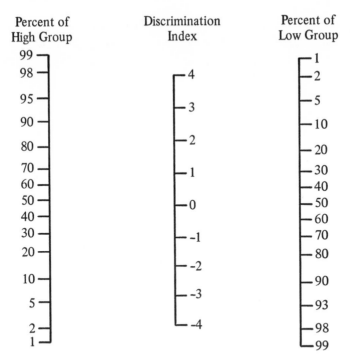

FIGURE 9.3. Nomograph for Determining Discrimination Index of Test Items.

its infancy. The early developmental years have brought a great deal of professional dialogue on the topics of item analysis, reliability, and validity as they pertain to criterion-referenced testing. Refer to Popham (1974), Gronlund (1973), Cox and Vargas (1966), and Popham and Husek (1969) for technical discussions and proposed approaches.

Millman (1974) has identified, after considerable review and tryout, three methods of analyzing and selecting criterion-referenced items. Crehan (1974) has identified five methods, some of which overlap with Millman's three. Several of these approaches are beyond the practical time, expertise, and computer-facility limits imposed upon most instructional personnel. Crehan (1974) identified two basic types of item analysis to be used in improving criterion-referenced instruments that can be easily conducted by occupational teachers.

The first approach involves the calculation of a *difference index.* The difference index, first tried by Cox and Vargas (1966), is an index of how well each item discriminates, not between a high group and a low group as with norm-referenced testing, but between two different administrations of the same instrument—one occurring prior to instruction and one following instruction. This index aids in identifying items that actually measure the intended learning. Items whose difference index does not increase in magnitude from pre-administration to postadministration, as Popham (1971) indicates, are suspect. Also, items whose index indicates a decrease in the number of students who answer them correctly from the first admin-istration to the second are either faulty or the interim instruction is causing confusion as to the subject content being measured.

The Cox–Vargas (1966) approach is procedurally summarized below.

STEP 1. Tabulate the number of correct responses for each item in the pretest. A form such as the one shown in figure 9.1, used with computing the easiness percentage for norm-referenced instruments, can be used in this step.

STEP 2. Tabulate the number of correct responses for each item in the posttest.

STEP 3. Divide the number correct on the pretest by the number of students in the pretest group.

$$\text{Pretest value} = \frac{\text{No. correct}}{\text{No. in group}}$$

STEP 4. Divide the number correct on the posttest by the num-ber of students in the posttest group.

$$\text{Posttest value} = \frac{\text{No. correct}}{\text{No. in group}}$$

STEP 5. Subtract the pretest value from the posttest value and multiply by 100. The remainder is the difference index. The for-mula for the difference index is:

$$DI \text{ (Difference index)} = \frac{\text{No. correct} - \text{post}}{N \text{ post}} - \frac{\text{No. correct} - \text{pre}}{N \text{ pre}} \times 100$$

where N = the number of students in the group.

This approach is useful in identifying items that should be looked at more closely in terms of revision or should be discarded. A second approach to analyzing criterion–referenced items com-bines the approach just described with the approach described beginning on page 265. Since the basic procedure is similar for this approach as it is for other approaches, a detailed process is not outlined here. Instead, the mathematical formula is presented with each component or factor identified. The resulting index is an adaptation of one formulated by Brennan (1972) and adapted by Crehan (1974). It is referred to here as the *Brennan Index* and it is calculated with the formula:

$$B = \left(\frac{N \text{ right}}{N_1} \right) - \left(\frac{N \text{ wrong}}{N_2} \right)$$

where B = Brennan's index
N_1 = number of students in the instructed group
N_2 = number of students in the uninstructed group
N right = number of students in N_1 who got item correct
N wrong = number of students in N_2 who got item correct

It is important to note that N_1 and N_2 are identified as instructed and uninstructed groups. These can correspond to either pretest and posttest measures or they can be two randomly selected groups— one receiving instruction while the other does not.

Additional Item-analysis Procedures—Appropriate for Norm-referenced and Criterion-referenced Tests

There are several additional ways of observing item character that can aid in meeting one or more of the purposes outlined earlier in this chapter. One way of looking at items without any statistical manipulation involves displaying item responses by individual respondents. A chart such as the one shown in table 9.1 presents item responses for each student in the class. The plus (+) sign indicates a correct response and a minus (–) sign indicates an incorrect response. It might also be noted that items have been grouped according to topical areas or specific segments of the table of specifications upon which the design of the instrument was originally based—in this case, a segment of the fire science program.

A completed chart such as the one shown in table 9.1 is useful in several ways: first, the chart can be used in identifying items that were responded to incorrectly by a majority of the class. This provides a simple difficulty index without actually conducting the specific item analysis using high and low groups. By knowing that an item was responded to incorrectly by a large number of students, the test constructor can look more closely at that item and the instructions relating to it to find out why it was missed.

TABLE 9.1. Summary Chart for Showing Individual Student Responses

Objective			Terminology—Fire Science										
	Fire Types			Flammable Liquids				Flammable Solids				Fighting Agents	
Content Area													
Items	1 2 3			4 5 6 7				8 9 10 11				12 13 14	
Students:													
Jake Gabe	+ + +			− − + −				+ + − +				− − +	
Jack Walter	+ + +			+ − + +				+ + + −				− + +	
Jack Daniels	+ − +			− − + +				− − + +				+ − −	
Hiram Walker	+ + +			− − + +				+ + + +				− + −	
Jill Smith	+ + +			+ − − +				− − − +				+ − −	
Frida White	− − −			− − + +				+ + + +				+ + −	
Carol Music	+ + +			+ + + −				− − − +				− + −	
Leroy Brown	+ + +			+ − + −				− + + −				+ − +	

Second, the chart can aid in identifying individuals who may be having trouble learning the course material. Frida White in Table 9.1 had considerable difficulty on the fire science mastery test. The instructor may wish, based upon this analysis, to prescribe remedial work for this student to bring her up to a level of mastery.

Another item-analysis technique that can be used with either norm-referenced or criterion-referenced items focuses on the in-dividual components of an item as opposed to identifying deficient items. A form such as the one shown in figure 9.4 is used to tally responses to each item alternative. The tally used for determining the easiness percentage (figure 9.1) can easily be used for this purpose. It is extra beneficial to know how the high group as well as the low group has responded to each item. By having a picture of item-response pattern, alternatives can be assessed as to their adequacy as distractors or foils. For example, a distractor for a multiple-choice item would be viewed as effective if it was chosen by few if any students in the high group and received a large segment of the low group's responses. In this case, it was attractive to those who did not score well on the test as a whole—an ideal situation.

Gronlund (1973) has suggested a third analysis technique, which is a simplified version of one suggested for criterion-referenced measures, although it has utility for any type of measure. This tech-nique requires the administration of a pretest and a posttest. How-ever, rather than making computations as suggested in the Cox-Vargas difference index, a chart such as the one shown in table 9.2

High Group

	A	B	C	D
1.	~~1111~~1 *		111	1
2.		~~1111~~111 *	1	1
3.		111	111	111 *
4.		~~1111~~1 *	1111	
5.	11	1	1111 *	111
6.	~~1111~~1 *	11	1	1
7.	1	1111	~~1111~~ *	
8.	~~1111~~	11		1111 *
9.	11	1	1111 *	111
10.	1111	1111 *	11	

	A	B	C	D
11.	11		~~1111~~11 *	1
12.	11	111		~~1111~~ *
13.		~~1111~~11 *	11	1
14.	~~1111~~ *	1	11	11
15.	11	11	~~1111~~ *	1
16.		1111	1	~~1111~~ *
17.	11	1	~~1111~~ *	11
18.	111	11	1111 *	1
19.	1111 *	11	111	1
20.		~~1111~~ *	11	1111

Low Group

	A	B	C	D
11.	11	~~1111~~	1 *	11
12.		111	111	1111 *
13.	11	1 *	111	1111
14.	~~1111~~1 *		1111	
15.	111	1111	1 *	11
16.	11	111	1111	1 *
17.	11	~~1111~~1	1 *	1
18.	~~1111~~	1	111 *	1
19.	11 *	111	111	11
20.	1	11 *	11	~~1111~~

*Correct Response

FIGURE 9.4. Tally Sheet Used in Identifying Adequate Item Alternatives.

TABLE 9.2.   *Item by Student Display for Pretest and Posttest*

	Item Number												
	1		2		3		4		5		6		7
	B A		B A		B A		B A		B A		B A		B A
James Walker	− +		− +		− +		− +		− +		− +		− +
Bill Smith	− +		− +		+ −		+ +		+ +		− +		− +
John Jones	− +		− +		− +		+ +		− +		− +		− +
Linda White	− +		+ +		− +		+ +		+ +		− +		− +
Bob Baker	− +		− +		+ +		+ +		+ +		− +		− +
Carol Black	− +		− +		− +		+ +		− +		− +		− +
Nancy Daniels	− +		− +		− +		+ +		+ +		− +		− +
Steve Brown	− +		− +		+ +		+ +		+ +		− +		− +

is developed. This chart (see table 9.2) incorporates a plotting of students against test items and space is provided for tabulation of both pretest and posttest responses. It can provide, in an easy glance, an indication of improvement for each student as well as aid in identification of items that may be discriminating in the wrong direction.

Use of Item-analysis Results

The primary purpose of an item analysis is to improve the instrument by identifying deficient items so they can be revised or discarded. Secondary functions include the facilitation of learning and the improvement of individual and group instruction.

Easiness Percentage.   The *easiness percentage* indicates the percentage of a group responding correctly to an item. This index is inappropriate for criterion-referenced instruments. The goal for these instruments is that all students achieve mastery. For norm-referenced tests, items that are too difficult or too easy are not the most desired. A number of testing authorities have shown that a difficulty level of 50 percent is ideal for maximizing reliability (internal consistency). In other words, items with an easiness percentage of 50 allow discrimination indices to obtain their maximum value. However, as suggested in chapter 8, some easy items should be placed at the beginning of an instrument to lower anxiety and produce some initial reinforcement in the testing situation. This may, though, lower reliability estimates. Payne (1968) suggests the limiting of item difficulties to a range between 30 and 70 percent and the use of caution in interpreting reliability coefficients for classroom tests. Some test developers recommend that difficulty indices for a test be selected such that they take the form of a normal curve—indices ranging from 0.20 to 0.80 with the majority of them clustering around 0.50.

Discrimination Indices. The discrimination index used for norm-referenced measures determines if an item can be used to differentiate between high-achieving students and low-achieving students. If all high achievers respond correctly and all low achievers respond incorrectly to an item, the item would discriminate perfectly with a value of +1.00 and correlate perfectly with the total test.

It is important that all items discriminate positively, regardless of degree, in the case of additive scoring, that is, if correct item responses are to be added to form a total score. If one item discriminated negatively, it would cancel out a positively discriminating item from the total score. In selecting items for retention in an instrument and for identifying those that need revision, Ebel (1972) suggests items above +0.40 should be chosen and those with indices below +0.40 should be improved or deleted.

Cox–Vargas Difference Index and Brennan's Index.   Both the Cox–Vargas difference index and the adapted Brennan index are appropriate for criterion-referenced measures and both require administration of the instrument to a student group prior to and following instruction. These two indices, like the discrimination index and the easiness percentage, aid in identifying items that are deficient. Rather than discriminating between low and high achievers, however, they determine how an item discriminated between naive and knowledgeable learners. Items that fall below 0.50 on either index should be observed for possible revision or replacement.

A side effect of using either of the criterion-referenced indices lies in the use of pretest scores. These scores can be used for making placement decisions for students with regard to the instructional program. That is, if a student demonstrates proficiency on several topics or course segments prior to instruction, he may be placed in advanced segments of the course, if it is individualized, or he may be given advanced assignments or projects. Additionally, pretest information for an entire class may be useful to an instructor in designing instruction to meet the group's specific needs without spending undue time and resources on areas which students have already mastered.

The use of the three chart-type analyses described in the previous section should not be overlooked in terms of the information they can provide for making placement and instructional design decisions as well as for improvement of instruments.

Limitations of Item Analyses

Small Sample of Students.   There are several limitations to item analyses that deserve mention: first, most item analyses conducted by teachers involve a relatively small number of individuals in the sample. Item analyses for standardized instruments are based upon hundreds of cases as opposed to twenty or forty in most classes. In the latter situation, a shift in one or two responses could ultimately affect decisions about items. Therefore, item-analyses information for small groups should be considered tentative and only an estimation. Other data and personal judgment should play key roles in ultimate decisions about item retention and revision.

Applicability to Speed Tests.   The item-analysis techniques described in this chapter are inappropriate for all items of tests that are designed to be speed tests. Speed tests as defined in chapter 3 are designed to include items of close to equal difficulty but long enough so that no one will complete the entire test. Obviously, not all items will be responded to, and to include these items in a strict item analysis would be in error.

Effect on Content Validity.   In norm-referenced measures, a low discrimination index for some items may result in deletion or revision for use in future tests. This could affect the content validity of the test, as indicated on page 33 of chapter 2. Ultimately, and what usually happens in the development of standardized instruments, is that subtests are considered and items are improved with specific content of the subtests in mind. This helps maintain direction on the focus of the test and aids in maintaining content validity.

Applicability to Essay Tests. Both Payne (1968) and Ahmann and Glock (1975) identify the lack of appropriate procedures for handling essay items in item analysis as a definite shortcoming. Even though procedures for analyzing objective items can be adapted for essay tests, the problem of reliable scoring and the tabulation of incorrect responses limits their use. The restricted type of essay item described in chapter 5 is the most easily handled of all essay items.

Payne (1968) makes a strong caution that is worthy of emphasis here when considering item analysis. It is: "Don't be blinded by statistics." In essence, he cautions that statistics in the form of any of the indices mentioned in this chapter should not be used exclusively in making test improvement decisions. These statistics should be used as simple tools and not as an automated machine.

HOLISTIC-INSTRUMENT EVALUATION

The preceding sections of this chapter focused on analyzing and evaluating the items of instruments. It would be incorrect to assume that an instrument made up of items that have appropriate difficulties and discrimination powers—either norm- or criterion-referenced—is an adequate total instrument. An analogous situation would be the measurement and evaluation of each part of a jeweled watch (an item analysis), having each part fall within acceptable quality control standards but just dumped into a cardboard box rather than assembled and adjusted to build a quality timepiece. This emphasizes the need to look at the total instrument in terms of its composition and its adequacy in meeting its desired purpose. In essence, a holistic view of an instrument implies that the whole is greater than the sum of its individual parts. Holistic-evaluation procedures will help determine which of these possibilities is the case.

Looking at an instrument holistically can assume two different approaches: validity assessment and reliability assessment.

Validity

Validity, as defined in chapter 2, refers to the degree to which an instrument or test measures what it was designed to measure. Validity is the most important characteristic of any instrument. No matter how good individual items are, no matter how high reliability coefficients might be, without high validity, an instrument is useless. Chapter 2 described four types of validity. The validity indices that are associated with these validity types are yielded in several different ways. Table 9.3 presents the four validity types, an indication of the information they provide, and a brief description of how they are determined. The sections following provide in more detail actual validation procedures with suggested uses to be made of results.

Content Validity. *Content validity* is concerned with determining the relationship a test's content has to the behavioral or achievement domain being focused on by instruction. Content validity, unlike the other three validity types, is assessed without any statistical computation or empirical analysis. Instead a logical analysis is done that involves the professional judgment of one or more knowledgeable individuals.

In determining content validity, interest in knowing if an instrument is relevant to instruction or other behavior-modification scheme is important. Obviously, this type of validity is most appropriate for achievement tests—cognitive, affective, or performance. In most occupational programs, it is impossible to assess the attainment of every objective with a single exam or instrument. Therefore, a sampling procedure must be used to choose a representative group of objectives for measurement. Content-validation procedures focus on identifying how well the chosen sample represents the total number of actual objectives. For example, if an instructor of secretarial science had 90 objectives relating to three broad content areas, a logical assessment of the number of items on a 30-item instrument that pertains to each of the three areas would be important. This judgmental process would have to consider the importance of each area as well as its size. Additionally, the difficulty or complexity of objectives in sampling would also have to be considered to insure that all easily attainable objectives were not chosen.

Content-validation procedures are simplified when a table of specifications has been used and other procedures for test development described in chapters 4 through 6 have been followed. If these procedures have been followed, the validation will involve a check on this system. The procedure outlined below assumes lack of adherence to the development procedures. If they have been followed, steps 1 through 3 may be omitted.

TABLE 9.3. Summary of Validity Types and Their Computational Method

Validity Type	Information Provided	Procedure
Content	How well the instrument reflects the subject matter of instruction or content of objectives.	Compare instrument with established objectives or table of specifications.
Predictive	How well the instrument predicts performance in future training, careers, or other activities.	Compare obtained scores with another measure obtained later in a follow-up study.
Concurrent	How closely the instrument compares with other instruments that focus on the same behavior.	Compare scores with scores from other instruments administered at nearly the same time.
Construct	How test scores can be explained in terms of psychological phenomena.	Use research methods to test psychological hypotheses.

STEP 1. Identify the major topical areas of instruction covered by the test. This may involve review of a course outline and/or review of class lesson plans or course activities.

STEP 2. Identify area of desired behavioral change. Focus on course goals to determine domains of learning (i.e., cognitive, affective, psychomotor, and perceptual) and specific levels within those domains (i.e., understanding, receiving).

STEP 3. Construct a chart that incorporates the information gleaned from steps 1 and 2. This chart is similar to the tables of specifications shown in tables 4.1 and 4.3 in chapter 4. If tables of specifications are already available, the first three steps can be omitted. Table 9.3 provides an example chart.

STEP 4. Establish an importance value or percentage to each topical area by each behavioral area. This value should represent the instructor's judgment of either time spent in instruction on each topic or overall judgment of importance of each topic. These values should total 100 percent for the entire content area. Table 9.4 shows

TABLE 9.4. Sample Content Validity Table of Specifications

Course Content	Types and Levels of Learning	
	Understanding	Doing
I. Fire behavior science		
1. Principles of com-		
bustion	20%	5%
2. Classes of fire	10%	5%
3. Flammable liquids	10%	50%
a. Identification		
b. Flashpoint		
c. Ignition point		
d. Transporting	——	——
	40%	60%

the division of content for a course segment. Note that the division for cognitive and performance is 40 percent and 60 percent respectively.

STEP 5. Have a knowledgeable individual review the instrument and categorize items into the topic–behavior chart. The reviewer should sort each instrument item into categories determined in steps 1 and 2. A chart similar to table 9.4 can be used for tabulation. Categorization should consider both subject matter divisions as well as learning domains.

STEP 6. Calculate percentages for each subject matter and learning domain. Divide the number of items in each category by the total number of items and multiply each dividend by 100.

STEP 7. Compare the first chart developed in steps 1–4 with the chart completed in step 6. The comparison of the two charts provides input for making judgments about content validity. It may be found that certain topical or content categories of items receive emphasis in the test that are disproportionate when compared to the original instructional design. Also, it is possible that a test may place too much emphasis on one learning domain at the expense of another. For example, a secretarial science course might have both knowledge and doing objectives, yet the test might emphasize the knowledge objectives without providing for the adequate sampling of doing objectives.

Another potential finding of content validation is the identification of items that cannot be placed into one of the selected categories by the test reviewer. That is, an item or items may have been included in an instrument when in fact they were unnecessary.

Predictive Validity. *Predictive validity* is concerned with how well an instrument predicts or forecasts performance in a future activity. Where content validity was most appropriate for achievement tests, predictive validity is appropriate for aptitude measures. As mentioned in chapter 1, aptitude measures are tools used in estimating the probability that, with appropriate instruction or training, an individual will be able to succeed in a particular occupation or career. Instruments can also be used to predict performance in advanced-training programs and other activities. Obviously, these types of measures are valuable to students and counselors in facilitating career decisions. They are also useful to corporate managers in selecting individuals for management and other types of positions. Therefore, for instruments to be adequate and useful in these settings, it is important that they possess high predictive validity.

Predictive validity, in simple terms, is the degree to which scores on an instrument correlate or relate to a future performance measure such as job success or success in an advanced-occupational program. *Correlation* is a simple mathematical calculation that results in a correlation coefficient. If two things correlate perfectly, that is, if they are directly related, the resulting correlation coefficient would be equal to +1.00. A simple example is the accelerator pedal in your automobile. As you push forward on the pedal (when the car is in forward gear) the car goes forward. Therefore, when the car is in forward gear, and you step on the gas pedal, you can predict perfectly that the car will go forward. If two things happen in opposite directions and always in opposing ways, they are said to correlate negatively perfect and possess a correlation coefficient of –1.00. An example might be applying brakes in your auto and the slowing of the car. As the brake pedal is moved forward, the car slows or stops. These are opposing happenings with a negative correlation.

Now, not all cars will perform perfectly the way described above. Some cars, when accelerated, may sputter and die. Likewise, when the brakes are applied in a number of automobiles, some may fail and some may stop more slowly than others. Some may have power brakes, which makes the relationship different. Therefore, correlations, over a number of cases, may range anywhere between +1.00 and –1.00.

The correlation coefficient is universally understood among all measurement specialists and an increasing number of instructional personnel. Therefore, it provides an excellent mode for expressing the degree of predictive validity.

Predictive validity, as previously mentioned, is determined by calculating the correlation between a set of scores on an instrument and a set of scores for a later performance that are achieved by the same individuals. One of the most useful and efficient correlation techniques for calculating predictive validity is *rank-order correlation* (rho). The following procedure outlines the entire predictive-validity procedure. Steps 2 and 4 through 8 are general rank-order correlation methods and can be applied to other types of validity and other needs.

STEP 1. Administer the instrument to a group of students. This administration will most likely be of an aptitude measure; however, often an end of course achievement measure may be used in a predictive way for counseling or selection purposes.

STEP 2. Rank order each student in the group according to his or her score and place names, scores, and ranks on a summary table. The summary shown in table 9.5 can be used for this purpose. Place test scores and ranks in columns 1 and 3 respectively.

STEP 3. After the students tested in step 1 have entered a job or advanced training program, obtain another measure of their actual job performance or success in the training program. This second measure or obtained score is the validation criterion and can be in many different forms. It may be an employer rating as suggested in chapter 6 or it may be an achievement test score or grade in an advanced training program. For example, here, consider employer ratings on a form ranging from 0 to 80 possible points.

STEP 4. Assign a rank to each student based upon the employer rating and enter scores and ranks on form. The scores and ranks should be entered in columns 2 and 4 of table 9.5 respectively.

STEP 5. Find the difference in each student's ranks by subtracting the rank in column 4 from the rank in column 3. Enter the difference in ranks for each individual in column 5 of table 9.5.

TABLE 9.5. Summary Table for Use in Correlating Two Measures

	1	2	3	4	5	6
Name	Test Score	Employer Rating	Test Rank	Employer Rating Rank	(D) Difference in Rank	D² Difference Squared
Bill	120	76	1	3	-2	4
Mary	119	75	2	4	-2	4
Zeke	117	71	3	5	-2	4
Carl	116	66	4	7	-3	9
Lloyd	113	80	5	1	4	16
Hazel	110	62	6	8	-2	4
Judy	109	59	7	9	-2	4
Bob	107	77	8	2	6	36
Mildred	106	68	9	6	3	9
Paul	105	48	10	13	-3	9
Jake	103	47	11	14	-3	9
Chuck	101	57	12	10	2	4
Tom	99	55	13	12	1	1
Burt	98	56	14	11	3	9
					Total D^2 =	122

STEP 6. Square each difference in rank (column 5) and enter the product in column 6. This results in differences squared and all numbers become positive.

STEP 7. Sum or add the differences squared in column 6 to find ΣD^2. In the example shown in table 9.5 the ΣD^2 =122.

STEP 8. Calculate the correlation coefficient (rho) using the formula:

$$\rho \text{ (rho)} = 1 - \frac{6 \times \Sigma D^2}{N(N^2 - 1)}$$

where: Σ = sum of that which follows
D = difference in rank
N = number in the group

Using the above formula with the example data printed in table 9.5, the correlation coefficient or validity coefficient is 0.73.

$$\rho = 1 - \frac{6 \times 122}{14(14^2 - 1)}$$

$$= 1 - \frac{732}{14(195)}$$

$$= 1 - \frac{732}{2730}$$

$$= 1 - 0.27$$

$$\rho = 0.73$$

A validity coefficient of 0.73 means that a pretty strong relationship exists between the test scores and the criterion measures, employer ratings in this case. This relationship can be viewed by observing the similarities in ranks of the two measures in columns 3 and 4 of table 9.5. For example, Bill had ranks of 1 and 3, Mary 2 and 4, Zeke 3 and 5, and Carl 4 and 7. If there had been a negative relationship or a low validity coefficient, ranks might have been 1 and 12, 2 and 13, 3 and 10, and so on.

A logical question is: "How good is a validity coefficient of 0.73?" This is a common question; however, there is no clear-cut answer nor is there a set of standards to which the value may be compared. The value becomes important to the use to which it will be put (the reason for which it was calculated) and the validities of other existing instruments that may be substituted.

As mentioned earlier, most instruments for which predictive validity is important are aptitude tests. This does not necessarily hold true in all cases, however. Interest measures, achievement measures, and measures of general mental ability are frequently used to predict success in some career or job. For example, all final examinations (achievement tests) for an advanced-level occupational course should possess high validity for predicting success in more advanced technical training or in employment after graduation. With validity correlates, the higher the validity, the more accurate the prediction can be. Therefore, in the case of our example, if standardized measures exist that have a higher predictive validity with the criterion we wish to predict and require the same time to administer and have the same cost, then the instrument with the highest validity should be used.

With locally developed instruments, attempts should be made to improve the instrument to increase its predictive validity. Subsequent validity checks should be made periodically to determine if the coefficient has changed.

In addition to using correlative coefficients and scattergrams to demonstrate predictive validity, simple expectancy tables can be easily constructed and used by occupational personnel to show the practical relationship between test scores and some criterion variable. The scores of the test and the employer ratings used in table 9.5, for example, can easily be plotted in the two-dimensional matrix with ranges of scores used to categorize each student's performance. Detailed procedures for developing expectancy tables are presented in chapter 12.

The expectancy table shown in table 9.6 is useful in demonstrating the relationship between students' original test scores and their future performances. For example, if a new student scored 115 on the test, it is fairly predictable that the individual would be rated over 65 by an employer. Likewise, an individual scoring below 102 would likely be rated below 65 by an employer.

TABLE 9.6. *Sample Expectancy Table Converted to Percentages*

Test Scores	Employer Ratings			
	45-54	55-64	65-74	75-84
111-120	0	0	40%	60%
103-110	33%	33%	17%	17%
90-102		100%		

When using locally developed expectancy tables such as the one shown in table 9.6, caution must be exercised because of the few cases that may be used in its formulation. Expectancy tables for standardized instruments usually include hundreds of individuals in each cell, which usually provide a more accurate demonstration of validity.

Concurrent Validity. Concurrent *validity,* as described in chapter 2, is very similar to predictive validity, and the techniques used to compute a concurrent validity coefficient are identical to those used to compute predictive validity. Concurrent validity is concerned primarily with determining how well an instrument measures what some other instrument measures. For example, an occupational instructor may wish to develop a paper and pencil test to replace a time-consuming work-sample test that requires individual administration. After its development, the instructor is interested in determining how well the paper and pencil test compares to the work-sample test in terms of its ability to measure the same achievement. The process used to determine the relationship between the scores on these two tests, then, is concurrent validation. It involves the administration of the work-sample performance instrument to a number of individuals and soon after administering the paper and pencil measure. Then the correlation or relationship between the two can be computed, which results in a concurrent-validity coefficient. Obviously, if the paper and pencil test does have high validity it would increase testing efficiency immensely because it would provide similar measures of students without requiring as much time, equipment, and observation. The procedure for conducting a concurrent validation is shown below.

STEP 1. Administer the existing measure, which has an established high validity.

STEP 2. Administer the newly devised instrument to the same individuals as soon after the administration of the first instrument as possible.

STEP 3. Compute the correlation between the two groups of scores using the rank-difference method presented in the preceding section or the Pearson Product Moment Method described in Appendix A.

STEP 4. Based upon the obtained coefficient, make decisions regarding the adoption of the new instrument or take action to improve it and recheck its concurrent validity.

As can be easily seen, the use of concurrent-validity procedures will not be an everyday occurrence for most instructional personnel. But in some cases such as the one described it is feasible. Generally, if a valid test already exists that does not require an extreme amount of time or that is not very costly, a new instrument usually will not warrant development and validation. Too much time and effort would be involved for the typical occupational instructor to undertake such a task.

Construct Validity. *Construct validity* is the form of validity that is the most abstract of the four validity types and has probably the least utility to occupational instructors. Construct validation is concerned with identifying psychological constructs or theoretical principles. The procedure followed involves structured inquiry involving a number of information sources and a number of research methods. There is no set procedure for determining construct validity nor does it result in a single-correlation coefficient. It usually begins with observing an instrument in a manner such as that used in content validation followed by the statement of hypothesis to be tested through research effort.

For example, an instrument may focus on the assessment of students' career interests. Career interest is a construct, just as intelligence, reasoning, and spacial ability might also be considered constructs. The instrument developed to assess career interests, in construct validation, is studied to learn more about what a resulting score really means. Gronlund (1973) suggests that content validation, predictive validation, and concurrent validation all may be used in determining construct validity in addition to the use of other empirical approaches. Cronbach and Meehl (1955) indicate that the construct as well as the instrument are being validated in this process. Therefore, much can be learned about the nature of career interests and how they can most adequately be measured through construct validation.

Reliability

Reliability is a second major concern in holistically evaluating an instrument. Reliability as defined in chapter 2 is the degree to which an instrument provides a trustworthy or consistent measure of whatever it does measure. The degree of consistency is another way of considering reliability. If an instrument has high reliability it is highly consistent in its measurement. Chapter 2 identified three types of reliability coefficients. The coefficients are designed to be used with norm-referenced instruments when variability in scores is desirable. The procedures for computing reliability for norm-referenced measures rely on classical test models, which are based upon variability. Therefore, the approaches discussed in this section are inappropriate for criterion-referenced tests. Measurement theorists are currently involved in extensive dialogue and testing of alternate approaches to reliability for criterion-referenced instruments and what is happening is very formative. A brief presentation is made at the end of this chapter on some of the more promising approaches but the specific offerings of procedures for calculation would be premature for the purposes of this text. Table 9.7 summarizes the three types of reliability coefficients discussed in chapter 2. Each type of reliability coefficient is presented with an indication of the information provided and the procedures used for calculation.

TABLE 9.7. Summary of Reliability Coefficients and Their Computational Method

Reliability Coefficient	Information Provided	Procedure
Stability	A measure of consistency from one administration of an instrument to another	Compare the results on two administrations of the same instrument to the same individuals with any time lapse ensuing.
Equivalence	To determine the likeness of two different forms of the same instrument	Compare two parallel forms of the same instrument by administering them in close succession.
Internal consistency (split half)	To determine how consistent segments of the test are with the total	Compare two halves (odd and even items) of the test and make correction for length with special formula.
Internal consistency (Kuder–Richardson)	To determine how consistent segments of the test are with the total	Apply special formula to test results.

Table 9.7 covers stability, equivalence, and internal-consistency reliability coefficients with two approaches to the latter. Following segments focus on a presentation of procedures and demonstration of use for each.

Stability.   *Stability* of an instrument is the degree to which an instrument measures consistently over a period. The calculation of a stability coefficient involves the readministration of the same instrument to the same group of individuals with a lapse of time between administrations. The method used, often called the *test–retest method,* incorporates the computation of the correlation between the sets of scores obtained from the two administrations. The test-retest approach attempts to determine, for example, if scores a-chieved on Monday morning are the same as they would be if the test were administered on a following Friday morning. It attempts to determine if the test is "robust" with respect to day-to-day differences in the individuals tested. To summarize, the procedure is as follows:

STEP 1. Administer the instrument.

STEP 2. Readminister the instrument after a time lapse.

STEP 3. Compute the correlation between the two instruments.

The correlation is equal to the stability coefficient. Most teachers will not often compute stability coefficients but in the selection of standardized instruments, it is an important criterion.

Equivalence. The *equivalence coefficient* provides a measure of how well two parallel forms of the same test measure the same thing. In other words, each test has been based upon a sampling of content from a content universe. The equivalence method makes a comparison between the two instruments to determine if they are both sampling the same behavior. The equivalence coefficient is determined by administering the equivalent forms of the instrument to the same students without a lapse of time between administrations. The steps involved are:

STEP 1. Administer form A to a group of students.

STEP 2. Administer form B to the same group of students immediately.

STEP 3. Compute the correlation between the two groups of resulting scores.

A resulting low equivalence coefficient indicates that there is little relationship between the two forms of the test and that the sampling of content is not equivalent for each test. Likewise, a high coefficient would indicate that both forms were measuring the same content.

Internal Consistency.   The *internal-consistency coefficient* provides an indication of how well each item or subsection of a test is consistent with the remaining items or subsections. It seeks to answer the question, how homogeneous is the instrument? There are two basic procedures for calculating the internal-consistency coefficient: the first of these is the split-half method. The *split-half method* is very similar to the equivalent-forms method. Rather than having two separate forms, one instrument is divided into two equal parts, then the scores for the two halves are correlated. The resulting correlation coefficient represents the correlation of two half tests. The Spearman-Brown Prophecy Formula is applied to the half-test correlation to provide an estimate of correlation or reliability for the whole test. The procedure is briefly described below.

STEP 1. Administer the instrument to a group of students.

STEP 2. Score the instrument in two halves. It is usually suggested that all even-numbered items make up one half while odd-numbered items form the other half.

STEP 3. Compute the correlation (rho or Pearson *r*) between the scores for the two halves.

STEP 4. Apply the Spearman-Brown Formula to the resulting correlation coefficient. This formula is:

$$\text{Reliability of total test} = \frac{2 \ \times \ \text{reliability of } \frac{1}{2} \text{ test}}{1 \ + \ \text{reliability of } \frac{1}{2} \text{ test}}$$

A high reliability coefficient for split halves denotes a high degree of equivalency between the two halves of the test and supports the notion that the two halves represent the sample-achievement universe.

A second procedure for determining internal consistency is the *Kuder–Richardson method.* This method does not require the splitting of the test or dual administration. Instead, a special formula called the Kuder–Richardson Formula 20 is used. This formula is based upon the proportion of persons scoring correctly on each item and the standard deviation[1] of the distribution of test scores. This formula is somewhat cumbersome unless a detailed item analysis has been conducted to determine the proportion responding correctly to each item.

---

1. See pages 371-373 in chapter 12 for computational instructions for the standard deviation.

An alternative to the Kuder–Richardson Formula 20 is a second formula that is not as accurate but is much easier to apply. This formula is the Kuder–Richardson Formula 21:

$$\text{Reliability coefficient } (KR\ 21) = \frac{K}{K-1}\left(1 - \frac{Mn(K-Mn)}{K(SD)^2}\right)$$

where: K = the number of items in the test
Mn = the mean or average score
SD = the standard deviation of the scores

The resulting coefficient provides a fairly accurate measure of internal consistency and a liberal estimate of Kuder–Richardson Formula 20. The ease in which the Kuder–Richardson Formula 21 can be applied makes it the most popular form of reliability index.

One should be cautioned when using speed tests or tests with speed components. These particular tests that have a built-in limitation to completion by students should not be analyzed for internal consistency by using the Kuder–Richardson Formula 21.

New Developments in Reliability Coefficients for Criterion-referenced Measures

As mentioned previously, the development of adequacy indices that are appropriate for criterion-referenced instruments is in its infancy. There is, however, a considerable amount of formative effort being expended in the development and tryout of a number of different approaches. It would be premature to suggest the use of any one of these approaches in this text or to offer specific procedural steps for each. However, several are given brief mention here for the benefit of those who at this time would seek ways of estimating reliability for locally developed criterion-referenced instruments.

Ivens' Agreement Index. Ivens (1970) provides a means for estimating reliability outside of the use of test-score variance. This measure is based upon the administration of an instrument in a test–retest fashion or upon using alternate forms. For each administration, the raw scores on each form for each student are converted to a percentage correct score. For each student, then the absolute difference between the two percentages is determined. The reliability coefficient is presented in the form of the percent of students with percent difference scores of a given size or less.

Berger–Carver Mastery Agreement Index.   The Berger (1970) and Carver (1970) index is similar to the Ivens index in terms of calculation except, rather than using percentages, the Berger–Carver index uses dichotomous categories. For each student, either a mastery or non-mastery category is achieved. Agreement between the two categories achieved by each individual on test–retest or parallel forms is determined. If all students who achieved mastery on the initial administration also achieved mastery on the second administration, then a perfect mastery-agreement index is achieved. The formula for this index is:

$$BC \text{ mastery agreement} = \frac{A + B}{N}$$

where: A = the number of students who scored above the mastery cutoff on both test and retest
B = the number of students who scored below the mastery cutoff on both tests
N = the total number of students

Marshall's Index of Separation.   Marshall (1973) has proposed an index based upon the assumption that two subpopulations exist—knowledgeable and unknowledgeable. For the knowledgeable population, the expected score is the number of items in the test. The formula for calculating Marshall's separation index is:

$$\text{Sep.} = 1 - \left(\frac{4}{nN} \right) \sum_{i=1}^{n} \frac{(X_i - X_i^2)}{n}$$

where: n = the number of test items
N = the number of students
X_i = a person's total score

Several other indices exist that are built upon adaptations of classical test theory. These include Harris' Index of Efficiency (Harris 1972), Hambleton–Novick Indices (Hambleton and Novick 1973), Ozenne's Sensitivity Indices (Ozenne 1971), Livingston's Coefficient (Livingston 1972), and the Coefficient of Reproducibility (Cox and Graham 1966; Ferguson 1971). Refer to these sources for a more detailed description and discussion of each.

REFERENCES

Ahmann, J. S., and Glock, M. D. *Evaluating Pupil Growth,* 5th ed. Boston: Allyn and Bacon, 1975.

Berger, R. J. "A Measure of Reliability for Criterion-Referenced Tests." Paper presented at the annual meeting of the National Council on Measurement in Education, Minneapolis, 1970.

Brennan, R. L. "A Generalized Upper-Lower Item Discrimination Index," *Educational and Psychological Measurement,* vol. 32, 1972, pp. 289-303.

Carver, R. P. "Special Problems in Measuring Change with Psychometric Devices." In *Evaluative Research: Strategies and Methods.* Pittsburgh: American Institutes for Research, 1970.

Costa, Irene, ed. *MERMAC Manual.* Urbana, Illinois: University of Illinois Press, 1971.

Cox, R. C., and Graham, G. T. "The Development of a Sequentially Scaled Achievement Test," *Journal of Educational Measurement,* vol. 3, 1966, pp. 147-150.

Cox, R. C., and Vargas, J. S. "A Comparison of Item Selection Techniques for Norm-Referenced and Criterion-Referenced Tests." Paper read at the annual meeting of the National Council on Measurement in Education, Chicago, Illinois, February 1966.

Crehan, K. D. "Item Analysis for Teacher-Made Mastery Tests," *Journal of Educational Measurement,* vol. 2, no. 4, Winter 1974, pp. 255-262.

Cronbach, L. J., and Meehl, P. E. "Construct Validity in Psychological Tests," *Psychological Bulletin,* vol. 52, 1955, pp. 281-302.

Downie, N. M. *Fundamentals of Measurement.* New York: Oxford University Press, 1958.

Ebel, R. L. *Essentials of Educational Measurement.* Englewood Cliffs, New Jersey: Prentice-Hall, 1972.

Ferguson, R. L. "Computer Assistance for Individualizing Measurement." University of Pittsburgh, Learning, Research and Development Center, March 1971.

Gronlund, N. E. *Preparing Criterion-Referenced Tests for Classroom Instruction.* New York: Macmillan, 1973.

Hambleton, R. K., and Novick, M. R. "Toward an Integration of Theory and Method for Criterion-Referenced Tests," *Journal of Educational Measurement,* vol. 10, 1973, pp. 159-170.

Harris, C. W. "An Index of Efficiency for Fixed-Length Mastery Tests." Paper presented at the annual meeting of the American Educational Research Association, Chicago, 1972.

Ivens, S. H. "An Investigation of Item Analysis, Reliability, and Validity in Relation to Criterion-Referenced Tests." Doctoral dissertation, Florida State University, August 1970.

Livingston, S. A. "A Criterion-Referenced Application of Classical Test Theory," *Journal of Educational Measurement,* vol. 9, 1972, pp. 13–26.

Marshall, J. L. "Reliability Indices for Criterion-Referenced Tests: A Study Based on Simulated Data." Paper presented at the annual meeting of the National Council for Measurement in Education, New Orleans, February 1973.

Millman, J. "Criterion Referenced Measurement." In *Evaluation and Education,* W. J. Popham, ed. Berkeley, California: McCutchan Publishing, 1974.

Millman, J. "Reporting Student Progress: A Case for Criterion-Referenced Marking System." Working Papers in Educational Research, no. 5, Cornell University, 1970.

Ozenne, D. G. "Toward an Evaluative Methodology for Criterion-Referenced Measures: Test Sensitivity." CSE Report No. 72. Los Angeles: Center for the Study of Evaluation, Graduate School of Education, University of California at Los Angeles, 1971.

Payne, D. A. *The Specification and Measurement of Learning Outcomes.* Waltham, Massachusetts: Blaisdell Publishing, 1968.

Popham, W. J. *Criterion Referenced Measurement.* Englewood Cliffs, New Jersey: Educational Technology Publications, 1971.

Popham, W. J., ed. *Evaluation in Education.* Berkeley, California: McCutchan Publishing, 1974.

Popham, W. J., and Husek, T. R. "Implications of Criterion-Referenced Measurement," *Journal of Educational Measurement,* vol. 6, no. 1, 1969.

Swanson, R. *Educational Statistics Workbook* (mimeo). Menomonie: University of Wisconsin-Stout, 1965.

Part III

Standardized
Instruments

Chapter 10

Characteristics, Development, and Selection of Standardized Instruments

Of the measurement procedures and techniques used in occupational education programs far more use is made of teacher-made and teacher-modified instruments than is made of published standardized instruments. The expense involved in developing and publishing standardized instruments, tends to restrict their use to measurement tasks where very large numbers of individuals are to be served. In education, the development and use of standardized instruments generally has been restricted to instruments used in career-guidance programs and to achievement tests for general education subject areas that enroll large segments of the student population.

Compared to the numbers enrolled in general education subject areas like English, math, and reading, there are relatively few students in any single occupational education subject area. Moreover, technical changes in occupations occur rather frequently and, across the nation, courses and programs in occupational education have varied considerably in their objectives, content, and method of instruction. Since standardized achievement tests are designed to reflect the common curricular goals and objectives at the time they are developed, very few of these tests relate to new technical developments in an occupation or to the goals and objectives of an innovative program.

For these reasons, it has not been economically feasible to develop and publish standardized achievement tests for use in occupational education programs. The only exception would be those instruments used to assess achievement in military occupational programs and those noncommercial standardized instruments developed by federal and state agencies for certifying or licensing personnel such as automotive and airplane mechanics, airplane pilots, health care specialists, barbers, cosmotologists, and welders. Although economic considerations have tended to restrict the development and use of standardized measurement procedures and techniques in occupational programs, some types of these instruments can make significant contributions to local occupational programs.

Occupational education teachers, administrators, and career-guidance personnel who use externally developed standardized measurement procedures and techniques often ask questions concerning (1) the nature of standardized instruments and how they are developed, (2) procedures for identifying and criteria for selecting instruments, (3) instruments that have demonstrated potential for occupational programs, and (4) how to make good use of the data and information obtained with these instruments. Answers to these questions are important if we are to obtain full benefit from standardized measurement instruments in our occupational programs. Many of the problems encountered in using measurement procedures and techniques in occupational programs have as their origin improper selection and/or use of standardized measurement instruments. This chapter focuses on providing answers to questions in these four areas of concern and on helping occupational teachers, administrators, and career-guidance personnel avoid problems stemming from improper use of standardized measurement procedures and techniques.

CHARACTERISTICS OF STANDARDIZED INSTRUMENTS

Standardized instruments are carefully developed and highly refined measurement procedures and techniques designed to be administered under carefully prescribed conditions for some specific purpose. In addition, standardized instruments can provide scores that have specified degrees of validity and reliability and that can be interpreted in a comparative manner. By definition, these instruments share a number of common characteristics or properties: first, standardized instruments have well-defined and uniform procedures and techniques for obtaining samples of performance. That is, the same set of test items is administered using the same set of directions and time limitations. Second, their procedures for scoring have been carefully prescribed. Third, normative data (scores obtained from representative samples of specified groups of individuals) have been prepared for all standardized instruments. Finally, they have estimates of validity and reliability that are based upon sound experimental research.

Many standardized tests have one additional quality. They have been published by commercial publishers. However, not all published instruments are standardized instruments—only those that have all the foregoing characteristics: uniform procedures for administration and scoring, norms, and sound estimates of validity and reliability.

Standardized instruments often have restrictions placed on their use. Those restrictions that are of importance to occupational teachers, administrators, and career-guidance personnel are concerned with maintaining the integrity of the test and with the level of expertise required in administering and scoring and in interpreting the obtained scores. For example, the Armed Services Vocational Aptitude Battery (ASVAB) used by the military services for assessing several vocational aptitudes are restricted to administration by qualified military personnel only. The interest here is in protecting the instruments from getting into the hands of unauthorized persons. Once standardized instruments are "out" their integrity is threatened if their prescribed conditions for testing cannot be met. In brief, these conditions generally cannot be met if one or more among those taking the test has had an opportunity to practice the items and experiences included in the test. It is for this reason that the military will not release their vocational interest and aptitude tests for civilians to use with nonmilitary occupational programs. Upon invitation, qualified military personnel will, however, administer these instruments to occupational students and assist teachers and career-guidance personnel to interpret and use the obtained scores.

In order to insure that the integrity of test materials is not compromised and that such materials are released only to those who are prepared to use and interpret them properly, test publishers classify their instruments and distribute them in accordance with established standards (American Psychological Association 1953). Three levels (A, B, and C) are included in the classification scheme used. Simplified descriptions of each level are as follows:

Level A

Level A includes tests that can be adequately administered, scored, and interpreted with the aid of the test manual and a general orientation to the kind of organization in which one is employed. Examples would include standardized achievement and proficiency tests that might be used in occupational programs. Such tests could be administered, scored, and interpreted by responsible occupational teachers, administrators, or career-guidance personnel.

Level B

Level B tests require some knowledge of test construction and use as well as supportive preparation in areas such as statistics, individual differences, personnel psychology, and guidance. Examples would include standardized general mental ability tests, special aptitude tests, and some interest inventories. These instruments can be used by those having suitable preparation; by those who are employed by an established school, government agency, or business and are authorized by their employer to use them in their employment; or by graduate students using them in connection with a course of study for such instruments.

Level C

Tests that require substantial understanding of testing and supporting preparation in psychological topics as well as many hours of supervised experience in their use are classified at the *C level.* Examples include individually administered general mental ability tests and personality tests. These tests can be used only by Diplomats of the American Board of Examiners in Professional Psychology; by persons with at least a master's degree in psychology and at least one year of properly supervised experience; by graduate students enrolled in courses requiring the use of such tests under the supervision of a qualified psychologist; by members of kindred professions with adequate training in clinical psychological testing; or by other professionals who have had training and supervised experience in administering and scoring the test in question and who are working with someone qualified to interpret the test results.

DEVELOPMENT OF STANDARDIZED INSTRUMENTS

There is no single prescribed set of procedures used by developers of the standardized instruments frequently used in occupational education programs. The general procedures that one might follow in developing paper and pencil standardized achievement tests for automotive mechanics are presented below. These same procedures typically are followed by individuals and test development agencies in developing most types of standardized instruments used in occupational programs.

Definition of Purpose

The first step in developing a standardized instrument would be to define its purpose—assessing student achievement in auto mechanics in this instance.

Subject-matter Index

The second step in our example would be to develop a *subject-matter index* or listing of all the knowledge and understanding related to auto mechanics that is to be included in the instrument. For this example, the subject areas would include engines, drive trains, braking systems, and electrical systems.

The purpose of this listing is to define, specifically, the knowledge and understanding that may or may not be appropriately included in the test. In addition, the listing assists in determining whether or not any important subject matter has been inadvertantly omitted and in determining the number of test items that will be devoted to each subject area.

Table of Specifications

Once the subject-matter index is completed, the next step is to develop a table of specifications for the test. The *table of specifications* is the plan or blueprint for the test. It includes (1) a listing of the subject areas to be covered by the test and (2) the number of test items to be devoted to measuring a specific level of knowledge, skill, or understanding for each subject area. Detailed suggestions for developing tables of specifications are presented in chapter 4 of this text.

Test Items

After the table of specifications has been prepared, the test developer then prepares individual *test items* designed to measure the knowledge, skill, and/or understanding specified for each subject area in the table of specifications. The total number of items to be developed would depend, of course, upon the number of items to be devoted to measuring each level of knowledge, skill, and/or understanding for each subject area, as per the table of specifications.

Great care is taken in development of each item and each passes through a rigorous editing process for technical accuracy, appropriateness of content, and clarity. After this review and editing process the items are set into test format along with instructions for administering and scoring the test.

First Draft Review

This initial draft of the test is reviewed by administering it to a sampling of persons employed as auto mechanics and generally recognized as being good mechanics and a sampling of individuals recognized as having little or no knowledge in this area. Their answer sheets are scored and item-analysis procedures are used to identify items and parts of items that do not appear to be performing adequately: those that are of little or no help in differentiating between knowledgeable auto mechanics and those who are unknowledgeable in this field. The purpose of this review and subsequent reviews of this type is to find and eliminate any remaining ambiguities or inaccuracies, and to improve or replace defective items. The review process continues until the test developer feels little or no improvement is to be gained from continuing the process.

Validity, Reliability, and Norms

The final draft of the instrument is administered to large samples of individuals representative of those for whom the test is being developed. In this example, the samples certainly include students enrolled in secondary and postsecondary vocational automotive programs. Estimates of predictive and/or concurrent validity and test reliability are computed using one or more of the procedures outlined in chapter 9.

Normative data are also formulated for each of the large samples of individuals included in these administrations of the test. The obtained scores from these reference groups are converted into norms or scores that can be used to interpret the obtained scores of individuals taking this test at some later date.

Test Manual

The final step in the development of this standardized achievement test for automotive mechanics, or any other standardized instrument, is the development of the test manual. Those who will be using the test need certain information about this test that will help them determine whether this test will be adequate for their purposes and to assist them in obtaining and interpreting the scores obtained with this test. Guidelines or standards for developing test manuals have been published by the American Psychological Association (French and Michael 1966). In brief, these guidelines call for test manuals to include concise directions for administering and scoring the test as well as extensive information concerning (1) how the test was developed, (2) its validity and reliability, (3) the basis for its norms, (4) the kinds of interpretations that are appropriate, and (5) the uses for which the instrument can best be employed. Preparation of an adequate test manual, then, completes the procedures for developing this example automotives achievement test. Again, similar procedures would be used to develop most other standardized instruments used in occupational programs.

SOURCES OF INFORMATION ON STANDARDIZED INSTRUMENTS

Occupational education teachers, administrators, and career-guidance personnel who have a measurement task that requires instrumentation to assist them in gathering needed information and data should look first to see if they can find some standardized instrument to meet their needs. Certainly others like themselves have been faced with the same or nearly the same measurement task. Perhaps a standardized instrument has been developed that would at least come close to meeting their need. There are several good sources of information about available standardized instruments. Each differs somewhat in regard to the types of information it has to offer about available standardized instruments. Most will be found to be helpful in their particular areas of strength. Brief descriptions of each of these sources and the types of information they contain follow.

Mental Measurements Yearbooks

The Mental Measurements Yearbook series edited by Buros (1938, 1941, 1949, 1953, 1959, 1965, and 1972) is undoubtedly the single most comprehensive and valuable source for locating and obtaining pertinent information about particular standardized instruments. In addition to indicating the usual authors, titles, publishers, costs, and the like, critical reviews are offered for each instrument included in these yearbooks.

Tests in Print

Tests in Print II (Buros 1974) presents a comprehensive bibliography of instruments that are useful in educational, business and industrial, and psychological applications. It provides general basic information about each test listed and includes references to *The Mental Measurements Yearbooks* and the critical reviews offered for each test. With its publication, the earlier work, *Tests in Print* (Buros, 1961) is now regarded as having primarily historical value.

Vocational Tests and Reviews

Vocational Tests and Reviews, edited by Buros (1975), is an extremely useful reference for personnel associated with occupational education programs. Using materials from *The Mental Measurements Yearbook* series and *Tests in Print II,* this work presents tests, reviews, and references for hundreds of vocational tests. Specific tests are described and criticized as to their usefulness and applicability.

Test Publishers' Catalogs

Test publishers' catalogs are the most current source of information concerning the availability of specific tests. The thrust here, of course, is in merchandising and little if any evaluative data and information is presented for any of the instruments included in these catalogs. A listing of test publishers who have instruments often found to be of value to occupational programs is presented in Appendix B.

Professional Journals

Journals published by professional associations periodically include reports of research efforts involving standardized instruments as well as critical reviews of such instruments. A listing of journals that have included articles focusing on measurement instruments that would be of interest to occupational teachers, administrators, and career-guidance personnel is presented in Appendix C.

Measurement Textbooks

Many texts concerned with educational and psychological measurement procedures and techniques sometimes present very detailed and helpful descriptions and discussions of selected standardized instruments. Several standardized instruments currently used in occupational education programs are presented in the following pages of this chapter. Occupational teachers, administrators, and career-guidance personnel might review these pages as well as the texts listed as references at the close of this chapter when seeking information on standardized instruments being considered for inclusion in their programs.

Test Manuals

The test manual prepared for a particular standardized instrument should provide the most comprehensive information about that instrument. In addition to estimates of validity and reliability, norms, and descriptions of the normative samples, the manual usually includes bibliographic listings of published research efforts involving that instrument. Because test manuals are prepared by test authors and publishers, the data and information presented in them sometimes tend to be subjective and partial with respect to the purported value of a particular instrument. One should not make selection decisions with respect to particular standardized instruments that are based solely upon data and information presented in their test manuals.

Instruments

One final source of information about standardized instruments sometimes passed by without much consideration is the instruments themselves. Often we fail to see the forest for the trees and do not consider this important source of information when selecting standardized instruments. However, securing a specimen set for a particular instrument and merely reviewing it to check out the types of items included and perhaps its procedures for scoring is not adequate.

The best approach to securing information about a particular test from the test itself should include sitting down and taking the test (the whole thing) and then administering it to at least one other person. These two activities provide valuable information and insights that are impossible to obtain from any other source.

Moreover, the value of such knowledge and insights will not be limited to making a decision about whether to use a particular test in the occupational program. The knowledge and insights gained will increase the effectiveness of both the administration and the interpretation of obtained scores, should the decision be to use that particular instrument in the occupational program.

Questions and Information Sources

Some questions commonly posed about standardized instruments are presented in table 10.1 along with the foregoing sources of information. Each source of information has been rated with regard to the level of contribution it would be likely to make in answering each of the questions presented in the matrix.

The one-, two-, and three-star ratings presented in the matrix indicate the amount of value each source of information would be in answering that particular question. For example, publishers' catalogs provide little or no information about test validity and reliability and receive a one-star rating in this regard. However, they are a primary, or three-star, source of information concerning the costs associated with particular instruments.

CRITERIA AND PROCEDURES FOR SELECTING STANDARDIZED INSTRUMENTS

Using standardized instruments in occupational programs has associated with it two basic questions: first, what contributions can standardized instruments make to the functions of measurement in occupational programs? Second, what criteria should be used in selecting instruments to be used in conjunction with the various functions of measurement in occupational programs? Answers to the first question are presented in the last section in this chapter. Answers to the second question are presented here.

Certain of the criteria for selecting standardized instruments are the same as those considered when building good locally developed instruments. The basic considerations for selecting an externally developed standardized instrument are (1) validity, (2) reliability,

TABLE 10.1. *Common Questions About Standardized Instruments and Possible Sources of Information*

Sources of Information

Questions	Mental Measurements Yearbooks	Tests in Print	Vocational Tests and Reviews	Test Publishers' Catalogs	Professional Journals	Measurement Textbooks	Test Manuals	Instrument Review
1. What instruments are available?	***	***	***	***	**	*		
2. What new instruments are available?				***	**			
3. What are the costs for a particular instrument and test-scoring services?	**		**	***				
4. In what type of occupational program has this instrument been found to be of value?				*	**		*	
5. What groups of individuals are included in the norms for a particular instrument?	***		***				***	
6. What do professionals think about a particular instrument?					**			
7. What level of preparation is required for using a particular instrument?				***				**
8. What does a particular instrument really measure?	**		**	*	**		***	***
9. How reliable are the obtained scores for a particular instrument?	**		**		*		***	

(3) interpretability of obtained scores, (4) efficiency in administration and scoring, and (5) costs. A discussion of each of these criteria and how they can be used in the selection of standardized instruments for occupational programs follows.

Validity

There are very few standardized instruments that can be considered perfectly valid. Few, if any, provide complete measurements of that which they were designed to measure—nothing more or nothing less. Acceptable levels of validity for instruments used in measuring occupational students' behavior generally range from nearly perfect, as in timing student performance in an automotive troubleshooting contest, to barely acceptable, as in assessing specific personal characteristics like honesty, loyalty, and attitude toward work. Generally, the question, "Is this a valid test?" is rarely appropriate. Appropriate questions concerning test validity focus on the extent to which the instrument in question has *sufficient validity* of the *type necessary* to satisfy the requirements for measurement accuracy demanded by the measurement task to be achieved for a *particular group of students.* For what individuals and for what purpose(s) is this particular instrument a valid instrument? This is the question that needs to be answered.

How Much Is Enough? How much validity should a standardized instrument have? One good but not too helpful reply is, "As much as possible." In most instances, the level of validity associated with a particular instrument is a function of balance between level of validity and resources available. There appears to be a direct relationship between level of validity attained and the amount of time available for testing, the amount and sophistication of the instrumentation, and the qualifications of those involved in the measurement process. Given even the present level of sophistication in measurement procedures and techniques, exceptionally valid standardized instruments can be developed for most measurement tasks associated with occupational programs *if* no limits are placed on time, personnel, and other resources.

The following are the important questions regarding validity when selecting standardized instruments for occupational programs.

How much time, effort, and talent are necessary to provide us useful measurements that have acceptable levels of validity? What would it cost us to obtain higher levels of accuracy or validity? What is the appropriate balance between our costs and validity for this particular measurement task?

The phrase "for this particular measurement task" is an important qualifier when comparing the levels of validity for two or more standardized tests. It is an error to think of measurement instruments as having either high, acceptable, or unacceptable levels of validity associated with them per se. The validity of a test can vary considerably from one testing situation to another. A test might provide a very adequate assessment of what it is designed to measure in one situation and not in another. For example, an electronics teacher might select a valid standardized achievement test to assess the knowledge, skills, and understanding achieved by students enrolled in his introductory course. This does not mean that this test would provide valid measures of student achievement in introductory electronics courses being taught by other teachers in other schools. Variations in course objectives, students' levels of scholastic ability, community attitude toward education, and actual course content serve to lessen the possibility of having standardized instruments that provide accurate measures of student achievement in occupational courses being taught in all schools. An expression of level of validity for a particular standardized instrument must be judged or weighed in terms of the specific situations in which the instrument has been normed and is intended to be used. The more the norming samples and the intended samples are alike, the more confidence we can have in the expressed validity coefficient.

What Type of Validity?   The types of validity discussed earlier have implications for various measurement purposes or tasks and the selection of standardized instruments to achieve these various tasks. Each task generally has associated with it the need for instrumentation having a particular type of validity.

Content Validity. For example, when assessing student achievement in an occupational program, content or face validity is of primary importance. We are interested in the extent to which the content included in the standardized test is a balanced and complete sampling of the knowledge, skills, and understanding we are attempting to develop in the occupational program. As indicated earlier, content validity is determined by comparing test content with the content, methods, and instructional objectives for the occupational program. To the extent that the content of the standardized test and instruction in the program are found to be congruent, the instrument being considered has content validity for this measurement task.

Predictive Validity. When assessing student interest, aptitude, or readiness for instruction in a particular occupational program, predictive validity is of primary importance. We are interested in the extent to which performance on the standardized instrument accurately predicts future success in the occupational program for which the obtained scores would be used as predictors. Of course, predictive validity is determined by correlating obtained scores with some measure(s) of success in particular occupational programs. To the extent that performance on the instrument in question is related to performance in some selected occupational programs, then the instrument is said to have validity for this measurement task, predicting success in selected occupational programs.

Concurrent Validity. If the measurement task is to develop quick and accurate descriptions of students' general mental abilities or personality characteristics, then concurrent validity would be of importance. The interest here would be in the extent to which scores obtained with the instrument in question are related to other obtained measures of general mental ability or personality characteristics that, themselves, have established levels of validity. To the extent that performance on the standardized instrument in question is related to other valid but time-consuming measures of particular ability traits or personality characteristics, the instrument would be a valid substitute for some established but costly or unavailable procedure and may be used for developing quick and accurate descriptions.

Again, the purpose for which the instrument is to be used is an important factor when considering validity as a criterion in test selection. Given a specific group of individuals (home economics students), a particular instrument may be valid for one purpose (measuring student achievement in a child-care course), but not for other purposes (assessing vocational interests or aptitudes). In this example, validity for the child-care achievement test has meaning only if it is content validity. The validity estimate in this instance must relate to certain instructional content and particular instructional objectives as well as a specific purpose.

Internal Validity. Test manuals for certain tests present estimates of validity that are based upon internal validation procedures. You will recall from the discussion on validity presented in chapter 2 that this approach to validity uses total test score as a criterion rather than some external criterion like success in the occupational program or success on the job after graduation.

The contribution that internal consistency procedures can make to test validation is extremely limited. Without validity data that are external to the instrument itself, it is difficult if not impossible to determine precisely what is being measured by the instrument. It is for this reason that the *Standards for Educational and Psychological Tests and Manuals* (French and Michael 1966) stipulates that "Item-test correlations should not be presented in the manual as evidence of criterion-related validity. . . . such correlations are not, in themselves, indicators of test validity; they are measures of internal consistency."

Standardized instruments with published descriptions that make reference to using internal validation processes should be viewed with extreme suspicion, particularly if no mention is made of results from validation processes using external criteria.

Valid for Whom? In some instances, even having an appropriate amount of the right type of validity still may not be enough to warrant selection of a particular instrument. A standardized instrument could have a more than adequate level of the appropriate type of validity and still not be a valid instrument for some particular situation. An instrument that is of great value to the decision-making process in one occupational program and with one group of occupational students may be of little or no value in some other occupational program or with other groups of occupational students. Therefore, when selecting a standardized instrument one should not ask only if the instrument has enough of the right type of validity.

For occupational education programs, the students and the manner in which the obtained scores are to be used are important factors in considering test validity as a criterion for selecting standardized instruments. The appropriate question would be, "How valid are the obtained scores on this test when it is used in the manner I want to use it and with the group with whom I want to use it?" Given a particular subject area (foods and nutrition), an instrument may be valid for assessing student achievement and determining final grades for one group of individuals (associate degree food service majors) and invalid as a diagnostic test for other groups (adult culinary arts classes). This same concept can be applied to levels of maturity as well. For example, an instrument may be valid for inventorying ultimate vocational interests of high school students, but invalid for inventorying vocational interests among other groups such as preschool or grade school children. Again, the validity of standardized instruments only can be considered in terms of having a sufficient quantity of the type necessary to meet the requirements of a specific measurement task to be achieved for a specific group of students.

Moreover, many standardized instruments for assessing vocational aptitude and interests have normative data for males only and sometimes only white middle-class males. Such instruments have questionable validity for career-guidance decisions that involve females and minority students from low-income families. Federal, state, and local equal opportunity statutes are serving to increase (1) the number of females who are enrolling in occupational programs leading to employment in traditionally male occupations and (2) the number of minority students from low-income families who are seeking enrollment in occupational programs. As the characteristics of our student population in occupational education shift, we must remember to select only those standardized instruments that have demonstrated adequate levels of validity with students having those characteristics.

Reliability

As with validity, test publishers include in the manual for each standardized instrument data and information concerning the reliability of that instrument. It is necessary to have a thorough understanding of reliability as a selection criterion for standardized instruments. Those who can interpret properly the estimates of reliability presented in test manuals also can develop some impression of the degree to which an instrument in question can produce consistently accurate obtained scores for whatever it is measuring. Such impressions are important to and helpful in interpreting the estimates of validity for a given instrument.

Impact on Validity. As indicated earlier, test reliability places serious restrictions on test validity. In statistical terms, a validity coefficient for a particular instrument cannot be any larger than the square root of the instrument's reliability coefficient. In more practical terms, an elastic rubber tape measure would not be a valid instrument for laying out building foundations or clothing patterns, primarily because such a tape would not produce consistently accurate (reliable) measurements. Given that only reliable instruments can produce obtained scores that are valid, estimates of reliability that have been derived for standardized instruments can be useful in making judgments concerning the validity of those instruments.

For example, a perfectly reliable instrument that produces consistently accurate (reproducible) obtained scores may have associated with it a series of relatively low validity coefficients. One interpretation of the instrument's validity would be that the instrument suffers not in its ability to produce accurate scores but rather in its ability to measure the variable it was designed to measure. On the other hand, instruments that have associated with them low levels of reliability suffer both in their ability to produce accurate (reproducible) scores and to measure the variables they were designed to measure.

How Much Is Enough?   Few, if any, measurement procedures and techniques used in occupational education programs are perfectly reliable. Most all are unreliable to a certain degree. What is an acceptable level of reliability for measurement instruments used in occupational education programs? As high as possible is one answer. However, a better approach would be to relate the question to the precision of the discrimination for which the obtained scores will be used. For example, comparing the average level of achievement for two large Foods and Nutrition I classes being taught by different methods of instruction requires an achievement test with a moderately high degree of reliability—a coefficient of at least 0.75. Whereas measurement of individual differences in student achievement for purposes of assigning grades to the students enrolled in these same two classes requires achievement tests having somewhat higher reliability—a coefficient of at least 0.90. However, these examples should not be used as arbitrary standards. There are other factors that should be considered.

Other Considerations.   Reliability estimates for standardized as well as locally developed instruments must be interpreted in terms of the nature and composition of the group for which they were computed and the methods used in computing them.

Restriction of Range. Changes in the range of ability levels present in the norm group used in computing a reliability estimate can produce dramatic changes in the size of the resulting coefficient. Reliability coefficients based on obtained scores from a group that exhibits little variation in the behavior measured by the instrument characteristically will be low. Obtained scores from groups that have wide variation in the behavior measured will produce higher reliability coefficients. In short, the reliability coefficient will vary with the range of levels of performance present in the group being tested, even though the nature of the instrument remains constant. Data in table 10.2 illustrate this point.

Table 10.2 presents the raw scores and rankings of fifteen students for two forms of a home economics achievement test. Only minor shifts in rank from one form of the test to the other are observed. A rank-difference correlation coefficient (Guilford 1965) computed from these data would approach 0.97. The shifting in ranks is not great enough to produce a low coefficient. However, if the coefficient were computed using only the top five students (a severe restriction in range of ability) the computed coefficient would drop to 0.50.

TABLE 10.2. Raw Scores and Ranks of Students on Two Forms of a Home Economics Achievement Test

| Student | Form I | | Form II | |
	Score	Rank	Score	Rank
A	60	1	59	2
B	59	2	61	1
C	57	3	51	5
D	55	4	55	4
E	52	5	57	3
F	51	6	50	6
G	50	7	48	8
H	48	8	49	7
I	46	9	45	9
J	45	10	44	10
K	42	11	39	13
L	41	12	43	11
M	40	13	40	12
N	38	14	38	14
O	37	15	37	15

The reason for such a dramatic drop in the size of the computed coefficient is the restriction in range of achievement in home economics among those being tested. Although the shifts in rank for the top-ranked five students are the same in both instances, the effect or importance of these shifts is exaggerated when the range is so restricted. In the group of fifteen, for example, student E's shift from a rank of fifth place to third represents a 12.5 percent shift—two ranks out of fifteen. However, this same change in rank represents a 40 percent shift (two ranks out of five) when the coefficient is computed using only the top five students.

It should be noted that the lower coefficient in this example is the result of restricting the *range* of ability in the group being tested. It is not the result of restricting the *size* of the sample. A reliability coefficient computed on the basis of five students randomly selected from the total range available in this example (i.e., students A, F, K, M, and O) would be 0.99—approximately the same as the coefficient computed using the total group of fifteen.

For simplicity, small numbers of students were used in this example. In actual practice, group size approaching 100 is required to insure a high degree of confidence in the obtained coefficient. However, the foregoing example demonstrates why the size of reliability (and validity) coefficients tends to be suppressed by restrictions in range. If one wants to estimate the reliability coefficient in one range from the known reliability in another range, Guilford (1965) presents a technique and formula for doing so.

Most standardized instruments are of value in discriminating with satisfactory precision among individuals representing a wide range of the behavior being measured. These same instruments, however, may not be able to discriminate equally well among individuals representing a narrow range of the selected behavior. Occupational teachers and career-guidance personnel have little difficulty finding instruments that discriminate between trainable, average, above-average, and genius levels of ability among their students. However, measurement procedures and techniques for occupational or any other school program have not been refined to the point where they can, without error, discriminate between students within the various levels of ability. Fine distinctions within the above-average range, for example, are very difficult to make. The reliability coefficients reported in test manuals for standardized instruments should be interpreted with one eye on the nature and composition of the group tested.

No reported reliability coefficient can be interpreted properly without knowledge as to the range of the behavior being measured in the group providing the obtained scores from which the coefficient was computed. A reliability coefficient of 0.60 derived from a group having a restricted range of the behavior being measured could well blossom to 0.95 if the same instrument were administered to a group having a broad sampling of that behavior. The same type of statement can be made for validity coefficients as well. Both are very much a function of the range of the behavior being measured that is present in the group being tested.

Equivalence of Groups. Closely related to restriction of range as a consideration in interpreting reliability coefficients is consideration of the equivalency of the ability levels of the group to be tested and that of the group used in computing the reliability for standardized instruments. When a single reliability coefficient is offered for a standardized instrument, there is a tendency to assume that the estimate of reliability holds for all groups that might be tested. Such an assumption is more often than not incorrect. For example, when standardized instruments are administered to groups that are incapable of responding with anything other than guesses, scores tend to cluster randomly around the chance level. No matter how accurate with some groups, instruments that produce unreproducible chance performances with other groups should not be used with these groups. The closer the resemblance between the group providing the scores used to derive the coefficient and the group whose behavior is to be assessed, the more meaningful the reliability coefficient becomes.

Part-score Reliability. Often reliability for standardized instruments is reported for only the total score on an instrument that is made up of several subparts that are scored individually and combined to form the total test score. When reliability data are not presented for the part scores it is sometimes assumed that each subpart has a level of reliability equal to that of the instrument as a whole. Such an assumption is more often than not incorrect.

The size of a reliability coefficient often is a function of the length of the instrument. The Spearman–Brown prophecy formula presented in chapter 9 can be used to estimate the extent to which lengthening or shortening a particular instrument will affect its reliability. As indicated in the earlier chapter, the longer the instrument the more reliable it is likely to be.

Normally, a part score based on only a portion of the items

included in an instrument cannot be expected to have the amount of reliability associated with the total score. Unwarranted confidence is given to part scores when they are treated as though they had the reliability of the total test score.

There are two important points relating to instrument length and reliability: first, if evidence of adequate reliability for each part score is not available, these part scores should not be used except as parts of the total score. Second, one method of increasing reliability that often produces very satisfactory results is to develop additional items that are equivalent to those in the instrument and simply lengthen the instrument.

Speed Tests. As indicated earlier, reliability estimates based on a single administration of the instrument are usually satisfactory. However, reliability estimates for instruments involving speed conditions are a definite exception to this generalization. Speed tests are composed entirely of simple tasks or items that almost anyone can answer or complete correctly. However, so many items are included in the test that most individuals cannot finish the test within the imposed time limit. Many clerical speed and accuracy, and simple arithmetic aptitude tests are speed tests and should not have reliability estimates reported for them that were computed using internal-consistency techniques.

Internal-consistency methods of obtaining estimates of reliability often provide exaggerated coefficients for such instruments. This is because speed tests are composed of such easy items that there tends to be a high correlation among items completed (they are generally all completed correctly) as well as a high correlation among those not attempted (they are all scored incorrect). Tests that are only somewhat dependent upon a speed factor and whose items are arranged from easy to hard in order of difficulty will produce internal consistency estimates of reliability that are inflated but not so seriously misleading. However, the only satisfactory method for obtaining an accurate estimate of reliability for a speed test is to use test–retest techniques. The same form can be used in both administrations, though it is preferable to use alternate forms. Therefore, it is important to view reliability coefficients reported for standardized instruments having a speed factor as being spuriously high if they have been derived using any of the internal-consistency techniques.

Normative Data

Measurements obtained with a standardized instrument are relative—relative to the performance of other individuals whose performance on that instrument is a matter of record. Therefore, standardized instruments, to be of optimum value, must be accompanied by useful relative standards of performance (norms) that can be used to interpret individual student performance on that instrument.

The standard of performance generally provided for standardized instruments used in occupational programs is the performance of one or more reference groups composed of individuals representative of those for whom the instrument was developed. The obtained scores for each reference group are converted to norms and presented in the test manual along with complete descriptions of the characteristics (age, sex, geographic location, socioeconomic background, and the like) of that reference group.

In order for norms to contribute meaningfully to the interpretation of student performance on the standardized instrument, the reference group used in developing the norms must have been chosen to represent adequately the characteristics of those for whom the instrument was developed and to whom a comparison of their performance will be of value. In fact, the APA *Standards for Educational and Psychological Tests and Manuals* (French and Michael 1966) includes the following essential recommendation: "Norms presented in the test manual should refer to defined and clearly described populations. These populations should be groups to whom users of the test will ordinarily wish to compare the persons tested."

The first question to ask about the norms for a particular standardized instrument is, "How close do the pertinent characteristics of the group used to develop the norms for this instrument match the characteristics of the occupational students to whom the instrument will be administered?" If both the former and the latter groups are of the same general ability level, age, and sex, and from similar socioeconomic backgrounds, for example, then the norms presented in the test manual should be of value. To the extent that they are not the same, the norms presented in the test manual would be of less value.

The APA *Standards* presents three additional recommendations for the development of test manuals that relate to norms. These too are helpful guides in judging the adequacy of normative information and data presented in test manuals.

1. Local norms are more important for many uses of tests than are published norms. In such cases the test manual should suggest appropriate emphasis on local norms and describe methods for their calculation.
2. Except where the primary use of a test is to compare individuals with their own local group, norms should be published in the test manual at the time of release of the test for operational use.
3. Norms should be reported in the test manual in terms of standard scores or percentile ranks that reflect the distribution of scores in an appropriate reference group or groups (French and Michael 1966).

Unless local personnel intend to develop and use local norms based on their students' performance alone, those standardized instruments that have inadequate norms are severely limited in the contribution they can make to the occupational education program.

Administration and Scoring

Another important consideration in selecting standardized instruments is the ease with which local personnel are going to be able to administer and score the instrument that is selected. Obviously, the directions for administration should be presented in the test manual such that the local personnel can duplicate the testing conditions that were used to obtain the validity, reliability, and normative data presented in the test manual. The directions for administration must be sufficiently clear and precise to make possible standardized testing conditions from one locale to another.

Likewise, procedures for scoring should be presented in the test manual so that these procedures will not vary from one locale to another. They too must be presented with sufficient detail and clarity so as to minimize the possibility of scoring error or deviation from the scoring procedures used to determine the obtained scores from which the validity, reliability, and normative data for the instrument were developed.

The nature of instruments with regard to the time needed to administer and score is often an important consideration in selecting standardized instruments. When school and other schedules make it inconvenient or difficult to accommodate the administration and scoring of a particular instrument, that instrument should be given careful consideration before being adopted for use. However, if the choice is between a somewhat "inconvenient" but very strong instrument and a "convenient" but significantly weaker instrument, the decision should be to select the stronger of the two and make the necessary adjustments to accommodate the inconvenience.

Cost

Cost seems to be a major consideration in most every aspect of occupational programs. However, the cost associated with the purchase of standardized instruments is so small (as compared to the costs of personnel services to administer adequately, score, and use the results) that costs for test booklets, for example, really should not be a significant factor to consider when selecting standardized instruments for the occupational program. Given two equally good instruments that vary in purchase price by even a few cents, of course, the least expensive should be selected. A few cents per student tested, taken over a large number of students, will save a few dollars. However, if a selection decision involves significant differences in personnel services and/or equipment costs to administer adequately, score, and use the results, then these costs should be related to the value added to the testing program through the additional costs. If the value added is great enough to justify the added expense and the resources are available, then the decision should be to select the best instrument regardless of costs. If these two conditions cannot be met, then obviously some other decision will have to be made.

However, if a selection decision does not involve excessive additional personnel services and/or equipment costs, then cost should not be a primary consideration in selecting one instrument over another. As a matter of fact, in some instances, the better of two instruments may actually cost less to purchase than its counterpart. In most instances, adequate validity, reliability, and norms are *far more important* considerations than either purchase price, costs for personnel services, or equipment costs.

Test Selection Procedures

The basic criteria for selecting standardized instruments have been introduced. Generally, before one attempts to make a decision regarding the selection or rejection of a particular instrument, a thorough review of the pertinent information relating to these criteria should be developed for that instrument. The discussion here shifts to a format for summarizing the pertinent information about a standardized instrument that will be useful to occupational teachers, administrators, and career-guidance personnel in reviewing and developing a thorough understanding of the pertinent information about any standardized instrument.

The format presented in table 10.3 is a useful guide for recording the facts and opinions that are important to the process of identifying, reviewing, and selecting from among the many available, standardized instruments for occupational programs. The format contains ten sections. Each has been numbered to assist in relating it to the discussion that follows.

Sections I and II are concerned with the local situation, for it plays a significant role in narrowing the field of instruments that would serve the need of the local occupational program. First, as indicated in the format, a clear statement of the purpose or measurement task for which the instrument will be used must be developed. It makes little sense to start looking for the best available measurement tool when the measurement task has not been clearly defined. Such a statement might be very general, as is our statement for the example review of the GATB presented in table 10.4 (obtaining a range of vocational aptitude data to be used in the high school career-guidance program), or somewhat specific (e.g., diagnosing learning difficulties among selected low achieving occupational students). In any event, it must be clearly stated before the search process can really begin.

Most occupational programs also have some built-in or local constraints that must be considered early in the search process. As indicated in section II of the format, these constraints should be listed right after the statement of purpose. For example, the time available for testing, financial resources, and the measurement expertise among the professional personnel who would be using the instrument would be constraining factors in many occupational education testing programs. An instrument for obtaining a range of vocational aptitude data for career-guidance purposes might,

TABLE 10.3. *Format for Reviewing Standardized Instruments*

I.   Measurement task for which the instrument will be used

II.   Constraints imposed by the local program

III.   General information about the instrument
  1. Author
  2. Title
  3. Type of instrument
  4. Publisher
  5. Date of publication

IV.   Interpretability
  1. Adequacy of norms
  2. APA level of classification
  3. Types of items employed
  4. Variables represented in obtained scores

V.   Validity
  1. Type(s) reported
  2. Criterion for each type
  3. Sample size(s)
  4. Result(s)
  5. Noteworthy comments

VI.   Reliability
  1. Type(s) reported
  2. Sample size(s)
  3. Result(s)
  4. Noteworthy comments

VII.   Efficiency in use
  1. Time required
  2. Scoring procedures
  3. Group or individual test
  4. Forms available
  5. Adequacy of directions
  6. Probable acceptance by students

VIII. Costs
  1. Instruments
  2. Answer sheets
  3. Scoring service
  4. Special equipment

IX.   Reviewers' comments
  1. Positive
  2. Negative

X.   General suitability for local purposes

for example, have to be (1) a group test (rather than an individually administered test), (2) suitable for use by high school students having a broad range of vocational aptitudes, and (3) suitable for administration and interpretation by the career-guidance personnel, occupational teachers, and administrative personnel currently employed in the district.

Once sections I and II of the format are completed, one would be ready to turn to Buros' *Tests in Print II, Vocational Tests and Reviews,* or *The Mental Measurements Yearbook* series and other sources of information on available standardized instruments to compile a listing of potentially useful instruments, always keeping in mind, of course, the statement of purpose and local constraints. The remaining eight sections of the format would be used in gathering pertinent facts and opinions for each of the instruments included in the compiled listing of potentially useful instruments.

Section III calls for some general information like author, title, type of instrument (e.g., achievement test, aptitude test, interest inventory, or general mental ability test), publisher, and date of publication. Except for publication dates, most of the information here is straightforward. Older instruments should be viewed with some caution. Advancing technological developments in the world of work cause standardized achievement tests in many occupational areas to become outdated rather quickly. Aptitude tests and interest inventories have a somewhat longer useful life span but here too normative data tend to lose their relevance as social and cultural patterns shift with our advancing technology. However, there are some older standardized instruments that are still very useful to occupational education programs.

Section IV of the format is concerned with the general interpretability of the scores obtained with the instrument in question. The first consideration here should be the adequacy of the norms presented in the test manual. Are the norms going to be useful for the purpose for which the instrument will be used? Are they up-to-date and based on a large enough norming sample composed of individuals having attributes, characteristics, and backgrounds similar to those to be served in the local occupational program? Unless local norms are developed, interpretation of obtained scores is extremely difficult if the norms are judged as being inadequate.

Instruments that require the employment of personnel who are extremely sophisticated in measurement procedures and techniques

TABLE 10.4. Example Review of the GATB

I. **Measurement task.** Obtaining a range of vocational aptitude data to be used in the high school career-guidance program.

II. **Local constraints.** To be administered and interpreted by present career-guidance personnel. Limited financial resources.

III. **General information.** U.S. Department of Labor developed test; General Aptitude Test Battery (GATB); vocational aptitude test battery; Superintendent of Documents, U.S. Government Printing Office, Washington, D.C. 20402, 1946-70.

IV. **Interpretability.** Provides occupational aptitude patterns (OAPs) for a broad range of occupations or clusters of occupations listed in the *Dictionary of Occupational Titles* (DOT). Can be administered and interpreted by local personnel or State Employment Office personnel. Item types include matching pictures of tools, comparing written names, basic arithmetic problems, arithmetic reasoning problems, vocabulary, visualizing three-dimensional pattern development, matching two-dimensional forms, placing and turning pegs in a pegboard, and assembling and disassembling rivets and washers. Nine aptitudes are represented in the obtained scores: general learning ability, verbal aptitude, numerical aptitude, spatial aptitude, form perception, clerical perception, motor coordination, finger dexterity, and manual dexterity.

V. **Validity.** An extremely large number of predictive and concurrent validity studies have been conducted in a broad range of occupational areas. Criteria used in these studies include instructor's ratings, grade point averages, supervisor's ratings, piece-rate earnings, lecture and laboratory grades, production records, course grades, scores on other tests, work samples, and the like. Sample sizes range from 30 or so to 200 plus. Obtained validity coefficients range from around 0.20 to 0.80 plus. Validity studies emanate from a continuing program of GATB research conducted through State Employment Services. Probably more validity data available for this battery than any other standardized test. Battery appears to be measuring some key vocational aptitudes.

VI. **Reliability.** A rather large number of test-retest reliability studies have been conducted with the intervals between testing ranging from one day to three years. Sample sizes range from around 25 to well over 500 subjects. The obtained coefficients range from the lower 0.70s to the mid 0.90s. Adequate reliability for the battery certainly has been demonstrated.

VII. **Efficiency in use.** About three hours are required for administering the entire battery. May be administered as a group or individual test. However, the testing apparatus needed for the finger and manual dexterity subtests would require individual or small group administration. May be hand or machine scored. Answer sheets can be hand scored locally or sent in a batch to National Computer Systems Inc., Minneapolis, Minnesota for machine scoring. Special forms of the test are available for the Spanish-speaking and for those deficient in reading skills. Directions for administering, scoring, and interpreting scores are clear and easy to follow. Appears to be accepted well among the general high school-aged population.

VIII. **Costs.** No testing fee is charged for students tested through the local State Employment Service. Tests supplied for counseling purposes to local school districts and other nonprofit organizations. Test booklets, answer sheets, and profile record cards are available for less than $0.50 per student. However, booklets are reuseable. Machine scoring available at a nominal cost per student. Special testing apparatus (pegboard and finger dexterity board) cost about $40 for the two. Both are reuseable. No other special equipment is required.

IX. **Reviewer's comments.** On a relative basis, the GATB is the best researched of the multiple-aptitude batteries. The large amount of validity data available make it a very useful tool for career-guidance. However, considerable change has occurred in the world of work since the GATB's development, which limits its usefulness in some occupational areas.

X. **General suitability for local needs.** The GATB would appear to be capable of providing a wide range of vocational aptitude data that would be useful to the school career-guidance program. Moreover, it could do so with present personnel and with reasonable expenditures of staff time, student time, and financial resources.

325

(APA level C instruments) may present problems in administration and interpretation for many occupational education testing programs. Therefore, it is wise to note an instrument's classification level early in the review and selection process and eliminate that instrument at this point in the review process if adequately prepared personnel cannot be made available for administering, scoring, and interpreting the obtained records of student performance.

Noting the types of items employed and the variables represented in the obtained scores is an important step in getting a "feel" for a particular instrument. This feel is particularly important when one begins to interpret obtained scores and make evaluative judgments that are based on these interpretations.

Information recorded for these last two areas should be based on the local reviewer's analysis of the items included in the instrument. This analysis should involve the local reviewer taking the test himself as well as administering it to at least one other person. These activities will assist greatly in identifying the abilities, traits, and the like that appear to influence the scores obtained with the instrument.

For achievement tests there is a simple yet effective technique for determining whether the items included in the test are consistent with the objectives for a particular occupational course. This technique uses a table of specifications similar to the one presented in table 4.1. Student-performance objectives for the course in which the test is to be used are listed in the appropriate column of the table. A percentage figure indicating relative importance in the course is then assigned to each of the listed objectives. After taking the test and gaining some feel for the knowledge, understanding, or skill each item seems to elicit, one can begin matching the item included in the test with the importance attached to each course objective. This is done by writing the number of each test item across from the objective to which it relates and under the appropriate type and level of learning, knowing, understanding, doing, or being. For test items that do not seem to relate to any of the course objectives, their numbers can be recorded on a separate sheet headed "unrelated items." Upon completion of this tabulation process, one can see quite readily the number of items that relate to each objective. Do these numbers generally correspond to the importance attached to each course objective? Are there very few unrelated items? If not, this particular test probably has little value for *this course.* However, if the answer to these two questions is yes, then there is little need to give further consideration to this test.

Section V of the format is concerned with the instrument's validity as reported in the test manual and as judged by the local reviewer and by reviewers reporting in Buros' *Vocational Tests and Reviews, The Mental Measurements Yearbook* series, professional journals, or some other source. The type(s) of validity studies reported in the manual (predictive, concurrent, or construct), the criterion used in each study, the number of subjects included in the sample for each study, and the validity coefficient that was derived from each study should all be noted in this section. In addition, noteworthy comments relative to the foregoing points (e.g., validity studies are outdated and sample size was extremely small), reviewers' comments regarding the instrument's validity, and the local reviewer's general impression of the instrument's ability *actually* to measure what it was designed to measure should be noted at the conclusion of this section.

Section VI of the format is concerned with the instrument's reliability as reported in the test manual and as judged by the local reviewer and by reviewers reporting in *The Mental Measurements Yearbook* series, professional journals, or some other source. The type(s) of reliability studies reported in the manual (test–retest, split halves, and the like), the number of subjects included in each study, and the reliability coefficients that were derived from each study should all be noted in this section. In addition, noteworthy comments relative to the foregoing points (e.g., coefficients are spuriously high because this is a speed test and split-halves procedures were used), reviewers' comments regarding the instrument's reliability, and the local reviewer's general impression of the instrument's ability to measure *consistently* what it purports to measure should be noted at the conclusion of this section.

Section VII is concerned with the instrument's efficiency in producing interpretable obtained scores or some of the more practical aspects of the instrument: the amount of time required to administer the instrument; the type(s) of scoring procedures that may be used; whether it can be administered to large group settings or must be administered on an individual basis; the number of forms of the instrument that are available; the completeness and clarity of instructions for administering, scoring, and interpreting obtained scores; and the manner in which the instrument will be perceived and accepted on its face value by students. Except for the latter two, answers to each of these concerns are straightforward and need little amplification here.

The local reviewer's reaction to the latter two concerns, adequacy of directions and instrument acceptance, should emanate from the experiences gained in taking the test oneself and in administering it to at least one other person. These experiences would provide an adequate foundation for evaluating the instrument in terms of its completeness and clarity of instructions for administering, scoring, and interpreting obtained scores as well as the manner in which it will be received by those to whom it will be administered.

Section VIII of the format is concerned with important costs associated with using the instrument in question. Here, too, the information is rather straightforward—purchase prices for items like test booklets and answer sheets as well as costs associated with scoring services (if needed or desired) and any special equipment required in administering the instrument. The most current information would be found in the publisher's catalog.

Section IX provides for general comments regarding the overall adequacy and/or worth of the instrument, both positive as well as negative comments. The best sources for such comments would be Buros' *Vocational Tests and Reviews, The Mental Measurements Yearbook* series, and professional journals that regularly publish reviews of standardized instruments.

Section X, the final section of this review format, provides for some general or overall comments by the local reviewer regarding the suitability of the instrument for the specified purpose for which the instrument would be used in the local occupational education testing program. These comments also could be positive as well as negative in nature. In any event, the reader should not be left in doubt as to what the local reviewer's final assessment would be regarding the instrument's suitability for serving the local purpose.

In order to make such a decision, it is going to be necessary to (1) integrate all of the foregoing data, information, and opinions; (2) determine which of the apparently contradictory points should be judged the most trustworthy; and (3) come to some conclusion based on the evidence presented as a whole. The outcome should be a decision based on a careful consideration of the stated local measurement task as well as the instrument's technical and practical features that will contribute to achieving the measurement task.

SELECTED STANDARDIZED INSTRUMENTS
USED IN OCCUPATIONAL PROGRAMS

The purpose of the listing presented here is to provide occupational teachers, administrators, and career-guidance personnel with a brief introduction to some examples of the types of standardized instruments that have been used with some degree of success in some occupational programs. The listing includes the following types of instruments: achievement, general mental ability, aptitude, interest, and attitude. Inclusion in this listing does not imply suitability for all occupational programs. As so aptly stated by Seibel (1968, p. 265): "Unless the teacher or test user looks beneath the superficial descriptions of a given test and actually examines the tasks to be performed there is no assurance that the test results will be meaningful or useful to him." In addition to having potential value for actual use in some occupational programs, these tests would be of value to occupational teachers, administrators, and career-guidance personnel who are preparing locally developed instruments of the types represented in the listing. Each instrument presented here contains well developed examples of the measurement procedures and techniques presented in part II. Local test developers are advised to review the instruments of the type they are developing as they begin to prepare their instruments.

In addition to the sources presented earlier in this chapter, listings of achievement and aptitude tests currently being used in many occupational programs have been prepared. The listings prepared by Denton (1973) and by Boyd and Shimberg (1971) are sources that should be reviewed. Those whose occupational programs enroll disadvantaged youths and/or adults would be interested in reviewing the listing of assessment tools for the disadvantaged prepared by the American Vocational Association Manpower Research Review Panel (Van Dorn 1973).

Achievement Tests

Ohio Trade and Industrial Education Achievement Test Program
Instructional Materials Laboratory, The Ohio State University Group tests—Grades 11-12

The trade tests section of this battery includes ten achievement tests in the following occupational areas: machine trades, automotive mechanics, electricity, electronics, mechanical drafting, printing, sheet metal, cosmotology, auto body, and welding. Each is designed to be administered in conjunction with an intelligence and an arithmetic test included in the program. These trade tests are not available on an individual basis. They are restricted for use as a group by schools that subscribe to the total program.

NLN Achievement Tests for Schools Preparing Registered Nurses
National League of Nursing, Inc.
Group tests—Students in state-approved programs preparing registered nurses

Basic achievement tests are available in the following nursing-related subject areas: anatomy and physiology, chemistry, microbiology, nutrition, pharmacology, medical-surgical nursing, public health nursing, obstetric nursing, nursing of children, and psychiatric nursing. Comprehensive achievement tests are available also in nursing-related subject areas including diet therapy and applied nutrition, pharmacology in clinical nursing, natural sciences, maternity and child nursing, disaster nursing, medical–surgical nursing, and communicable disease nursing.

Fire Performance Rating System
McCann Associates
Individual scale—Firemen

This rating scale covers 100 traits thought to be important for fire service personnel. It is to be completed by immediate supervisors and yields seven summary ratings: fire ground work, station work, personality traits and work habits, fire ground command, supervision, administration, and total.

General Mental Ability Tests

SRA Verbal Form
Science Research Associates, Inc.
Group test—Grades 7–16 and adults

A self-scoring test of general mental ability that provides three scores: quantitative (numerical ability), linguistic (verbal ability), and total score.

SRA Pictorial Reasoning Test
Science Research Associates, Inc.
Group test—Ages 14 and above

A "culture-free" test of general mental ability designed to be used with individuals from all the major subcultural groups in the United States to assess their learning potential for occupational training and employment when reading difficulties make use of more verbal tests inappropriate.

California Short-Form Test of Mental Maturity
CTB/McGraw-Hill
Group test—Grades 9–12 and 12–16 and adults

This is a short form of the *California Test of Mental Maturity* that provides seven scores: logical reasoning, numerical reasoning, verbal concepts, memory, language total, nonlanguage total, and total score.

Aptitude Tests

Differential Aptitude Tests
Psychological Corporation
Group tests—Grades 8–12 and adults

This is a battery of eight tests designed to provide, for career-guidance purposes, aptitude scores in the following areas: verbal reasoning, numerical ability, abstract reasoning, clerical speed and accuracy, mechanical reasoning, space relations, spelling, and grammar.

General Aptitude Test Battery (GATB)
United States Government Printing Office
Group test—Ages 16 and over and grades 9–12 and adults

This battery was developed for use in the occupational counseling program of the U. S. Training and Employment Service. Nine scores are provided: intelligence, verbal, numerical, spatial, form perception, clerical perception, motor coordination, finger dexterity, and manual dexterity. Orders for this instrument must be approved by a local State Employment Service office.

Nonreading Aptitude Test
United States Government Printing Office and National Computer Systems, Inc.
Group test—Disadvantaged grades 9–12 and adults

This is a nonreading adaptation of the foregoing *General Aptitude Test Battery.*

Interest Inventories

Ohio Vocational Interest Survey (OVIS)
Harcourt Brace Jovanovich, Inc.
Group test—Grades 8–12

This survey provides 24 scores relating to the following types of work: manual, machine, personal services, people or animal care, clerical, inspection and testing, skilled crafts, customer services, nursing and related technical services, skilled personal services, training, literary, numerical, appraisal, agriculture, applied technology, promotion and communication, management and supervision, artistic, sales, music, entertainment, and performing arts. Cannot be locally scored.

Strong Vocational Interest Blank for Men (SVIB)
Measurement Research Center
Group test—Males, ages 16 and over

This is an occupational interest inventory that has nearly 100 scoring scales of the following types: basic interests, occupational interests, and nonoccupational interests.

Strong Vocational Interest Blank for Women (SVIB-W)
Measurement Research Center
Group test—Females, ages 16 and over

This inventory has slightly fewer scoring scales than the SVIB and they are of the same types: basic interests, occupational interests, and nonoccupational interests.

Kuder Occupational Interest Survey
Science Research Associates, Inc.
Group test—Grades 11–16 and adults

This is an occupational interest survey that has 106 scoring scales for men (77 occupational and 29 college major) and 74 scales for women (47 occupational and 27 college major).

Attitude Tests

Study of Values: A Scale for Measuring the Dominant Interests in Personality
Houghton Mifflin Company
Group test—Grades 10-16 and adults

This scale provides six scores in the following areas: theoretical, economic, aesthetic, social, political, and religious.

Vocational Preference Inventory, Sixth Revision
Consulting Psychologists Press, Inc.
Group test—Grades 12-16 and adults

This is a personality test that uses occupational item content. It provides eleven scores: realistic, intellectual, social, conventional, enterprising, artistic, self-control, masculinity, status, infrequency, and acquiescence.

Edwards Personality Inventory
Science Research Associates
Group test—Grades 11-16 and adults

This is a personality inventory that provides fifty-four scores (11-15 each with one of the five available test booklets).

REFERENCES

American Psychological Association. *Ethical Standards of Psychologists.* Washington, D.C.: 1953.

Boyd, J. L., and Shimberg, Benjamin. *Directory of Achievement Tests for Occupational Education.* Princeton, New Jersey: Educational Testing Service, 1971.

Buros, O. K. *Tests in Print II.* Highland Park, New Jersey: Gryphon Press, 1974.

Buros, O. K., ed. *The Mental Measurements Yearbooks.* Highland Park, New Jersey: Gryphon Press, 1938-72 (irregular).

___. *Vocational Tests and Reviews.* Highland Park, New Jersey: Gryphon press, 1975.

Denton, William T. *Student Evaluation in Vocational and Technical Education.* Columbus, Ohio: ERIC/CVTE Ohio State University, 1973.

French, J. W., and Michael, W. B., co-chairmen. *Standards for Educational and Psychological Tests and Manuals.* Prepared by an American Psychological Association, American Educational Research Association, and National Council on Measurement in Education joint committee. Washington, D.C.: American Psychological Association, 1966.

Guilford, J. P. *Fundamental Statistics in Psychology and Education.* New York: McGraw-Hill, 1965.

Holmen, Milton G., and Hector, Richard. *Educational and Psychological Testing— A Study of the Industry and Its Practices.* New York: Russell Sage Foundation, 1972.

Seibel, Dean W. "Measurement of Aptitude and Achievement." In Whitla, Dean K., ed., *Handbook of Measurement and Assessment in Behavioral Sciences.* Reading, Massachusetts: Addison-Wesley Publishing, 1968.

Van Dorn, Ronald, ed. "Manpower, Human Assessment and the Disadvantaged," *American Vocational Journal,* vol. 48, no. 1, 1973.

Part IV

Obtaining and Using Measurement Information

Chapter 11

Administering Teacher-made and Standardized Instruments

The process of administering teacher-made instruments should not overlook any technical considerations. The standardization of procedures, establishment of adequate testing conditions, orientation of the students, and many other technical considerations should not be taken for granted. These technical concerns can greatly influence the way individual students perform the measurement tasks, which, in turn, may affect the overall accuracy and validity of the obtained scores.

Standardized instruments generally include specific instructions to the administrator and proctor for establishing conditions and standardizing the administration. This standardization usually includes the exact words that the test proctor reads to all students with specific instructions on how to handle student questions and how to time the particular segments or sections of the instruments. There are good reasons why the standardization of procedures as used in standardized instruments should be applied to the administration of teacher-made instruments as well.

First, it is important to maximize the test-taking performance of each individual being tested. If the test administrator for one group slightly changes the administrative procedures from those used with another group, the maximum performance of both groups may not be obtained. For example, an instructor might do more to motivate one group by giving more positive encouragement prior to administration. This could affect student performance in that group.

Second, standard procedures become very important when group comparisons are to be made among classes or schools, or to state or national norms. For example, when a group of X-ray technicians is being examined in fifty different locations on a national certification test, it is important that each group and individual has an equal opportunity to pass the examination. It would be unfair if one group received more time or had the opportunity to ask for clarification of certain items when another did not have a similar opportunity. The need for consistency is easily identified on large-scale testing and certification efforts but is not as often seen by occupational instructors within their classrooms and laboratories.

If an instructor is testing the achievement of three different sections of the same course, all to be graded as one group, the emphasis on consistent procedures should prevail. Otherwise, it is possible that a student in one section who is actually superior to a student in another section but was not given an equal testing opportunity, may score lower.

Standardizing the administration of instruments to different groups, then, is important. Also of importance is the administration of individual tests. To most educators the term individual tests brings to mind a specific type of intelligence test that is administered on a one-to-one basis. The Wechsler and Stanford–Binet tests are examples of such tests. However, as emphasized in chapter 6, tests of psychomotor and perceptual performance in many cases are individually administered. For example, a dental hygiene student is evaluated by an examiner in the task of teeth cleaning. For individual tests, it becomes very important that each individual being examined has equal opportunity to perform. This concern is amplified if more than one examiner is involved in assessing a group of students.

An additional concern for individuals responsible for test administration is in meeting the needs of individuals with special handicaps or disadvantages. When confined to self-contained classrooms or homogeneously comprised classrooms for special students, measurement tasks are generally designed for these students. However, with an increasing emphasis on mainstreaming or placing special students into regular classrooms, there is a need not only to alter many instructional techniques for these individuals, but also to expand the measurement expertise of instructors. Attention is placed throughout the section on administrative considerations on this concern, and a specific section focuses on administration of instruments to special students.

GENERAL PREADMINISTRATION
CONSIDERATIONS

Test administrators should prepare themselves before testing. The following suggestions will help test administrators prepare themselves for administering standardized instruments but the principles should be applicable to locally developed measures as well. Affirmative responses are indicative of an administration that will not jeopardize the accuracy and value of the obtained test scores.

1. Thoroughly study the content of the test manual.
2. Personally take the test under the same conditions specified in the test manual.
3. Make certain that the testing environment is in a state of readiness (absence of undue tension or anxiety, an understanding of the fact that one can expect to find some hard items that most people cannot answer, etc.).
4. Understand and accept the notion that a test is necessarily a frustrating experience, since it is designed to include many items that an individual will fail. The task of the test administrator is to make this frustration as mild as possible.
5. Refrain from any special coaching on the subject matter of the test in an attempt to reduce anxiety or frustration.
6. Rehearse by reading aloud *all* the directions and noting the timing for each section when giving the test for the first time.
7. Make sure that an adequate supply of pencils, erasers, and scratch paper is available when needed.
8. Try to anticipate the questions that might be asked just before giving the signal to begin.
9. Make arrangements so that those being tested will not be interrupted. ("TESTING–DO NOT DISTURB" signs prevent many unnecessary interruptions.)

PREADMINISTRATION CONSIDERATIONS
FOR SPECIAL STUDENTS

Prior to the administration of any measurement instrument, it is important to determine if any students have handicaps that might adversely affect their performance. In some situations it is possible that a homogeneous group of deaf or blind students exists. However, especially with current emphasis on mainstreaming handicapped and disadvantaged students, a group or class of students may include individuals possessing a variety of handicaps.

Whatever the makeup or degree of homogeneity, it is necessary to look closely at the prevalent handicaps and to take measures that will minimize the handicaps' effects on test performance.

Reading Level

One of the greatest limitations of many measuring instruments for special students is that the reading level is too high or vocabulary is inappropriate. Generally, the reading level of an instrument can be lowered by decreasing sentence length and minimizing the use of complex language or terms. Individuals may be physically normal with some type of learning or educational disadvantage resulting from mental retardation, deafness, language barrier, etc. Regardless of the case, simplification of language can improve the measuring process. If deaf students are among the respondents and if sign language or manual communication will be used to present items, extra care should be taken to insure that each word used in the instrument is within the manual vocabulary of the students so that difficult words that require finger spelling can be minimized. It may also be necessary to translate reading material to the native language of a non-English student.

Brailling

If blind students are being measured, it may be necessary, as a prerequisite to test administration, to have the instrument brailled so that blind students can read the instrument without oral prompting or reading. If brailling equipment or braille service is not immediately available, it may be necessary to prepare instruments in advance of normal scheduling. Additionally, it may be advantageous to place each brailled item on a separate card or sheet. This could save effort and time in revising tests and in developing alternate forms of instruments. In addition to brailled tests, the use of an oversize print typewriter may be helpful for students with partial vision to provide a readable test.

Answer Sheets

For blind students or students with motor impairments, it may be necessary to use special answer sheets. For multiple-choice or dichotomous-response items, it is often useful to provide additional or larger spaces for responses. In the case of blind students, a brailled answer sheet can be used or a sheet of paper can be folded vertically in four places (as shown in figure 11.1) to provide four kinesthetically

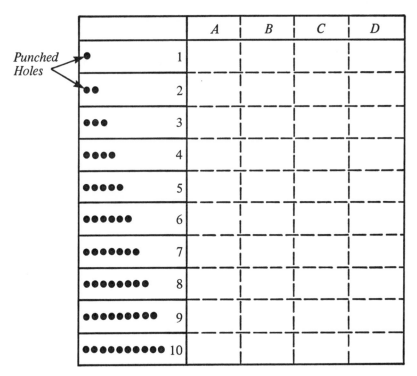

FIGURE 11.1.   Kinesthetic Answer Sheet for Blind Students.

identifiable columns. The sheet can then either be punched along the horizontal to indicate item location or additional folds can be made.

For motor-impaired or spastic individuals, larger item-response categories can be used on the answer sheet. These larger categories, such as the ones in figure 11.2, can provide ease and accuracy in response.

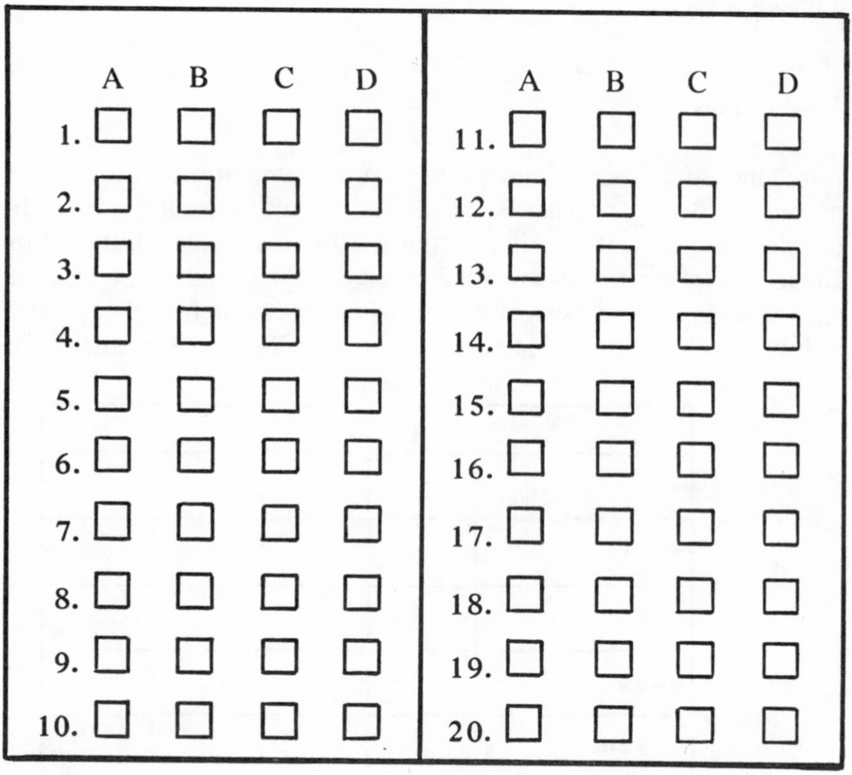

	A	B	C	D		A	B	C	D
1.	□	□	□	□	11.	□	□	□	□
2.	□	□	□	□	12.	□	□	□	□
3.	□	□	□	□	13.	□	□	□	□
4.	□	□	□	□	14.	□	□	□	□
5.	□	□	□	□	15.	□	□	□	□
6.	□	□	□	□	16.	□	□	□	□
7.	□	□	□	□	17.	□	□	□	□
8.	□	□	□	□	18.	□	□	□	□
9.	□	□	□	□	19.	□	□	□	□
10.	□	□	□	□	20.	□	□	□	□

FIGURE 11.2. Answer Sheet with Enlarged Response Spaces for Motor-impaired Students.

ADMINISTRATION CONSIDERATIONS

Traxler (1951) has identified five sources or kinds of errors that have been identified as affecting test administration. These include: incorrect timing, lack of clarity in directions, expectations about guessing, physical conditions, and student motivation. The following pages focus on a discussion of these potential error sources with suggestions for overcoming or avoiding them.

Setting Time Limits

Timing has been often cited as the greatest cause of error in the administration of tests. This error has generally been related to the administration of standardized instruments and has focused specifically on failure to read timing directions correctly, lack of understanding on the part of examiners of the need for precise timing, faulty time pieces, and careless scheduling or planning. These problems have been observed with standardized testing programs but the same problems occur in classroom-testing situations as well.

Time limits become important in conjunction with the choice of a power or speed test. In chapter 3 a *power test* was defined as one that samples an individual's broad range of skill and ability without emphasis on time limits. A speed test, on the other hand, has definite time limits that place emphasis on responding rapidly.

Teacher-made tests in occupational education are usually power tests. However, for some students with special needs and/or low reading abilities, a normal power test might place undue emphasis on time and may, for them, make the test more of a speed test. Under these circumstances, the results of a test may provide more of a reading skill measure than an occupational skill measure.

In administering a measure, then, there are several suggestions:

1. Establish time limits in accordance with the purpose of the test—power or speed.
2. Base time limits on a trial run of the instrument. As a general guide, allow students about twice the time it takes an instructor to read through and complete the test.
3. Notify each student of the time limits in writing and orally.
4. Specify time limits and their importance to test proctors or administrators and insure that these limits are clearly communicated to the students prior to administration.

Establishing Adequate Testing Conditions

The most neglected of all test administration concerns has been the physical conditions of the testing area. Educational agencies vary as do individual classrooms and laboratories in their adequacy for testing. General factors such as light, heat, ventilation, and noise have been proven to affect adversely test performance of many individuals. More specifically, limitations related to amount of writing space have had an effect on performance—especially on speed tests. Tables, armchairs, full desks, or lapboards provide writing space of varying size and desirability. Some become less desirable and adequate when separate answer sheets are used. The following suggestions for establishing and maintaining adequate physical conditions are offered:

1. Noise should be minimized in the testing situation to insure that students hear the oral instructions given by the examiner or proctor. Also, noise control is important to minimize distraction to the students.
2. Provide a room that has adequate lighting, heat, and ventilation. These factors often affect a student's motivation, and improper control of the environmental components can distract students.
3. Seat students in desks or at tables that provide adequate space for writing or otherwise responding to the instrument.
4. Schedule testing so that individuals are not overburdened with too much testing in one day or within several days. Fatigue may affect performance.
5. The time of day for administering an instrument should be considered. The first thing in the morning, immediately following lunch, and the end of the day should be avoided whenever possible for the administration of instruments.
6. Make special arrangements for handicapped students. These arrangements might include special tables for paraplegic students, grouping to facilitate use of the same brailled test by blind students, grouping of deaf individuals to aid in manual interpretation of the instrument, or grouping of students who may need to have directions translated into their native language.
7. Seat students in alternate desks or chairs at tables to provide adequate working space and to minimize the temptation of copying or cheating.

Orienting Students

Orientation of students to the measuring activity is important to build the proper motivation, reduce anxiety, and insure correct interpretation of items. Research has shown that motivation affects test-taking performance of individuals. It is therefore important to maximize the motivation of students to gain an accurate measure of their achievement level or other related skill. Printed directions, as suggested in chapter 8, should be self-explanatory; however, they should also be emphasized orally by the test administrator or proctor. This should help eliminate the possibility of misinterpretation or failure to focus on the directions. Also, by orally presenting directions, it is possible for students to ask for clarification on certain aspects of the test format. Emphasis can also be placed on factors such as time limits, scoring procedures and weights, and, of great importance, the purpose of the test. The following suggestions are offered for orienting students to the testing situation:

1. *Try to raise students' interest and concern for accurate test scores.* An attempt has been made to identify incentives that will increase or maximize test performance. These incentives include monetary reward, pep talks, and prizes. But the incentive demonstrated to be most successful is concern for accurate measurement on the part of students.

2. *Action should be taken to minimize student anxiety in the test-taking situation.* Fear is a common reaction to many testing situations. Fear of punishment, not wanting to disappoint parents, fear of peer rejection, and fear of not maintaining an adequate self-concept are all sets common to taking tests. Try to minimize fear and anxiety.

3. *The purpose of testing and the use to be made of results should be made clear to all students.* By knowing the purpose, anxiety about the testing situation can be reduced for many students. In the administration of diagnostic tests and affective instruments, communication of the purpose is especially important. In some cases it may be advantageous to distribute a statement of purpose prior to test administration.

4. *The test administrator should project a positive and humane attitude regarding the testing situation.* The personality of the examiner has a lot to do with the motivation of students to tests. Of course, an examiner cannot change his or her personality, but a positive and friendly attitude can help maximize the motivation of students.

5. *Provide consistent and complete oral directions.* Oral directions should not supplant but should supplement printed directions. It is important that each individual and each group receive the same directions. Therefore, notes or read directions should be used. However, care should be taken not to remove the personal element of the situation through too much regimentation.

6. *Provide opportunity for students to clarify purposes, directions, scoring, and time limits.* After the oral directions have been given, an opportunity should be provided for students to ask questions about anything that was said. It is especially important to be sure that special-needs students understand all directions. In some cases, they may require additional time or personnel. In providing the time for questions, it is important for the proctor or test administrator not to give information that might give one group or one individual an unfair advantage over others. *Common sense* is usually the best judge in determining how much information to give in response to questions.

Provide for Practice

A common practice in standardized testing programs is the provision of sample or practice items on the first page or cover of the test booklet. Usually the sample items are presented as part of the printed directions and provide the correct responses to the sample items. By including sample items, the provision for practice is made that is designed to insure proper interpretation of the directions. In addition, by having the opportunity to respond to one or several sample items and learning the correctness of responses, reinforcement is provided and anxiety toward the instrument may be reduced.

Locally developed paper and pencil tests can include practice items similar to those used with standardized instruments. Often, the first item on a test or the first item of each test section can be completed at the time oral directions are given. It may be extra important to use trial items if unfamiliar answer sheets are used or if special adaptations in the test or answer sheet have been made for special-needs students.

The need for practice on performance measures is probably greater than the need on paper and pencil tests. Except for special cases, most paper and pencil measures use a format and response mode familiar to most advanced elementary and older students. However, with performance tests, especially individually administered tests, there is a chance that most students will not be familiar with the test format. The format for responding to identification tests can easily be clarified through the use of a sample item or two. With simulation and work-sample types of performance tests, the student must have the opportunity to become familiar with the simulator or equipment used in the testing to insure an accurate measure of students' actual ability to perform. Either a related task or practice of the task to be evaluated can provide an opportunity to learn the specifics of the equipment and to help minimize anxiety about the test. Several suggestions will help summarize some of the aforementioned concerns.

1. Include a sample item on paper and pencil tests if the item types used are not familiar to all students or if special answer sheets are being used.
2. Discuss the sample items after giving students the opportunity to respond. If possible it may be useful to walk around the room and observe each individual's response to check that he/she is responding appropriately.
3. Focus specific attention on special-needs students if adaptations in testing or responding have been made. It is important that everyone have an equal testing opportunity.
4. When identification tests are used, provide a sample item or segment of the test as practice. It is also important to provide feedback regarding responses and format.
5. Provide the opportunity for students to become accustomed to simulator or work-sample equipment prior to actual testing. This may involve going through a related task or practicing the task to be observed.

Indicate How Guessing Will Be Treated

Guessing at the correct response on items in which knowledge is lacking does not provide useful information for understanding an individual's performance level. However, specific directions about not guessing may give the chance taker an undue advantage over a student who has knowledge but lacks confidence. So, directions often tell the respondent to guess if the correct response is unknown.

There exists a controversy among measurement specialists regarding the use of special formulas that make corrections for guessing. Most of the concern, however, is with standardized tests that assume that there will be some items that will be unanswerable by some students without guessing. In some of these cases a correction-for-guessing formula may be appropriate. Speed tests that are designed to inhibit completion of the entire test also may appropriately use a guessing formula for scoring.

Basically, the correction-for-guessing formula is:

$$\text{Score} = \frac{\text{number right} - \text{number wrong}}{\text{number of alternatives} - 1}$$

In the case of a four-alternative multiple-choice item, the formula would appear as follows:

$$\text{Score} = \text{right} - \frac{\text{wrong}}{3}$$

For a true–false test the denominator in the fraction would be 2 – 1 or 1. This formula simply requires counting the number of right answers and wrong answers and substituting these numbers into the formula. For a student who had 40 items right and 6 items wrong on a four-alternative multiple-choice test, the score would be equal to 38 as computed below.

$$40 - \frac{6}{3} = 38$$

This formula operates under the assumption that the student had a 25 percent chance to guess correctly and that for the 6 he guessed incorrectly, he guessed 2 correctly. The formula computes this and subtracts the two items. The following suggestions are offered relative to guessing:

1. Use guessing formulas sparingly. Usually, standardized achievement tests and teacher-made speed tests are the only appropriate uses.
2. Be sure to inform students in writing as well as in oral directions of how guessing will be handled.
3. Use caution in computing scores to avoid error.

Answering Student Questions

Ample opportunity should be provided for students to ask questions prior to the beginning of testing. These questions should be related to directions and practice items. Content-related questions should be discouraged and avoided. Content or subject matter questions should be handled in a review session prior to testing.

Questions may also arise after testing has begun. These should be handled in a manner that will minimize disruption of others in the testing group. This can be accomplished by asking students to raise their hand if they have a question. Then the teacher or test proctor should go to the individual student for the question. If the question relates to an item that appears to be ambiguous, it might be worthwhile to interrupt the entire class to highlight and clarify the item. If the question is specific to the student, the need to interrupt the entire group should be avoided.

Handling Obvious Cheaters

There may, in any testing situation, be the possibility for cheating or unfairly using aids. By adhering to the suggestions made in previous sections of this chapter, the opportunity for cheating will be decreased. For example, if students feel the need for accurate assessments of their performance to aid in placement, etc., their desire to cheat will be diminished.

There are, however, several additional actions that the teacher or proctor can take to minimize cheating. First, in the giving of oral directions, the teacher should emphasize that "eyes should focus on one's own test and answer sheet." Also, a suggestion can be made to guard one's answer sheet from others' views. These two instructions will prevent most cheating.

Second, if a student is observed looking at another's answer sheet, a stern look from the teacher should be the first form of action. If it persists, a second step should involve an oral reminder to the class to keep their eyes on their own papers. A third action, if the first two are not corrective, should be a specific directive to the student observed cheating such as, "Mr. Jones, would you watch your own paper, please." If this does not bring action, the last step should be to negate the test score of the individual observed cheating.

ADMINISTERING TESTS TO SPECIAL STUDENTS

The introduction to this chapter and the section on preadministration concerns emphasized the need to make special testing arrangements for students with special needs. Many special-needs students, such as some paraplegic individuals, will require no special administration considerations. However, there may be a great need to facilitate testing of others.

For mentally retarded individuals it will be necessary to use appropriate language in the instrument and in many cases the instrument will need to be administered orally with much simplification and clarification. It may be necessary with some students to administer the instrument individually.

For deaf students, it may be sufficient to simplify the language and vocabulary used on printed instruments. However, the verbal and reading skill of many deaf individuals may require that the instrument be administered by interpreting it through a total communication approach giving the opportunity for lipreading, sign language, and finger spelling. If a large group of deaf students is being tested, it may be possible to interpret the instrument to the entire group at once. If only one or two students in the class are deaf, a special tutor or proctor may aid in interpreting the test individually.

In testing the blind or partially sighted students suggestions were made in a previous section to braille the instrument or to use oversize type. Another alternative is to read the instrument aloud to the blind students. This approach has a disadvantage when used in a group setting, in that it requires all students to progress through the test at the same speed. One way to overcome this disadvantage is to use a separate tape recording for presenting the test to individual students, providing the opportunity to stop and start the recorder.

When testing students whose native language is not English, it may be necessary to use the services of a bilingual specialist. The bilingual specialist could either translate the directions and questions orally or prepare the instrument in the students' native language.

There are many more types of handicaps or learning disabilities that could require special attention in test administration, many of which are beyond the scope of this chapter. Often advice in testing these special students can be obtained from a special consultant or from special education teachers who are employed in most educational institutions.

REFERENCE

Traxler, A. E. "Administering and Scoring the Objective Test." In Lindquist, E. F., ed., *Educational Measurement.* Washington, D. C.: American Council on Education, 1951, pp. 329–416.

Chapter 12

Scoring, Reporting, and Interpreting Test Results

SCORING TESTS

The most important aspect of scoring students' performance on measurement instruments is accuracy. The very best of instruments quickly becomes absolutely useless if it is not scored correctly. Occupational education teachers, administrators, and career-guidance personnel must recognize this point and consciously strive for complete accuracy in scoring the instruments they use in their programs. There is enough uncontrollable error represented in most test scores and additional error should not be introduced through inadequate scoring techniques, especially when this type of error is controllable.

Scoring Objective Instruments

Objective instruments are instruments with scoring procedures such that no matter which of several qualified scorers score a student's performance, the same score will be obtained. For example, true-false and multiple-choice type tests are usually considered to be objective tests. Given the scoring key for a test of either type, several qualified teachers, secretaries, or even students could score these tests and come up with the same raw scores. Machine-scored instruments also are objective instruments. No matter how often an answer sheet is put through the test-scoring machine, the same raw score should result.

There are, however, three commonly recognized potential sources of error when scoring objective type instruments: (1) simple counting errors, (2) errors in the scoring key, and (3) errors in recording scores.

Avoiding Counting Errors. Errors in counting occur when one is counting the number of correct or incorrect responses that are on a student's answer sheet or test paper after it has been corrected or marked. Using a contrasting-colored felt-tipped pen or pencil to mark correct or incorrect responses on the answer sheet will help considerably to avoid making counting type errors. In addition, some find it advisable to check their work by counting the "right" or correct responses first and recording that number. Then they count the "wrong" or incorrect responses and subtract that number from the total points possible. The rights plus wrongs should equal total points possible. If not, there is an error somewhere in the process and it should be found before going on to correct the next student's test.

Using Scoring Keys. One of the most common errors is that of using a scoring key in which one or more of the keyed correct answers is actually an incorrect answer. The mistake is made in the process of developing the scoring key. Usually, it is because the individual constructing the key feels very familiar with the test items and does not read each item carefully before marking the correct answer on the answer key. Yes, even occupational teachers who develop their own tests quite often err when building their answer keys. The best approach to avoiding such errors is to read carefully as you build the scoring key and have a knowledgeable colleague check the accuracy of newly developed keys.

Recording Scores. The final common source of error in scoring is in recording a score incorrectly. This type of error occurs with sub-jective tests, too. Anyone who has thought or read 132 and then recorded something like 123 will understand this type of error. Frequently, it occurs as the occupational teacher, for example, is recording scores on tests, papers, or projects in a gradebook.

Scoring Subjective Instruments

Subjective instruments are far more prone to error in scoring than are objective instruments. The scores obtained are often based to some degree on the scorer's subjective judgment. Grading essay-type or even short-answer-type tests does not always produce the same obtained score regardless of who is doing the grading. On the contrary, the scorer's subjective judgment is an important factor in scoring subjective-type instruments. The best approach to controlling the degree to which subjective judgment can influence obtained scores is to develop well-structured items that call for well-defined responses.

Using Answer Keys. In the case of essay- and short-answer-type tests, one of the best ways to lend additional objectivity to the scoring process is to develop an answer key for each test item. The answer key here is merely a listing of all the points, ideas, or statements that will be counted as correct answers as the test is scored. As the listed points are identified in the student's written answers they should be underlined in a contrasting color. One or more points is awarded each time one of the listed items appears in the appropriate place within the student's written responses. The underlining makes it easier to tally those parts of the essay response for which credit is to be awarded. The natural tendency for scorers to be influenced by and award credit for neat penmanship or long, well-phrased answers that really are not what the test developer was looking for, will be avoided if such procedures are followed when scoring essay-type tests.

Short-answer and completion-type tests should be scored using a similar procedure if subjectiveness in scoring is to be minimized. The example in figure 12.1 demonstrates this point.

Item 1 in figure 12.1 should be scored correct because the student has entered the correct terms. If terms such as tallness or fatness are entered, they should be scored incorrect because they do not appear on the key. Likewise, item 2 should be scored incorrect if the answers entered do not match either of the two acceptable sets of answers presented on the key.

Maintaining a Consistent Mental Set. Even when using an answer key to score well-developed subjective-type instruments, scores often

Sentence Completion Items

1. The three dimension planes in mechanical drawing are _height_ , _length_ , and _width_ .

2. In three-view orthographic projections, edges that appear as lines in the top view will appear as _points_ in the front view and as _lines_ in the side view.

Sentence Completion Answer Key

1. (height)   (length)   (depth, width, thickness)
2. (points)   (lines)   or   (lines)   (points)

FIGURE 12.1.   Example Completion-type Items and Associated Answer Key.

can be influenced both positively and negatively by the mental set or attitudes that the scorer brings to the scoring process. This is particularly true when scoring essay-type tests where there is opportunity and necessity for the scorer to make interpretations as well as judgments.

Actually for most classroom situations, it matters not so much whether the scorer has a positive or negative mental set or a good or poor attitude toward the task or students. What matters is that the mental set and attitude be consistent across all test papers as they are scored. Potential unfairness can be seen in having an occupational teacher score one-half of his students' essays on a day when nothing seems to go right and the second half three days later when everything is coming up roses.

Therefore, it is a good idea for teachers to score the first item(s) on the test for *all* students and then proceed to the second item(s) and so on throughout the instrument. Moreover, it is also a good idea to mix up the test papers between each item or set of items that are to be scored to insure that the same papers are not always scored first and last throughout the scoring process.

If this approach to scoring subjective-type instruments is used and the teacher has need to stop when the task is only partially complete, he can return to the task with even a different mental set and each student's paper will receive equivalent treatment throughout the process of scoring the remaining half of its answers; that is, unless the teacher is paying attention to and is influenced by whose paper he is scoring. This is another potential source of inconsistency that must be guarded against to insure equivalent treatment of each student's responses.

Anonymous Scoring.   The best approach to avoid being influenced by knowledge of *whose* test is being scored is to grade all tests in the blind; that is, to score each test without being aware of whose test it is.

One approach to anonymous scoring that is particularly popular with students is to cover each student's name on his/her test paper or answer sheet shortly after the test administration period has begun. One simple way of doing this is to distribute the answer sheets or test booklets the students will be writing their answers on, ask them to write their names in the space provided, and then walk through the class folding and stapling over student names as per the following diagram in figure 12.2.

FIGURE 12.2.   Example Fold and Staple Technique for Concealing Students' Names.

Students react most favorably to this process because it indicates that their teacher is trying to insure that he will not bring personal biases into the scoring process. After all tests have been scored, the stapled corner can be opened to reveal the student's name for purposes of recording test scores and to return the scored instruments to students so that each item can be reviewed and discussed in class.

REPORTING NORM-REFERENCED TEST RESULTS

As indicated in chapter 2, norm-referenced testing in occupational programs is always concerned with reporting and making comparisons between students and their respective levels of performance on some particular measurement instrument. A variety of scores, measures of average performance, and measures of dispersion have been developed to assist occupational teachers, administrators, and career-guidance personnel make these comparisons. A discussion of the most useful of these approaches to reporting and comparing student performance on locally developed and standardized instruments is presented here.

Raw Scores

Occupational teachers who want to obtain the maximum amount of information about a particular student from a particular instrument should review the student's performance on each item included in the instrument. Determining the reasons why a student correctly completed or missed each item would provide the most complete assessment of that student's level of development in the area(s) measured by the instrument. Such a detailed analysis would provide a clear and extensive picture of the student's strengths and weaknesses in regard to the knowledge, skills, understanding, and/or affects that are being measured. However, except in some special instances, there are too many students enrolled in occupational courses for teachers to use this individualized item-by-item approach with any degree of efficiency or effectiveness.

One simple, efficient, and effective means of describing students' achievement or level of development in occupational programs is to use a single-score approach where some one score is used to signify a student's level of performance on a particular instrument. The most often used score in this approach to describing student performance is the student's raw score. It generally represents either the number of items answered correctly (for objective-achievement tests), the number of points awarded by the scorer (for essay-type tests), or the number of responses that fall into a particular affective category (for attitude and interest surveys).

Advantages of Raw Scores. Raw scores are easy to obtain. After tests or other instruments have been administered in occupational courses, each is scored. The score that is assigned to each student's test paper or answer sheet as a result of the scoring process is the raw score.

When criterion-referenced mastery tests are used, students can look at their raw scores and determine how well they did on the test. For example, if they see their raw score is 90 and they remember that there were 100 points on the examination, then they know they did pretty well on this exam. Likewise, those whose scores were only 25 on the same exam would know that they did not perform very well. However, looking at raw scores alone does not *always* provide students (or anyone else) with accurate feedback regarding how well they performed on an examination. This is particularly true for norm-referenced instruments.

Disadvantages of Raw Scores.   Suppose, for example, you are asked to interpret one student's raw score of zero on a five- or even a ten-item quiz in a foods class. Of course, a zero raw score usually means that the student failed to answer correctly any of the items included in the quiz. Does this mean that the student has zero knowledge, understanding, or skills in the area(s) covered by the quiz? Does this mean that the student should be placed in a more elementary level in the home economics program because he or she was unable to answer even the simplest of the items included in the quiz? Probably not would be a good answer for both of these questions.

With regard to the first question, it must be remembered that the items included in the quiz are a *sampling* of all the possible questions that might have been asked on the quiz. How can one be certain that if another sampling of items would have been included on the quiz the student would not have answered several of them correctly? One cannot be certain that this might not be the case. Therefore, it is dangerous to conclude that a zero raw score means zero learning has occurred. Likewise, a raw score of ten on a ten-point quiz may not be indicative of 100 percent learning in the area covered by the quiz. It only means that the student answered correctly ten of the ten sample items included in this particular quiz. Moreover, he or she may have guessed correctly on one or more of the ten items.

As for the second question regarding the student being in the wrong class, it, too, is difficult to answer without having some additional information. It would be helpful to know, for example, if any other students in the class scored a zero on the quiz also. For, if a significant number did, then perhaps the instruction, through no fault of the students, was inadequate.

Similar types of problems occur with nonzero raw scores, too. For example, suppose that Mary, Rose, and Dale obtain raw scores of 10, 20, and 30 respectively on a 35-item unit test in a data processing course. What can be said about the differences in these scores? The differences in raw scores are in 10-point increments. Can it be said with certainty that the differences in learning between each of these students are equal?

Perhaps Mary answered correctly the ten easiest items on the test. Rose may have answered these ten easy items plus ten more of moderate difficulty. Finally, Dale probably answered those same twenty items plus ten others of a rather high difficulty level. If this is the case, then it can readily be seen that while the differences between these three raw scores are equal, the differences in the learning that each represents are not. This is because all test items tend to vary in their level of difficulty. When those answered correctly are added or summed to obtain a raw score, unequal units of the behavior being measured are included in the raw score.

As indicated in chapter 2, most obtained scores are on an ordinal scale of measurement. That is, they have neither a zero point nor equal intervals between them. These weaknesses have made it difficult to interpret adequately raw scores and have led to the development of other types of scores that are more useful in interpreting a student's test performance.

Frequency Distributions

As indicated in the preceding discussion, raw scores for criterion-referenced mastery tests provide occupational students with some information regarding their performance. They indicate how many of the items included in the instrument were answered correctly. However, in norm-referenced testing the real meaning of a raw score depends upon how it compares with the raw scores obtained by others who have taken the same test. High raw scores generally do not indicate high level of performance or ability if almost everyone in the group tested obtained equally high scores. Likewise, low raw scores generally do not indicate low levels of performance or ability if nearly everyone of those tested also obtained low raw scores. Raw scores achieve their maximum usefulness only when they can be compared with the raw scores of others from the student's peer group who have taken the same test.

One simple technique for allowing occupational students to compare their raw scores on a given test with the raw scores of their fellow students is to develop a frequency distribution. A simple frequency distribution for a 35-item achievement test administered in two sections of an occupational course is presented in table 12.1.

TABLE 12.1. Example Frequency Distribution for Scores on a Thirty-five-item Achievement Test.

Raw Score	Tally	Frequency
31	1	1
30	1	1
29	111	3
28		0
27	1111	4
26	̶1̶1̶1̶1̶ 11	7
25	̶1̶1̶1̶1̶ 1111	9
24	̶1̶1̶1̶1̶	5
23	11	2
22		0
21	1	1
20	11	2
19		0
18	1	1
		$N = 36$

The raw-score column on the left in table 12.1 presents the highest and lowest raw scores obtained for the two administrations (31 and 18) respectively, and all possible scores between the highest and lowest scores. The tally column is used to tally or record the actual number of students who obtained each of the scores included in the score column. The frequency column indicates the total number of students in the two sections who obtained each of the listed raw scores. Only one student obtained a score greater than 30. Nine received a score of 25. Students can take one look at this frequency distribution and get a quick impression of how well or how poorly they did on this 35-item achievement test. Frequency distributions are easy to develop and can be of considerable help in providing a quick impression of how well or how poorly a student has performed on a particular instrument.

Ranks

Another technique that can be used to clarify the meaning of raw scores on a particular instrument is to determine the ranking that each has within the total group. The highest raw score would receive a rank of one, the second highest a rank of two, the third highest a rank of three, and so on down the distribution of scores. An average rank is assigned to each raw score when two or more students achieve that score. Ranks for the frequency distribution in table 12.1 are presented in table 12.2.

TABLE 12.2.   Assigning Ranks for Each Score in a Frequency Distribution.

Raw Score	Tally	Frequency	Rank
31	1	1	1
30	1	1	2
29	111	3	$4 = (3 + 4 + 5) \div 3$
28		0	
27	1111	4	$7.5 = (6 + 7 + 8 + 9) \div 4$
26	++++ 11	7	13
25	++++ 1111	9	21
24	++++	5	28
23	11	2	31.5
22		0	
21	1	1	33
20	11	2	34.5
19		0	
18	1	1	36
			$N = 36$

To be able to say that students with raw scores of 31 and 30 rank first and second among their peers adds considerable meaning to these scores. However, if we compare the raw scores and ranks of students from two classes that differ in size, then we must also indicate the size of each class. To rank tenth in a group of twelve students is very different from ranking tenth in a group of 120 students. The most efficient way to report ranks and to account for differences in group size is to use percentile ranks.

Percentile Ranks

The *percentile rank* for a given raw score is the percentage of students in the group tested who obtained raw scores that were smaller than the given raw score. Thus, a percentile rank of 90 for a raw score of 40 means that 90 percent of those included in the group tested have raw scores that are smaller than 40 and only 10 percent have raw scores greater than 40.

Computing Percentile Ranks.   The following formula can be used to compute the percentile rank for any raw score in a frequency distribution:

$$\text{Percentile Rank} = \frac{\text{Number below score} + \frac{1}{2}\text{ of those at score}}{\text{Total number in the group}} \times 100$$

For example, the percentile rank for a raw score of 23 in the preceding frequency distribution would be computed as follows:

$$Pr \text{ for the score } 23 = \frac{4 + 1}{36} \times 100 = 13.89 \text{ or } 14$$

The percentile rank 14 was obtained by summing the frequencies for all scores below 23 (i.e., $1 + 2 + 1 = 4$), adding to this sum one half of the frequency for the score 23 ($2 \div 2 = 1$), dividing this total ($4 + 1$) by the total number of the group (36), multiplying the result by 100, and then rounding it to the nearest whole number.

The percentile rank for a raw score of 29 in this distribution should be higher than 14. The percentile rank for a raw score of 29 in this distribution would be computed as follows:

$$Pr \text{ for the score } 29 = \frac{31 + 1.5}{36} \times 100 = 90.28 \text{ or } 90$$

The percentile rank for the raw score 29 is much greater than that for the raw score 23. This is because a far greater percentage of the total group scored less than 29 (31 of 36) than scored less than 23 (4 of 36).

When discussing the procedure for computing percentile ranks questions often arise concerning the reasoning for including one half of those at the score in the numerator of the fraction included in

the formula. This practice is based upon a widely accepted measurement convention that a test score occupies a range extending
one-half unit above and one-half unit below the score. That is, a
raw score of 15 is said to occupy the interval between 14.5 and 15.5.
Moreover, all students having the same score in a frequency distribution are said to be equally distributed throughout the interval
around their obtained raw score. If, for example, the raw score
held in common is 15, then one half of them would, by convention,
be in the range 15 to 15.5 and one half in the range 14.5 to 15.
Because a percentile rank is the rank for the *exact* score, one half
of those at the score (those falling in the range one-half unit below
the given score) are counted as being below the exact score when
computing the percentile rank for that score.

Interpreting Percentile Ranks.   Percentile ranks lend themselves to more
precise interpretation than either raw scores or ranks. Percentile
ranks provide immediate knowledge as to how well a student has
performed in comparison to others who have taken the same test.
Where the conditions of class size or size of the group being tested
affect the interpretation of simple rankings, percentile ranks have
this consideration built in. A percentile rank of 70 in a group of 20
students is equivalent to a percentile rank of 70 in a group of 200 or
even 2,000 students.

However, the manner in which raw scores tend to cluster in the
frequency distribution must also be considered when interpreting
percentile ranks. The actual differences in students' performances
for successive percentile ranks in the center of the distribution are
much smaller than the differences for successive percentile ranks
near the tails of the distribution. Thus, a given difference in percentile ranks reflects a small difference in raw scores in the middle
of the distribution and a larger difference in raw scores near the tails
of the distribution.

It must also be remembered that percentile ranks are relative
scores rather than absolute scores. That is, a given obtained score
may be transformed into a relatively high percentile rank in one
group of scores and a relatively low percentile rank in another
group of scores. Lyman (1971) offers a descriptive scale for interpreting percentile ranks. Lyman's scale is presented in table 12.3.

The following scale should be viewed as a good starting point
for interpreting percentile ranks. It is not an inflexible standard.

TABLE 12.3. Ranges of Percentile Ranks and Associated Descriptive Terms for Interpreting Percentile Ranks Falling Within Each Range.

Percentile Ranks	Descriptive Terms
95 or above	Very high; superior
85–95	High; excellent
75–85	Above average; good
25–75	About average; satisfactory or fair
15–25	Below average; fair or slightly weak
5–15	Low; weak
5 or below	Very low; very weak

The descriptive terms may be varied and either more or less rigorous standards may be used if the nature of the group of students tested warrants such action.

Occupational teachers who use standardized instruments in their programs often encounter the term percentile. This term and percentile rank are closely related but should not be confused. A percentile is a score in a distribution of scores below which a given percentage of the scores in that distribution lie. For example, in the frequency distribution we have been working with, about 80 percent of the scores fall below the midpoint of the score 27. The 80th percentile in this distribution, therefore, would be 27. The percentile rank for the score 27 would be 80. Remember, a *percentile* is the *score* below which a certain percentage of the scores in the distribution fall. A *percentile rank* is the *percentage* of students in the distribution who have scores that fall below a certain score.

Measures of Central Tendency

Occupational students can get a rough interpretation of a raw score if they can see how it compares with the average score in the frequency distribution. "How did I do? Was I above the average?" are common questions by students seeking to make some interpretation of their raw scores as test results are made known to them. Making comparisons with the average performance on the test is a simple way of comparing one student's performance with the performance of the total group. In addition, comparing the average performance of two groups of students is one way of determining which of the two groups, as a whole, has achieved the most. Occupational teachers should be familiar with three measures of central tendency or average group performance: mean, median, and mode.

The Mean. The *mean* or the arithmetic average of a group of scores is the most common of these measures of central tendency. The mean score in a frequency distribution of test scores is computed in the same manner that all arithmetic averages are computed. All the scores in the distribution are added together or summed and the total is then divided by the number of scores included in the distribution. The formula for computing the mean is:

$$Mn = \frac{\Sigma X}{N}$$

where *Mn* represents the mean score, Σ (the Greek letter sigma) indicates that which follows is to be summed, *X* represents each score included in the distribution, and *N* represents the total number of scores in the distribution. The mean, therefore, is defined as being equal to the sum of all the scores in the distribution divided by the number of scores in the distribution. For example, the mean score for the set of scores 10, 10, 11, 12, 14, 15, 15, 17 would be computed as follows:

$$Mn = \frac{10 + 10 + 11 + 12 + 14 + 15 + 15 + 17}{8} = \frac{104}{8} = 13$$

The easiest, quickest, and most accurate way of determining the mean for a group of scores is to enter each in a calculator, obtain their sum, and then divide this sum by the number of scores included in the group.

The Median. Another commonly used measure of central tendency is the median (*Md*), the middle score in a frequency distribution or the 50th percentile. The *median* is defined as that point in a group of *ranked scores* above or below which one half or 50 percent of the scores fall.

For small distributions, one can determine the median without a great deal of calculating. For example, consider the distributions presented in table 12.4: one having an odd number of ranked scores and the other an even number of ranked scores.

When there is an odd number of scores, the median will be the

TABLE 12.4. *Determining the Median in Small Distributions Having Odd and Even Numbers of Obtained Scores.*

Odd Numbers of Scores		Even Number of Scores	
Scores	Tally	Scores	Tally
30	1	30	111
29	1]	29	1
28	1	28	1*
27	1* ← Md = 27	27	1* ← Md = 27.5
26	11	26	11
25		25	1
24	1	24	
23	1	23	1
	N = 9		N = 10

middle score. For example, in table 12.4, in the frequency distribution where $N = 9$, the middle score would be the 5th score counting from either the top or the bottom of the distribution. The median for this distribution, therefore, would be 27. This score is indicated with the asterisk.

There is an even number of scores in the frequency distribution where $N = 10$. A little different but no more complicated procedure must be followed to compute the median. Here, the middle two scores are averaged to determine the median—$(27 + 28) \div 2 = 27.5$. The median is 27.5: the point below which 50 percent of the scores lie. Count them. It should be noted here that in both of these distributions the scores were arranged in descending order of magnitude (30 to 23) *before* counting to determine the median. Likewise, in determining the median for a large number of scores, the first step is to arrange the scores, from lowest to highest, in a frequency distribution and complete the f (frequency) and cf (cumulative frequency) columns as presented in table 12.5.

Actual computational steps in determining the median for this distribution or for any large frequency distribution are as follows:

1. Determine the number of scores needed to constitute 50 percent of the scores. In this example, $N \div 2 = 18$.

2. Locate in the cf column the largest number that is equal to or less than that which constitutes 50 percent of the scores. In this example, 11 is the highest number of the cf column that is equal

TABLE 12.5. Calculating the Median in Large Distributions of Obtained Scores.

Scores	Tally	f	cf
31	1	1	36
30	1	1	35
29	111	3	34
28			
27	1111	4	31
26	H̶H̶ 11	7	27
25	H̶H̶ 1111	9	20
24	H̶H̶	5	11
23	11	2	6
22			
21	1	1	4
20	11	2	3
19			
18	1	1	1
	N = 36		

to or less than 18. The eighteenth score is to be found within the next highest *cf* value, 20 in this example. The score associated with *cf* 20 is 25. You will recall from the discussion of percentile ranks that this score actually ranges from 24.5 to 25.5 and that all having attained this score by convention are equally distributed across this range.

3. The next step is to determine at what point the 18th score lies within the range 24.5 to 25.5. There are 9 students who scored 25 and therefore are included in this range. The cumulative frequency through 24.5 is 11. Subtracting these 11 from 18, we find that we are looking for the 7th of the 9 students included in the range 24.5 to 25.5.

4. Calculate seven-ninths of one by dividing 7 by 9. Add the result (0.78) to the lower limit of the range (24.5) and the final result (25.28) is the median, middle score, or 50th percentile for the distribution.

The foregoing procedures are expressed in the formula:

$$Md = X_{LL} + \frac{\frac{N}{2} - cf_{LL}}{fX}$$

where Md = the median

X_{LL} = the lower limit of the range for the middle-obtained score in the distribution

cf_{LL} = the cumulative frequency up to X_{LL}

fX = the frequency of the middle-obtained score

Applying this formula to the foregoing frequency distribution:

$$Md = 24.5 + \frac{\frac{36}{2} - 11}{9}$$

$$= 24.5 + \frac{18 - 11}{9}$$

$$= 24.5 + .78$$

$$Md = 25.28$$

the calculated median is the same as that calculated by following the foregoing four-step procedure.

The Mode.   Another common but not frequently used measure of central tendency is the mode (*Mo*). The *mode* is simply the most frequently occurring score in the frequency distribution. Determining the mode in a group of scores is really quite easy. After the scores are ordered in a frequency distribution, the frequency (*f*) column is examined and the obtained score that occurred most frequently is the mode for that distribution. In situations where two or more scores tie for occurring most frequently, the distribution is referred to being bimodal, trimodal, or etc. and is considered to have a corresponding number of modes.

Using Measures of Central Tendency.   The mean, median, and mode each provide a little different measure of central tendency or average performance for any distribution of scores. All three can be used in interpreting individual scores, since each provides a measure of central tendency with which individual scores can be compared. They also are used frequently to compare the average performance of two or more groups of students on a single test and to compare one group's performance on two tests. In short, they provide quick, simple, and useful summaries for a distribution of test scores.

In most occupational programs where relatively large numbers of students are being given achievement and other types of tests, the obtained scores will form a "normal" frequency distribution. A model normal distribution is presented in table 12.6.

Table 12.6. Example Frequency Distribution Where Obtained Scores Take the Shape of a Normal Distribution.

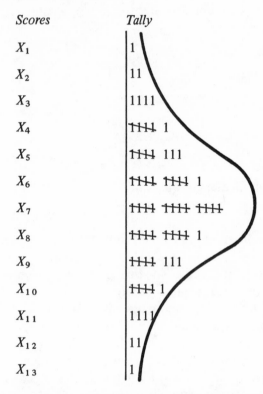

Scores	Tally
X_1	1
X_2	11
X_3	1111
X_4	┼┼┼┼ 1
X_5	┼┼┼┼ 111
X_6	┼┼┼┼ ┼┼┼┼ 1
X_7	┼┼┼┼ ┼┼┼┼ ┼┼┼┼
X_8	┼┼┼┼ ┼┼┼┼ 1
X_9	┼┼┼┼ 111
X_{10}	┼┼┼┼ 1
X_{11}	1111
X_{12}	11
X_{13}	1

From the model presented in table 12.6, it can be seen that in a normal distribution the three measures of central tendency—mean, median, and mode—all fall at the same point in the distribution. The score X_7 is the mean or arithmetic average, the middle score, as well as the most frequently occurring score in this distribution. Therefore, when the distribution of students' scores is normal it makes little difference which measure of central tendency is used as a reference point in interpreting individual scores. Interpretations describing a student's performance as being so many units above or below the mean, median, or mode all have the same meaning when scores for the group tested are normally distributed.

As long as these measures of central tendency are used only

as reference points for interpreting individual scores in a group of normally distributed scores, it does not make much difference which of the three is used. There are, however, some conditions that make the use of one of the three more appropriate than the use of another.

Sometimes it is a matter of convenience, and the need for further calculations. For example, if standard scores are to be computed for all raw scores in a distribution, then the mean might be used because it would have to be computed in the process of computing the standard scores anyway.

There are, however, some situations in which the characteristics of the mean, median, or mode make it the most appropriate reference point for interpreting individual scores or for summarizing a distribution of scores. One example would be a situation where one or a few scores in a distribution are extremely different from the others. In such situations the mean does not provide a good picture of the average or typical performance because it is influenced so by extreme scores. Consider, for example, the following hourly salaries for ten students selected at random from a cooperative vocational program:

- $1.25
- $1.27
- $1.35
- $1.65
- $1.70
  - $\leftarrow Md = \$1.75$
- $1.80
- $1.82
- $1.95
- $2.10
  - $\leftarrow Mn = \$2.24$
- $7.35

The mean hourly salary for this group of students is $2.24. This is higher than all salaries in the group except one. The median salary for the group is $1.75. Obviously, the latter provides a more accurate picture of the typical salary for students enrolled in the cooperative program. It should be noted that such extremes in a distribution of scores are not only the result of an occasional extremely nontypical performance. As the numbers of students included in a sample become smaller the opportunity to obtain extreme examples of typical performance becomes larger. In either case, the mean becomes the less appropriate measure of central tendency.

Measures of Dispersion

To know a student's test score and that it is above or below the average performance for the group provides a rough indication of that student's relative performance. A more precise interpretation requires knowledge as to how far above or below the average performance for the group this student's score falls. Comparing the score with the mean, median, or mode of the distribution of scores, of course, permits statements like "this score is 3 points above the mean" and "that score is 7 points below the mean." However, additional information is needed if more precise interpretations of relative performance are to be made. In the foregoing example, seven points below the mean could indicate an average or very poor performance, depending upon the range of performance for the total group. If the scores for the total group ranged from 42 to 58 with a mean of 50, then 7 points below the mean would be interpreted as a relatively poor performance. However, if the scores for the group ranged from 18 to 100 with a mean of 50, then 7 points below the mean might be interpreted as a relatively average performance. Refined interpretation of individual test scores requires knowledge as to the range and manner in which the scores are dispersed in the frequency distribution.

The Range.   The simplest measure of dispersion is the *range*. It is defined as the difference between the highest and lowest obtained scores in a frequency distribution. It is computed using the formula:

$$R = \text{highest score} - \text{lowest score}$$

where R indicates the range and highest and lowest score indicate the highest and lowest obtained scores in the distribution, respectively. From the formula it can be seen that the range is entirely dependent upon the two extreme scores in the distribution. Therefore, its usefulness is limited in that it cannot provide any information as to the manner in which the scores are dispersed *within* the distribution.

The Standard Deviation.   The *standard deviation* is a measure of dispersion that is dependent upon the relative position of *every* score in the frequency distribution. It provides a very precise measure of the degree to which the scores within the distribution deviate from the mean. In brief, it is obtained by taking the square root of the average of the squared deviation from the mean score of the distribution. The standard deviation is defined by the formula:

$$SD = \sqrt{\frac{\Sigma\, x^2}{N}}$$

where SD = the standard deviation
        Σ = the summation of that which follows
        x = represents a score's deviation from the mean score ($x = X - Mn$)
        N = the total number of scores included in the frequency distribution

The standard deviation continues to remain a confusing type of measure for some occupational teachers, administrators, and career-guidance personnel. Generally, the confusion is a result of attaching more complexity to the standard deviation than is warranted. The basic features of the standard deviation are really quite elementary:

1. It is a measure of the *spread* among scores.
2. It is based upon each score's *deviation* from the mean score.
3. It is computed by squaring each score's deviation from the mean, *averaging* these squared deviations, and taking the *square root* of the average squared deviation.

The simple example in table 12.7 illustrates the above three basic features of the standard deviation and demonstrates how it can be computed from the formula which defines it.

The first step in computing the standard deviation from the formula presented in table 12.7 is to determine the mean for the distribution of scores. In this example, $Mn = 630 \div 7$ or 90. After the mean is determined, a line is drawn across the distribution at that point and the deviation from the mean score (x) is calculated

TABLE 12.7.   *Calculating a Standard Deviation from the Definition Formula.*

	Scores	x	x^2	
	95	+5	25	$SD = \sqrt{\dfrac{\Sigma x^2}{N}}$
	94	+4	16	
	93	+3	9	
$Mn = 90$	91	+1	1	$= \sqrt{\dfrac{112}{7}}$
	87	-3	9	
	86	-4	16	
$N = 7$	84	-6	36	$= \sqrt{16}$
	$\Sigma X = 630$		$\Sigma x^2 = 112$	$SD = 4$

for each score using the formula $x = X - Mn$. The deviations from the mean are entered in the column as they are calculated. The x^2 column is then completed by squaring corresponding deviations from the mean score in the x column. All squared deviations in the x^2 column are summed and this sum and the number of scores in the distribution are substituted in the above formula. In this example, the sum of the squared deviations is 112, N is 7, and the standard deviation is 4.

The above formula is commonly used in defining the standard deviation and, as was just demonstrated, it can be used to compute the standard deviation for any distribution. However, the process is simplified considerably if a calculator is used and the standard deviation is computed directly from the obtained scores. J. P. Guilford (1965) offers a formula and an eight-step procedure for computing the standard deviation in this manner. A slightly modified version of his formula and procedures follows.

$$SD = \frac{1}{N}\sqrt{N \Sigma X^2 - (\Sigma X)^2}$$

1. Square each score or measurement.
2. Sum the squared measurements to find ΣX^2.
3. Multiply ΣX^2 by N to find $N \Sigma X^2$.
4. Sum each score or measurement to find ΣX.
5. Square the ΣX to find $(\Sigma X)^2$.
6. Find the difference $N \Sigma X - (\Sigma X)^2$.
7. Find the square root of the number found in step 6.

8. Divide the number found in step 7 by N (the total number of scores in the group).

Sample data used previously to illustrate computing the standard deviation from its definition formula are presented again in table 12.8. The example presented here illustrates how a calculator and the Guilford formula can be used in computing the standard deviation directly from a distribution of obtained scores.

TABLE 12.8. *Calculating the Standard Deviation Directly from a Distribution of Obtained Scores Using the Guilford Formula.*

Scores (X)	X^2	
95	9,025	$SD = \dfrac{1}{7} \sqrt{N \Sigma X^2 - (\Sigma X)^2}$
94	8,836	$= \dfrac{1}{7} \sqrt{7\,(56{,}812) - (630)^2}$
93	8,649	$= \dfrac{1}{7} \sqrt{397{,}684 - 396{,}900}$
91	8,281	$= \dfrac{1}{7} \sqrt{784}$
87	7,569	$= \dfrac{28}{7}$
86	7,396	$SD = 4$
84	7,056	
630	56,812	

It should be noted that the calculator formula for computing the standard deviaton is derived from the definition formula. As is the case with the two examples presented here, the standard deviations obtained for a given group of scores will be the same no matter which of these formulas are used.

Knowledge of the standard deviation for a group of scores contributes much to the ability to make interpretative statements about individual scores within the group and the group of scores as a whole. This is because for normally and near-normally distributed groups of scores there are some dependable relationships that exist between frequency distributions, mean scores, and standard deviations. To aid in presenting and clarifying these relationships the model frequency distribution presented earlier in this chapter has been rotated from a vertical to a horizontal axis and modified as presented in figure 12.3.

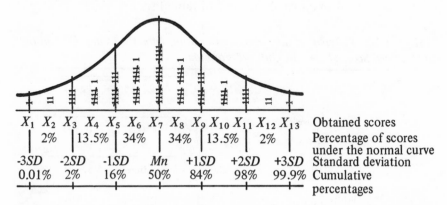

X_1 X_2 X_3 X_4 X_5 X_6 X_7 X_8 X_9 X_{10} X_{11} X_{12} X_{13}	Obtained scores
2% 13.5% 34% 34% 13.5% 2%	Percentage of scores under the normal curve
-3SD -2SD -1SD Mn +1SD +2SD +3SD	Standard deviation
0.01% 2% 16% 50% 84% 98% 99.9%	Cumulative percentages

FIGURE 12.3. Example Normal Distribution Showing the Obtained Scores and Their Percentages Under the Normal Curve, Standard Deviations, and Cumulative Percentages Under the Normal Curve.

The relationships in the model presented in figure 12.3 that are important to interpreting individual students' test scores are summarized below:

1. The total area under the curve represents the total number of scores in the frequency distribution.
2. Normally, about 99 percent of the obtained scores in a frequency distribution fall within ±3 standard deviations from the mean score.
3. The distribution is generally symmetrical with 50 percent of the obtained scores distributed on either side of the mean.
4. Each standard deviation from the mean generally contains a given percentage of the total number of the obtained scores.
5. The cumulative percentage of the number of obtained scores falling below a given obtained score is directly related to the percentage of obtained scores included within each standard deviation.

With an understanding of these five relationships, one can make meaningful interpretations of students' obtained scores. For example, consider an obtained score of 48 in a distribution having a mean of 40 and a standard deviation of 4. Using the foregoing model, we can see that 48 represents an excellent performance relative to the rest of the students in the group. It is two standard deviations above the mean and therefore greater than about 98 percent of the scores in this group. A score of 32 in this distribution (Mn = 40 and SD = 4) represents a relatively poor performance. It is two standard deviations below the mean and represents a performance that is greater than only 2 percent of those in the group.

The important related benchmarks that should be memorized so they are readily available for use in interpreting students' test scores are few. They are presented here.

- Deviation from the mean   − 2 SD − 1 SD 0 +1 SD + 2 SD
- Cumulative   percentages   2%   16% 50% 84%   98%

Skewness. It should be noted that the relationships expressed in the foregoing model hold only if the obtained scores are normally distributed. The relationships are not applicable to distributions that deviate significantly from normal. A quick way to check for non-normality or *skewness* in a distribution is to compare the mean and median scores for the distribution. The effects of variation in mean and median scores in a distribution of scores can be expressed graphically as presented in figure 12.4.

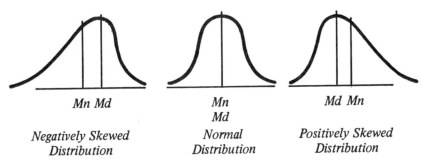

Mn Md	*Mn*	*Md Mn*
	Md	
Negatively Skewed	*Normal*	*Positively Skewed*
Distribution	*Distribution*	*Distribution*

FIGURE 12.4. Example Shapes of Negatively Skewed, Normal, and Positively Skewed Distributions.

Skewness in a distribution is defined by the formula:

$$Skewness = Mn - Md$$

where *Mn* and *Md* represent the mean and median of the distribution respectively. As can be seen in figure 12.4, when these two values are equal, the distribution is normal. When they are not, the distribution is skewed, either positively or negatively. Extreme scores at one end of a distribution do not affect the median (the middle score). However, as indicated in the earlier discussion of the mean, such scores tend to draw the mean toward their end of the distribution. In practice, skewed distributions should not present problems in interpreting students' scores in occupational programs where relatively large numbers of students are included in the group being tested and where there are very few, if any, students whose performance will cause extreme shifts in the mean score for the group.

Standard Scores

In addition to aiding in interpreting student scores, the standard deviation also is a useful statistic for (1) comparing the distributions for two or more groups of students who have been measured on some variable and (2) serving as the basis for standard scores. For example, the standard deviation for the ages of students enrolled in evening occupational classes is generally greater than that for the ages of students enrolled in daytime occupational classes. When this is the case, we can assume that students enrolled in daytime occupational classes are more homogeneous than their evening school counterparts with respect to age. The standard deviation could be used in making these same types of observations for most any other similar variable.

As for serving as the basis for standard scores, both *z*-scores and *T*-scores are based on the standard deviation.

The z-Score. The *z*-score is the basic form of standard score. It is defined by the formula:

$$z = \frac{X - Mn}{SD}$$

where z = the *z*-score
X = a student's obtained raw score
Mn = the mean
SD = the standard deviation for the total group of scores

From the formula it can be seen that a z-score is simply a measure of how many standard deviations a raw score is from the mean of the scores included in the distribution. A graphic description is presented in figure 12.5.

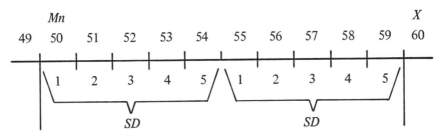

FIGURE 12.5. Graphic Description of the Relationship Between an Obtained Score, the Mean, and the Standard Deviation When Calculating z-Scores.

If, as pictured in figure 12.5, a student's obtained score (60) is ten units from the mean score (50) when the standard deviation is five units, then the z-score for that student would be two. Substituting the data in the foregoing formula, the result is the same.

$$z = \frac{X - Mn}{SD}$$

$$= \frac{60 - 50}{5}$$

$$z = 2$$

Once the mean and standard deviation have been computed for a distribution of scores, the process of computing z-scores for that distribution is rather straightforward. The distribution of scores used earlier in this chapter to demonstrate computing the standard deviation by hand will be used here in computing the associated z-scores. Again, a calculator is a useful tool. However, if one is not available, all computations can be completed by hand as shown in table 12.9.

After each score in the distribution is listed and the mean and standard deviation are calculated, the $(X - Mn)$ or deviation from the mean column is completed. Each entry in this column is then divided by the standard deviation to obtain the z-scores. Z-scores then, not raw scores, are recorded in the occupational teacher's gradebook.

TABLE 12.9. *Calculating z-Scores from a Distribution of Obtained Scores.*

	Scores (X)	(X - Mn) z	
	95	+5 ÷ 4 = +1.25	
	94	+4 ÷ 4 = +1	$z_{95} = \dfrac{X - Mn}{SD}$
Mn = 90	93	+3 ÷ 4 = +.75	
	91	+1 ÷ 4 = +.25	
	87	-3 ÷ 4 = -.75	$= \dfrac{+5}{4}$
SD = 4	86	-4 ÷ 4 = -1	
	84	-6 ÷ 4 = -1.50	
			$z_{95} = 1.25$

T-Scores.   There are, however, some objections to using z-scores as records of student performance. The primary objection is based upon the inherent difficulties that usually accompany negative numbers and decimals. It is too easy to make arithmetic errors when working with them. To overcome this objection, a slightly modified standard score (the *T*–score) can be used. *T*-scores have all the desirable characteristics of z–scores but no decimals or negative numbers. They are defined by the formula:

$$T = 10z + 50$$

where *T* and z represent *T*-score and z-score respectively.

From the formula it can be seen that *T*-scores are really transformed z-scores. The transformation process involves multiplying the z-score by the constant 10 (and rounding to the nearest whole number to eliminate decimals) and then adding another constant (50) to eliminate negative numbers. As an example, the z-scores +2.8 and –2.53 would be transformed to *T*-scores as follows:

$$
\begin{aligned}
T &= 10z + 50 \\
  &= 10\,(+2.8) + 50 \quad \text{and} \\
  &= 28 + 50 \\
T &= 78
\end{aligned}
\qquad
\begin{aligned}
T &= 10z + 50 \\
  &= 10\,(-2.53) + 50 \\
  &= (-25) + 50 \\
T &= 25
\end{aligned}
$$

It should be noted that in working with standardized tests, one finds normative data in the form of rather large standard scores. These are *T*-scores or some other standard score the test producer has developed by multiplying z-scores by some constant and adding to this product another constant.

Unique Properties of Standard Scores. Both *T*-scores and *z*-scores have some interesting and unique properties that are helpful in interpreting them. Unlike raw scores, for example, they stand alone. That is, one does not need to know all the other scores in the distribution before he or she can relate a *T*-score or *z*-score to the performance of others in the group tested.

Frequency distributions of raw scores that have been converted to *z*-scores always have a mean of zero and a standard deviation of one. *T*-scores, because they are *z*-scores multiplied by ten and then added to by fifty, have a mean of fifty and a standard deviation of ten. Therefore, we know that a *z*-score of +2.0 usually represents an excellent performance. It is two standard deviations above the mean and equal to or better than about 98 percent of those in the group tested. Remember the important benchmarks?

- Deviation from the mean $\quad -2\,SD \ -1\,SD \ 0 \ +1\,SD \ +2\,SD$
- Cumulative percentages $\qquad\quad 2\% \qquad 16\% \ 50\% \ 84\% \qquad 98\%$

Likewise, we know that a *T*-score of 40 generally represents a relatively poor performance. It is equal to or better than only about 16 percent of those in the group tested.

Summarizing Students' Test Scores. It is important that some form of standard score be used in summarizing students' performance on a series of tests in the occupational program. This is particularly true in situations where scores from tests of differing lengths and levels of difficulty have been given during the year and the teacher wants to summarize these scores for each student and have each test contribute a *controlled* amount of weight to the final grade. Standard scores provide one of the most accurate ways to achieve this end. This phenomenon is demonstrated in the following exercise.

Assume that a vocational welding teacher gives two examinations during the semester: one performance test and a paper and pencil achievement test. Assume further that the performance test contains a maximum of 20 points and the written exam has 135 possible points. To make the example interesting, assume also that the semester grade is to be weighted two-thirds performance test and one-third written exam. The frequency distributions for the example are presented in table 12.10.

Because it was the welding teacher's desire to have the performance

TABLE 12.10. Frequency Distributions Showing the Effect of Forming Composite Scores from Raw Scores Instead of z-Scores.

Students	Performance Test		Written Test		Composite Scores	
	Raw Score &	z- Score	Raw Score &	z- Score	Raw Score & Rank	z-Score & Rank
Matt	8	-2.5	132	+2.8	148 (1)	+1.2 (3)
Bob	13	0	93	+0.2	119 (5)	+0.2 (7)
John	10	-1.5	88	-0.1	108 (7)	-2.9 (10)
Jen	14	+0.5	100	+0.7	128(3)	+1.7 (2)
Bill	13	0	86	-0.3	112 (6)	-0.3 (8)
Tim	13	0	94	+0.3	120 (4)	+0.3 (6)
Dick	15	+1.0	75	-1.0	105 (8)	+1.0 (5)
Joyce	12	-0.5	122	+2.1	146 (2)	+1.1 (4)
Pete	18	+2.5	46	-3.0	80 (10)	+2.0 (1)
Lea	14	-0.5	64	-1.7	92 (9)	+2.7 (9)

test count twice as much in the semester grade, both the raw scores and z-scores for the performance test were multiplied by two and then added to the written test score in forming the composite scores presented in table 12.10. Note that in several instances students' positions in the total group shifted significantly when their composite scores were based upon z-scores rather than raw scores. Of special interest is Pete, whose composite level of performance shifted from tenth in the group to first. All shifts in rank were due to the fact that the 135-item written test actually has the potential for contributing more than four times its proportionate share to the raw score-based composite even though the performance-test score was doubled in computing this composite. This is because when these raw scores are combined, the total possible for the composite score is 175 (135 written and 2 × 20 performance). In Pete's case, when raw scores are used to compute his composite, his top performance-test score, even when multiplied by two, cannot contribute enough—not even enough to begin to offset his poor showing on the written test. Forming composite scores from raw scores is a little like the recipe for making mule–rabbit stew. All it takes is a little mule and a little rabbit: one mule and one rabbit.

However, when z-scores are used to compute a composite score, each test score contributes equally unless it is weighted or multiplied by some factor to increase the percentage of its contribution to the composite score. This is because *z*-scores are based upon the number of standard deviation units there are between the raw scores and mean. Thus, the potential for longer or more difficult tests to contribute a disproportionate share to the composite is nullified. For many occupational students, especially those like Pete, the manner in which their teacher summarizes their test performances in computing final grades does make a difference.

The grading chart presented in table 12.11 is adapted from a similar chart developed by Robert Swanson, University of Wisconsin-Stout. It provides a useful format for summarizing several measures of a student's performance and controlling the actual weight that each contributes to the student's final grade. The number and types of measures included on such a chart will be based upon the number and type of assessments that will be used to determine students' final grades. The procedures for using this chart (or a similar chart designed to serve a particular occupational program) are as follows:

1. Record students' obtained raw scores in the appropriate columns as each becomes available.
2. Compute and record in the appropriate columns *T*-scores for each of the obtained raw scores.
3. Decide what weight is to be given to each test, examination, project, observation, or assignment included on the form and record these weights in the spaces provided. For example, unit tests might receive a weight of 0.5, while mid-term and final exams each receive weights of 1.0, and the term project a weight of 2.0. Course objectives should be the basis for determining these weights.
4. Multiply each student's *T*-score for each of the tests, examinations, projects, or the like by the appropriate weight and record these products in their respective columns on the chart.
5. Sum each student's weighted *T*-score to obtain his or her total *T*-score.
6. Use students' total *T*-scores as the basis for determining and assigning final grades.

Aids for Computing Standard Scores.   Several devices have been developed that occupational teachers will find useful in transforming raw scores into standard scores. The Standard Score Conversion Chart developed by Porter (1965) and pictured in figure 12.6 is one such device.

TABLE 12.11. *Example T-score Grading Chart.*

Students' Names	Unit Test I (a)*		Unit Test II (b)		Mid-Term Exam (c)		Unit Test III (d)		Unit Test IV (e)		Final Exam (f)		Term Project (g)		T_a x (wt.)	T_b x (wt.)	T_c x (wt.)	T_d x (wt.)	T_e x (wt.)	T_f x (wt.)	T_g x (wt.)	Total T-Score	Final Grade
	Raw Score	T-score	Raw Score	T-Score	Raw Score	T-Score	Raw Score	T-Score	Raw Score	T-Score	Raw Score	T-Score	Raw Score	T-Score									

*Headings (a) through (g) will vary in nature and number as the measurement techniques vary from one occupational program to another.

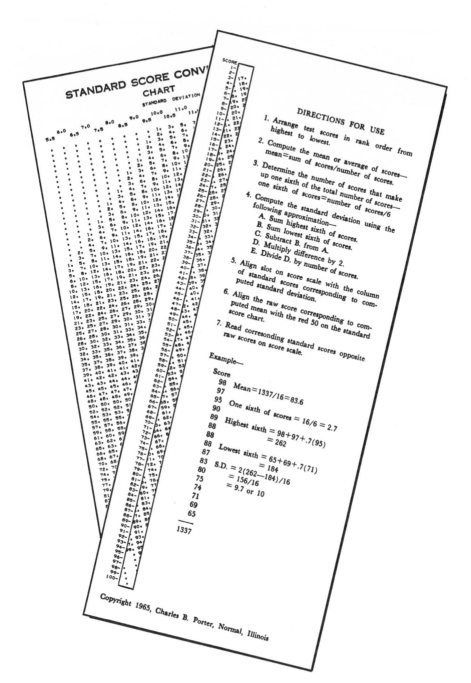

FIGURE 12.6. Standard Score Conversion Chart for Computing T-Scores from Raw Scores.

This two-part chart is designed to convert raw scores into *T*-scores for frequency distributions having standard deviations that range from one to twenty by one-half point intervals. Moreover, its directions for use include instructions for quickly computing a good estimate of the standard deviation using the formula:

$$SD = \frac{2 \text{ (Sum of highest } 1/6 \text{ of scores} - \text{Sum of lowest } 1/6 \text{ of scores)}}{\text{Total number in group}}$$

The formulas for computing the standard deviation that were presented earlier in this chapter will produce more precise calculations of this measure of dispersion. However, the above formula will provide a quick and useful estimate for most distributions of students' scores in occupational programs. Once the standard deviation and the mean score are known for a distribution of raw or obtained scores, the two parts of the conversion chart are aligned with respect to these two values. *T*-scores then can be read directly from the chart for each raw score in the distribution. Occupational teachers will find devices of this type to be useful and time-saving aids for calculating *T*-scores.

Comparing Standard Scores and Percentiles. Percentile ranks have some advantages over standard scores. First, they are easily understood by students and parents, who generally do not have a background in educational statistics. In addition, they can be interpreted exactly even when the distribution of obtained scores is not a normal distribution. However, percentile ranks tend to make small differences in obtained scores that are near the mean look larger than they are. Likewise, they tend to make large differences in obtained scores near the ends of the distribution look smaller than they are. Finally, it is not appropriate to use percentile ranks to compute statistics such as standard deviations, correlation coefficients, and standard errors of measurement.

Standard scores are more difficult for lay persons to understand and interpret, particularly when the distribution of scores deviates from the normal curve. However, differences in standard scores are equivalent to differences in the obtained scores from which they are computed. Their use in computing standard deviations, correlation coefficients, standard errors of measurement, and other statistics yields the same result as would obtained scores. In summary, it might be said that researchers and others with some background in statistics prefer to use standard scores and those concerned with interpreting scores to students and parents prefer to work with percentile ranks.

AIDS FOR SUMMARIZING AND INTERPRETING NORM-REFERENCED TEST SCORES

The time and effort expended to develop, administer, and score the tests administered in occupational programs would be in vain if the results were not communicated to others, particularly to students and their parents. Several good techniques have been developed to aid in summarizing and interpreting students' performance on norm-referenced instruments. Some of the most useful of these techniques are presented here.

Norm-referenced Grades

Local district regulations generally stipulate that the scholastic achievement or progress of occupational as well as other students be monitored, summarized, and reported by their teachers. Moreover, in occupational programs this process generally includes (1) the use of achievement tests of some type (quizzes, unit tests, final exams) and (2) the assignment of grades or other summative descriptions of student performance in the classroom, shop or laboratory, or on the job.

Important Characteristics of Grades.   Grades should be valid summaries of students' achievement in the occupational program. They should not be based upon or influenced by a teacher's or an administrator's capricious or subjective assessment of student achievement. Obviously, if they are to be valid indices of student achievement and not be influenced by irrelevant factors, then grades should be based on data and information obtained by using valid measurement procedures and techniques of the types presented in this text. For most occupational programs, assigned grades are either of the pass–fail or letter-grade type. In either case, they represent a summary of all the data and information that were considered in determining the grade. For effective communication to occur, the meaning of each symbol used must be defined. Grades which do not have the same meaning to both the teacher and students and/or parents are of little or no value. The most widely used system of letter grades is the A through E (or F) system where A represents outstanding achievement; B, above average; C, average; D, below average; and E or F, failure.

When letter grades are assigned to a frequency distribution of raw scores, they actually represent a type of percentile rank. That is, the letter A is assigned to some of the highest scores in the distribution. B is assigned to some of the next highest; C is assigned to those in the middle or average range of the distribution; and so on down through the letter grades D and E or F. The percentage of students receiving any particular letter grade will vary some from one test to another, but letter grades do provide occupational students with a general idea of how well they performed on a test in comparison to others in their course.

Assigning Grades. Assigning grades in a strict norm-referenced system calls for assigning a small and like percentage of A's and E's or F's, a somewhat larger percentage of B's and D's, and a major portion of C's.

One popular technique for determining the cutoff points in the distribution of scores is to divide the distribution into five sections, each containing 1.2 standard deviations. Scores falling 2.0 and 1.2 standard deviations above the mean, for example, would be assigned the letter grades of A and B respectively. This system is based on the "normal curve" and the assumption that student achievement is a normally distributed trait among the students in the classes in which the system is used. This assumption is not always valid, particularly when a class is composed of gifted, handicapped, or disadvantaged students. The distribution for learning in such classes would not approximate the normal curve.

Table 12.12 shows the results of applying the foregoing described system for assigning grades to a class of 26 students where learning appears to be normally distributed. The test scores shown have a mean of 14 and standard deviation of 3.5. Cutoff points for each grade classification were established at points 1.2 and 2.4 standard deviations above and below the mean score. The anticipated percentages of students who would receive each grade if the distribution were truly normally distributed is indicated in the column to

TABLE 12.12. Norm-referenced System for Assigning Grades Applied to a Typical Distribution of Test Scores.

Test Scores	Tally	Grades	Anticipated Percentages	Actual Percentages
25				
24	/	A	3.6%	0%
23				
22	11			
21		B	23.8%	11.5%
20				
19	1			
18	111			
17				
16	11			
15	1			
14	~~THH~~ 11	C	45.2%	80.8%
13	111			
12	111			
11				
10	11			
9				
8	11	D	23.8%	7.7%
7				
6				
5				
4				
3		F	3.6%	0%
2				
1				

Mn = 14   *N* = 26   *SD* = 3.5

the right of the grades in table 12.12. The actual percentages are indicated in the next column. Careful comparison of these two columns reveals that this system should not be applied rigidly.

To do so, even in this instance where the distribution of scores does not deviate very much from normal, would appear to lead to a few injustices. For example, no students would receive A's, even though those scoring 22 are nearly a full standard deviation above the next highest scoring student. Students scoring 19 and 18 would receive C's and B's respectively, even though they are only one point apart, and those scoring 18 are quite far removed from an average or C-level performance.

This, however, does not mean that the system is completely without value. A slight shifting of the cutoff points between some grade classifications usually clears up problems such as those cited above. For example, if the cutoff points for the A and B classifications were each moved one point closer to the mean (as indicated by the broken lines in table 12.12), then all of the foregoing problems would be resolved. The only question that might remain regarding this distribution would be whether to shift the cutoff point between the D and C classifications one point closer to the mean also. The decision should be based upon the answer to one question: "Is the score 10 more representative of an average or a below-average performance?" If the answer is the latter, then the cutoff point should be shifted one point closer to the mean score. Otherwise, it should remain where it is.

Thus, this norm-referenced system for assigning grades, if applied with some flexibility, can be a useful tool in summarizing a student's achievement and reporting it in terms that are readily understood by students, parents, school administrators, and the like. However, if rigidly applied, in most occupational programs, it loses its value very quickly. Again, this is particularly true in programs that are serving groups of students where learning is not a normally distributed trait.

Standard Error of Measurement

One indispensible aid in interpreting students' test scores is the *standard error of measurement.* It is a quantitative expression of the magnitude of the error component in a test score. It is used to define confidence limits around an observed score in which one would be reasonably sure to find the true score.

Theoretical Definition. As indicated in chapter 2, true score is a hypothetical concept. One simple explanation of this concept is constructed around administering a large number of truly equivalent forms of a hypothetical test to one individual at one sitting with absolutely no learning occurring throughout the testing period. From what we know about human performance, we could assume that the scores obtained for each form of the test would not be the same. From what we know about the distribution of random variables, we could assume that the obtained scores would be normally distributed. The mean score for this distribution would be our best estimate of this individual's true score. The standard deviation of this distribution would be the standard error of measurement for this test.

If the standard deviation is large, we know that the reliability for this test is low. If the standard deviation is small—this individual obtained nearly the same score on each of the various forms of the test—we know that the reliability for this test is high. The reliability estimate for a test is, in part, the basis for the standard error of measurement.

Computing the Standard Error.   The formula for computing the standard error of measurement for a particular distribution of scores is:

$$SEm = SD \sqrt{1 - r_{xx}}$$

where SEm = the standard error of measurement
SD = the standard deviation of the distribution of scores
r_{xx} = the reliability coefficient for the test

As an example, the standard error of measurement for a test having a standard deviation of 5 and a reliability coefficient of 0.84 would be computed as follows:

$$SEm = 5 \sqrt{1 - 0.84}$$
$$= 5 \sqrt{0.16}$$
$$SEm = 2$$

Using the Standard Error.   The standard error of measurement is a useful aid in interpreting test scores. It provides a good estimate of the probable margin of error in obtained scores. Occupational teachers who know the standard error of measurement for each of the tests used in their program can make meaningful probability statements about the accuracy of scores obtained with those tests.

For example, if the $SEm = 2$ for the final examination in their course, then they could say with certainty that for about two-thirds of the students, obtained scores are no greater than 2 points ($\pm$ 1 SEm) away from their true scores on the examination. Using similar reasoning, occupational teachers can say with some certainty that for about 95 percent of the students, obtained scores are no greater than 4 points (±2 *SEm*) away from their true scores. The same reasoning can be extended to include 99 percent of the students' obtained scores by moving to limits that are ± 3 *SEm*.

Tests that have a large standard error of measurement associated with them should be revised. However, of equal importance is the need to consider the magnitude of the standard error of measurement when interpreting students' test scores. If it is assumed that students' obtained scores are necessarily their true scores and obtained scores are treated as true scores, then misinterpretation will certainly result. Several examples are presented in chapter 2. An additional example is presented here.

Occupational teachers often experience difficulties in drawing the necessary fine line between test scores that are "borderline" cases when they are converting scores to letter grades. If the standard error of measurement for the test used to obtain the scores is very large, their difficulties are justified. For example, suppose an occupational teacher made the distribution of A and B grades presented in table 12.13 on the basis of the indicated test scores when the standard error of measurement of the test was 2 points.

TABLE 12.13. *Sample Partial Frequency Distribution Showing Raw Scores, Frequency, and Letter-grade Ranges for Each Score.*

Test Score	Tally	Grade
97	1	
96		
95	11	A
94	1	
93		
92	1	
91	1	
90		
89	11	B
88	1	
87	111	

A standard error of 2 points would indicate that the teacher can be two-thirds confident that the students' obtained scores are no more than 2 points away from their true scores. Consider the score 91. Two out of three with this score will have a true score somewhere within the range 89 to 93. Thus, it can be seen that even with a test having a relatively small standard error of measurement, there is a pretty good chance that if the true scores could be known, there would be considerable exchanging of letter grades among these borderline cases. Imagine how many incorrect grades are assigned among borderline cases when the standard error of measurement is in the magnitude of five to six points (SD = 10 and r = 0.70).

Occupational teachers, administrators, and career-guidance personnel should not attach too much significance to small differences in obtained scores, particularly when the standard error of measurement is very large. As indicated in chapter 2, the standard error of measurement for most popular tests of general mental ability ranges from five to eight points. This statistic is obviously a very useful aid in interpreting obtained scores.

Student Profiles

Another useful aid for summarizing and interpreting student performance is student profiles. *Profiles* are graphic devices that provide an excellent overall picture of a student's strengths and weaknesses. Publishers of standardized tests usually make profile forms available with their tests. For those that do not and for locally developed instruments, profile sheets can be easily prepared and duplicated in quantities such that each student can have an individual profile sheet. An example profile sheet for Differential Aptitude Test (DAT) scores (Bennett et al. 1961) is presented in figure 12.7.

One useful technique for constructing and interpreting individual student profiles involves the students in the construction process. This technique involves either preparing an enlarged sample profile form, constructing a sample profile form on a blackboard, or projecting a sample profile form using an overhead projector. A sample set of scores and the big profile form are used in explaining to an entire class or group of students what each of the sample scores means in terms of local and/or national norms and how scores are plotted on the profile form. After these explanations, students are given an individual profile form and copies of their own scores rather than an already completed individual profile.

Students, with a minimum of supervision, can construct their own individual profiles. Each student plots his/her score in the appropriate places on the profile form: first, for the national norms

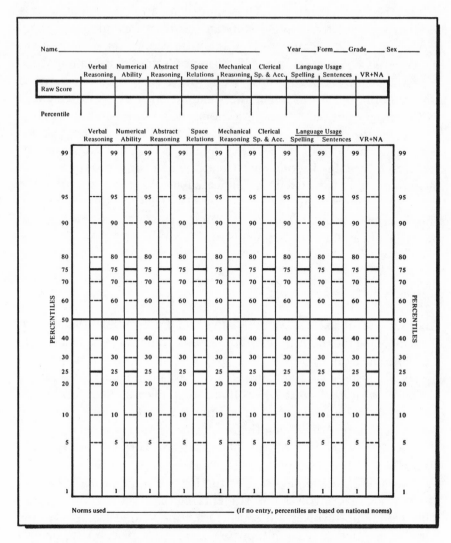

FIGURE 12.7.   Form for Plotting a Student's Aptitude Profile Based on His/Her Differential Aptitude Test *Scores.*

(if used), connecting them with a solid line to form the profile; then, for the local norms, connecting them with some contrasting (dotted or broken) line to form the profile. Thus, profiles for large numbers of students can be developed with a relatively small amount of teacher and/or clerical support time.

However, the real advantage to using this technique is that students seem to gain a more thorough understanding of their individual profile, its peaks and valleys, and their own relative strengths and weaknesses. Of course, all students should understand that their individual profiles are a private matter. They should be encouraged to talk with their teachers and/or guidance personnel if they have questions or concerns about their profiles and what they indicate. But, each should also understand that he/she is under no obligation to share his/her profile or test scores with others and likewise should not seek to see the test results of others. Such an understanding is to protect students' privacy in this regard and to prevent embarrassment.

Profiles also can be used to plot levels of student achievement or development over time. A series of weekly ratings by teachers and employers for each student is displayed through use of the profile form shown in figure 12.8.

Weekly ratings by teachers and employers are entered into the profile for each major area of concern. Lines are drawn to connect weekly ratings so that a graphic picture of each student's progress as viewed by each of the two raters can readily be seen.

Similar profile forms could be developed for most any occupational program where the skills to be developed are developed in stages over a significant period. Speed in performance (as in typing skills), accuracy of performance (as in shorthand skills), strength of performance (as in welding skills), and tolerances in performance (as in machining skills) and similar performance variables can be profiled. These profiles then become useful aids in reporting and interpreting student progress in the occupational program over some specified period.

When appropriate, locally developed profile forms, like their published counterparts, should provide full information about the scores reported on the form including type of score reported (raw scores, percentile ranks, etc.) and the instrument(s) (title, form, etc.) used. The type of norms used also should be identified and places should be provided for the student's name and the testing date(s). Finally, if any deviations from usual testing conditions or scoring procedures are used, such deviations should be noted also on the profile form.

ILLINOIS SCHOOL FOR THE DEAF- DIVISION
OF VOCATIONAL REHABILITATION
Evaluation and Career Planning
Summer Program 1975

		WEEK 1		WEEK 2		WEEK 3		WEEK 4		WEEK 5		WEEK 6	
		TEACHER	EMPLOYER	TEACHER	EMPLOYER	TEACHER	EMPLOYER	TEACHER	EMPLOYER	TEACHER	EMPLOYER	TEACHER	EMPLOYER
20.	**THE QUALITY OF THIS STUDENT'S WORK IS:**												
1.	Superior	o	o	o	o	o	o	o	o	o	o	o	o
2.	Above average	o	o	o	o	o	o	o	o	o	o	o	o
3.	Average	o	o	o	o	o	o	o	o	o	o	o	o
4.	Below average	o	o	o	o	o	o	o	o	o	o	o	o
5.	Unsatisfactory	o	o	o	o	o	o	o	o	o	o	o	o
a.	Does not apply	o	o	o	o	o	o	o	o	o	o	o	o
b.	Insufficient information	o	o	o	o	o	o	o	o	o	o	o	o
21.	**THE QUANTITY (AMOUNT) OF THIS STUDENT'S WORK IS:**												
1.	Superior	o	o	o	o	o	o	o	o	o	o	o	o
2.	Above average	o	o	o	o	o	o	o	o	o	o	o	o
3.	Average	o	o	o	o	o	o	o	o	o	o	o	o
4.	Below average	o	o	o	o	o	o	o	o	o	o	o	o
5.	Unsatisfactory	o	o	o	o	o	o	o	o	o	o	o	o
a.	Does not apply	o	o	o	o	o	o	o	o	o	o	o	o
b.	Insufficient information	o	o	o	o	o	o	o	o	o	o	o	o
22.	**I WOULD RATE THIS STUDENT'S PERSONAL HABITS:**												
1.	Adequate	o	o	o	o	o	o	o	o	o	o	o	o
2.	Adequate but inconsistent	o	o	o	o	o	o	o	o	o	o	o	o
3.	Inappropriate	o	o	o	o	o	o	o	o	o	o	o	o
4.	Generally poor	o	o	o	o	o	o	o	o	o	o	o	o
5.	Very inadequate	o	o	o	o	o	o	o	o	o	o	o	o
a.	Does not apply	o	o	o	o	o	o	o	o	o	o	o	o
b.	Insufficient information	o	o	o	o	o	o	o	o	o	o	o	o

FIGURE 12.8. *Form for Summarizing Teachers' and Employers' Ratings of a Student's Growth in Work Habits and Personal Habits.*

Expectancy Tables

As an aid in interpreting measures of student performance, expectancy tables are used to develop easily understood statements regarding a student's chances of succeeding in a situation unlike the test or situation in which the performance measures were obtained. For example: "Of the entering students with mechanical aptitude scores at or below this level, only one-third of them complete the auto mechanics program at this school."

Publishers of standardized tests often develop and include in their test manuals expectancy tables to aid users in interpreting scores obtained with these tests. However, some of the most useful expectancy tables are locally developed. Procedures for developing expectancy tables involve (1) administering a test or gathering other pertinent data for a relatively large number of students, and (2) observing and recording these students' success with an activity one is interested in predicting.

For example, in some occupational programs it is useful to be able to relate students' grades in the program to their ability to pass the externally administered licensing or certifying examination on their first attempt. A grid of the type presented in table 12.14 would be used in developing such an expectancy table.

TABLE 12.14. Example Form for Tallying and Organizing Two Sets of Data When Developing an Expectancy Table.

	Certification Exam Results				
GPA's	Fail		Pass		Totals
3.5 - 4.0		(0)	⊢⊢⊢ ⊢⊢⊢ 11	(12)	12
3.0 - 3.5	1	(1)	⊢⊢⊢ ⊢⊢⊢ ⊢⊢⊢ 1	(16)	17
2.5 - 3.0	111	(3)	⊢⊢⊢ ⊢⊢⊢ ⊢⊢⊢ 1111	(19)	22
2.0 - 2.5	⊢⊢⊢ 1	(6)	⊢⊢⊢ ⊢⊢⊢ 111	(13)	19
1.5 - 2.0	⊢⊢⊢ ⊢⊢⊢ 1	(11)	⊢⊢⊢ 11	(7)	18
1.0 - 1.5	⊢⊢⊢ 111	(8)	1	(1)	9
0.5 - 1.0	11	(2)		(0)	2
0 - 0.5	1	(1)		(0)	1
Totals		32		68	100

Grade-point intervals are indicated down the left column and the pass-fail results of students' first attempt at the licensing or certifying examination are tallied for each level of grade-point average. Each tally shows the student's grade average in the occupational program and whether he passed or failed the examination on his first attempt. When all tallying is completed, the tallies in each cell of the table are summed and the number recorded in that cell. Next, all row and column numbers are summed at the right and bottom of the table respectively. As an accuracy check the sums at the right side of the table should equal the sum of the column totals along the bottom of the table. This data may then be organized into an expectancy table of the format presented in table 12.15.

TABLE 12.15. Expectancy Table Showing for Each Level of Grade-point Average the Number and Percentage of Students Expected to Receive Passing and Failing Marks on the State Licensure Examination on the First Attempt.

| Total | Number Pass–Fail | | Occupational Program | Percent Pass–Fail | | Total |
No.	Fail	Pass	Grade-point Average	Fail	Pass	Percent
12	0	12	3.5 – 4.0	0	100	100
17	1	16	3.0 – 3.5	6	94	100
22	3	19	2.5 – 3.0	14	86	100
19	6	13	2.0 – 2.5	32·	68	100
18	11	7	1.5 – 2.0	61	39	100
9	8	1	1.0 – 1.5	89	11	100
2	2	0	0.5 – 1.0	100	0	100
1	1	0	0 – 0.5	100	0	100

This table then can be used in discussing with students their progress in this occupational program. For example, if a student inquires as to how well he is doing in the program, his present grade-point average could be used to provide a good indication as to the probability of his passing the licensing or certifying examination on the first attempt. Of those graduating from the program with averages in the 2.0 to 2.5 range, about one-third of them fail on their first attempt. Likewise, students with averages less than 1.5 rarely, if ever, pass the examination on their first attempt and those above 3.5 rarely, if ever, fail on their first attempt.

When interpreting student grade-point averages in relation to their probable performance on the licensing or certifying examination, their attention can be directed toward their current grade-point averages and that area of the table that corresponds to their estimated grade-point averages at the end of program. The probability of their finding success at the end of the program then can be read directly from the table. Moreover, as data for additional students are added to the table, these predictions become more accurate.

Expectancy tables also can be prepared in a chart or graph format as shown in figures 12.9 and 12.10.

Note how the probability for attaining success increases as the level of the predictor variable increases. Expectancy charts can be very effective in dramatizing the relationship between the charted variables. As indicated in chapter 9, they are an excellent way of demonstrating the validity of instruments used in obtaining measurements of the predictor variables.

Whether to use a chart or table format or to use a large or small number of cells are questions that must be addressed when developing these aids for interpreting test information and data. In all cases, optimum format and cell size are that which best summarize the relationship to be illustrated. Each of the foregoing expectancy tables and charts could have been presented in a different form. However, if there is one guiding principle in preparing expectancy tables and charts, it is to maintain a reasonable relationship between the number of cells used and the number of students included in the sample; the fewer the students, the fewer the number of cells that should be used.

A collection of expectancy tables and/or charts are most helpful tools. Occupational teachers who can relate relative achievement in their programs to probable success on the job are in a good position to provide meaningful assistance when students have unrealistic appraisals of their abilities. Career-guidance personnel who are able to relate measures of aptitude, interest, and general mental ability to probable success in advanced occupational education programs are in a good position to provide meaningful input for students' career-preparation decisions. In these and many similar situations, expectancy tables are useful aids in interpreting students' test scores in relation to their chances for success in some future occupationally oriented endeavor.

REPORTING CRITERION-REFERENCED TEST RESULTS

Just as the philosophical bases for criterion-referenced measurement differ from norm-referenced measurement, so do some of the

Occupational Program Grade-point Average	No. in Group	No. Rated Satisfactory or Above	Percent Rated Satisfactory or Above
3.5 – 4.0	10	10	
3.0 – 3.5	16	14	
2.5 – 3.0	20	16	
2.0 – 2.5	18	14	
1.5 – 2.0	14	9	
1.0 – 1.5	4	2	
0.5 – 1.0	0	0	
0 – 0.5	0	0	
Total	82		0% 20% 40% 60% 80% 100%

FIGURE 12.9. Expectancy Chart Showing Percentage of Occupational Program Graduates Expected to Receive Satisfactory or Better Supervisory Ratings on the Follow-up Study of First-year Graduates.

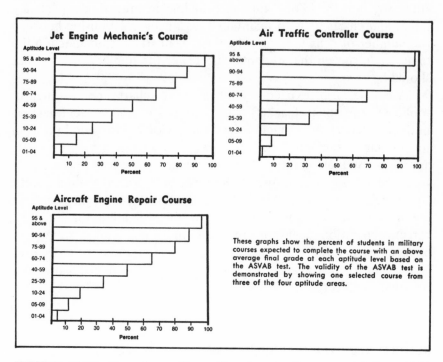

FIGURE 12.10. Expectancy Charts Showing the Percentage of Students in Military Courses Expected to Complete the Named Courses with an Above-average Final Grade at Each Aptitude Level as Measured by the Armed Services Vocational Aptitude Battery.

methods of scoring, reporting, and interpreting the measurement results obtained with these two approaches to measurement. Criterion-referenced approaches are concerned with students attaining a predetermined level of mastery rather than being concerned with comparing levels of performance among students within a particular group.

Levels of Mastery

The establishment of levels of mastery for criterion-referenced measurements are decisions made by some recognized authority. For example, an office occupations teacher might set 60 words per minute as the level of mastery he would expect to be achieved by all first-year typing students. Manufacturers' specifications serve to identify the mastery level for auto mechanics students as they learn to perform operations such as aligning automobile front ends, regulating the electrical output from alternators (generators), or adjusting the fuel flow through carburetors. Government agencies indirectly establish mastery levels with their licensure and certifying exams in certain skill areas such as cosmotology, health care, barbering, welding, truck driving, airplane navigation, and pilot programs. In each of the foregoing and similar types of situations the expected level of mastery is arbitrarily set at some level beyond a recognized level of minimum usefulness, but not at a level that is beyond practical necessity. That is, most office education teachers recognize that being able to type only 30 to 40 words per minute is generally not fast enough in the business world. However, to insist that each of their students be able to type 100 words per minute is beyond practical expectation in all but very specialized assignments. Therefore, 65 words per minute has been somewhat arbitrarily established as an acceptable level of mastery for first-year typing students. Similar thought processes are used to establish levels of mastery for students enrolled in most all occupational programs.

Identifying Deficiencies

Once established, the levels of mastery can be used with appropriate testing procedures in identifying deficiencies in an occupational student's ability to perform at or above an established level of mastery. For example, if the level of mastery for welding students is producing flat butt welds capable of withstanding a 60,000 psi tensil test, then it is anticipated that each student in the program should be able to produce such welds that would meet or exceed the 60,000 psi test. Students who cannot are obviously deficient in their ability to perform one or more of the following operations: select an appropriate welding rod, set the welder at the appropriate amperage, strike an appropriate arc, maintain an appropriate distance between rod and base metal, move the rod over the base metal in an appropriate line and at an appropriate speed, and properly clean the weld between each pass. Only after the deficiency or deficiencies are identified and this information is conveyed to the student, will the student and his instructor be able to begin working on the operation(s) with which the student is experiencing difficulty. Therefore, it is apparent that establishing levels of mastery and using them as the basis for identifying deficiencies in the ability to perform necessary operations is important to the teaching–learning process in many occupational areas. However, probably the most recognized reason for determining levels of mastery and identifying deficiencies in students' abilities to perform at or above these levels is to serve as a basis for assigning student grades.

Criterion-referenced Grading

Procedures for assigning criterion-referenced grades are of the pass–fail type. The criterion or minimum level for a passing performance on an achievement test is established prior to the administration of the test, and generally prior to the instruction that is to be covered by the test.

For example, early in an office occupations course, the teacher informs the students that one of the objectives for this course is for each student to be able to type at 60 words per minute without error when given the standard typing test at the end of the course. In this instance, the teacher would administer the typing test at the end of the course. For those students whose test performance was at or above 60 words per minute, the teacher would assign a pass grade. For those whose performance was below the established passing level, the teacher would assign a fail grade.

Pass–fail grades also can be assigned on the basis of student performance on paper and pencil achievement tests. In this instance, the occupational teacher establishes a minimum passing score prior to the administration of the test. For example, a raw score of 75 might be the minimum passing score on a 100-item multiple-choice exam in consumer homemaking. Students who score at or above 75 on the test receive a pass grade. Those who score 74 or lower receive a fail grade.

However, once the pass–fail grade is recorded, much valuable information is lost. For example, students who can accurately type at 58 words per minute and at 30 words per minute each receive the same failing grade. Likewise, students who score 75 and 98 on the 100-item multiple-choice achievement test each receive the same passing grade. Such a loss in precision is tolerable in student-grade reports but would not be tolerable if one were formally testing research hypotheses concerning the effectiveness of two methods of teaching shorthand or consumer homemaking, for example. In these latter two instances, raw scores rather than pass–fail should be used.

The big advantage that criterion-referenced pass–fail grading has is that *all* students who can perform at or above the established criterion level receive a passing mark. No student is forced by the grading system to be viewed or to view him or herself as being a failure or among the lowest achievers in the class. This is not the case with norm-referenced grades.

INTERPRETING TEST RESULTS

If a test or series of tests is worth administering in the occupational program, then the obtained scores or records of student performance should be communicated to one or more of the following groups: the students, their parents, other teachers, the administrators, and the career-guidance personnel. There are several general principles or guidelines that should be kept in mind as one proceeds to interpret test scores to individuals from these groups. Some of the more important of these principles are presented here.

Timing

Sometime prior to the time that an instrument is administered, students are usually informed that they will be taking a test. At that same time, they are usually told something about what type of test(s) to expect, the purposes of the test(s), and how the test results will be used. After going through this process of introduction and the processes of taking the test, it seems only reasonable that students should receive feedback as to their performance as soon as possible after taking the test.

Students are more likely to be interested in reviewing their tests and their test performance if the interest generated in the introductory and test-taking phases of the process has not subsided. Very few students would be interested in test scores from tests they can barely remember taking. Moreover, in the case of locally developed instruments, they would be even less interested in reviewing the instrument for the purpose of obtaining some specific knowledge or understanding that they missed on the test or for the purpose of helping their teacher clarify and improve items on the test that need clarification.

In most occupational programs there will not be enough time available for the teacher to present to each student his test score(s) and explain what they mean. Of course, some students will need such individual attention. But, for most students, an in-class presentation of the scores and review of the test as soon as possible after the test has been administered will satisfy the needs of most students and conserve considerable amount of teacher time.

Finally, teachers who habitually allow large periods to elapse between test administration and reporting the results to their students will, after a few tests, find it difficult to get their students interested in taking tests. It is difficult for students to participate in any activity when feedback as to their performance is not soon forthcoming. Testing is no exception to this truism and the error component of each student's obtained score is magnified when students are not interested and bring an "I don't care" attitude to the testing situation.

Knowledge of the Test

A thorough knowledge of the test is important to those who would interpret students' performance on the test. For most locally developed achievement tests, knowing the test is not much of a problem for occupational teachers. They prepared the test, therefore, they should know it perhaps better than anyone else. Occupational teachers should, however, be aware that locally developed instruments, like standardized instruments, do not always measure precisely what they were designed to measure. The *actual* (which may not be the planned) rationale underlying the items included in a test should form the basis for interpreting the obtained scores.

This concept is particularly important when interpreting scores obtained with standardized instruments. Test titles and even test manuals do not always describe accurately the behavior(s) actually measured. Therefore, it is important that the test manual be read very carefully by those who would interpret the obtained scores and that the test be taken in whole and under actual testing conditions by these individuals before they begin to interpret student performance.

Knowledge of the Scores Used

As indicated earlier in this chapter, there are important differences in the various types of scores that might be used to summarize and report student performance on a test. Raw scores, percentile ranks, z-scores, and T-scores, for example, must receive different interpretations. It follows, then, that one must know what type of score he is interpreting, the shape of the frequency distribution for other scores in the group, as well as the magnitude of the score. Very large errors in interpretation can be made when the shape of the distribution is skewed and/or when different types of scores are confused with one another.

Knowledge of Norms

Whether local norms or external norms are being used to interpret students' performances on a given test, one cannot begin to make meaningful comparisons and interpretations unless he is thoroughly familiar with the norm groups. The important characteristics of norm groups (e.g., age, sex, occupation, education, race, and geographic location) are generally presented in test manuals for standardized instruments. Local norms should also be so defined. Knowledge of these characteristics is a must for those who would provide meaningful interpretations of test scores.

Knowledge of the Students

A single test score rarely provides an accurate picture of a student's traits, such as abilities, interests, or aptitudes. When possible, data and information from other sources should be brought to bear on the interpretation of individual test scores. This is particularly important when interpreting scores for disadvantaged and/or handicapped students when their particular shortcoming would seem to influence test performance. For example, highly emotional and slow-reading occupational students generally have difficulty with achievement tests, particularly those presented in a written format. Thus, their obtained scores may underestimate their actual level of achievement in the occupational program. The temptation to seize upon a single score and interpret it in isolation must be avoided. Individual scores should be interpreted in light of all known student-related factors that are pertinent to the score.

Effective Communication

Whether interpreting test scores to students, parents, other teachers, or career-guidance and administrative personnel, much is lost if the message is not communicated effectively. In extreme cases of misinterpretation, no interpretation at all would have been better than the misinterpretation. An adequate interpretation generally requires that all pertinent information be communicated. What the test was designed to measure, the composition of the norm group used, and how this particular student's performance compares to that of the norm group, his classmates, or some standard criterion are the types of questions that should be answered.

Several good techniques or aids for reporting and interpreting test scores were presented earlier in this chapter. Percentile ranks, standard scores, norms, profiles, and expectancy tables and charts are all useful aids for effective communication. Occupational personnel who know and understand these aids will find them to be almost indispensable for adequate interpretation of students' scores.

Exercising Caution

Remember, test scores do have an error component. They generally are based upon only a sampling of behavior. They are easily influenced by extraneous variables like disposition, emotion, and physical condition. They generally are not direct measures of ability, interest, aptitude, and the like. Rather, they are reflections of such variables. Most important, test scores only *suggest* the appropriateness of certain conclusions. They should *never* be offered as proof of anything.

Occupational education personnel are on safe ground if their interpretations of students' test scores are based upon comparisons with the performances of meaningful norm groups (norm-referenced testing) or with previously established levels of performance (criterion-referenced testing). Interpretative statements should begin with "When compared with the performance of students like yourself," or "The minimum acceptable score was set at . . . and your performance was . . . ." Interpretative statements that begin with "Your score means that you will . . ." are rarely appropriate.

REFERENCES

Bennett, G. K. et al. *Differential Aptitude Tests—Directions for Administration and Scoring.* New York: The Psychological Corporation, 1961.

Guilford, J. P. *Fundamental Statistics in Psychology and Education.* New York: McGraw-Hill, 1965.

Lyman, Howard B. *Test Scores and What They Mean.* Englewood Cliffs, New Jersey: Prentice-Hall, Inc., 1971.

Porter, Charles B. *Standard Score Conversion Chart.* Bloomington, Illinois: Illinois State University Foundation, 1965.

U.S. Department of Defense. "Vocation Test Identifies Students' Strongest Aptitude Area," *Commanders Digest.* Washington, D.C.: U.S. Government Printing Office, vol. 15, no. 25, June 1974, pp. 3–7.

Chapter 13

Using Measurement
Data and Information
in Occupational Programs

The initial chapter in this text opened with the premise that measurement procedures and techniques, when properly applied, are useful in monitoring student progress and can provide for occupational programs assurance that the "right" students are receiving the "right" instruction from the "right" teachers. The discussion of specific functions of measurement in occupational programs that followed focused on their relationship to this premise or overall goal for measurement in education.

This concluding chapter of the text is organized around these same functions of measurement in occupational programs. The focus here, however, is on suggested ways of *using* the results of measurement efforts in order to maximize their value in monitoring student progress, aiding career guidance, classifying and placing students, aiding program evaluation, aiding curriculum improvement, improving instruction and hypothesis testing, and assessing teaching effectiveness.

The level of assistance provided by various types of instruments for the foregoing functions of measurement in occupational programs is summarized in table 13.1.

From the table it can be seen that the amount of assistance provided by each type of instrument varies significantly with the

TABLE 13.1. Use of Measurement Instruments in Occupational Education.

Types of Instruments

Functions of Measurement in Occupational Programs	Locally Developed				Standardized				
	Cognitive Achievement Tests	Performance Achievement Tests	Attitude Instruments	Interest Inventories	General Mental Ability Tests	Aptitude Tests	Interest Inventories	Attitude Measures	Achievement Tests
Monitoring student progress	***	***	*		***				**
Aiding career guidance	***	***	**	**	***	***	***	***	*
Classifying and placing students	**	**	*	*	***	***	***	***	*
Aiding program evaluation	***	***	*						*
Aiding curriculum improvement	***	***							*
Improving instruction and hypothesis testing	***	***							*
Assessing teaching effectiveness	***	***	*					*	*

nature of the function. For example, locally developed achievement tests can make significant contributions to all of the functions of measurement in occupational programs, whereas standardized tests of general mental ability and standardized instruments for assessing affective behaviors like interests and attitudes are quite limited in this regard.

With this final chapter, the text has come full circle. It started with the functions of measurement in occupational programs, moved to basic measurement concepts and specific procedures and techniques for obtaining and reporting pertinent types of data and information, and now concludes with suggestions for using this data and information to fulfill the functions of measurement in occupational programs.

MONITORING STUDENT PROGRESS

Standardized and locally developed measurement procedures and techniques are indispensible aids for monitoring student progress in occupational programs. Without such aids, administrators, teachers, parents, and the students themselves would be forced to rely on subjective judgments as to the progress students were making in the program. Procedures for adequately monitoring student progress in occupational programs generally involve two basic steps: (1) using achievement measures of some type (e.g., quizzes, unit tests, final exams, rating scales) to assess student achievement, and (2) assigning for each student a grade or some other evaluative description that characterizes his or her level of performance in the classroom, shop or laboratory, and/or on the job. Obviously, if these grades are to be valid indices of student progress in the occupational program, they should be based upon valid data and information obtained in step one above. As indicated in chapter 12, grades should neither be based upon nor influenced by a teacher's or administrator's capricious or subjective assessment of student progress.

There are four basic reasons for monitoring student progress. Each is related to a need for this type of data and information by one or more groups of individuals, namely, school administrators, teachers, guidance personnel, parents, and students. A discussion of how data and information from monitoring student progress in occupational programs is used by each of these groups follows.

Facilitating Program Administration

Most local districts require occupational teachers periodically to prepare for each student a grade or some other qualitative descriptor of his or her record of achievement in the occupational program. This record of performance is useful to occupational teachers, administrators, and/or career-guidance personnel as they:

1. Confer with parents regarding their children's progress in the occupational program
2. Compare and contrast the efficiency and effectiveness of the occupational program from year to year
3. Prepare recommendations for graduates of the occupational program seeking either employment or furthering of their education at another institution

The viability and impact of these activities would be reduced significantly if each student's performance in the occupational program were not systematically monitored, recorded, and made available to appropriate school personnel.

Facilitating Instruction

Occupational teachers should obtain and review the records of their students' performance in the occupational program to identify areas in their instruction that (1) have been covered adequately, or (2) are in need of new or additional learning experiences to achieve the instructional objective(s). When student progress is monitored during an instructional unit in the occupational program and their performance indicates that they have achieved the objective(s) for that unit of instruction, then it is time for the teacher to conclude that unit of instruction. This would be the case even if the occupational teacher had completed the first few class days of a two-week unit of instruction. For to continue the instruction beyond the point where a large majority of the students have attained the instructional objective(s) is to invite a loss of interest in the instructional program on the part of the students—and justifiably so.

Likewise, the instructional program is impaired significantly if units of instruction are routinely concluded as scheduled even if large numbers of students have not attained the instructional objective(s) established for the unit. This is particularly true when, as is the case with much occupational education, one's mastery of the objectives for the succeeding unit(s) of instruction is dependent upon one's mastery of the objectives for the present unit.

Occupational teachers should routinely monitor their students' progress in the program and use the obtained data and information continually to refine or improve their instruction to its highest possible level of efficiency and effectiveness. Anticipated levels representing satisfactory student performance should be established for each convenient subunit of instruction (e.g., 85 percent of the students will be able to make satisfactory pipe welds in the horizontal position upon completion of this unit of instruction). Demonstrations and student practice of this welding technique should be halted and shifted to the next welding technique or unit of instruction when the 85 percent level of demonstrated performance is attained by the class. Again, to do otherwise will: (1) decrease the efficiency and effectiveness of the instruction, and (2) risk losing student interest in the instructional program. To do so will serve to: (1) optimize the efficiency and effectivenss of the instruction, and (2) maintain or perhaps even increase student interest in the instructional program.

If, on the other hand, only 35 percent of the occupational students can make satisfactory pipe welds in the overhead position after the planned instruction has been completed, then the instruction should be improved or modified to achieve the anticipated 85 percent level of demonstrated performance. To do otherwise will, in this example: (1) cause an ineffective and inefficient unit of instruction to remain so, and (2) increase the chances for students to fail to learn to weld pipe in a vertical position. To do so will, in this example: (1) improve the efficiency and effectiveness of this unit of instruction, and (2) more adequately prepare the students to achieve the objectives established for the instructional unit on pipe welding in a vertical position.

Facilitating Learning

Probably the most important reason for monitoring student progress in the occupational program is to share the obtained information and data with the occupational students. Providing each student with up-to-date feedback with regard to his or her performance in the occupational program will serve as a significant facilitator in the learning process.

For example, occupational students who receive high marks, praise, and recognition for their achievement as a result of the monitoring process are, more likely than not, going to study harder and learn even more in order to maintain, if not increase, the level of recognition they receive. Occupational students, like most everyone else, need and enjoy being recognized for their achievements. Those who are on the receiving end of positive reinforcement for their attention to learning in the program will want this recognition to continue. Consequently, they will strive to maintain or increase its frequency and level and their learning will be facilitated in the process.

The process of monitoring student progress also can serve to facilitate learning for occupational students who, if left to their own, would not learn very much in the occupational program. For example, the mere fact that students are aware that their progress in the occupational program is being monitored through a series of tests or quizzes often induces some students to study harder and be prepared for each upcoming test or quiz. Many otherwise lackadaisical occupational students are induced to study diligently to prepare for a short quiz, a unit, or final exam. Thus, the monitoring process serves to facilitate students' learning in the occupational program on a concomitant basis.

Regular monitoring of student progress in the occupational program also facilitates learning on a more direct and controlled basis. Occupational teachers often make testing experiences into very effective learning experiences by reviewing with their students all achievement tests shortly after they have been scored and graded. This practice provides many opportunities for students to pick up specific knowledge, skills, and understanding that for some reason were not attained during the regular instruction. Occupational students often draw closure on some understanding or relationship as a result of discussing with their teacher the particular test item that was designed to measure student attainment of that understanding or relationship. In many instances the test review session is the students' last opportunity to clarify misconceptions and to fill in minor gaps in their occupational preparation prior to employment. Moreover, these sessions provide the occupational teacher with a final opportunity to facilitate learning in those areas of his or her instruction that were not 100 percent effective the first time around.

Occupational teachers should be sure to inform their students well in advance of any tests, quizzes, or other procedures for monitoring student progress that are used in the occupational program. Likewise, the information and data obtained in the process of monitoring student progress must be shared with the students as soon as possible after they are obtained. Obviously, the impact that monitoring student progress can have on facilitating learning will be reduced significantly if one or both of the foregoing conditions (providing adequate announcement and providing immediate feedback) cannot be met. Occupational teachers who provide their students with a schedule of tests to be administered during the semester and who provide students with nearly immediate feedback regarding their progress will facilitate learning for an important segment of the students enrolled in their classes—those who did not learn material the first time around.

DIAGNOSING LEARNING DIFFICULTIES

Many local districts have implemented testing programs to monitor student progress in developing a variety of scholastic skills. The Iowa Tests of Basic Skills is a good example of a battery used to monitor student progress continuously from elementary grades through high school. Systematic procedures for monitoring student progress also can be useful in diagnosing learning difficulties among students who are having a seemingly inordinate amount of difficulty in achieving the instructional objectives established for the occupational program in which they are enrolled. Learning difficulties in electronics programs, for example, often are found to be due to the students' lack of background in and/or aptitude for mathematics. If standardized instruments with appropriate norms are used in making this diagnosis, then those concerned are automatically provided with good estimates as to how many grade levels individual students are behind in mathematics and whether they have the aptitude for eliminating the deficit through remedial study.

Occupational teachers who periodically monitor student progress and review with their students the achievement tests and quizzes used in this process have an excellent opportunity to identify learning difficulties. Shortly after these tests or quizzes have been administered and graded, they should be returned to the students and each test item should be discussed in class or in individual conferences with the students. This dialog between the teacher and students usually provides, among other important insights, insights regarding the types and nature of learning difficulties that are operant among the students.

Prior to the discussion period, occupational teachers should make note of areas in the test in which extraordinary numbers of students experienced difficulty. Individual students who experienced extraordinary levels of difficulty throughout the test should be noted also. During the discussion period the teacher should be sure to focus on the identified problem areas in the test and check or remember the names of students who appear to be experiencing learning difficulties that cannot be corrected by making reasonable modifications in the course content or methods of instruction. These students, of course, should be referred to the appropriate guidance personnel so that arrangements can be made for more detailed and intensive diagnostic testing followed by reclassification and placement in the occupational program to accommodate better their individual needs, interests, aptitudes, and/or abilities.

AIDING CAREER GUIDANCE

Standardized and locally developed instruments make one of their most significant contributions to occupational education when students who are sincerely interested in identifying their career-related interests, strengths, and weaknesses are administered instruments that cause them to focus on their vocational interests, aptitudes, and abilities. When properly administered, scored, and interpreted in light of other appropriate information and data, the information and data obtained using such instruments can be of much value in assisting students with their career development decisions. The keys to success here are three: (1) proper application of the criteria for selecting standardized instruments, (2) proper application of the procedures for preparing locally developed instruments, and (3) adequate preparation to insure sincere interest on the part of the students.

Using Standardized Measures

Instruments like the Strong Vocational Interest Blank for Men (SVIB), General Aptitude Test Battery (GATB), or the California Short-Form Test of Mental Maturity that might be included in a local district's battery of career-guidance tests administered to all students should be carefully selected from among those offered by reputable test publishers. Moreover, records of student performance obtained with these instruments should be presented to the students and their parents or guardians in a format that they will understand. Derived scores such as percentile ranks, local and national norms, individual and group profiles, and expectancy tables are useful formats for presenting and interpreting for career-guidance purposes student performance on standardized tests.

Normally, responsibility for interpreting results from standardized instruments focusing on attitudes, interests, aptitudes, personality, and general mental abilities belongs to local career-guidance personnel. They are usually the best trained in the use and interpretation of such instruments.

As a general rule, scores obtained with the instruments should always be interpreted in light of all available pertinent data and information. For example, students who have achieved success working part-time in a particular occupation and/or have high grades in classes that relate to a particular occupation should not be discouraged from pursuing that occupation just because their score on some standardized instrument indicates a low probability of success in that particular occupation. Likewise, students should not be encouraged or pressured to enter a career field in which they have scored high on an aptitude test, when their apparent abilities and/or expressed interests lie elsewhere. Measurements in the affective domain are quite easily influenced by factors such as one's interest in taking the test, cultural background, and prior training. Students' "aptitudes" and "vocational interests," for example, have been known to shift markedly as their interest in using a battery of career-guidance tests to determine their true aptitudes and interests increased. Given the best of available instruments, efforts taken to increase students' interest in using these instruments to assist them in discovering their interests, aptitudes, and abilities can only increase the validity of the obtained responses.

Using Locally Developed Measures

Locally developed teacher-made or teacher-modified tests for occupational programs are generally of the achievement-test type and
are designed to determine the degree to which students have attained
the instructional objectives for a particular course or unit of instruction. Occasionally, standardized achievement tests are used to assess
student attainment of objectives in occupational programs. The role
that locally developed and (occasionally) standardized achievement
tests play in evaluating and reporting student progress in occupational
programs is very apparent. Not so obvious, however, is the role that
these achievement tests play in aiding career development.

Most occupational education students view their record of
achievement in an occupational program as an index of their having
what it takes to succeed in that occupation. This is a reasonable
practice. Short of trial periods of employment in a particular occupation, the best career-guidance information a student can obtain
regarding his or her suitability for that occupation would be his or
her record of performance on achievement tests that accurately
reflect the important cognitive, affective, psychomotor, and perceptual aspects of that occupation. Many students, after having
given considerable attention to career planning, have enrolled in the
occupational program of their choice only to learn after the first
few achievement tests administered in the program that they do not
have the aptitudes, interests, abilities, and/or motivation to be
successful in that occupation.

Thus, it behooves occupational teachers and/or career-guidance
personnel to (1) insure that the achievement tests selected, modified,
or developed for their programs are truly reflective of the personnel
requirements of the occupation, (2) provide students with reports
of their performance on achievement tests as soon as practical after
testing, and (3) include records of student performance on achievement tests in occupational courses among the data and information
used to assist students in making their career-development decisions.

CLASSIFYING AND PLACING STUDENTS

Traditionally, the measure of success for occupational programs has
been in the numbers and success of those who complete the programs.

Traditionally, the surest means of having an excellent program has been to select and admit only those who demonstrate levels of abilities, aptitudes, and interests that, based on past experience, indicate an extremely high probability of success. The current move toward more accountability in education has caused many vocational educators to rethink these traditional viewpoints. Evans (1971), for example, suggests that *value added by education* should be the criteria for evaluating the success of occupational programs and students should be selected who will gain most from the program, regardless of the level at which they start. Student selection, classification, and placement, then, should focus on (1) accepting *all* students who are sincerely interested in developing occupational skills, (2) classifying them according to their present level of development and readiness for occupational preparation, and (3) placing them in a program of studies that is consistent with their career-development needs.

Selecting Occupational Students

Selection decisions focus on who will be admitted to the program and who will not. These are hard decisions to make, primarily because in occupational education we must be concerned with those who are rejected as well as those who are accepted.

However, our objective should be to admit all students who have interest in and can benefit from the occupational program—not to select for admission only those who have more than enough ability to succeed in the program.

Classifying and Placing Occupational Students

If we were to follow Evans's suggestion, then, measurement procedures and techniques would be used to make classification and placement decisions rather than selection decisions. All who sought entry to the occupational program would be selected for occupational preparation. The measurement task would be to classify and place each student with respect to such variables as vocational interest, aptitude, and level of readiness in communication skills and mathematics. The primary objective of the classification and placement process would be to start each student in the occupational program at a level where the value added by education would be maximized. Classification and placement decisions of this type require the use of some rather sophisticated measurement procedures and techniques such as: diagnostic tests in relevant basic skill areas like mathematics and verbal skills; aptitude, interest, and personality tests in relevant affective areas; and expectancy tables to aid in interpreting the data and information obtained with the foregoing tests.

Currently available standardized instruments and most locally developed instruments are sophisticated enough for us to select those students who have more than enough ability to succeed in our occupational programs. Errors will be made in many instances. But, overall, if the objective is to admit to occupational programs only those students who will definitely succeed, then we can come close to meeting this objective 100 percent by employing carefully selected standardized and/or locally developed instruments to assist us in making selection decisions. Cutoff points and/or prediction formulas can be prepared and levels of acceptance set so that we virtually can be assured of selecting only those students who will succeed in our occupational programs.

AIDING PROGRAM EVALUATION

Data and information obtained from locally developed, criterion-referenced, and externally administered assessments of student performance can be useful input for evaluating occupational programs. An explanation of ways in which these types of assessments can be used toward this end follows.

Using Locally Developed Assessments

Normally, it is desirable to use data and information from external sources when evaluating occupational programs. Employers' ratings of occupational program graduates' performances on the job and performance tests administered by advisory council members would be two examples of locally developed techniques for obtaining external information and data. The data and information obtained using these techniques can be used to answer questions regarding program effectiveness and to identify related trends. For example, if employers' ratings of graduates' performances are generally adequate but lower than those obtained for first-year graduates from the same program during the previous two years, then one could conclude that the program is satisfactory but its effectiveness is on a downward trend.

Occupational programs that are based upon specified performance objectives can use data and information from internally administered achievement tests to evaluate the effectiveness of the program, too. For example, a competency-based program for preparing auto mechanics would have associated with it a series of objectives calling for the students to be able to perform some service or repair in accordance with manufacturer's specifications and within some specified flat-rate time. Achievement tests for such a program would be designed to assess students' abilities to perform each of the repairs or services as per the manufacturer's specifications within the time allowed. Obviously, a record of the students' pass–fail performance on these locally administered achievement tests would provide valuable information regarding the effectiveness of the program. For example, if 95 percent of the students pass their performance tests in each competency area the very first time they are tested, one probably would conclude that this is a very effective program.

Using Standardized Externally Developed Assessments

Because there are so few well-developed and readily available standardized achievement tests in occupational education subject areas, occupational teachers and administrators rarely need to consider them as sources of evaluative input when evaluating the efficiency and effectiveness of their occupational programs. However, for those occupational programs leading to certification and licensure (e.g., cosmotology, aviation, welding, heavy equipment operation, nursing, and allied health occupations), student performance on the standardized instruments administered by the certifying or licensing agency can be one valuable source of data and information for evaluating the efficiency and effectiveness of the occupational programs in which the students receive their technical preparation for these exams.

In some instances the only information revealed by the agency is whether the students passed or failed the examination. If even this bit of information is collected for a significant number of students (perhaps as few as twenty-five), then quite often some evaluative conclusions concerning the effectiveness of the program can be drawn. For example, if under normal circumstances, only 60 percent of those students completing the cosmotology program pass the state licensing examination, then one might conclude that the program is not very effective. If the per-student costs for this program are steadily increasing and at the same time the percentage of graduates who pass the licensing examination is decreasing, then one might conclude that the efficiency of the program is questionable and in need of further investigation.

More refined conclusions regarding program efficiency and effectiveness can be drawn in those instances where feedback from the examining agency is not limited to pass–fail information alone. Often the agencies report the extent to which a student's obtained score is above or below the cutoff score for passing the examination. The availability of this added information makes it possible for our evaluative conclusions to be a little more precise. Suppose, for example, that data from the 100-point certifying examination taken by graduates of the welding program indicate that 80 percent passed and, of the 20 percent who failed, half of them missed achieving the passing mark by less than 5 points. One could conclude that this program is quite effective and could be even more so with, perhaps, a little more individualized instruction and/or practice time, particularly for those whose performance on the examination was so close to the passing mark.

In any case, data and information from externally administered instruments, where possible, should be combined with input from other sources such as student follow-up or employer surveys before any specific conclusions regarding the occupational program are finalized.

AIDING CURRICULUM IMPROVEMENT

Externally developed measurement instruments are recognized sources of information and data that are useful in improving curriculum in educational programs. As indicated earlier in Chapter 10.

however, the use of standardized achievement tests in occupational programs has, for economic reasons, not been as extensive as it has been in other subject areas in education. Thus, the opportunities for using data and information from standardized testing programs to improve courses of study are somewhat limited for occupational programs.

Identifying New Course Content

However, when the opportunity presents itself, it is good practice for occupational teachers to use data and information from standardized or other published achievement tests for the purposes of locating types of learning that were not included in the course of study. Suppose, for example, the data from a standardized examination revealed that 95 percent of the students in an ornamental horticulture course missed an item concerned with classifying some rather uncommon coniferous and deciduous trees, and these trees were not included in the course of study for the course. The occupational teachers and perhaps the advisory committee for the ornamental horticulture program should analyze the knowledge required in this occupation and decide whether the course of study should be upgraded by including in it a discussion of these trees. If, after analyzing the knowledge requirements of this occupation, this content is determined to be important enough to be included in the course of study, then the course of study should be modified to include this content. If not, the course of study should not be modified. Under no circumstances should its presence on a standardized or other published achievement test be the sole rationale for including a particular bit of content in a course of study.

Do Not Use Tests as Course Outlines

Likewise, neither standardized nor locally developed achievement tests should be used as outlines for courses of study in occupational programs. Most achievement tests used in occupational programs present only a sampling of the knowledge, skills, and understanding that are important to the occupation upon which they are based. Much essential content is necessarily excluded, otherwise, these tests

420

normally would be too long. Some is excluded because it does not lend itself to measurement via paper and pencil techniques. In addition, many achievement tests of this type include items concerning content that is important to the occupation but not essential for job entry and would be known only by those with long experience in the occupation. Often, such items are included to insure that the instrument is capable of assessing achievement at all levels of development in this occupation. Thus, to use achievement tests as outlines for courses of study would lead to serious gaps in the needed course content that would be filled with content of the "nice-to-know" variety.

Do Not "Teach the Test"

Occupational teachers should not be overly concerned with covering all the course content presented in a standardized achievement test, and "teaching the test" so that their students will look good when compared with other students. Chances are the students included in the norming sample were in a course similar to the one that they are teaching and were not exposed to all the course content covered by the test either. Therefore, students with preparation equal to that received by the norming sample should neither have an advantage nor be at a disadvantage. Each should do as well on the test as his or her equal in the norming group.

IMPROVING INSTRUCTION AND HYPOTHESIS TESTING

The use of measurement procedures and techniques to test hypotheses formally or check out informally hunches concerning the teaching–learning process in occupational education is credited with making significant improvements in occupational education. However, there are other ways to make significant improvements in instruction, some of which have not been used to their full potential. Ways in which data and information from locally administered and externally administered achievement tests and hypothesis testing can be used to improve instruction follow.

421

Using Locally Administered Tests to Improve Instruction

Occasionally, when occupational teachers score achievement tests for a new course or unit of instruction, they find that some of their students did not perform as well as the teacher had anticipated. First, the teacher should check to see if the scoring key for the test is correct. Marking the wrong "correct" answer on the test key is a common malady among teachers. Finding no errors in any of the scoring processes, the teacher then should make note of the "troubled areas" or areas of instruction that did not appear to come across as well as intended. When these tests are distributed and reviewed with the students, particular attention should be paid to student questions and comments in those areas of the test previously identified as troubled areas. Throughout the discussion the occupational teacher should make note of apparent voids in knowledge and/or misunderstandings expressed by the students, particularly those that appear to be responsible for the students' poor performance in selected segments of the test. These notes then become the basis for improving the instruction in the identified troubled areas.

Often the identified troubled areas of instruction can be smoothed out by modifying the instruction in the occupational course in one or more of the following ways:

1. Including in the instruction additional examples of on-the-job applications
2. Starting the instruction in that area on a more basic level
3. Providing more opportunities for students to practice using newly acquired knowledge, understanding, or skills
4. Incorporating into the instruction one or more visual aids to help clarify the points made
5. Revising the student performance objectives to clarify for the students the intent of the instruction

Using Externally Administered Tests to Improve Instruction

Occasionally, data and information from standardized achievement tests are also available for improving occupational programs. For example, some certifying and licensing agencies like the Federal

Aviation Agency provide feedback on examinations that indicate (1) pass-fail information, (2) how far above or below the passing mark the obtained score was, and (3) the areas of competence judged to be unsatisfactory. When this type of feedback is available to occupational teachers for the students who graduate from their programs and who take certifying and licensing examinations administered by external agencies, it can be most useful in identifying areas of instruction in their courses of study that are in need of improvement. The emphasis here, however, would be on identifying the *types* of knowledge, skills, and understanding that appear to have been taught ineffectively, rather than identifying *specific items* on the test that were missed by the students.

Instruction in the course should be improved by taking appropriate steps to insure that adequate learning experiences are provided for all the knowledge, skills, and understanding included in the course of study. Steps taken to insure that students can respond correctly to specific test items are of little value. Most types of knowledge, skills, and understanding included in these instruments could be measured using any one of a large number of possible test items. The futility of attempting to improve instruction by attempting to "teach the test" or individual items on the test is evident. Improvements in instruction that are based upon analysis of student performance on externally administered licensure or certification examinations must focus on insuring adequate instruction in the *types* of knowledge, skills, and understanding that the testing agency considers to be important to the occupation.

Hypothesis Testing to Improve Instruction

Hypothesis testing, whether on an informal "checking-out-hunches" or a formal "experimental-research" basis, is an integral part of using measurement-derived data and information to improve instruction. After identifying areas of their instruction that do not appear to have been very successful, most occupational teachers will come to some conclusions regarding these problem areas. They usually identify some tentative causes of the problems and form one or more hunches about how the instruction could be modified to overcome the suspected problems. The process of testing one or more of the hunches will involve making the necessary modifications in the instruction and then comparing student test performance after the modified instruction with the test performance recorded by the earlier students. Improved student performance usually means the teacher's hunch was correct. The end result then is improved instruction for future students.

However, sometimes the teacher's hunch is not correct. The "improved" instruction does not produce added learning as evidenced by an increase in the level of student performance for the problem areas of the achievement test. The occupational teacher then should return to the initial stages of the process and either develop a new hunch to be checked out in the same informal manner or develop a hypothesis to be tested using formal experimental research methods.

The actual design and analysis of experimental studies to test formal hypotheses are beyond the scope of this text. However, it should be noted here that the studies conducted to compare the effects of two or more instructional methods require data and information that can only be obtained using one or more of the measurement procedures and techniques presented in this text. Such data then might be analyzed by comparing students' performance on a pretest administered prior to the instruction with these same students' performance on a posttest administered after the instruction, as depicted in figure 13.1. Or, they might be analyzed by comparing the average test performance of a group of students who received the instruction with that for a similar group of students who had not received the instruction, as depicted in figure 13.2. Finally, they might be analyzed by comparing observed levels of student performance with some predetermined or anticipated level of performance, as depicted in figure 13.3.

Normally, if the instruction is effective and if the pretests and posttests are equivalent tests, we would expect students to perform significantly better on the posttest (after instruction) than they did on the pretest (before instruction). If this is not the case, then the instruction needs to be improved.

Normally, if the instruction is effective, we would expect the average test performance for the students who received the instruction to be significantly higher than the average test performance for the students who did not receive the instruction. If this is not the case, then the instruction needs to be improved.

Normally, if the instruction is as effective as we think that it

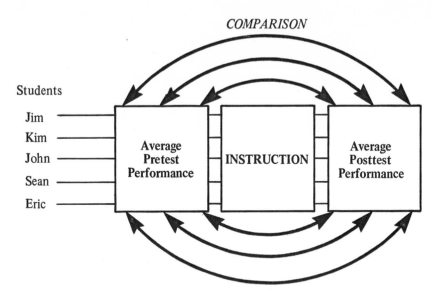

FIGURE 13.1.   Comparing Pretest Performance with Posttest Performance.

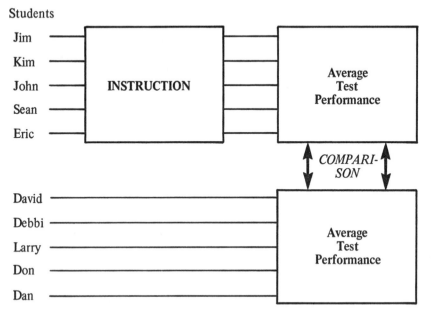

FIGURE 13.2.   Comparing Performance of Students Who Have Received Instruction with Students Who Have Not.

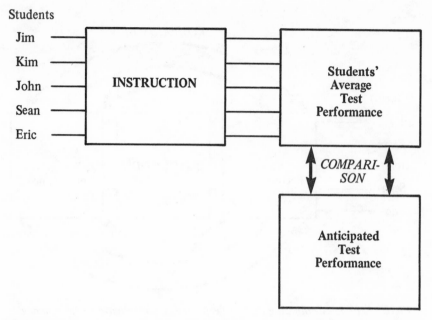

FIGURE 13.3.   Comparing Observed Student Performance with a Predetermined or Anticipated Level of Performance.

should be, the students should be able to perform at or above the level of mastery to which the instruction was designed to bring them. If the students do not reach the anticipated level of mastery as evidenced by their failure to perform at the anticipated level, then the instruction needs to be improved.

For an exhaustive treatment of these and other research designs to test hypotheses concerned with improving instruction or with determining the impact that variables such as age, sex, or cultural background of the learner have on the learning process, refer to Campbell and Stanley (1966) and Isaac and Michael (1971). Again, it should be noted that all hypothesis testing, no matter how sophisticated the research design, will require valid data and information of the types that can only be derived using one or more of the measurement procedures and techniques presented in this text.

ASSESSING TEACHING EFFECTIVENESS

Feedback concerning the degree to which graduates from occupational programs are successful with certifying, licensing, and other job-related standardized instruments can serve as one source of input in assessing teaching effectiveness. The three types of feedback discussed earlier (pass–fail information, data indicating level of performance above or below the cutoff point, and data and information concerning areas of competence judged to be unsatisfactory) can be useful input for assessing teaching effectiveness.

Supervisors' Assessment

Student success on relevant externally administered standardized licensing or certifying exams and/or on locally administered achievement tests is strong evidence of effective teaching. Not so certain, however, are the implications for teaching effectiveness that are sometimes attached to a lesser record of student performance on such exams.

It is important for occupational education teachers, their immediate supervisors, and other administrators to bear in mind that, in both instances, this one bit of input is not the whole picture. Such data must be viewed in light of other pertinent factors, circumstances, conditions, and data from other sources. No attempt should be made openly to compare the teaching in individual occupational programs on the basis of student performance on internally or externally administered achievement tests. Such practice can only lead to a spirit of rivalry and lack of cooperation between teachers, and eventually to improperly prepared occupational program graduates.

Occupational Teachers' Self-evaluation

Finally, it should be recognized that measurement procedures and techniques make their greatest contribution to assessing teaching effectiveness in occupational programs when the occupational teachers themselves, in the privacy of their offices, laboratories, and classrooms, review their students' performances on the tests and quizzes they have developed, administered, and scored and seriously ask themselves the basic question, "Could I have been more effective in my teaching?"

SUMMARY

It is important to note that there is little, if anything, inherent in the measurement procedures and techniques presented in this text that determines the amount of contribution they can make to each of the functions of measurement for occupational programs. It is how these instruments are used that determines the level of their contribution. For example, achievement tests are commonly used in monitoring student progress and in assigning grades in the occupational program. However, occupational teachers who review achievement tests and the results of these tests after they have been scored can use this experience to achieve the following additional ends:

1. Monitoring student progress
2. Aiding career guidance
3. Classifying and placing students
4. Aiding program evaluation
5. Aiding curriculum improvement
6. Improving instruction and hypothesis testing
7. Assessing teaching effectiveness

If occupational teachers fail to review achievement tests with their students after they have been scored, then some good opportunities to serve the above seven ends will be missed.

In order to realize the full contribution that measurement procedures and techniques can make in the development, conduct, and evaluation of occupational programs, occupational teachers, administrators, and career-guidance personnel must themselves engage in using the obtained information and data in ways described within this chapter. To do so requires time and effort. However, such effort also has its rewards, namely, improved efficiency and effectiveness of the occupational program and better-prepared graduates entering the world of work.

REFERENCES

Campbell, D. T., and Stanley, J. C. *Experimental and Quasi-Experimental Designs for Research.* Chicago: Rand McNally, 1966.

Evans, R. N. *Foundations of Vocational Education.* Columbus, Ohio: Charles E. Merrill, 1971.

Isaac, S., and Michael, W. B. *Handbook in Research and Evaluation.* San Diego: Robert R. Knapp, 1971.

List of Appendices

Appendix A

Guide for Computing the Product-Moment Correlation Coefficient

1. Begin with pairs of raw scores to be analyzed. Columns 2 (*X*) and 3 (*Y*) represent Scores of Mechanical Aptitude and Scores on a Computer Programming Examination for 20 students.
2. Compute scores for column 4 (*XY*) by multiplying column 2 by column 3.
3. Compute scores for column 5 (*X²*) by squaring each score in column 2.
4. Compute scores for column 6 (*Y²*) by squaring each score in column 3.
5. Sum each column of scores, columns 2 through 6.
6. Substitute needed totals in the following formula:

$$r = \frac{\Sigma XY - [(\Sigma X)(\Sigma Y)/N]}{\sqrt{\left[\Sigma X^2 - \frac{(\Sigma X)^2}{N}\right]\left[\Sigma Y^2 - \frac{(\Sigma Y)^2}{N}\right]}}$$

where:
r = Product-moment correlation coefficient
Σ = The sum
X = Any test score of one characteristic
Y = Any test score of another characteristic
N = Number of pupils

By substitution, the calculation is:

$$r = \frac{137,085 - [\,(2142)\,(1256)\,/\,20\,]}{\sqrt{\left[\,232,750 - \dfrac{(2142)^2}{20}\,\right]\left[\,84,188 - \dfrac{(1256)^2}{20}\,\right]}}$$

$r = .61$

TABLE A.1. *Computation of a Coefficient of Correlation for Ungrouped Data.*

Pupil	Mechanical Aptitude Test (X)	Computer Programming Test (Y)	XY	X^2	Y^2
Jim	135	66	8,910	18,225	4,356
Sam	130	90	11,700	16,900	8,100
Ruth	120	68	8,160	14,400	4,624
Mary	117	85	9,945	13,689	7,225
John	116	81	9,396	13,456	6,561
Louise	114	47	5,358	12,996	2,209
Ralph	113	69	7,797	12,769	4,761
Mae	112	77	8,624	12,544	5,929
Quinton	111	65	7,215	12,321	4,225
Sandra	109	56	6,104	11,881	3,136
Larry	107	89	9,523	11,449	7,921
Norma	106	49	5,194	11,236	2,401
Frank	101	57	5,757	10,201	3,249
Milton	100	58	5,800	10,000	3,364
Dave	97	71	6,887	9,409	5,041
Joe	95	60	5,700	9,025	3,600
Bill	94	38	3,572	8,836	1,444
Sally	90	31	2,790	8,100	961
Margaret	88	40	3,520	7,744	1,600
Sue	87	59	5,133	7,569	3,481
Total	2,142	1,256	137,085	232,750	84,188

Appendix B

Some Publishers of Standardized Instruments Used in Occupational Education Programs

American Guidance Service, Inc.
Publishers' Building
Circle Pines, Minnesota 55014

College Entrance Examination Board
888 Seventh Avenue
New York, New York 10019

CTB/McGraw-Hill
Del Monte Research Park
Monterey, California 93940

Educational Testing Service
Princeton, New Jersey 08540

Harcourt Brace Jovanovich, Inc.
Test Department
757 Third Avenue
New York, New York 10017

Houghton Mifflin Company
110 Tremont Street
Boston, Massachusetts 02107

Learning Concepts, Inc.
2501 North Lamar
Austin, Texas 78705

Scholastic Testing Service, Inc.
480 Meyer Road
Bensonville, Illinois 60106

Science Research Associates, Inc.
259 East Erie Street
Chicago, Illinois 60611

South-Western Publishing Company
5101 Madison Road
Cincinnati, Ohio 45227

The Bobbs-Merrill Company, Inc.
Test Division
4300 West 62nd Street
Indianapolis, Indiana 46206

The Psychological Corporation
757 Third Avenue
New York, New York 10017

Western Psychological Services
12031 Wilshire Boulevard
Los Angeles, California 90025

Appendix C

Professional Journals That Periodically Contain Reviews of Standardized Tests

- *American Education Research Journal*
- *British Journal of Educational Psychology*
- *British Journal of Educational Studies*
- *Educational and Psychological Measurement*
- *Journal of Consulting Psychology*
- *Journal of Counseling Psychology*
- *Journal of Educational Measurement*
- *Journal of Projective Techniques and Personality Assessment*
- *Measurement and Evaluation in Guidance*
- *Occupational Psychology*
- *Perceptual and Motor Skills*
- *Personnel and Guidance Journal*
- *Personnel Psychology*

Name Index

Subject Index